ALTERMODERN

TATE TRIENNIAL

ALTERMODERN

ALTERMODERN

TATE TRIENNIAL

Edited by Nicolas BOURRIAUD

Tate Publishing

First published 2009
by order of the Tate Trustees
by Tate Publishing,
a division of Tate
Enterprises Ltd,
Millbank, London SW1P 4RG
www.tate.org.uk/publishing

On the occasion of the
exhibition

ALTERMODERN:
TATE TRIENNIAL

Tate Britain
3 February – 26 April 2009

The exhibition at Tate
Britain is supported by
Calouste Gulbenkian
Foundation

A catalogue record for
this book is available
from the British Library.

ISBN 978 1 85437 817 0

Distributed in the United
States and Canada by Harry
N. Abrams, Inc., New York

Library of Congress Control
Number: 2008938612

Designed at M/M (Paris)
Printed in Spain by Grafos

Measurements of artworks are given
in centimetres, height before width

CONTENTS

SPONSOR'S FOREWORD

The Tate Triennial provides a unique glimpse at the state of contemporary art in Britain which itself reflects a collective mood – our preoccupations, our pleasures and concerns. Artists do not work in isolation and this Triennial highlights the connections that exist between different cultures within Britain and also internationally, connections which are increasingly important for all of us. Over the past three years, the Calouste Gulbenkian Foundation, which has its headquarters in Lisbon, has been extremely pleased to support the Gulbenkian Curator, Nicolas Bourriaud, enabling him to develop his knowledge of British art and place it in its wider international context. The result is an exhibition of works that are sensuous, witty and sometimes challenging, and from which Bourriaud has developed a new and thought-provoking analysis. The Foundation has a long history of association with Tate. Forty years ago, we initiated its seminal post-war exhibition of international contemporary art, *Painting and Sculpture of a Decade: 54–64*. In 1969 we made a substantial contribution to Tate's rebuilding programme. And we supported the last Triennial in 2006, our fiftieth anniversary year. We identify with Tate's willingness to take artistic risks, to build vigorous international connections, and with its increasing desire to reach out and involve people from all cultures: principles at the heart of our own work. We are impressed by the 2009 Triennial and hope those who visit leave enriched and connected to the concerns of others from cultures at home and abroad.

ANDREW BARNETT
Director
Calouste Gulbenkian Foundation,
UK Branch

DIRECTOR'S FOREWORD

Altermodern is a new term, coined by Nicolas Bourriaud, to describe a discernible, insistent sensibility that has emerged in contemporary art in Britain in tandem with recent social and cultural change across the world. Altermodern is a phenomenon belonging to the global era, and Tate Britain's exhibition explores this new, alternative form of the 'modern' by bringing together a diverse group of works of art that in various ways embrace and express such a proposition. But at the same time, emphatically, the show is also a presentation of a series of works as remarkable for their own individuality and agenda as for the contribution they make to this emerging, fascinating debate.

Nicolas Bourriaud is Tate Britain's Gulbenkian Curator of Contemporary Art and he has led this extraordinary project from its inception, with particular support from Tate curators Lizzie Carey-Thomas and Carolyn Kerr. He has worked with them on the development of the ideas and the exhibition, on the selection of the work and on the orchestration of the surrounding debate. Notably, they organised a series of one-day Prologues, events over the past year that launched and interrogated the idea of altermodern – with the generous participation of artists, writers, philosophers, curators and academics – in advance of determining the final form of the show. The vitality and diversity of this discussion reflects the spirit of the art that was ultimately selected and installed in our exhibition galleries to form this, the fourth Tate Triennial.

We are very grateful to all the artists, galleries, and other lenders of works of art who have agreed to be part of this extraordinary adventure. And I would like to thank, in addition, the Calouste Gulbenkian Foundation for providing the project with fundamental support from the outset.

STEPHEN DEUCHAR
Director
Tate Britain

CURATOR'S ACKNOWLEDGMENTS

The realisation of the 2009 Triennial exhibition was an inspiring and challenging endeavour, which required the total commitment of Tate Britain. I would particularly like to thank Nicholas Serota for his encouragement, Stephen Deuchar and Judith Nesbitt for their trust in the project and their constant support, and Siân Ede and the Calouste Gulbenkian Foundation, without whom all this would not have been possible.

The development of the four 'Prologues' to the Triennial and the process of creating the exhibition allowed me to work with many other Tate team members to whom I am very grateful. I would like to thank Kelli Dipple, Andrew Wilson, Will Gompertz, Ann Gallagher, Cedar Lewisohn, Paul Goodwin, and Clarrie Wallis for the discussions we had, which were fundamental to the direction of the project. I also want to thank Rebecca Fortey, Celeste Stroll and Deborah Metherell for their fantastic work on the catalogue; Helen Beeckmans and Daisy Mallabar in the press office for their energy and commitment, and Alice Teng for her efficiency. Other Tate staff who have helped to bring the exhibition to fruition include Felicity Allen, Alistair Ashe, Hans Biorn Lian, Kirstie Beaven, Helen Beeckmans, Christopher Burns, Louise Butler, Indie Choudhury, Rachel Crome, Dan Crompton, Kelli Dipple, Sionaigh Durrant, Claire Eva, Bronwyn Gardner, Fiona Gaskin, Clare Gill, Paul Goodwin, Vanessa Griffiths, Mikei Hall, Rebecca Hellen, Dania Herrera, Franziska Herzog, Duncan Holden, Bettina Kaufmann, Madeleine Keep, Gil Leung, Kirsteen McSwein, Roger Miller, Fergus O'Connor, Antoinette O'Loughlin, Doris Pearce, Tony Powers, Kenneth Price, Shuja Rahman, Marilena Reina, Michaela Ross, Andy Shiel, Hattie Spires, Katharine Stout, Liam Tebbs, Piers Townshend, Kate Vogel, Victoria Walsh, Piers Warner, Tina Weidner, and Eve Wilson.

And, most importantly, the curatorial team with whom I have been closely and enthusiastically collaborating, and who have worked tremendously hard in the conception and the organisation of the show: Carolyn Kerr, Lizzie Carey-Thomas, Sofia Karamani and Jamie Kenyon, to whom I want to send all my gratitude.

Working alongside Tate Staff, we could not have done without the invaluable contributions of Malcolm Clark and Dave Williams, Mtec; Simeon Corless; Richard Cottrell, Cottrell & Vermeulen Architecture; Richard Eaton; Michael Falzon, MC; Designers Limited; Adrian Fogarty; M/M (Paris); Philip Miles; Anna Nesbit; Tim O'Loghlin; Paul Ragsdale, Alan Baxter Associates, and the Museums, Libraries and Archives Council.

I would also like to thank the arists' representatives and all those who have helped to produce works for the exhibition, including Albion, London; Alex Bradley, White Cube, London; Cabinet, London; Judith Carlton; Bridget Chew; Lorenzo Fiaschi, Adrien De Melo and Lubi Reboani, Galleria Continua, San Gimignano; doggerfisher, Edinburgh; Giancarlo Francenella and Laura Francenella, Il Museo internazionale della Fisarmonica, Castelfidardo; Friedrich Petzel Gallery, New York; Frédéric Giroux, galerie Frédéric Giroux, Paris; Carol Greene, Greene Naftali Gallery, New York; June Gwak, Arario Gallery, Beijing; Jane Hait, WALLSPACE, New York; Sara Harrison, Hauser & Wirth, London; Hales Gallery, London; Herald St, London; HOTEL, London; Robin Klassnik and Clare Fitzpatrick, Matt's Gallery, London; Aude Levère; Galerie Jan Mot, Brussels; Capucince Motte and Pierre Rouart, Galerie Motte-Rouart, Paris; Paradise Row, London; Mélanie Meffrer Rondeau; Joshua Smith; Rob Tufnell, Ancient & Modern, London; Nicky Verber and Ash L'Ange, Herald St, London; Michael Ward-Bergeman; Workplace Gallery, Newcastle; Toby Webster/Modern Institute, Glasgow. And all private collectors who wish to remain anonymous.

Above all, I would like to thank all the Prologue participants and artists without whom the exhibition would not have been possible.

No acknowledgments would be complete without sending a personal thought to Tom Morton, Skye Sherwin-White, Patrick Brill, J.J. Charlesworth, Jessie Fortune-Ryan, Shezad Dawood, Hans-Ulrich Obrist, Charles Avery, and all the other friends who enlightened my London life during the last two years.

And finally, I want to dedicate this exhibition to Sinziana Ravini, for all the inspiring discussions we had, and more.

NICOLAS BOURRIAUD
Gulbenkian Curator
of Contemporary Art
at Tate Britain

ALTERMODERN
Nicolas BOURRIAUD

A COLLECTIVE EXHIBITION, when based around a theoretical hypothesis, needs to establish a balance between the artworks and the narrative that acts as a form of subtitling. It needs to develop a space-time continuum where the curator's voice-off, the statements of the artists, and the dialogues woven between the artefacts can co-exist. This hybrid arrangement is best compared with the production of a film, and cinematographic metaphors provide the clearest introduction to an event like *Altermodern*. According to Wim Wenders, analysing the relationship between image and narrative in the cinema, 'the narrative resembles a vampire attempting to drain the image of its blood'.[1] His observation could belong in any manual of the curator's ethics. It seems to me that that the fundamental question that exhibitions ought to be repeatedly asking concerns the interpretation of forms: what is the message they convey today? What is the narrative that drives them? We have an ethical duty not to let signs and images vanish into the abyss of indifference or commercial oblivion, to find words to animate them as something other than products destined for financial speculation or mere amusement. The very act of picking out certain images and distinguishing them from the rest of the production by exposing them is also an ethical responsibility. Keeping the ball in the air and the game alive: that is the function of the critic or the curator. Wenders pursues his reasoning by opposing text and form: 'Images are highly sensitive, rather like a snail, which retreats into its shell when you touch its horns. They don't want to work like a horse, carrying or fetching things – messages, meanings, arguments or morals. Yet that is precisely what a story demands.' [2] A fair riposte to the German director would be that this contradiction has its limits, since images are neither so naive nor so devoid of meaning, and that to believe in their basic 'purity' is an equally dangerous delusion. When a camera registers them, doubtless they are 'pure' in the sense he intends, but as soon as they are projected and shared they assume a host of meanings, and the battle begins anew. Every exhibition is the record of such a battle.

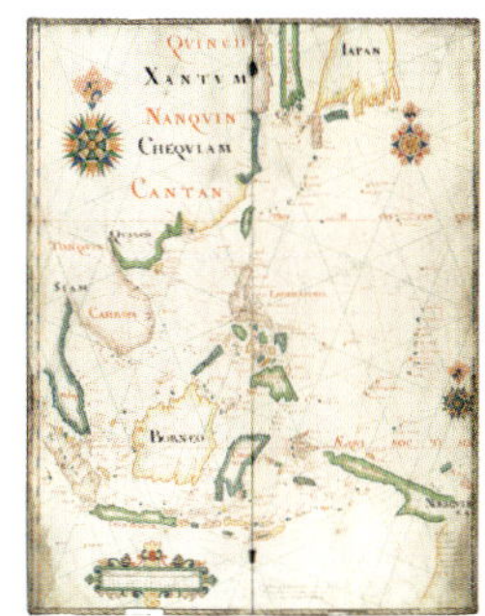

A MAP OF AN EAST INDIAN ARCHIPELAGO FORMATION, made by Nicholas Comberford and published in London in 1665. Collection of the National Maritime Museum, London.

'THE FIGURE IN THE CARPET' (THE TALE OF AN EXHIBITION)

USUALLY AN EXHIBITION BEGINS WITH A MENTAL IMAGE with which we need to reconnect, and whose meanings constitute a basis for discussion with the artists. The research that has preceded the Triennial 2009, however, had its origins in two elements: the idea of the archipelago, and the writings of a German émigré to the UK, Winfried Georg Sebald. The archipelago (and its kindred forms, the constellation and the cluster) functions here as a model representing the multiplicity of global cultures. An archipelago is an example of the relationship between the one and the many. It is an abstract entity; its unity proceeds from a decision without which nothing would be signified save a scattering of islands united by no common name. Our civilisation, which bears the imprints of a multicultural explosion and the proliferation of cultural strata, resembles a structureless constellation, awaiting transformation into an archipelago. We should add that the modernism of the twentieth century, and today's mass cultural movements, amount to agglomerations that we could describe as 'continental'.

As for Sebald's writings – wanderings between 'signs', punctuated by black and white photographs – they appear to me as emblematic of a mutation in our perception of space and time, in which history and geography operate a cross-fertilisation, tracing out paths and weaving networks: a cultural evolution at the very heart of this exhibition. The two concepts – the archipelago and Sebald's excursions – do not intertwine arbitrarily: they represent the paths I followed led by my initial intuition: that of the death of postmodernism as the starting point for reading the present.

The term 'altermodern', which serves both as the title of the present exhibition and to delimit the void beyond the postmodern, has its roots in the idea of 'otherness' (Latin *alter* = 'other', with the added English connotation of 'different') and suggests a multitude of possibilities, of alternatives to a single route. In the geopolitical world, 'alterglobalisation' defines the plurality of local oppositions to the economic standardisation imposed by globalisation, i.e. the struggle for diversity. Here we are back with the image of the archipelago: instead of aiming at a kind of summation, altermodernism sees itself as a constellation of ideas linked by the emerging and ultimately irresistible will to create a form of modernism for the twenty-first century. Why is this imperative necessity? The historical role of modernism, in the sense of a phenomenon arising within the domain of art, resides in its ability to jolt us out of tradition; it embodies a cultural exodus, an escape from the confines of nationalism and identity-tagging, but also from the mainstream whose tendency is to reify thought and practice. Under threat from fundamentalism and consumer-driven uniformisation, menaced by massification and the enforced re-abandonment of individual identity, art today needs to reinvent itself, and on a planetary scale. And this new modernism, for the first time, will have resulted from global dialogue. Postmodernism, thanks to the post-colonial criticism of Western pretensions to determine the world's direction and the speed of its development, has allowed the historical counters to be reset to zero; today, temporalities intersect and weave a complex network stripped of a centre. Numerous contemporary artistic practices indicate, however, that we are on the verge of a leap, out of the postmodern period and the (essentialist) multicultural model from which it is indivisible, a leap that would give rise to a synthesis between modernism and post-colonialism.

Let us then call this synthesis 'altermodernism'. It cannot be placed *after* the modernist phenomenon any more than after this aftermath: it does not 'overtake' anything, any more than it 'harks back' to a previous period. There is no question of a return to the principles or the style of twentieth-century modernism, nowadays the object of a revival far from our preoccupations. If today we can envisage a form of modernism, this is only possible starting from the issues of the present, and assuredly not by an obsessive return to the past, whatever its attributes.

Altermodernism can be defined as that moment when it became possible for us to produce something that made sense starting from an assumed heterochrony, that is, from a vision of human history as constituted of multiple temporalities, disdaining the nostalgia for the avant-garde and indeed for any era – a positive vision of chaos and complexity. It is neither a petrified kind of time advancing in loops (postmodernism) nor a linear vision of history (modernism), but a positive experience of disorientation through an art-form exploring all dimensions of the present, tracing lines in all directions of time and space. The artist turns cultural nomad: what remains of the Baudelairean model of modernism is no doubt this *flânerie*, transformed into a technique for generating creativeness and deriving knowledge.

Thus the exhibition brings together three sorts of nomadism: in space, in time and among the 'signs'. Of course, these notions are not mutually exclusive, and the same artist can simultaneously explore geographical, historical and socio-cultural realities. We need to be clear that nomadism, as a way of learning about the world, here amounts to much more than a simplistic generalisation: the term enshrines specific forms, processes of visualisation peculiar to our own epoch. In a word, trajectories have become forms: contemporary art gives the impression of being uplifted by an immense wave of displacements, voyages, translations, migrations of objects and beings, to the point that we could state that the works presented in *Altermodern* unravel themselves along receding lines of perspective, the course they follow eclipsing the static forms through which they initially manifest themselves.

Thus Simon Starling relocates a piece of furniture designed by Francis Bacon from one continent to another by radio waves. Katie Paterson transmits moments of silence from the Earth to the Moon and back, and we are placed in telephone communication with the melting of a glacier. Tris Vonna-Michell, whose exhibit comprises the narrative of a planetary drift, conceives of his exhibitions as linked series. Darren Almond teleports the bus shelters of Auschwitz into a gallery, photographs Chinese landscapes, or sets off to film the Great Wheel of Chernobyl frozen into immobility at the moment of the nuclear disaster. Franz Ackermann invents the age of painting with GPS. Joachim Koester follows the route of the Hashishins in Iran after retracing Kant's daily walks in Könisberg or – as related in *Dracula* – Jonathan Harker's trek in the Carpathians. Rachel Harrison's inspiration to invent a kind of formal anthropology comes from one of Charles Darwin's voyages on the *Beagle*. Walead Beshty passes exposed film stock through airport X-ray scanners, or captures the cracks occurring in Perspex sculptures as they travel to exhibitions in Fedex boxes. Subodh Gupta exports commonplace utensils from India; reassembled as digitised images, they take on a significance that transcends cultural divides. Pascale Marthine Tayou employs colonised forms of African art to suggest the parameters of a truly globalised culture. The tendency of these works is to emphasise the fact that, in this era of the altermodern, displacement has become a method of depiction, and that artistic styles and formats must henceforth be regarded from the viewpoint of diaspora, migration and exodus.

These differing modes of displacement indicate, more generally, a *fragmentation* of the work of art. No longer can a work be reduced to the presence of an object in the here and now; rather, it consists of a significant network whose interrelationships the artist elaborates, and whose progression in time and space he or she controls: a circuit, in fact. Seth Price, in an essay defining the theoretical issues of his work, refers to the 'collective authorship' and 'complete decentralisation' that define our new cultural framework, to arrive at the conclusion that 'distribution is a circuit of reading', and that the artist's task 'becomes one of packaging, producing, reframing and distributing'.[3] Put another way, we could say that every artist manifests themself on their individual *wavelength*, especially by that progressive repetition of formal elements we used to call *style*. And this personal wavelength conveys in its emanations signs that are both heterogeneous (belonging to differing registers or cultural traditions) and heterochronic (borrowed from differed periods). Thus with *Feature*, Shezad Dawood has made a film that juxtaposes elements lifted from the western and the 'gore movie' in a narrative framework where Samuel Beckett has a fresh encounter with Buster Keaton. In an equally fantastical vein, Marcus Coates applies the archaic methods of shamanism to the contemporary world, seeking out 'animal spirits' to cure social problems in Israel or the Galapagos Islands. What is cutting-edge in these frolics is not the summoning-up of the past to express the present; it is the visual language with which this business is transacted – that of travelling and nomadism. There are no longer cultural roots to sustain forms, no exact cultural base to serve as a benchmark for variations, no nucleus, no boundaries for artistic language. Today's artist, in order to arrive at precise points, takes as their starting-point global culture and no longer the reverse. The line is more important than the points along its length.

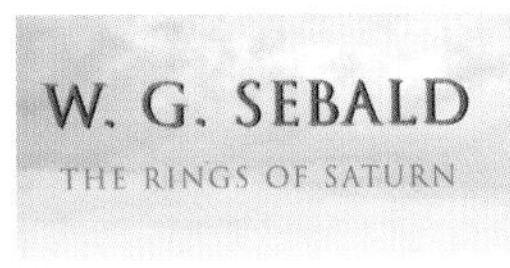

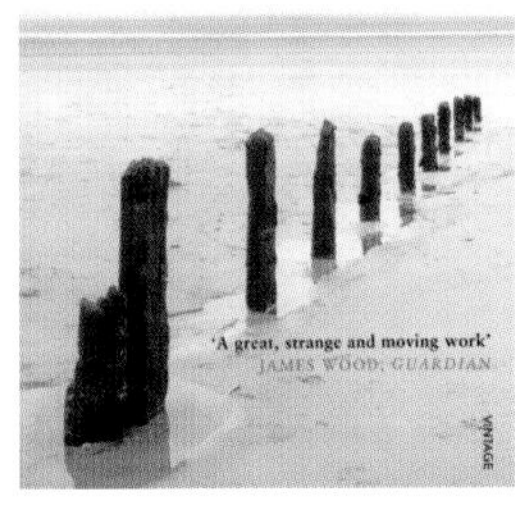

COVER OF THE 2002 edition of W.G. SEBALD's *The Rings of Saturn*, a book that provided one of the important starting points for the conception of the exhibition.

Strictly speaking, then, the exhibition assembles works whose compositional principle relies on a chain of elements: the work tends to become a dynamic structure that generates forms before, during and after its production.[4] These forms deliver narratives, the narratives of their very own production, but also their distribution and the mental journey that encompasses them. Loris Gréaud, for instance, produces electroencephalograms of his own brain as he think about an exhibition; this is transformed into a computer programme, then into light emissions and finally into electrical impulses releasing vibrations in the exhibition hall – before, as likely as not, being used somewhere else. Lindsay Seers ceaselessly re-edits the documentary of her life, from her childhood in Mauritius to life in London, in installations that explore the origins of the photographic image.

As they follow the receding perspectives of history and geography, works of art trace lines in a globalised space that now extends to time: history, the last continent to be explored, can be traversed like a territory. In Sebald's *The Rings of Saturn*, the narrator journeys on foot across the landscapes of England's East Coast. He travels through various layers of time, mingling the past, the imaginary and the future. He ploughs through the works of Sir Thomas Browne in search of the burial-place of the philosopher's skull, comments on Rembrandt's *Anatomy Lesson of Dr Tulp*, meets Joseph Conrad en route to the Congo, recalls a film about herring-fishing, muses on ethnic cleansing in the Balkans or great naval battles and their pictorial representation, before discussing Chateaubriand and introducing us to the history of silkworm culture. The narratives are embedded in images or encounters, and Sebald constructs a kaleidoscope of fragments that reflect the footsteps of history. Later, Tris Vonna-Mitchell wrote a piece meant for a website dedicated to Sebald: 'That was in 2003, and through this serendipitous moment, the work started off as a text or prose piece, and just unfolded into this labyrinth of associations and narratives. Three years after this, I went back through my computer files and I saw those documents and photographs, these tunnels and web searches ... and the project still goes on.'[5]

The journey format, as it appears so frequently in the works of today's artists, goes hand in hand with the generalisation of hypertext as a thought process: one sign directs us to a second, then a third, creating a chain of mutually interconnected forms, mimicking mouse-clicks on a computer screen. With Nathaniel Mellors, Olivia Plender, Ruth Ewan or Spartacus Chetwynd, references to the past are coordinated according to a system of cognitive logic. To understand the present means carrying out a kind of rough-and-ready archaeological investigation of world culture, which proceeds just as well through *re-enactments* as through the presentation of artefacts – or again, through the technique of mixing. For example, Ewan installs a giant accordion from an Italian museum; it plays old revolutionary songs to accompany the reproduction of archival documents. Chetwynd, in the same work, can scramble Milton, Marx and Sesame Street; one of the constant features of her oeuvre is a playful use of forms not considered as relics of the past but as living tools that we need to grasp in order to create new narratives. In a similar way, Peter Coffin extracts the narrative potential of existing works of art by employing an audiovisual setup that parasitically appropriates their meaning and puts them to work as fictional characters.

These journeys in time result in a modification of the way in which signs are indexed with their period. In the case of Charles Avery, the artist produces not only signs, but also the context that gives them coherence, through the narrative of an imaginary world: he is the explorer of a universe inside which the idea of contemporaneity is abolished in favour of a voluntary confusion of eras and genres. Olivia Plender's comic-format book on the life of a fictitious artistic genius in 1960s London and her explorations of the archives of utopian communities or magic circles utilise forms not really belonging to any recognisable *present*. And Matthew Darbyshire links different landmarks from periods chronologically far apart, connecting for instance architecture of Stalin's era, fragments of Tate Britain and the facelifting of British public buildings, his aim being a transhistoric meditation on contemporary space. As for David Noonan's images, they seem to originate from a parallel world, once again defying precise localisation. These works peregrinate through time and space, released from the fetishistic obsession with contemporaneity. Most probably this is why they are better at describing our present, both heterochronic and heterotopic.

CREDIT CRUNCH: POSTMODERN COMES OUT OF MOURNING

THE TERMS 'MODERN', 'POSTMODERN' OR 'ALTERMODERN' do not define styles (save as ways of thinking), but here represent tools allowing us to attribute time-scales to cultural eras. In order to understand why the collapse of the globalised financial system in Autumn 2008 appears to mark a definite turning-point in history, it is necessary to re-examine modernism from the point of view of world energy consumption.

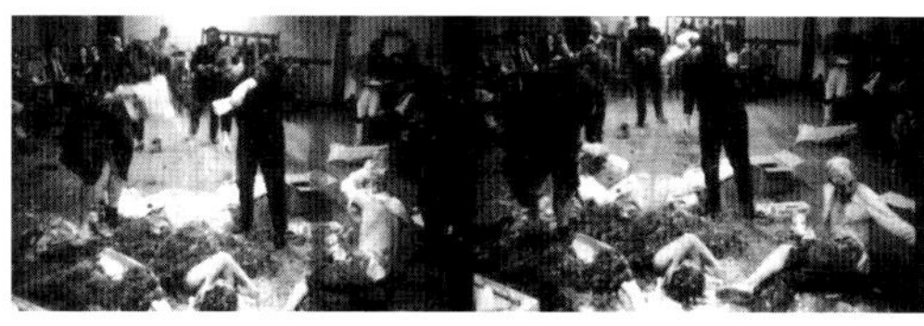

OTTO MÜHL and **HERMANN NITSCH** of the Viennese Actionists performing *Ten Rounds for Cassius Clay* at the *Destruction in Art Symposium*, 13 September 1966. Photographs by Tom Picton in Tate Archive.

In an enlightening text published in 2004, Peter Sloterdijk defined the modern way of living as a 'fast-burn culture', a specific condition of civilisation in the era of a 'superabundance of energy'. 'Today', he continues, 'our lifestyle still depends upon being able to squander stocks of fossil fuels. In other words, we have gambled on a sort of explosion. We are all fanatical believers in this explosion, worshippers of this rapid liberation of a massive quantity of energy. I get the impression that the focal point of today's adventure films – "action movies" – is that other primitive symbol of modern civilisation: the explosion of a car or a plane. Or rather, of a huge fuel tank that is the archetype of the religious movement of our times.'[6] This relationship between modern life and the explosion appears both literally and metaphorically throughout the twentieth century, from the Futurist eulogising of war to the 'sudden liberations of great quantities of energy' in the performances of the Gutai group or the Viennese

Actionists, not to mention the fragmented forms of Dadaism, the self-destructive machines of Jean Tinguely or the 'blown-up' imagery of pop art.

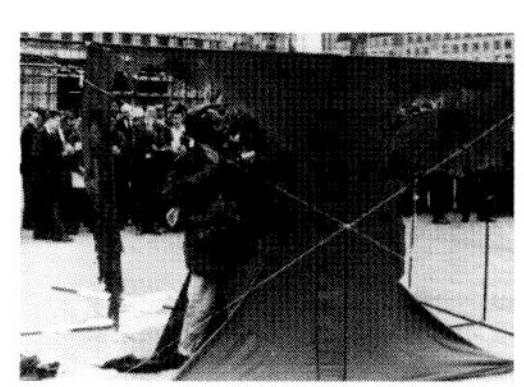

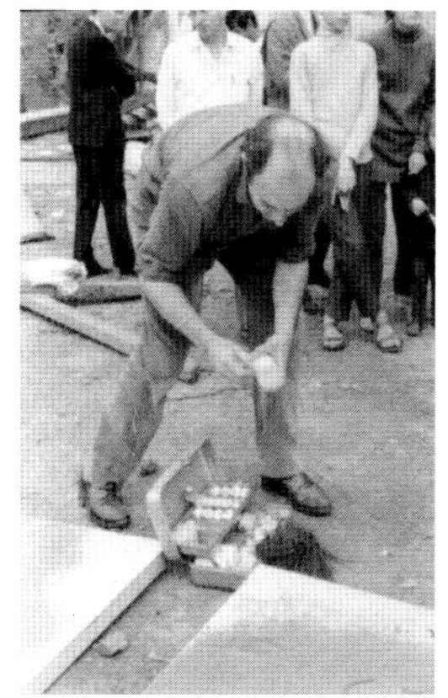

It is significant that the appearance of the term 'postmodern' coincided exactly with the 1973 oil crisis, the event that caused the entire world, for the first time, to realise that reserves of fossil fuels were limited: the end of Sloterdijk's 'superabundance'. In other words, our future was all of a sudden mortgaged. It is also no accident that the term 'postmodern' became current in the second half of the 1970s, popularised first by the architect Charles Jencks and then by the philosopher Jean-François Lyotard. Jencks's ideas constituted a criticism of modernism in architecture, notably the functionalism of the Bauhaus or Le Corbusier, whilst Lyotard sought to lay down a new paradigm (essentially epistemological) that would extend the life of modernism. Postmodernism thus developed in the wake of the energy crisis and the ending of the boom that the French call the 'thirty glorious years' (1945–75), just as a fit of depression succeeds a traumatic loss: that of the ideologies of carefree superabundance and progress, technical, political or cultural. The oil crisis of 1973 could well represent the 'primitive scene' of postmodernism in the same way as, according to Sloterdijk, oil gushing from a well symbolises twentieth-century modernism. The latter was the fateful moment when the economy was founded on an unlimited confidence in the availability of energy, and culture on an infinite projection into the future. These were the two principles swept away by the oil crisis, and whose disappearance gave birth to what we call the postmodern.

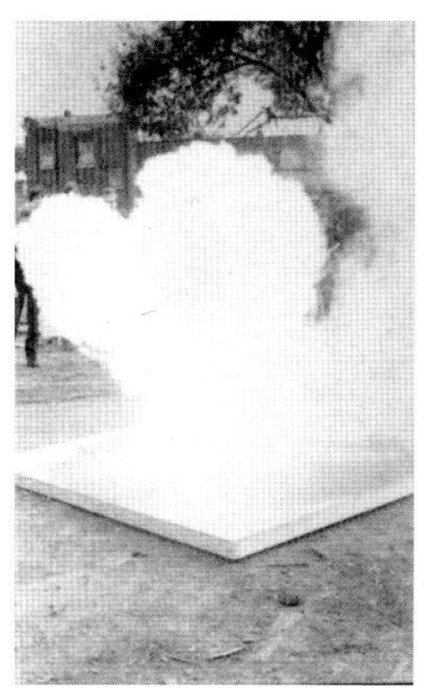

Since the crisis of 1973, the economy has never again been based on the exploitation of raw materials. Capitalism has since disconnected from natural resources, reorienting itself towards technological innovation – the choice of Japan – or 'financiarisation', the route adopted at the time by the United States. And now, when the economy is cutting its ties with concrete geography, culture for its part is divorcing from history; two parallel processes tending towards the abstract.

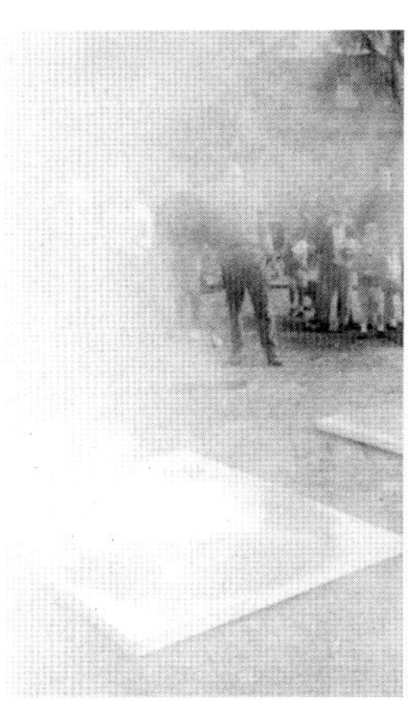

In the view of Bernard Stiegler, here resuming the essential thread of Jean-François Lyotard's theories on the 'libidinal economy', capitalism functions through the channelling of desires; yet, he adds, 'desire underwent a downward tendency', forcing the system to 'exploit instinctive impulses', all real passions having disappeared among alienated individuals who had lost control of their

[TOP] **GUSTAV METZGER**, *Acid Action Painting*, Nylon, hydrochloric acid, metal, South Bank Demonstration, 3 July 1961. [BOTTOM] **PRO-DIAZ** produing *Painting with Explosion* at the *Destruction in Art Symposium*, 1966, organised by Gustav Metzger. Photographs by Tom Picton in Tate Archive.

own lives.[7] After exhausting the consumer's desires, capitalism was thereafter reduced to exploiting his reflexes and gut reactions; sustainable sources of energy had dried up, just as with the oil crisis. In art, this assault upon our instincts was translated as a rapid rotation of works and the ascendancy of the sensational and the spectacular: those aimed simply at releasing a vast quantity of (non-renewable) energy at first sight. Gustav Metzger, master of the energy-burst, self-destruction and ecological disaster, has found his true place in this tableau of our times; a believer in the continuous development of culture, his work anticipates the evolution of capitalism and its culture, assembling the elements of a form of modernism capable of outliving the cult of the explosion.

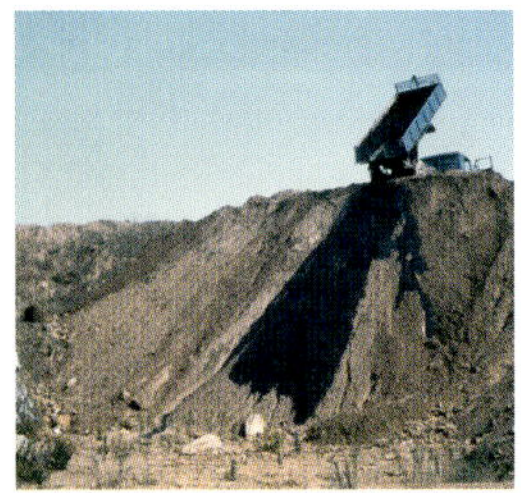

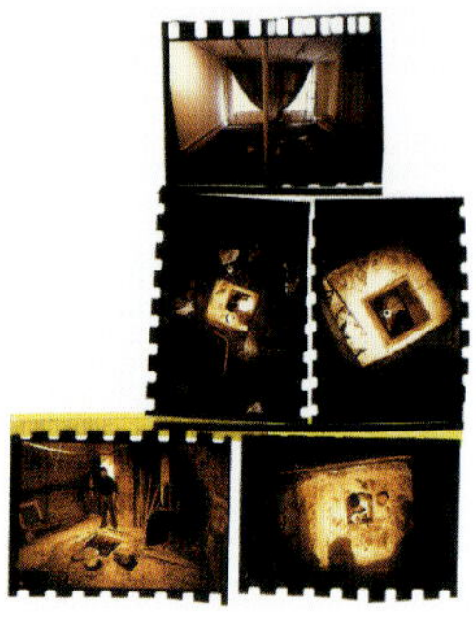

[TOP] **ROBERT SMITHSON,** *Asphalt Rundown, Rome 1969*, 1969
[BELOW] **GORDON MATTA-CLARK,** *Rendez-vous, Sous-sol (Descending Steps for Batan)*, 1977, views of the project site under Yvon Lambert Gallery, Paris.

I wrote earlier that postmodern culture had its roots in the idea of the end of history; more precisely, it posits the end of history considered as a linear narrative. In this respect, Lyotard defines the postmodern as the end of 'grand narratives', future scenarios that history is fated to fulfil, like a film-maker following a pre-defined script. The disappearance of these 'metanarratives' (Marxism, in particular) ushers in a culture of improvisation and time-loops: if there is no more script, we have henceforth to react to a 'context', or deal in short-term measures. Forms are no longer indexed to a narrative defining them as belonging to precise historical moments, but rather embedded in the 'text' of culture, with no reference save to themselves. Palimpsests, pastiches, textuality... Signs have lost all contact with human history and are self-generating in an infinite Brownian motion, a labyrinth of signs.

It seems difficult, in retrospect, to define the postmodern otherwise than as a period of pause and levelling, brief as befits a historical moment entirely determined by the one before – a marshy delta on the river of time. We can now identify those last twenty-five years of the 1900s as an interminable 'afterwards'; after the myth of progress, after the revolutionary utopia, after the retreat of colonialism, after the battles for political, social and sexual emancipation. As a theory, postmodernism has developed in reaction to a teleological view of the world, a vision we find both in the historicism of a critic like Clement Greenberg – for whom the history of art presented itself like a train en route toward the realisation of an idea – and in the various politico-aesthetic utopias that typified the century of the avant-garde. This, however, would be to reduce modernism to its most immediately 'progressist' aspect: its identification with ambitions for political change and the most radical artistic movements, i.e. those anxious to excise everything superfluous and return to the root of things. In fact, in the cases of Marcel Duchamp, Robert Filliou, On Kawara or Gordon Matta-Clark, we would have considerable difficulty in discerning the slightest tendency in this direction; their vision of history was not 'progressist', but apprehended time in all its complex and multiple dimensions. With each of these four artists, any movement towards the past – symbolism with Duchamp, Oriental philosophy with Filliou and Kawara, archaeology with Matta-Clark – was superimposed upon another towards the future, making them precursors of our heterochronic time. As for Robert Smithson, whose visual meditations on the notion of entropy or the concept of 'ruin in reverse' still remain so influential among the new generation of artists, he appears to be the first truly postmodern artist in that he anticipates and directly confronts the question of modernity *in relation to energy sources*: his entire corpus forms the narrative of a classic 'oil crisis'.

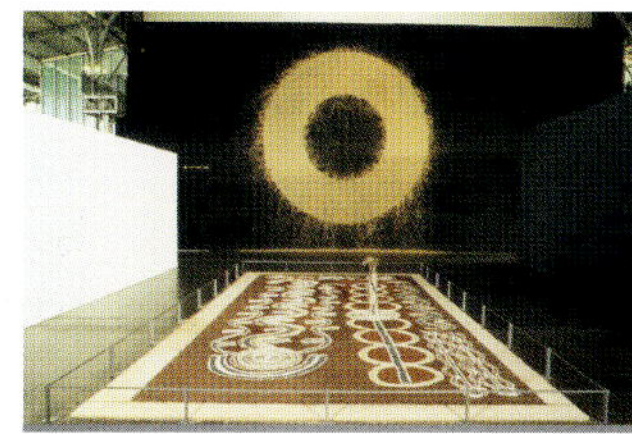

INSTALLATION VIEW of the *Magicians of the Earth* exhibition at Centre Georges Pompidou, Paris 1989

Postmodernism is the philosophy of mourning, a long melancholic episode in our cultural life. History having lost its direction and ability to be read, nothing remained but to come face to face with an immobilised space-time in which, like reminiscences, arose mutilated fragments of the past: the 'museum's ruins', as Douglas Crimp labelled postmodernism in 1980.[8] This purely depressive attitude profoundly impregnated the first postmodern period, characterised as it was by the borrowing of identifiable forms of art history and the theme of the 'simulacrum', an image that substitutes itself for reality within reality itself. Grieving for a lost reality ... Crimp defined the image as 'an object of desire, the desire for the signification that is known to be absent'.[9] H. Frederic Jameson, in his seminal essay on postmodernism, sees its dominant trait as schizophrenia, or, to be more exact, one of the most destructive effects of it – the loss of the mind's ability to perceive time as something ordered, an incapacity to organise experience as a collection of coherent and meaningful sequences, leading to the abandonment of the attempt in favour of a fascination with a kaleidoscopic present.[10] For Slavoj Zizek, depression proves to be 'a perfectly postmodern posture', for it 'allows us to survive in a globalised society while keeping faith with our lost "roots"'.[11] Finally, according to Freud, one of the symptoms of depression associated with mourning is a process that induces the patient to adopt certain characteristics of the deceased, to the point of identifying himself/herself partially or totally with that person. This kind of depression and identity substitution, endemic to postmodernism, can be recognised in the variety of neo-avant-garde devices that have surfaced since the latter half of the 1990s: formal quotes from the vocabulary of geometrical abstraction, the adoption of politically radical concepts in critical texts, etc. The result has been to denude modernism of its meaning by transforming it into a form of nostalgic obsession.

Unable any longer to determine the direction of history, we have had to pronounce its end. The eternal reversions to modernist forms in the 1980s have been succeeded by the relativisation of history itself through the medium of post-colonial thinking. This second postmodern period was less melancholy – but multiculturalist. It had its beginnings in the end of the Cold War. 1989 was the year not only of the collapse of the Berlin Wall but also of the exhibition that, for all the controversy it provoked, marked the symbolic inauguration of planetary art. Organised by Jean-Hubert Martin at the Centre Pompidou, Paris, it was entitled *Magicians of the Earth*. At this moment, history seemed to break free from a profound Ice Age imposed by the silent confrontation of the two political blocs. The grand modernist narrative was succeeded by that of globalisation, which does not designate a cultural period properly speaking, but a geopolitical standardisation and the synchronisation of the historical clock. With the door thrown open to artistic traditions and cultures other than those foisted on the world by the West, post-colonial postmodernism followed along the trail blazed by the world economy, enabling a re-evaluation from the ground up of our visions of time and space: a 'horizontalisation' of the planet on which we need to build today.

What better characterises this period than the mythification of origins? The meaning of a work of art, for this second-stage postmodernism, depends essentially on the social background to its production. 'Where do you come from?' appears to be its most pressing question, and essentialism its critical paradigm. Identification with genre, ethnicity, a sexual orientation or a nation sets in motion a powerful machinery: multiculturalism, now a critical methodology, has virtually become a system of allotting meanings and assigning individuals their position in the hierarchy of social demands, reducing their whole being to their identity and stripping all their significance back to their origins. Thus postmodernism has moved on from the depression of the Cold War to a neurotic preoccupation with origins typical of the era of globalisation. It is this thought-model that today finds itself in crisis, this multiculturalist version of cultural diversity that must be called into question, not in favour of a 'universalism' of principles or a new modernist esperanto, but within the framework of a new modern movement based on heterochrony, a common interpretation, and freedom to explore.

MODERNISM AND HETEROCHRONY: FROM 'POST' TO 'ALTER'

CERTAIN ARTISTS WERE HOSTILE TO THE LINEAR TIMELINE of modernism based on a projection into the future. Such was the case with Marcel Duchamp, whose repertoire includes a vast catalogue of traditional craftwork, outdated or anachronistic (the croquet box of *Three Standard Stoppages* 1913–14, the door in *Etant donnés ...* 1946–66, etc), thereby introducing a vision of contemporaneity very different from what was then in vogue. Reusing the tools of the past in order to confound the present, Duchamp went so far as to describe his masterpiece *The Bride Stripped Bare by Her Bachelors, Even* 1915–23 as a *retard en verre*: a 'delay in glass'. Duchamp's 'delay', more significant than it would seem, thus overleaps the opposition between futurist projection and nostalgic glances at the past, an opposition that structures our view of twentieth-century art. But there is more to modernity than a kind of futurism. It is significant that a number of today's artists operate in a space-time characterised by this 'delay', playing with the anachronistic, with multi-temporality or time-lag. We could say that the ageless drawings of Charles Avery, the paintings of Spartacus Chetwynd or Shezad Dawood, the iconographic materials of Olivia Plender, Peter Coffin, Matthew Darbyshire and Ruth Ewan, or Tacita Dean's and Joachim Koester's references to the origins of the cinema – like those of Navin Rawanchaikul to Bollywood posters – all deal in the aesthetics of heterochrony: their work displays none of the obvious signs of contemporaneity, save perhaps in the process of their constitution, in the assembling of their parts into meaningful networks. Here what is 'contemporary' is the structure of the work, its method of composition: the very fact that it brings together heterochronic elements – delay (analogous to 'pre-recorded') coexists with the *immediate* (or 'live') and with the anticipated, just as documentary coexists with fiction, not according to a principle of accumulation (postmodern baroquism), but with the aim of revealing our present, in which temporalities and levels of reality are intertwined.

RAILS AND NETWORKS: THE 'VIATORISATION' OF FORMS

THE PREDOMINANT AESTHETICS OF THIS CONCERN with intemporality reside to all appearances in the massive usage of black and white, for instance in the 16mm silent films projected by Joachim Koester, the iconography of David Noonan, Tris Vonna-Michell or Charles Avery, the drawings of Olivia Plender, Tacita Dean's series *The Russian Ending*, or the entire universe of Lindsay Seers. Today, black and white labels images as belonging to the past and the world of archives – at the same time, however, guaranteeing the authenticity of their content, by the single fact that their technique pre-dates Photoshop. In the books of W.G. Sebald, the narrative is punctuated by similar photos, which, according to the author, are there to emphasise the truth of the story. With Sebald, then, narrative is not in conflict with image. But this is a different form of narrative from that employed by Wim Wenders, who sees images in the form of a line, in a fixed order, with a fixed chronology. The cinema, whose birth was contemporary with that of the locomotive, handles narrative spontaneously like 'a train passing in the night', to quote François Truffaut; that is to say, like narrative rails organising the passage of images. What better metaphor for history as twentieth-century modernism perceived it than that of the train? Rosalind Krauss stated: 'Perspective is the visual correlative of causality: things arrange themselves one after the other according to rules.' If pictorial modernism has done away with the monocular, centrist (spatial) perspective, it has substituted for it 'a temporal perspective, i.e., history'.[12] There still remains the question, a far more difficult one, of whether the era of the worldwide web and global hypermobility is really giving rise to new ways of perceiving human space. The term 'postmodern' can be applied to art that is refractory to these two types of perspective: spatial and temporal. 'Altermodern', on the other hand, combines both; the space-time circumscribed by the oeuvre of the new generation of artists, from Koester to Chetwynd, via Avery or Dean, presents itself in the form of a Möbius loop. In their productions, perspective is simultaneously geographical (mobility, displacement and cultural nomadism as methods of composition) and historical (heterochrony as a spontaneous take on the world). Simon Starling or Darren Almond, for example, displace objects in space to illuminate their history; they could be said to 'viatorise' them (from Latin *viator*, 'traveller'). For them, historical memory, like the topography of the contemporary world, exists only in the form of a network. Signs are displaced, 'viatorised' in circuits, and the work of art presents itself in the form of this dynamic system.

But what is a network? A connected chain of distinct elements in time or space. Various materials can serve as a 'glue' to hold the component elements together, yet one of them today assumes a particular importance: storytelling. Among the artists who have contributed to the theoretical development of this concept, Philippe Parreno explains that 'Pre-production, production, post-production, these narrative instances depend upon each other. In the course of the chaining of these sequences, a narrative unfolds.'[13] Exhibiting a work composed as a network of signs – like a computer screen reacting to a sequence of hypertext links – allows us to bypass another form of contradiction that has become unproductive: that of form and narrative. Liam Gillick defines this new structure as a 'discursive framework' or a 'discursive model of practice'. This is not to be understood as an urge to replace form by the formulaic, for 'the discursive is what produces work but is also the produced work itself in the form of critical and impromptu exchanges'.[14] In the same way as Parreno, he envisages the production of a work of art as a form of sequencing, like the continuous passage of an image to a text, from a narrative to a sign. 'This discursive is a production cycle, rather than a fixed performative moment in time ... It occupies the increasing gap between the trajectory of modernity (understood here as a flow of technologies and demographic development) and the somewhat melancholic imploded self-conscious trajectory of modernism.'[15]

A STRATEGIC UNIVERSALISM

If the postmodern critical process *par excellence* was the detailed explanation of signs by their origins, the vital thing today, starting from the standpoint of the extreme globalisation of world culture, is to grasp afresh the emblematic gesture of modernity – the exodus. This may be defined as a wrenching separation from the traditions, customs, everything in fact that anchors an individual to a 'territory' and the habits of a culture petrified by fixed ways of doing and saying things. But what exactly is being transformed and carried off? To answer this question, we must re-examine the very notion of territory – cultural or otherwise – from the viewpoint of 'viatorisation'.

For sociologist Marc Augé: 'Culture has never been a spontaneous product that any one territory could appropriate. This illusory definition resurfaces today because there no longer is any territory. It is one of the illusions maintained by globalisation. Contemporary art acquiesces in this ambivalence, even when seeking to make it its subject.'[16] In a world every inch of which is under satellite surveillance, territory takes the form of a construction or a journey.

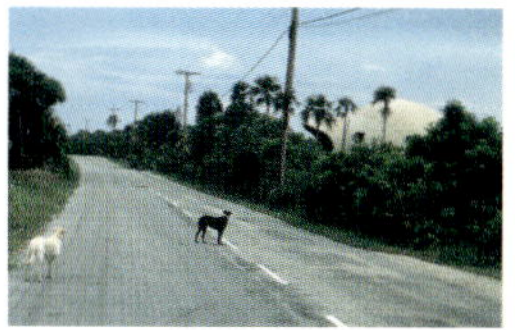

TACITA DEAN, *Bubble House (with Dogs)*, 1999

And so the artist, *homo viator*, turns nomad. They transform ideas and signs, transport them from one point to another. All modernity is vehicular, exchange-based, and translative in its essence; the variety apparently announcing its arrival today will become more extreme as it develops, for the first time in human history, on a planetary scale. And just as alterglobalisation does not seek cumulative solutions to the steamrollering effect of economic globalisation – rather a concatenation of singular responses within models of sustainable development – altermodern has no desire to substitute for postmodern relativism a new universalism, rather a networked 'archipelago' form of modernity. The movement is also taking shape under the urgent pressure to answer very basic questions: how do we live in this world that we are told is becoming 'global', but which seems to be buttressed on particular interests or tensed behind the barricades of fundamentalism – when not upholding icons of mass culture as role models? How to represent a power that is becoming ever more furtive as it slips into bed with economics? How, finally, to make art anything but a secondary type of merchandise in a system of values entirely oriented towards this 'general and abstract equivalent' that is money, and how can it bear witness against 'economic horror' without reducing itself to sheer militancy.

'When they created cities', argues J.M.G. Le Clézio, 'when they invented concrete, tar and glass, men invented a new jungle – but have yet to become its inhabitants. Maybe they will die out before recognising it for what it is. The [Amazonian] Indians have thousands of years' experience of it, which is why their knowledge is so perfect. Their world is not different from ours, they simply live in it, while we are still in exile.'[17]

NOTES

1. **WIM WENDERS**, *La Logique des images. Le Souffle de l'ange*, Paris 1995 p.149.

2. Ibid.

3. **SETH PRICE**, 'Dispersion', 2002, on www.distributed history.com

4. 'Fragmented narratives', **T. VONNA-MICHELL** interviewed by **ANDREW HUNT**, in *Untitled*, no.45, Spring 2008, p.27.

5. For a full description of the practice of chaining, in relation to the techniques of sampling and websurfing, see **N. BOURRIAUD**, *Postproduction*, New York 2002.

6. **PETER SLOTERDIJK**, 'La pensée sphérique', *BAM* no.2, *Vies modes d'emploi*, 2004, p.192.

7. **BERNARD STIEGLER**, *Réenchanter le monde: la valeur-esprit contre le populisme industriel*, Paris 2006.

8. **DOUGLAS CRIMP**, with photographs by **LOUISE LAWLER**, *On the Museum's Ruins*, Cambridge, Mass. 1993.

9. Ibid., p.183.

10. **FREDRIC JAMESON**, *Postmodernism, or the Cultural Logic of Late Capitalism*, Durham, NC 1991.

11. **SLAVOJ ZIZEK**, *Vous Avez Dit Totalitarisme?*, Paris 2004, p.167.

12. **ROSALIND KRAUSS**, 'A View of Modernism', in *Artforum*, Sept. 1972.

13. **PHILIPPE PARRENO** and **HANS-ULRICH OBRIST**, *The Conversation-Pieces*, Cologne 2007.

14. **LIAM GILLICK**, 'Maybe it would be better if we worked in groups of three?', *Hermes Lecture*, Eindhoven 2008, p.29.

15. Ibid., p.30.

16. **MARC AUGÉ**, *L'Art du décalage*, www.multitudes.samizdat.com, 5 June 2007.

17. **JEAN-MARIE GUSTAVE LE CLÉZIO**, *Haï*, Paris 1971, p.36.

Navin RAWANCHAIKUL, Stéphane GOXE and Jordi VIDAL, Tris VONNA-MICHELL, Okwui ENWEZOR, J.J. CHARLESWORTH

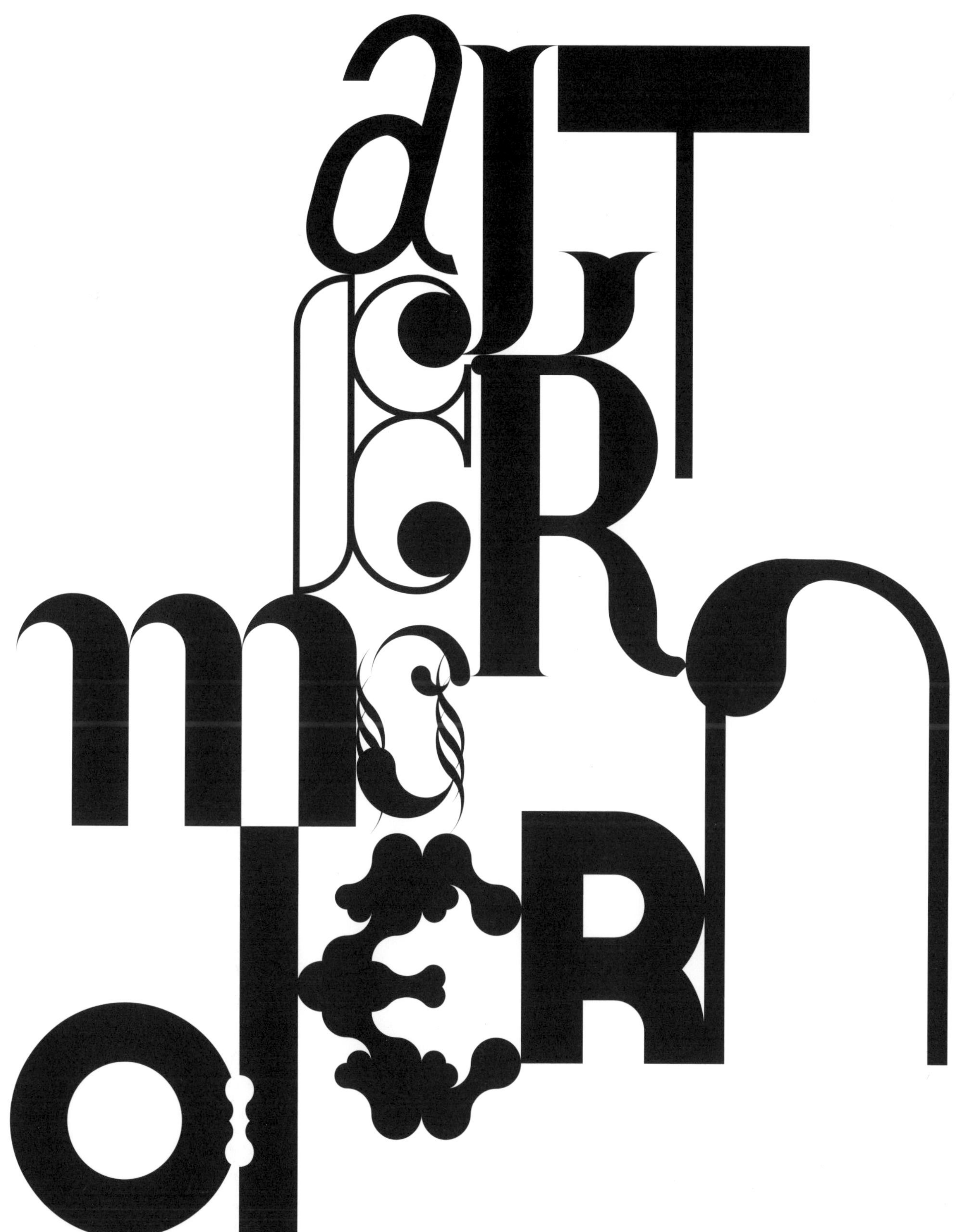

Altermodern was the first in a series of four one-day events, the Prologues, preceding the Tate Triennial exhibition. With contributions from prominent writers, art historians, artists and philosophers, each Prologue comprised lectures, performances, films and discussions attempting to introduce and provoke debate around the Triennial's themes.

The first Prologue opened the debate with the proposition that the period defined by postmodernism has come to an end and what can be called 'altermodernity' has taken its place. Art made in the times we live in belongs to the global era, and is conceived and produced as a reaction against standardisation and nationalism. The art is characterised by artists' cross-border, cross-cultural negotiations; a new real and virtual mobility; the surfing of different disciplines; the use of fiction as an expression of autonomy.

SATURDAY 28 APRIL 2008
TATE BRITAIN

14:00
MILLBANK ENTRANCE
NAVIN RAWANCHAIKUL
Navins of Bollywood

14:00 and 15.15
AUDITORIUM
STÉPHANE GOXE and JORDI VIDAL
Servitude and Simulacra

16:00
GALLERY 62
TRIS VONNA-MICHELL
Auto Tracking: From Cellar to Garret

16:30
AUDITORIUM
OKWUI ENWEZOR chaired by J.J. CHARLESWORTH
Specious Modernity: Speculations on the End of Postcolonial Utopia

MODERNITY AND POSTCOLONIAL AMBIVALENCE

Okwui ENWEZOR

FROM *GRAND* MODERNITY TO *PETIT* MODERNITY

THERE IS A DUAL NARRATIVE that is often taken to be characteristic of modernity: the first is the idea of its unique Europeanness, and the second is its translatability into non-European cultures. This narrative argues for the mutability of modernity, thus permitting its export and enhancing its universal character while putting a European epistemological stamp on its subsequent reception. The travelling character of this dimension of modernity as export understands modernity as emerging from Europe, say from the mid-fifteenth century, and slowly spreading outward like a million points of light into the patches of darkness that lie outside its foundational centre. Modernity in this guise was projected as an instrument of progress. The guiding concepts often associated with it – instrumental rationality, the development of capitalism – emerged in the debate between theological and scientific reason, and provided the foundation for the period of European Renaissance and Enlightenment, in which two structures of power and domination that marked the Middle Ages – feudalism and theological absolutism – collapsed. Scientific rationality and individual property that formed the basis of capital accumulation were triumphant. This collapse shifted the scales of sovereign power from the theological to the secular.

The chief principles of secularism – individual liberty, political sovereignty, democratic forms of governance, capitalism, etc. – defined its universal character and furnished its master narrative. Thus emerged the rightness of the European model, not only for its diverse societies, but also for other societies and civilisations across the rest of the world. Most importantly, the export of European modernity became not only a justification for, but a principal part of global imperialism. Among serious critics, the master narrative made the claims of universality susceptible to epistemological and historical distortion when deployed in the service of European imperialism. There is good reason for the criticism. Some historians on the right, such as Niall Ferguson, have argued that modern European imperialism, specifically that of the British Empire, was actually a good thing, not to be regretted, as it bestowed a semblance of modernity on those privileged enough to have been recipients of the Empire's civilising zeal.[1] So on the one hand there is *grand* modernity in all its European manifestations in reason and progress, and on the other is what could be called *petit* modernity, which represents the export kind, a sort of quotation, which some would go so far as to designate a mimic modernity through its various European references.

It is this relation between *grand* and *petit* modernity that has contributed to the widespread search for facilities of modernity that represent what the Indian Marxist historian Dipesh Chakrabarty would call modernity's heterotemporal history.[2] Chakrabarty argues that the various scenes of modernity observed from the point of view of a heterotemporal composition of history reveals the extent to which experiences of modernity are shot through with the particularities of each given locale, therefore deregulating any idea of one dominant universalism of historical experience. Such experiences, he argues, are structured within specific epistemological conditions that take account of diverse modes of social identity and discourse. Throughout the twentieth century, all across the world, diverse cultural contexts made adapting or translating modernity into specific local variants a pathway towards modernisation, by acquiring the accoutrements of a modern society. Because of colonial experience this resulted in what could be referred to as *grand* modernity writ small in cultures – Chakrabarty's case study was India – perceived to be in historical transition from colonialism to postcolonialism. In comparing different types of modernity, and in our attempts to describe their different characteristics we are constantly confronted with the persistent tension between *grand* modernity and *petit* modernity. How can this tension be resolved? And how can the fundamental historical experiences and the particularities of locale that attend them be reconciled or even compared? It strikes me that all recent attempts to make sense of modernity and bend it toward the multiple situated *petit* modernities – again Chakrabarty would have called these 'provincialities' – are premised on finding a way to render the divergent experiences and uses of modernity, namely the necessity to historicise and ground them in traditions of thought and practice.

FORMS OF TRANSFORMATION: MODERNITY AS META-LANGUAGE

To **historicise modernity** is not only to ground it within the conditions of social, political and economic life, it is also to recognise it as a meta-language with which cultural systems become codified and gain modern legitimation. The idea of modernity as a meta-language has been particularly acute for me over the past year. To travel in China and South Korea recently is to encounter this meta-language in action and in many guises. All around cities like Seoul, Busan, Shanghai, Beijing, Chengdu, Hangzhou, Guangzhou, Hong Kong and Taipei, etc., the clatter of machinery erecting impressive infrastructures sounded like the drill of the Morse code typing out the meta-language of modernisation. These structures – from museums, opera houses and theatres to stadiums, sporting centres, high-speed train lines, airports, stock exchanges, shopping malls and luxury apartments – bring alive to our very eyes brand new urban conditions and cultural spheres that were not remotely imaginable a generation ago. The cities of East Asia have become the playground of global architects enjoying the patronage of both public and private developers.

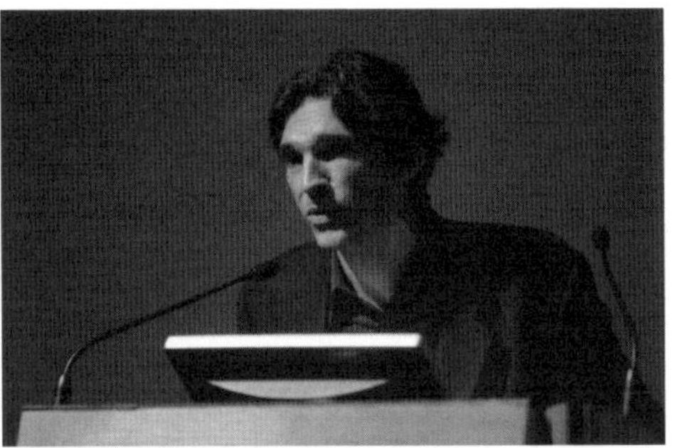

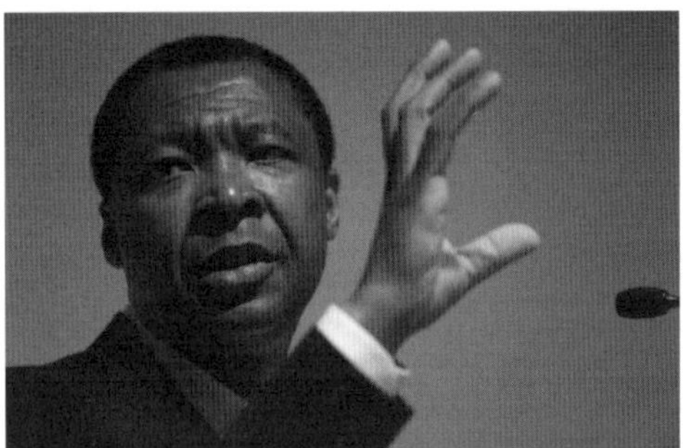

OKWUI ENWEZOR [BELOW] responding to **NICOLAS BOURRIAUD**'s [TOP] definition of the new 'modern': 'altermodern'. The session was chaired by London-based writer, curator and arist **J.J. CHARLESWORTH**.

In fact, over the course of the last sixteen months,[3] I have had occasion to travel repeatedly to South Korea and China. On numerous trips, as part of my research work as a curator, this situation of urban transformation and social renewal was visible everywhere. Underscoring the experiences of these trips is an observation of the scale of growth of the contemporary art world: artists, galleries, collectors, exhibition spaces, museums and art fairs all are making their way to Beijing and Shanghai. In China alone, the restless imagination and ambition shaping the landscape of contemporary art is breathtaking. Along with this shift, especially among intellectuals and artists, a reverse phenomenon of migration is occurring, namely the relocation back to an Asian context from which many of them had emigrated years before. Yet it is not only the infrastructures of the state and private speculation that are being revived, but the artistic and intellectual cultures of many cities are also being remapped. New centres are definitely emerging, but rather than cultural and intellectual capital being concentrated in a limited number of cities, it is being dispersed in many cities as the reverse migration of ideas continues to explode and expand the cultural parameters of new China and South Korea.

THE BAZAAR OR WORLD'S FAIR OF MODERNISATION

I **have witnessed** and marvelled at the breathtaking speed and scale of the modernisation occurring in both countries. Of course, the economies of these two countries – along with their modernisation, both in depth and in breadth – pale in comparison to Japan's, the immediate East Asian reference that lies equidistant to its two newly modernising neighbours. Both China and South Korea's financial strengths derive from a massive export economy. China, of course, is known as the factory of the world, a designation made possible by the fact that its factories are disproportionately the production centres of cheap global consumer goods that have transformed the 'Made in China' brand into a ubiquitous logo of global commerce. South Korea's industrial power, on the other hand, is characterised by a focus on advanced technology and heavy industry. Each of these two countries has built up its infrastructure through the combination of *grand* and *petit* modernity, bringing together successful models from both East and West. That is, they are both undergoing modernisation based on the acquisition of instruments and institutions of Western modernity – I mean this in a superficial sense – within a relatively short span of time, yet without the wholesale discarding of local values that modify the importations.

The ongoing, large-scale process of modernisation in China and South Korea underscores part of the energy, excitement and sense of newness coursing through the various strata of each country, making them contemporary emblems of a new modernity. Travelling in Europe, on the other hand, conveys no such sense of energy, excitement or newness. Europe, on the contrary, feels old and dour in its majestic petrification. In fact, many European cities feel less like part of our time. With their miles of imperious ceremonial architecture and in the quaintness of the narrow, tourist-friendly, cobble-stoned streets, walking through these cities feels like being in a museum of modernity. The museumification of Europe is in fact the intention: the display of heritage, historical glory and dead past. Preservationists of this heritage and glory play the role of morticians of modernity.

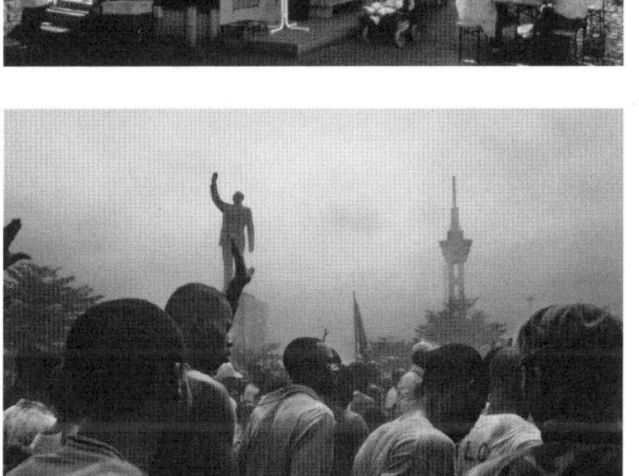

In his lecture and subsequent essay, **Enwezor** drew on works such as **Thomas Hirschorn**'s *Bataille Monument* 2002 [top] and [below] **Guy Tillim**'s *Congo Series* (this work showing supporters of Jean-Pierre Bemba on their way to a rally in Kinshasa, July 2006).

Yet ancient cities like Beijing and Hangzhou – in a country that possesses a very old civilisation and society – in contrast feel nothing like museums. Where vestiges of the past exist, they tend to be peripheral rather than central to modern Chinese cities. These cities, if anything, could be likened to temporary exhibitions of city-making, a succession of dizzying obsolescence; a bazaar or world's fair of modernisation. The cities' skylines are full of glass boxes crowned with the pitched green roofs of the classical Chinese pagoda. This hybridisation may appear absurd to us now, until we remember that, not too long ago, post-modern architecture in the West was busily inventing these trumped-up styles of the classical and the modern based on a similarly invented autochthonous Western past. Like latter-day biennales, Chinese cities are theatres of the grand statement, a lot of which have no other purpose than to impress and inspire awe. This has been achieved by what some have argued as indiscriminate modernisation and urbanisation schemes that have erased much of the cultural heritage of old China, sweeping out and destroying many old neighbourhoods and putting in their place unremarkable architecture.[4] Chinese bureaucrats, urban planners and developers, like latter-day Baron Hausmanns, are simply unsympathetic to any idea that cities like Beijing need to be historicised, that is to say museumified. Modernity is a continuous project. Its principal features, they may reason, are at best contingent. By this conjecture, I want to seek out what is currently at play in the relations of discourse in which the particularities or provincialities – I take this to mean the conditions and situations that generate them – of modernity are situated through the practice, production, dissemination and reception of contemporary art, far from any claims to a *grand* heritage or an arriviste, mimic *petit* translation.

THE ALTERMODERN AND HABITATIONS OF CONTEMPORARY ART

If the current spate of modernisation in China effectively lays waste to heritage and historical glory and instead emphasises contingency, might it not be reasonable to argue for the non-universal nature of modernity as such? This certainly would be true when applied to contemporary art. We are constantly entertained and exercised in equal measure by the notion that there is no red line running from modernism to contemporary art. For the pedagogues of the existence of such lineage, the chief emblem of this unbroken narrative can be found in the attention given to the procedures and ideas of the Western historical avant-gardes by contemporary artists. On the other hand, I take the view of this claim, *pace* Chakrabarty, as a provincial account of the complexity of contemporary art. To understand its various vectors, we need then to *provincialise modernism*. There is no one lineage of modernism or, for that matter, of contemporary art. Looking for an equivalent of an Andy Warhol in Mao's China is to be seriously blind to the fact that China of the Pop art era had neither a consumer society nor a capitalist structure, two things that were instrumentalised in Warhol's critique and usage of its images. In that sense, Pop art would be anathema to the revolutionary program – and, one might even claim, to the avant-garde imagination – of such a period in China that coincides with the condition and situation that fostered Warhol's analytical excavation of American mass media and consumer culture. But the absence of Pop art in China in the 1960s is not the same as the absence of 'progressive' contemporary Chinese art during that period, even if such contemporary art may have been subdued by the aggressive destruction of the Cultural Revolution.

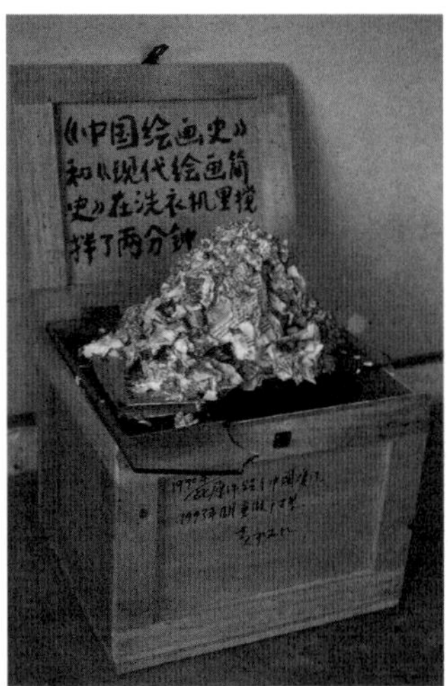

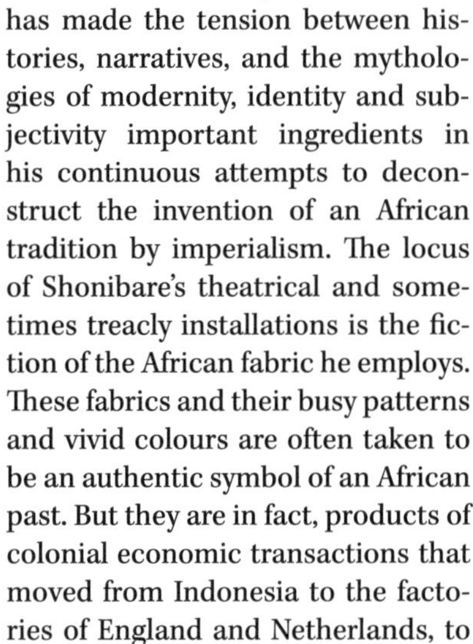

If we are to make sense of contemporary art during this period in China and the United States, then we have to wield the heterotemporal tools of history-writing; in so doing, we will see how differently situated American and Chinese artists were at this time. Despite the importance of globalisation in mediating the recent accounts of contemporary art – a world in which artists like Huang Yong Ping, Zhang Huan, Xu Bing, Matthew Barney, Andreas Gursky and Jeff Koons, for instance, are contemporaries – we can apply the same mode of argument against any uniform or unifocal view of artistic practice today. When Huang Yong Ping, in the work *A History of Chinese Painting and a Concise History of Modern Painting washed in a Washing Machine for Two Minutes* 1987 (Walker Art Centre, Minneapolis: below centre), washed two art historical texts – the first by Wang Bomin and the latter, one of the first books of Western art history published in China, Herbert Read's *A Concise History of Modern Painting* – in a washing machine, the result is a mound of pulped ideology, a history of hybridisation rather than universalism.[5] If we apply the same lens, say, to the work of Yinka Shonibare, a Nigerian artist working in London, we will again see how he has made the tension between histories, narratives, and the mythologies of modernity, identity and subjectivity important ingredients in his continuous attempts to deconstruct the invention of an African tradition by imperialism. The locus of Shonibare's theatrical and sometimes treacly installations is the fiction of the African fabric he employs. These fabrics and their busy patterns and vivid colours are often taken to be an authentic symbol of an African past. But they are in fact, products of colonial economic transactions that moved from Indonesia to the factories of England and Netherlands, to the markets of West, East and Central Africa, and ultimately to Brixton. These artists inhabit what could be called the provincialities of modernity and have incisively traced diverse paths of modernity through them. By examining these different locales of practice, as well as the historical experiences that inform them, we learn a lot more about the contingent conditions of modernity than about its universalism. Here again, Chakrabarty offers a useful framework in this regard by dint of what he refers to as 'habitations of modernity.'[6]

What could these habitations of modernity be? On what maps do they appear? And in what forms and shapes? The search for the habitations of modernity seems to me the crux of the 'altermodern' , the subject of the 2009 Tate Triennial exhibition and the accompanying discursive projects organised by Nicolas Bourriaud, its curator. In his outline to the altermodern project, Bourriaud lays out an intellectual and cultural itinerary, a jagged map of simultaneity and discontinuity; overlapping narratives and contiguous sites of production that form the basis of contemporary art practice globally. The chief claim of the altermodern project is simple: to discover the current habitations of contemporary practice. Thus the altermodern proposes the rejection of rigid structures put in place by a stubborn and implacable modernity and the modernist ideal of artistic autonomy. In the same way, it manifests a rebellion against the systematisation of artistic production based on a singular, universalised conception of artistic paradigms. If there is anything that marks the path of the altermodern, it would be the provincialities of contemporary art practice today – that is, the degree to which these practices, however globalised they may appear, are also informed by specific epistemological models and aesthetic conditions. Within this scheme, Bourriaud sets out to exmaine for us the unfolding of the diverse fields of contemporary art practice that have been unsettled by global links. But, more importantly, these practices are measured against the totalising principles of *grand* modernity.

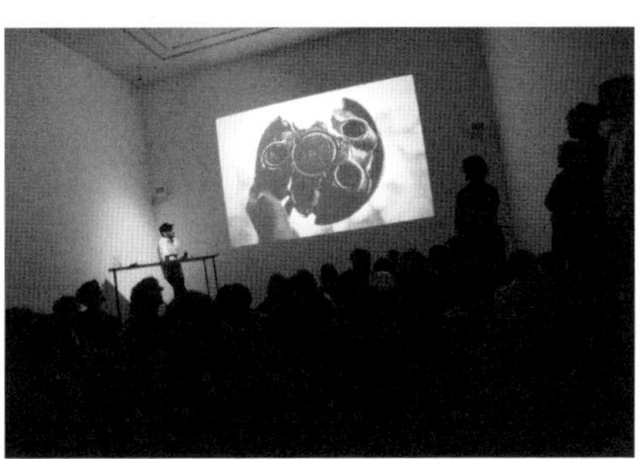

TRIS VONNA-MICHELL uses the tradition of storytelling to make energetic performances that take the audience on a mental and physical journey. His narratives, both fictional and non-fictional, explore the ways history is passed on. *Auto-Tracking: From Cellar to Garret* was a new performance piece, conducted in six acts (each lasting approx. 7 mins). It reworked previous narratives exploring notions of personal and historical spaces and monuments, which are embodied, fabricated or sought for. The spoken-word monologue interwove past and current verbal scripts, performed between interludes of audio field-recordings.

At the core of the altermodern's jagged map is its description of what its author refers to in his introductory paper as the 'offshore' location of contemporary art practice.[7] However, I will foreground the location of these contemporary practices as indicative of a drive toward an off-centre principle, namely the multifocal, multilocal, heterotemporal and dispersed structures around which contemporary art is often organised and convened. This multiply located off-centre – which might not be analogous to Bourriaud's notion of offshore-based production – is not the same as the logic of decentred locations. Rather, the off-centre is structured by the simultaneous existence of multiple centres. In this way, rather than being the decentring of the universal, or the relocation of the centre of contemporary art, as the notion of the offshore suggests, it becomes instead, the emergence of multiplicity, the breakdown of cultural or locational hierarchies, the absence of a singular locus or a limited number of centres.

TOWARD THE EXCENTRIC: POSTCOLONIALITY, POSTMODERNITY AND THE ALTERMODERN

To a large extent, the discursive feature of the altermodern project seems to me a return to earlier debates that shaped postcolonial and postmodernist critiques of modernity and the aesthetic principle of the universal. At the same time, they launched an attack on modernism's focus on a unifocal rather than dialogic modernity. Embracing these critiques, Bourriaud's project sets out to explore the excentric[8] and dialogic nature of art today, including its scattered trajectories and multiple temporalities, by questioning and provincialising the idea of the centre, by decentring its imaginary, as Chakrabarty posits in his provocative book *Provincializing Europe*.[9] Yet this excentric dimension of modern and contemporary art is not necessarily a rejection of modernity and modernism; rather it articulates the shift to off-centre structures of production and dissemination; the dispersal of the universal, the refusal of the monolithic, a rebellion against monoculturalism. In this way, what the altermodern proposes is a rephrasing of prior arguments. The objective is to propose a new terminology, one that could succinctly capture both the emergence of multiple cultural fields as they overspill into diverse arenas of thinking and practice, and a reconceptualisation of the structures of legitimation that follow in their wake. In his text, Bourriaud makes concrete what he sees as the field of the altermodern, describing his model as

> an attempt to redefine modernity in the era of globalisation. A state of mind more than a 'movement', the altermodern goes against cultural standardisation and massification on one hand, against nationalisms and cultural relativism on the other, by positioning itself within the world cultural gaps, putting translation, wander-

> ing and culture-crossings at the centre of art production. Offshore-based, it forms clusters and archipelagos of thought against the continental 'mainstream': the altermodern artist produces links between signs far away from each other, explores the past and the present to create original paths.
>
> Envisioning time as a multiplicity rather than as a linear progress, the altermodern artist considers the past as a territory to explore, and navigates throughout history as well as all the planetary time zones. Altermodern is heterochronical. Formally speaking, altermodern art privileges processes and dynamic forms to unidimensional single objects, trajectories to static masses.[10]

THE OFFSHORE, OFF-CENTRE AND PROCEDURES OF RELATION

THE FORMULATION of the altermodern reflects precisely Eduoard Glissant's theory of the 'poetics of relation,'[11] an idea predicated on linkages and networks of relations rather than on a singular focal point of practice. Bourriaud's idea of the altermodern addresses the cultural geography of relations of discourse and practice. He rightly reads contemporary art as that which always exceeds the borders of spatial confinement, beyond the limited geography of the nation and its totalised identity. The altermodern is structured around trajectories, connections, time zones: heterochronical pathways. Such relations suggest that the project is strongly in accord with a large corpus of scholarship and literature that has made conceiving an alternate system for evaluating modernity, one in which the off-centre contexts of contemporary art are a core intellectual principle. But have not the practices of art always been predicated on trajectories and detours, on dynamic forms and modes of production and dissemination? Is the role of contemporary art not always the constant refusal of orthodoxy; to display attentive vigilance against closure; to challenge all doctrinaire, unitary discourses on which some of the most powerful theses of classical modernism rest?

While Bourriaud identifies the shift in recent art as the desire to mobilise new localities of production, which he perceives today as proper to the field of artistic practice, a related field of historical research (as I have noted several times) has been examining the dimension of the off-centre principle of art-historical discourse for some time. The result of these research projects is slowly entering mainstream art-historical production. In the last decade, several scholars have explored the structure of the heterochronical (think, for instance, of Chakrabarty's notion of the heterotemporal method of organising historical frames) conception of modern and contemporary art history.

One such project is a recent exhibition, *Turns in Tropics: Artist-Curator*, developed for the *7th Gwangju Biennale* by the Manila-based Filipino art historian and curator Patrick Flores. In his exhibition project, he proposes an agenda of experimental and conceptualist practices from the late 1960s to early 1980s in Southeast Asia by four artists working in contexts in which the spirit of modernity was not only transforming the splintered identity of the nation, but rapid modernisation was also recalibrating the canons and languages of artistic practice.[12] Flores's emphasis of location represents a distinct cultural ecology, as it were, a habitation of modernity. His research explores not only the shifts in the language of artistic modernity – between the traditional and the experimental, from academic painting to conceptualism – it also interrogates the effects and receptions of modernity by these postcolonial artists in relation to their belonging to the nation.

In doing so, he directs attention to a text stencilled on a sculpture by the Malaysian artist Redza Piyadasa, which states that 'Artworks never exist in time, they have "entry points."'[13] In this text Piyadasa's sculpture declares the contingency of its own history. In fact, it historicises its own ambivalence towards canonical epistemology. What the stencilled text seems to be questioning is the idea of art as a universal sign that is a frozen historical datum. Instead, artworks are dynamic forces that seek out relations of discourse, map new topologies, and create multiple relations and pathways. Piyadasa's statement anticipates and echoes Bourriaud's own suggestion for altermodernist art, both in its claim for the trajectories of art, but also in the shifting historical and temporal dimension of the apprehension of such art.

While none of the four artists whose works were examined in the exhibition have appeared in standard, so-called mainstream surveys and accounts of experimental art and conceptualism of the late 1960s to the present, new off-centre historical research such as Flores's consistently drives us to the harbours of these archipelagos of modernity and contemporary art. The work of Ray Albano from the Philippines, Jim Supangkat from Indonesia, Piyadasa and the younger Thai artist, curator and art historian Apinan Poshyananda, have clear structural affinities with the work of their contemporaries practicing in the West. Yet their work – made with an awareness of, and in response to, specific historical conditions – shares similar objectives with the work of other postcolonial artists from different parts of the world, including those living and practicing in Europe.

These objectives would be familiar to emerging scholars such as Sunanda Sanyal, whose research focuses on modernism in Uganda;[14] Elizabeth Harney, who has written extensively about negritude and modernism in Senegal;[15] or the magisterial writing on modern and contemporary Indian art by the eminent critic Geeta Kapur.[16] Art historian Gao Minglu has engaged equally rigorously with contemporary Chinese art, and with the same objective.[17] In a similar vein of historical archaeology, the Princeton art historian Chika Okeke-Agulu has studied and written persuasively on the generative character of young modern Nigerian artists in the late 1950s during the period of decolonisation.[18] But by no means am I suggesting that many of the artists examined in these various research studies are obscure in their own artistic contexts. Their artistic trajectories belong exactly in the heterotemporal frames of historical reflection and the chronicles of their art are part of the heterochronical criticism and curating that has been part of the discourse of twentieth- and twenty-first-century modernity. However, viewed with the lens of a univocal modernist history, one that is predicated on the primacy of centres of practice – what Bourriaud refers to as the 'continental "mainstream"' – can these practices be understood as forming more than an archipelago, and in fact exceed the altermodernist impulse? They certainly do expand the purely modernist notion of artistic competence. These issues are at the core of recent writings and research by the British-Ghanaian art historian and cultural critic Kobena Mercer, who explores the diverse off-centre contexts of late modernism and contemporary art in a series of anthologies focused on artistic practices and artists in Africa, Asia and Europe.[19] Similar issues were mapped in the seminal 1989 exhibition, *The Other Story*, a project curated by the Pakistan-born British artist and critic, Rasheed Araeen at the Hayward Gallery, wherein he examined the contributions of hitherto unrecognised non-western modernist artists to European modernism.[20]

These surveys and situations of off-centredness are emblematic of the large historical gaps which today, in the era of globalisation, need to be reconciled with dominant paradigms of artistic discourse. In seeking to historicise these contexts of production and practice, a dialogic system of evaluation is established. It resolutely veers away from the standard and received notions of modernity, especially in the hierarchical segmentations that have been the prevailing point of entry into its review of off-centre practices.

MODERNITY, POSTCOLONIALITY AND SOVEREIGN SUBJECTIVITY

Whatever the entry point for the altermodern artists, there remain some boundaries between the locations of contemporary artistic practice and the historical production of modern subjectivity. These boundaries are tied up with the unfinished nature of the project of modernity. Consequently, I want to examine in more detail some ideas of modernity that could be related to the way hierarchies operate in the recognition and historicisation of artists and their locations of practice. The course I will follow could be likened to navigating the different levels and segments of *grand* and *petit* modernity, albeit with degrees of separation designating stages of development, movements, breaks in cultural logics, ossification of epistemological models, and transitions to which we ascribe the norms of the modern world. One logic of modernity to which the altermodern responds is globalisation, a series of processes synonymous with the emergence of a worldwide system of capitalism. We could understand this modernity, in its teleological unfolding, as part of the current manifestation of globalisation as a force-field of winners, near winners and losers. (The losers being, obviously, those thoroughly subordinated and utterly disenfranchised by modernity's centuries-long progression from the worlds of indenture, slavery, imperialism and colonialism, to the aggressive, retributive wars of recent memory.)

This field of retributive conduct has at its disposal the overwhelming capacity to erase and deracinate subjectivities that inhabit the cultural localities of *petit* modernity. This makes the large claims ascribed to *grand* modernity less an avatar of enlightened cultural and material transformation, and more a structure with a dark core. It seems fairly impossible to think of modernity without linking it to concepts such as sovereignty, equality and liberty as they have been developed across domains of life and social practices. *Pace* Michel Foucault's theory of biopower,[21] a range of thinkers have focused on this dimension of modernity, a space in which the master and slave dialectic is writ large. This dialectic, developed by Hegel, dissociates sovereignty from the practice of self-governance, and instead embeds it in the interrogation of the relations between power and subordination.

However, subordination is directly linked to how power exposes the subordinated to structures of violence, to acts of historical erasure. In this area of analysis, Giorgio Agamben's extension of biopower and *biopolitics* was an attempt to sketch out the conditions around which what he calls *naked life* is summoned: a state of living in which individual sovereignty is exposed to its most basic, barest dimension, to execution.[22] In terms of ideas surrounding modernity and colonialism, this thinking has been singularly illuminating, and has been taken up by other thinkers. The feminist literary scholar Judith Butler, for example, in a recent reflection on the prosecution of the war on terror and the hopelessness of prisoners caught in its principal non-place, Guantanamo Bay, addressed the issue of naked life in the essay 'Precarious Life.'[23]

Pushing further the frontier of this thinking is the powerful writing of theorist Achille Mbembe, especially in an essay in which he summarises the dimensions of biopower, bare and precarious life as the zone of *necropolitics*. In the essay Mbembe explored the fundamental relationship between modernity and violence, particularly in the apparatuses of the colonial regime, such that 'To exercise sovereignty is to exercise control over mortality and to define life as the deployment and manifestation of power.'[24] For Mbembe, *necropolitics* is the condition under which conducts related to sovereignty – as he amply demonstrates by citing the policy of apartheid in South Africa or the predicament of the Palestinians in the occupied territories – are inextricably bound up with exercises of control over existence, of individual lives and their narratives. Most examinations of the artistic work coming out of South Africa during the apartheid era confirms how artists were overwhelmingly preoccupied with the structures of violence and its direct manifestation as part of the condition of colonial modernity and thereby establishes art as one exploration of the question of sovereignty. Here, resistance to violence and the rigorous assertion of sovereign subjectivity becomes in itself the subject and narrative of art and cultural production.

Facing away from culture, Mbembe in his critique, for example, sees political theory as tending to associate sovereignty with issues of autonomy, be it that of the state or of the individual. He argues however, that

> The romance of sovereignty, in this case, rests on the belief that the subject is the master and the controlling author of his or her own meaning. Sovereignty is therefore defined as a twofold process of *self-institution* and *self-limitation* (fixing one's own limits for oneself). The exercise of sovereignty, in turn, consists in society's capacity for self-creation through recourse to institutions inspired by specific social and imaginary significations.[25]

To distinguish this relation of *self-institution* and *self-limitation*, the central concern he notes targets instead 'those figures of sovereignty whose central project is not the struggle for autonomy but *the generalised instrumentalisation of human existence and the material destruction of human bodies and populations*.'[26] Two of Mbembe's historical examples are South Africa and Palestine. In the fate of these two spaces, he identifies the fundamental rationality of modernity, arguing, 'that modernity was at the origin of multiple concepts of sovereignty – and therefore of the biopolitical.'[27] Artworks such as those by William Kentridge, in films such as *Ubu Tells the Truth* 1997, and Paul Stopforth, in his 1980 drawing series *Death of Steve Biko*, to name only two instances from South Africa; and by Emily Jacir in her exhibition *Where We*

Come From 2003, dealing with the emotions of separation, confinement, banishment and exile experienced by Palestinians – all form part of the artistic responses to the concepts of sovereignty and the biopolitical.

It strikes me that the idea of the altermodern, as it deviates from the limits placed on life and subjectivity by the instrumental violence of modernity, cannot be captured by focusing alone on shifts in locales of practice or by strategies of resistance against domination. The altermodern is to be found in the work of art itself; the work of art as a manifestation of pure difference in all the social, cultural and political signs it wields to elaborate that difference. It is the space in which to fulfil the radical gesture of refusal and disobedience, not in the formal sense, but in the ethical and epistemological sense. Such a stance – what I take to be altermodern – with difference writ large as the fundamental quest of the object of art, can be identified in such diverse works as the installations of Thomas Hirschhorn, the radiant paintings of Chris Ofili, the splayed anatomies of Marlene Dumas, the paintings on animal sacrifice as a metaphor for human suffering by Iba Ndiaye, the 2008 film *Hunger* by Steve McQueen and many more.

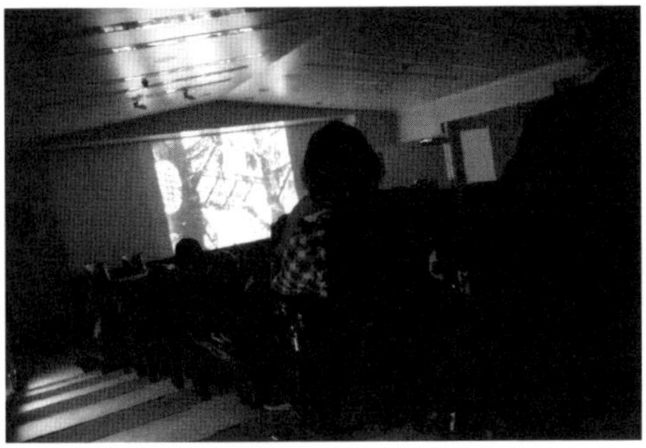

FRENCH PHILOSOPHER **JORDI VIDAL**'s *Servitude and Simulacra*, co-directed with **STÉPHANE GOXE** was screened at the Altermodern Prologue. It is at once a filmic essay about contemporary thought, a curated exhibition commentated by its author, and a supplement to his book of the same title. **VIDAL** has produced polemical statements against postmodernism and its reduction of modernism's promise of social equality and justice.

FOUR MODERNITIES

IN NAVIGATING the different segments of modernity, one could well imagine the different levels of its development or in the hierarchical layers of its construction, as the zones of differing concepts of life and death, subject and non-subject, as the sites of the biopolitical, as the scenes of struggle of sovereignty, as domains of exception. Here I am employing the segments metaphorically to situate the hierarchies of modernity, and in so doing to catch its over-spill into domains of everyday practice, crucially art.

Considering this over-spill, and following the schema of the hierarchies of modernity, especially as it bears on cultural and artistic practice, I want to conceptualise what I see as the four domains of modernity. The first three domains lays out the architecture for thinking the link between differing zones of life and, indirectly, cultural practice. The fourth and last is sceptical of attributes of modernity as such. It is obvious that when the concept of modernity is broached in recent scholarship, the defining characteristic is overwhelmingly skewed toward the idea of one single modernity, that being the idea that modernity is essentially a project fundamentally connected to the development of Western capitalism and imperialism. Fredric Jameson's book, *A Singular Modernity*,[28] partly suggests this. In fact, he was brutally sceptical of recent attempts to expand the definitions of modernity into such things as 'alternative modernity', 'African modernity', 'subaltern modernity' or other such designations. To him modernity is inextricably bound to capitalism, and globalisation is its current and main feature. But by perceiving all other modernities as flowing from this one single, grand narrative as the fount of historical development, what emerges is a narrower, unifocal, monocultural and less heterochronical perspective of modernity.

However, new debates have been historicising the discourses of modernity in other to propose a more heterogeneous, multifocal, polycentric, broader interpretation of categories of modernity. Many of the recent scholarship do insist that there has never been a single modernity but multiple modernities, as S.N. Eisenstadt has argued.[29] The economist and philosopher Amartya Sen also applies a multifocal interpretation of modernity as he lays out and describes the changing modalities of modernity based on a broad view of the human community and identity.[30] Björn Wittrock develops a comparative analysis of early modernity, examining particularly the dimensions of the public sphere in the Indian subcontinent,

Europe, China and Japan.[31] The French *Annales* historian, Fernand Braudel, also argues for the diachronic dimension of modernity as a long process of slow evolution in which there are no linear, unidirectional flows of time. Rather than a singular causality, he places a strong emphasis on the study of microsystems and events – on trade and cultural exchanges among competing interests in the Mediterranean, for example – that provide a more complex, but overarching world picture.[32] In the context of twentieth-century globalisation, Arjun Appadurai argues for a modernity seen and experienced predominantly through a scalar analysis of mediated exchanges telegraphed by representations such as images, sound, technology and ideas.[33] The philosopher Kwame Appiah has recently examined modernity through the lens of cosmopolitanism,[34] a view that appears to be in accord with some of the objectives of the altermodern conception of contemporary art.

There are four categories that I identify as emblematic of the conditions of modernity today: *supermodernity*, *andromodernity*, *speciousmodernity* and *aftermodernity*. For the sake of our focus on visual modernity, my categories may simplify the point. But they will nonetheless serve as points of entry for the photographic images I will reference later.

A. *SUPERMODERNITY*

THE FIRST CATEGORY postulates the essential forms of modernity through the general character and forms it has taken in European and western culture. This category of modernity emerges directly from the grand narrative of modernity. It is the zone of what I call *supermodernity*, to borrow Marc Augé's term. *Supermodernity* represents the idea of the 'centre'. It is a domain of power, and is often understood as greatly evolved, or highly '*advanced*' or '*developed*'. It is generally acknowledged as fundamental to the development of the entire framework of global modernity, namely the world system of capitalism. Therefore, it is foundational to all other subsequent claims and discourses of modernity. All of them follow in the wake of *supermodernity*. The main coordinates of *supermodernity*, as developed through the Enlightenment, are marked by notions such as *freedom*, *progress*, *rationality* and *empiricism*. It is through these ideas that the concepts of sovereignty and autonomy emerge.

To understand the nature of the next two categories of modernity requires paying close attention to the four coordinates exemplified in *supermodernity*, because they are the framing devices that allow us to describe whether a cultural sphere is pre-modern, modern or anti-modern, insofar as it concerns the world of modernity that we have inherited since the ages of discovery and imperialism. *Supermodernity* is deeply embedded in structures of power and has at its disposal superior and formidable infrastructures of force to continuously maintain and advance its agenda. More importantly, it tends to represent our view of modernity in relation to cultural positions and political contexts that may subscribe to the idea of modernity for which Bourriaud has gone searching for new possible artistic imaginaries that deviate from or may even blaspheme against its suppositions. For six centuries, *supermodernity* has been stubbornly resilient and has remained the example to which other modernities respond. This is the modernity that is well-captured in Mbembe's *necropolitics*, because of its capacity to standardise zones of living and practice.

B. *ANDROMODERNITY*

THIS BRINGS US to the next category of modernity, its second level. If *supermodernity* understands and claims for itself the sole category of the developed and advanced, we can designate the next level, which – because of historical circumstances – is imagined as not to have evolved to the same tertiary degree, as *developing* modernity. It is not difficult to guess which segments of the global order occupy this circle of modernity. Specifically, developing modernity today refers to broad swaths of Asia, especially China, India, South Korea, etc. In a true sense, this circle of modernity is caught in a cycle that I designate as *andromodernity*, meaning that it is a hybrid form of modernity, achieved through a kind of accelerated type of development, while also devising alternative models of development. *Andromodernity*, as such, is a lesser modernity since its principal emphasis is development or modernisation, as Jürgen Habermas would have it.[35] Because it is still modernising, *andromodernity* has neither the global structure of power nor the infrastructure of economic, technological, political and epistemological force to promulgate its own agenda independent of the systems (museums, markets, academies) of *supermodernity*. It therefore lacks, for the moment, the capacity for world dominance. Moreover, much of its development is seen to be based principally on the affective elements of modernity, that is they are deeply embedded in the process of modernisation; in the way things appear to be modern (hence the obsession with acquiring the accoutrements of a modern society, even if socially, there are distinctive differences between various zones of life.)

C. *SPECIOUSMODERNITY*

THIS BRINGS US to the next circle, which relates to the state of Islamic modernity today, especially in the present state of rebellion into which it is plunged. According to some detractors of the rise of political Islam and the extremist strains that have emerged out of the radicalisation of politics in Muslim societies, the problem of this rebellion is essentially one of modernity, the idea that these societies have never been modernised. One reason given for this state of affairs within Islam is the lack of democratic participation, which encourages and, in fact, foments authoritarian rule by either the clergy in theocratic Iran or the absolute monarchies in the Arabian peninsula or dictatorships such as Saddam Hussein's Iraq and Bashar al-Assad's Syria. The absence of democratic participation, the argument goes, makes it impossible to bring into existence modernising forces that would bring about modernity. When it is pointed out that countries like Egypt, Syria, Iraq, Iran, Lebanon and Turkey, have each undergone periods of radical secularisation throughout the twentieth century, such instances are often dismissed as superficial attempts at modernisation; therefore what they left in their wake is a kind of *speciousmodernity*. On the inverse, the long process of reform taking place within Muslim societies today is just as often labelled as a nihilistic, anti-modern movement. Whether specious or not, anti-modern or not, it is nevertheless the case that Muslim societies are radicalised, and within that radicalisation lies the seed of a biopolitical gesture that is a response to the programs of colonial modernity. Political Islam is thus not a consequence of a *speciousmodernity* that never assimilated into its structures an authentic modernity based on the four rationalities of *supermodernity*, but part of a postcolonial form of address seeking new models and political cultures.

The rise of Islamic radicalism throughout the Middle East, and the incipient revolution that exploded with the overthrow of the Shah Reza Pahlavi and the Peacock Throne in Iran, and with it, the sacking and occupation of the American embassy in Teheran by university students, unleashed a radical postcolonial force that is distinct from the forces of decolonisation in the 1950s and 1960s. The overthrow of the Shah not only revived political Islam, it placed it at the centre of global discursive formations in which it has remained since the founding of Al-Qaeda in the 1990s. Though political Islam was already well financed – both ideologically and intellectually with the formation of the Muslim Brotherhood by Hassan Al-Bana in Egypt in the 1920s, and its intellectual transformation by its chief ideologue Sayyid Qutb – the first demonstration of political Islam's will to globality was the theocratic organisation of its power in Iran in 1979.[36] The Islamic revolution in Iran signalled the changed context of superpower politics or, *pace* Mbembe, *necropolitics*. It not only introduced a new actor on the ideological landscape – an actor who decides on the limits of life and controls and mobilises the organisations of death – it also imagined a new political community separate from and permanently antagonistic to structures of power and infrastructures of force specific to *supermodernity*. As such, the early 1980s inaugurated a remarkable cultural and political shift in global terms.

The signal event of this historical shift was the return of Ayatollah Ruhollah Khomeini to Teheran from exile in Paris after the triumph of the resistance against the Shah. As the spiritual leader of the Islamic theocracy that has governed Iran to date, Khomeini presided over the radical ideological repositioning of Iran away from the epistemological and cultural dominance of the West to Islamic ethics, not only as a system of governance but as a worldview based on the Koran as the supreme tool of religious, political, cultural, social and economic conduct and identity. The revolution in Iran was not just an act of insurrection against *supermodernity*, attacking the dominant assumptions of imperialism that accompany it; the revolution posited itself as an instrument of spiritual and therefore social and cultural purification from the stain of Western, godless decadence. In the end the revolution, though political in the pedestrian sense, was in fact, about culture and identity: Islamic modernity as a counter-model and real alternative to *supermodernity*. This position of political Islam is in remarkable accord with the idea of the altermodern.

Thus, the test for the power of persuasion of *supermodernity* can be partly analysed through the sanguine postcolonial lessons of the Islamic revolution and the various struggles – for better or worse – that have been undertaken by social and political forces radicalised by their resentment of the machinations of the West in Muslim societies. Structuring this radicalisation, and all the splintered cultural ideas and ideologies that rise from it, is the collision of two irreconcilable positions: on the one hand a Western ethnocentric exceptionalism that continues to prescribe a civilising ethos for the Muslim world, and on the other, an Islamic fundamentalism that mercilessly attacks the West and its allies with nihilistic violence. This meeting is a collision of political forces and cultural logics, an altermodernist relation marked by a face-off between colonial modernity and postcolonial modernity. However, the distance between colonial modernity and postcolonial modernity is one of degrees, for each incorporates and contradicts the other. Each is the mirror of the other. Their strained interpretation of the other is what has produced the kind of cultural antagonism that currently bedevils Western and postcolonial discursive formations, further enervating the competing institutional structures, epistemology, ideals, faith and identity.

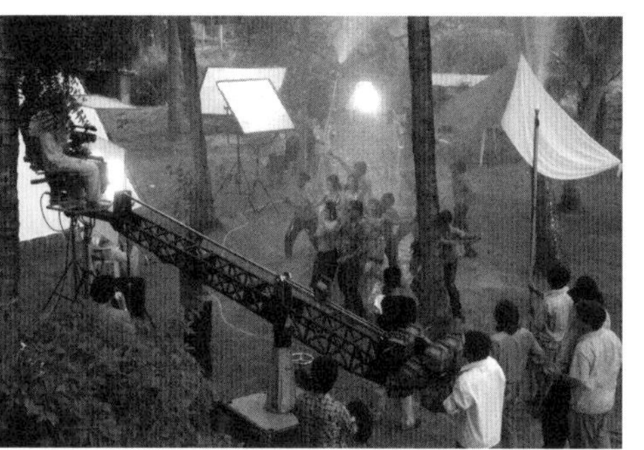

NAVIN RAWANCHAIKUL is a Thai artist who divides his time between Thailand and Japan, and whose family roots are Indian and Hindu-Punjabi. For the Altermodern Prologue he showed *Navins of Bollywood* 2006, which borrows from Bollywood song and dance cinema, and is part of the artist's ongoing investigation into identity through his global search for other 'Navins'.

D. *AFTERMODERN*

So far, we have addressed the three dominant ideas of current thinking about modernity. The fourth idea concerns an area of the world – Africa – seen to be the most opaque to the persuasions of *supermodernity*. Africa is located in the nethermost part of modernity, relegated to an epistemology of non-existence that has never been modern, to literalise Bruno Latour's idea that the world has never been modern.[37] Africa shares part of the scorn about its non-modernity that is also directed at the Muslim world. But Islamic societies do enjoy greater respect than Africa, because, there is a classical Islamic past which Africa is said to lack. German philosopher G.W.F. Hegel made this explicit, when he wrote:

> Africa proper, as far as History goes back, has remained – for all purposes of connection with the rest of the world – shut up; it is the Gold land compressed within itself – the land of childhood, which lying beyond the day of self-conscious history, is enveloped in the dark mantle of Night. Its isolated character originated, not merely in its tropical nature, but essentially in its geographical condition.[38]

If Africa is no part of historical consciousness, thereby lacking 'Spirit,' how can it lay claim to any experience of modernity if not from an education derived from the master narrative of *grand* modernity? If the Muslim world is speciously modern and Africa not yet modern, then the two societies exist in anti-rational systems of theocratic fundamentalism or tribal ethnocentrism. Each of these societies is reduced to cultural spheres whose experience of modernity have been developed out of oppression and violence and therefore in need of reconciling to modernity. However, Islamic societies tend to fare better than African ones in debates around modernity. Africa is a zone which many reflexively and categorically declare as the antithesis of the modern imagination, a place of the absence of modernity, where every aspect of the conditions of living specific to modernity has been effaced or erased. By this thinking, Africa is the true epigone of modernity. If Bourriaud posits the entire structure of his project as *altermodernist*, Africa, it may be said, at the very least is *aftermodern* not only because the narratives of modernity in Africa are predicated on an encounter of antagonism but also in the invention of a new African character of modernity that emerges after the end of modernity. The modernity to which Africa responds, and which it struggles to disaggregate from its social context, is the architecture of colonial modernity. It is in this sense that situations of modernity in Africa are *aftermodern*, because, having no relation to history-making, its modernity can only emerge after the end of the modern. Such modernity, more than in other parts of world, would be based in large part on a project of disinheriting the violence of colonial modernity.

This is partly what the recent images produced by South African photographer Guy Tillim seem to suggest: that parts of Africa – Congo, Angola, Madagascar, Ghana and Mozambique – have undertaken inconclusive projects of modernisation. Tillim's photographs depict processes of anomie. Viewed through a conventional lens, these images tend to convey and confirm the idea that modernisation has been marked by failure in Africa. To a large extent, the images are products of a certain ethnography of modernity, in the same way that my perception of European cities evokes the spectral nature of a museum of petrified modernity.

Tillim has been photographing in Africa for more than a decade now. His images can be superficially described as reportage, a mode of photographic production that can either oversimplify complex situations or may illuminate aspects of such situations as worthy of examination. Working with the verve of a photojournalist and an aid worker, over the years Tillim has carefully inserted himself and his camera into spaces that would normally be off-bounds for most photographers. He has made various African cities the haunt of his photographic enterprise, for instance photographing over a period of six months in the tough tenements of Johannesburg, in modernist buildings that have entered a state of ruin as the urban context of the post-apartheid city became replaced by a sense of siege. Likewise, Tillim has roamed all over Africa, to various regions of conflict, searching or, as some would say, scavenging for images of societies in near-collapse. On first encountering many of Tillim's images, the tendency is to view his photographs as the work of a zealous sensationalist or an ethnographer inscribing fantasies of visual frisson against the backdrop of social collapse.

The recent series of work by Tillim, like his Jo'burg series, initially gave me pause, but looking more carefully at the selection of scenes and the organisation of the larger compendium, the logic of his approach revealed a study of contrasts between postcolonial state failure in Africa and the notion of a continent in the throes of entering *aftermodernity*. To my mind it is in the intersection between these contrasts, the promise and failure of decolonisation, and the slow process of a counter-modernity that is about to take root in Africa. Tillim summarises this vision of a yet to come modernity, writing about his images:

> These photographs are not collapsed histories of post-colonial African states or a meditation on aspects of late modernist era colonial structures, but a walk through avenues of dreams. Patrice Lumumba's dream, his nationalism, is discernible in the structures, if one reads the signs, as is the death of his dream, in these de facto monuments. How strange that modernism, which eschewed monument and past for nature and future, should carry such memory so well.[39]

Throughout different parts of Africa new discourses and patterns of modernisation are not only rethinking the entire agenda which colonial modernity bequeathed the continent, but social scientists and researchers have also been articulating possible theories for a type of modernity and a structure of modernisation that can take hold in Africa. This modernity, it is hoped, is one that will emerge at the end of the project of *supermodernity*. It will perhaps mark not only an ideal of the altermodern, but will initiate a new cycle of the *aftermodern*.

Tillim succinctly articulates that spirit of the yet-to-come: 'In the frailty of this strange and beautiful hybrid landscape struggling to contain the calamities of the past fifty years, there is an indisputably African identity. This is my embrace of it.'[40] His photographic project is an expression of the hope that showing the decaying legacy of colonial modernity in Africa is not an attempt to mourn the loss of some great past, but a possible *tabula rasa* for a future composition. It disarms and dispossesses the colonial inheritance, and shows, as Jürgen Habermas argues, that modernity is an incomplete project.[41]

NOTES

1. **NIALL FERGUSON**, *Empire: The Rise and Demise of the British World Order and the Lessons for Global Power*, New York 2004. In a subsequent work, **NIALL FERGUSON**, *Colossus: The Price of American Empire*, New York 2004, Ferguson actually argues for an expanded American adaptation of the British model.

2. **DIPESH CHAKRABARTY**, *Provincializing Europe: Post-colonial Thought and Historical Difference*, 2nd ed., Princeton 2007, p.xvii.

3. These trips, totalling around 15 visits – 4 to China and 11 to South Korea – took place between June 2007 and early November 2008. They were made while I worked in Gwangju, South Korea, as artistic director of *Gwangju Biennale*, an event founded in 1995, in the wake of South Korea's transition to democracy in the 1990s. The biennale form, an exhibition model that combines massive scale with unabashed theatricality, is itself a product of a certain idea of cultural modernity that has made its way from the late nineteenth century in Europe to the explosion it presently enjoys all over the world, and more so in Asia in the twenty-first century.

4. **NICOLAI OUROUSSOFF**, 'Lost in the New Beijing: The Old Neighborhood', *New York Times*, 27 July 2008; and 'In the Changing Face of Beijing, a Look at the New China', *New York Times*, 13 July 2008. In a comparative analysis of China and Persian Gulf cities like Dubai, Ouroussoff explored how the idea of modernisation on a massive scale has shifted visionary architecture that, in the past, was largely viewed sceptically by architects and was, for the most part, peripheral to new theories of urbanism. With the advent of these changes in China and in Dubai, Abu Dhabi, Bahrain and Doha, etc., the new frontier of urban experimentation has moved to the East and declined in the West. See Ouroussoff, 'The New, New City', *New York Times*, 8 June 2008.

5. In a commentary about the intention of the work, **HUANG YONG PING** says, 'In China, regarding the two cultures of East and West, traditional and modern, it is constantly being discussed as to which is right, which is wrong, and how to blend the two. In my opinion, placing these two texts in the washing machine for two minutes symbolises this situation and well solves the problem much more effectively and appropriately than debates lasting a hundred years.' Quoted in **GAO MINGLU**, *The Wall: Reshaping Contemporary Chinese Art*, exh. cat., Albright Knox Art Gallery, Buffalo and Millennium Museum, Beijing 2005, p.129

6. **DIPESH CHAKRABARTY**, *Habitations of Modernity: Essays in the Wake of Subaltern Studies*, Chicago 2002.

7. **NICOLAS BOURRIAUD**, published statement from a brochure outline for the 'Altermodern' program, Tate Britain, London April 2008.

8. In 2001, the first African Pavilion in the Venice Biennale in the exhibition *Authentic/Excentric*, curated by Salah Hassan and Olu Oguibe, argued for this sense of a dispersed zone of practice. For a productive curatorial and critical exploration of the idea of the excentric nature of contemporary, see the accompanying catalogue, **SALAH HASSAN AND OLU OGUIBE** (eds.), *Authentic/Excentric: Conceptualism in Contemporary African Art*, Ithaca 2001.

9. **CHAKRABARTY** 2007, p.4.

10. **BOURRIAUD** 2008.

11. **ÉDOUARD GLISSANT**, *Poetics of Relation*, trans. Betsey Wing, Ann Arbor 1996.

12. The four artists in the exhibition: Ray Albano (Philippines), Redza Piyadasa (Malaysia), Jim Supangkat (Indonesia) and Apinan Poshanyanda (Thailand). All played multiple roles as influential artists, curators, critics and historians in each of their individual national contexts in the development of the discourses of modernity and contemporary art.

13. **PATRICK D. FLORES**, 'Turns in Tropics: Artist Curator' in Okwui Enwezor (ed.), *Annual Report: A Year in Exhibitions*, Gwangju 2008, p.263.

14. **SUNANDA K. SANYAL**, 'Transgressing Borders, Shaping an Art History: Rose Kirumira and Makerere's Legacy' in Tobias Döring (ed.), *African Cultures, Visual Arts and the Museum: Sights/Sites of Creativity and Conflict*, Matatu, 25–6, Amsterdam and New York 2002, pp.133–59.

15. **ELIZABETH HARNEY**, *In Senghor's Shadow: Art, Politics, and the Avant-Garde in Senegal, 1960–1995* Durham 2004.

16. **GEETA KAPUR**, *When Was Modernism: Essays on Contemporary Cultural Practice in India*, New Delhi 2000.

17. **MINGLU 2005**; and **GAO MINGLU**, *The Ecology of Post-Cultural Revolution Frontier Art: Apartment Art in China, 1970–1990s*, Beijing 2008.

18. **CHIKA OKEKE-AGULU**, 'The Art Society and the Making of Postcolonial Modernism in Nigeria', unpublished lecture, Princeton University, 2008. See also the remarkable study of the relationship between negritude, postcolonialism and modernism in Harney 2004 and Gao Minglu 2005. These studies are among a growing list of scholarship directed at excavating the multifaceted histories of modern and contemporary art across divergent historical and cultural geographies. The studies illuminate the basic fact that buried within official Western mainstream art history are complex tendencies, narratives and structures of practice that do not easily conform to the teleological construction of modern and contemporary art. These histories, at the same time, reveal the diverse temporalities of modern art by showing that there is no single genealogy of artistic modernity or sense of innovation. Yet whatever lacunae these histories inhabit, they do reveal modernity as a series of trajectories moving in multiple directions, and they are equally informed by cultural, ideological, formal and aesthetic logics.

19. **KOBENA MERCER** (ed.), *Cosmopolitan Modernisms* (2005); *Discrepant Abstraction* (2006); *Pop Art and Vernacular Cultures* (2007); and *Exiles, Diasporas and Strangers* (2008); Annotating Art's Histories, London and Cambridge 2005–8.

20. See **RASHEEN ARAEEN**, *The Other Story: Afro-Asian Artists in Post-War Britain*, exh. cat., Hayward Gallery, London 1989. This landmark exhibition and its accompanying catalogue was one of the earliest attempts to employ postcolonial and postmodern critiques to examine the institutional exclusions of the practices of artists who were not deemed to properly belong within the mainstream canon of historical legitimation.

21. **MICHEL FOUCAULT**, 'Right of Death and Power Over Life', in *The History of Sexuality: An Introduction*, trans. Robert Hurley, I, New York 1990, pp.135–59.

22. **GIORGIO AGAMBEN**, *Homer Sacer: Sovereign Power and Bare Life*, trans. Daniel Heller-Roazen, Stanford 1998.

23. **JUDITH BUTLER**, *Precarious Life: The Powers of Mourning and Violence*, London and New York 2004.

24. **ACHILLE MBEMBE**, 'Necropolitics', trans. Libby Meintjes, Public Culture, vol.15, no.1, Winter 2003 p.12.

25. Ibid., p.13.

26. Ibid., p.14.

27. Ibid., p.13.

28. **FREDRIC JAMESON**, *A Singular Modernity: Essay on the Ontology of the Present*, London and New York 2002.

29. **SHMUEL N. EISENSTADT**, 'Multiple Modernities', in *Daedalus*, vol.129, no.1, Winter 2000, pp.1–29.

30. **AMARTYA SEN**, *Identity and Violence: The Illusions of Destiny*, New York 2006.

31. **BJÖRN WITTROCK**, 'Early Modernities: Varieties and Transitions', in *Daedalus*, vol.127, no.3, Summer 1998, pp.19–40.

32. **FERNAND BRAUDEL**, *The Mediterranean and the Mediterranean World in the Age of Phillip II*, trans. Sian Reynolds, Berkeley 1995; for a more overarching study of the historical development in relation to modernity, see **FERNAND BRAUDEL**, *A History of Civilizations*, trans. Richard Mayne, London and New York 1993.

33. **ARJUN APPADURAI**, *Modernity At Large: The Cultural Dimension of Globalization*, Minneapolis 1996.

34. **KWAME ANTHONY APPIAH**, *Cosmopolitanism: Ethics in a World of Strangers*, New York 2007.

35. See **JÜRGEN HABERMAS**, *The Philosophical Discourse of Modernity: Twelve Essays*, trans. Frederick Lawrence, Cambridge, Mass. 1987.

36. The Iranian revolution marked a shift from the modern politics of Gamel Abdel Nasser's pan-Arabism.

37. See **BRUNO LATOUR**, *We Have Never Been Modern*, trans. Catherine Porter, Cambridge 1993.

38. **G.W.F. HEGEL**, *The Philosophy of History*, trans. J. Sibree, New York 1956, p.91.

39. This is an excerpt from an email statement sent to the author by **GUY TILLIM** on 25 September 2008.

40. Ibid.

41. **HABERMAS** 1987.

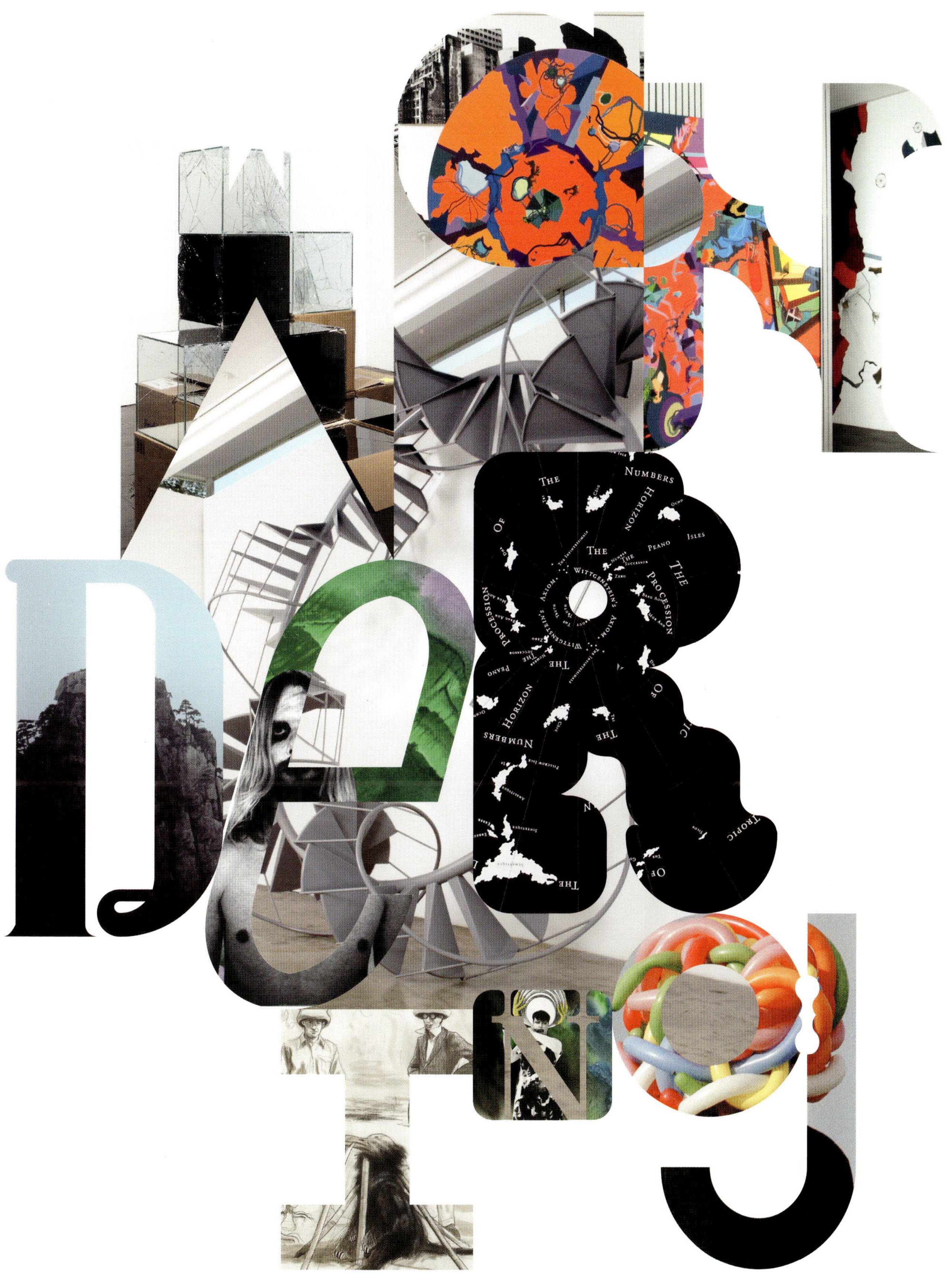

The
Numbers
Horizon
Peano
Isles
The
Procession
Wittgenstein's
Axiom
Of
Tropic

Franz ACKERMANN

I AM TRYING TO REWORK REAL IMPRESSIONS OR EVENTS, as well as reevaluate them. The material is the first thing in question when it comes to artistic action. Real events are represented more effectively using an already conveyed, processed form.

Authenticity, truth, reality: fundamental notions are shaken. Appearance, illusion, surface and colour provide me with the means with which to confront the viewer with my mostly two-dimensional works, physically and haptically, and therefore 'spatially'.

A painted plane becomes space – space that can be experienced and walked through.

From place to passage: the physical movement is getting more and more existential. (The time one spends in front of a picture shorter and shorter?)

The conditions of travel, and its very notion, exist in a state of radical change: streams of migration meet streams of tourism. In my travels I am trying to clarify these aspects 'on-site'. 'Mental maps', these small watercolours on paper seem like my most important companion.

By Fax. Berlin, 12 October 2008

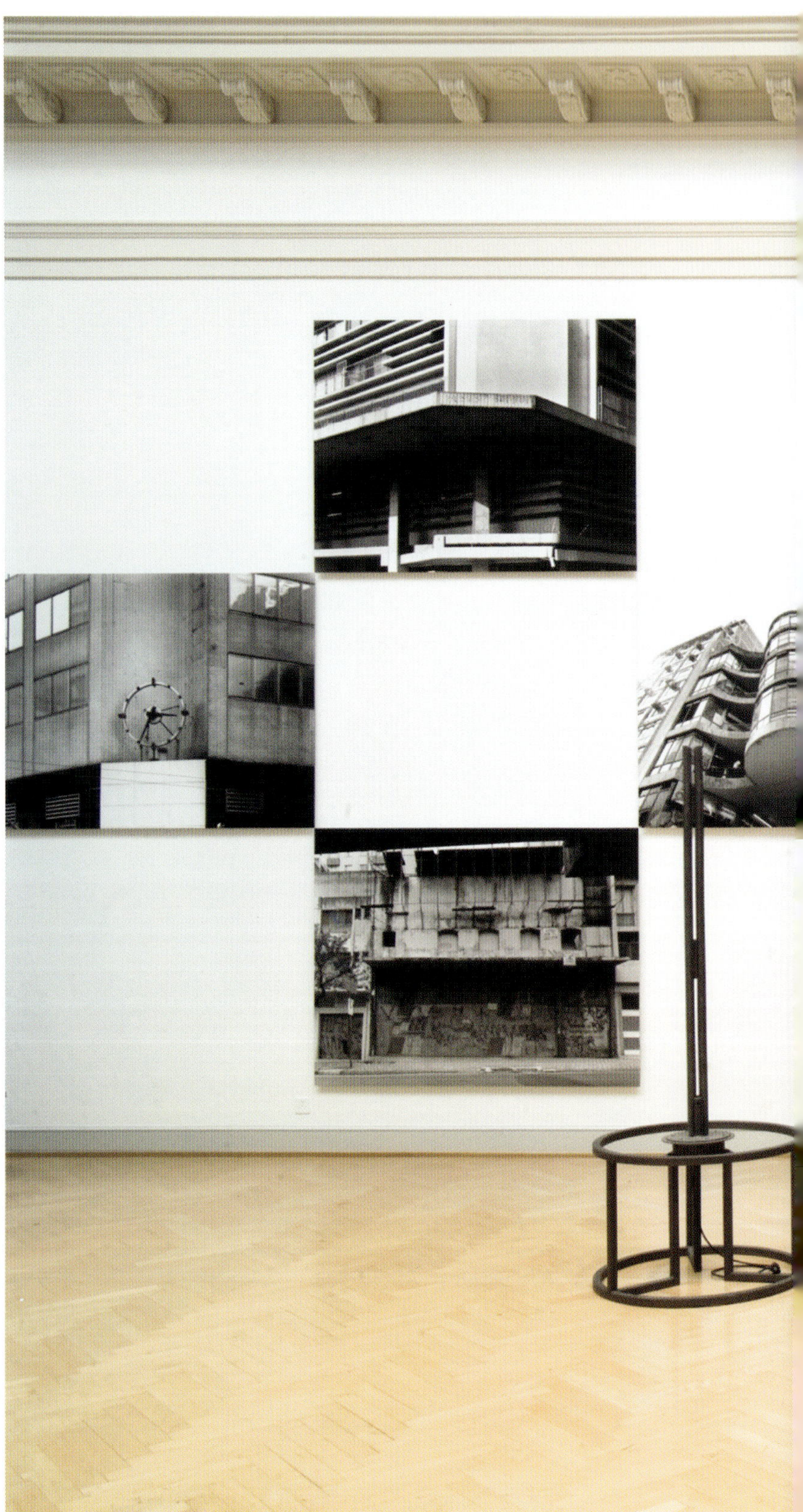

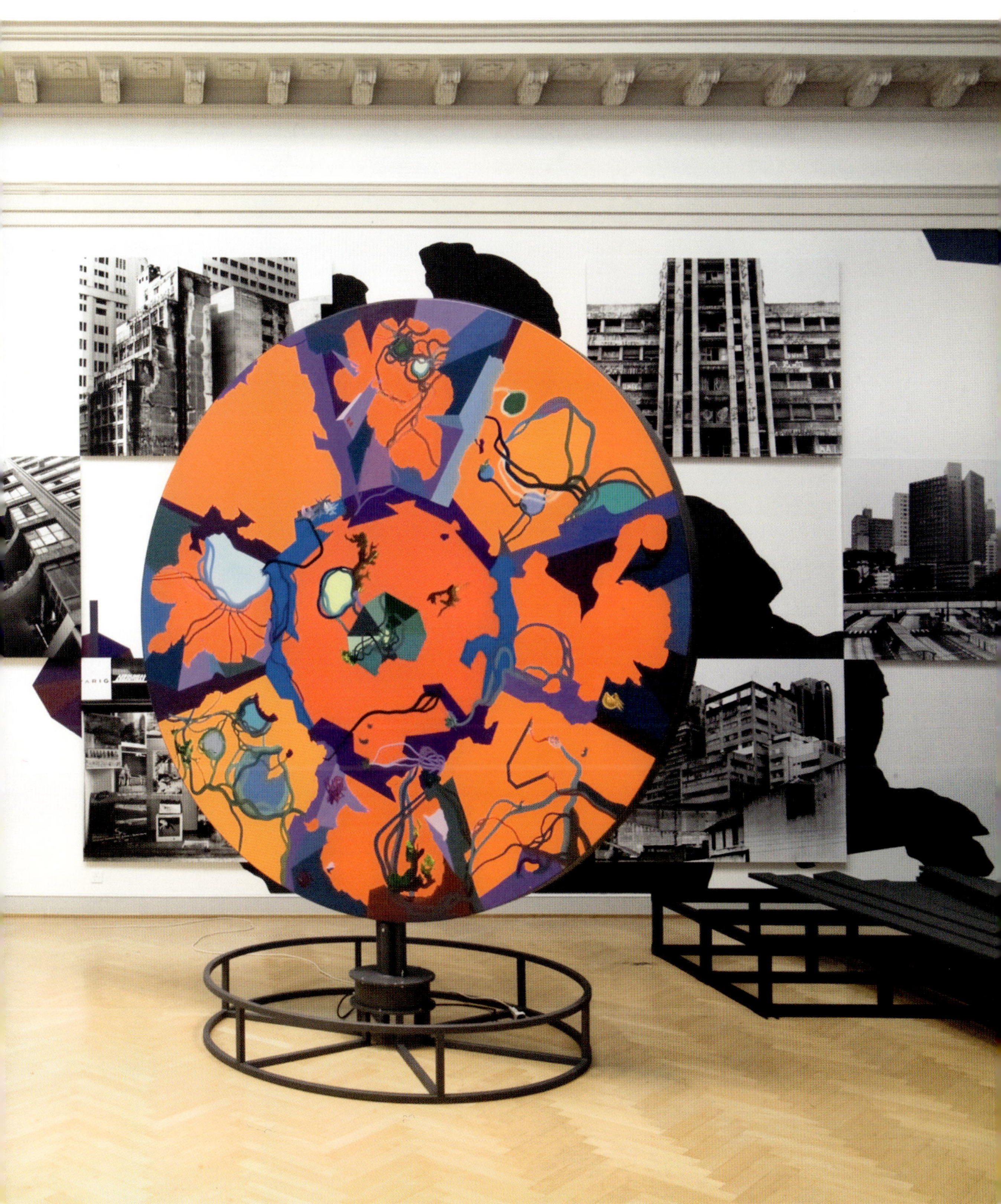

FRANZ ACKERMANN — **Installation view, *Franz Ackermann,* at Kunstmuseum St Gallen, 2008, courtesy neugerriemschneider, Berlin**

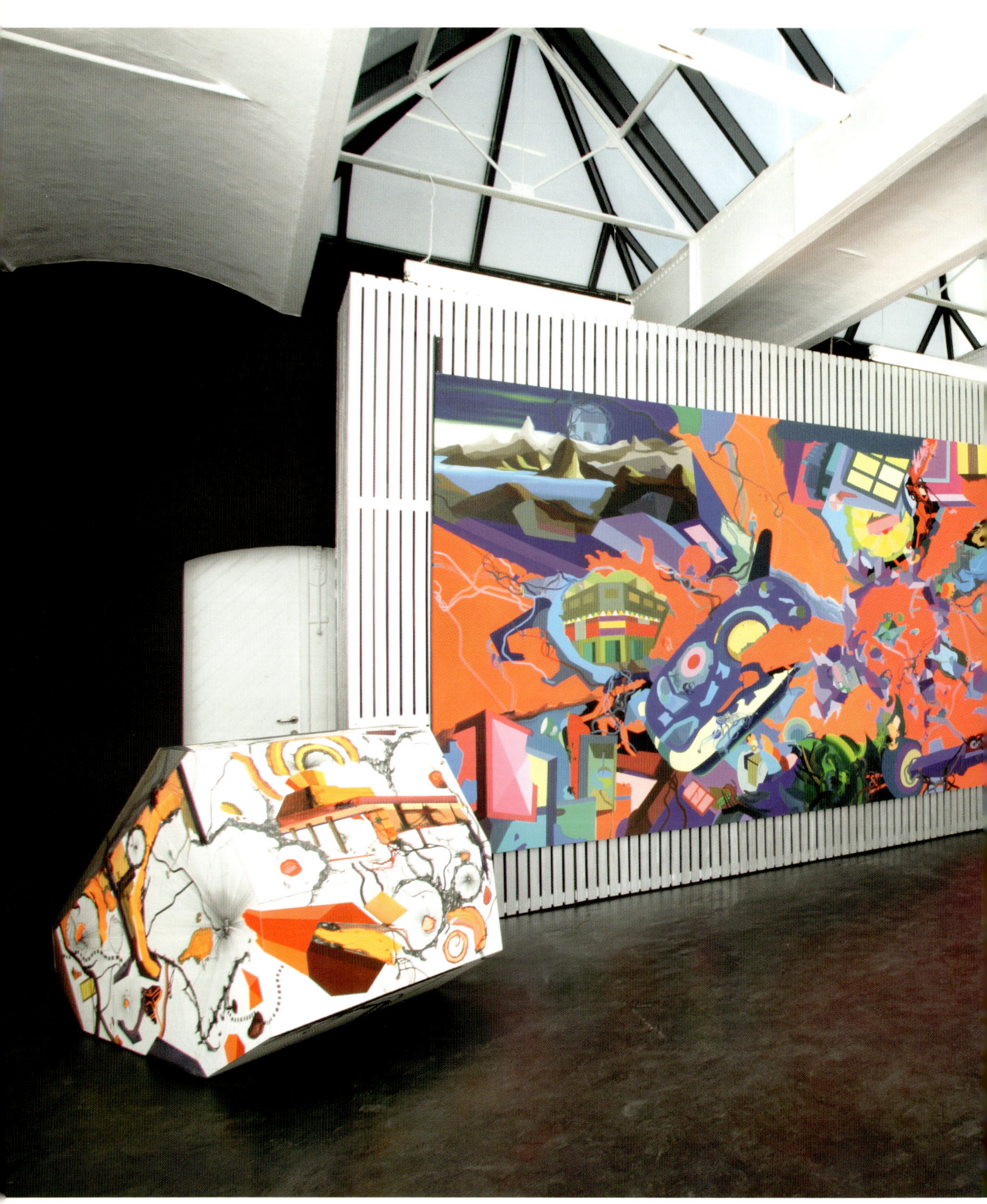

FRANZ ACKERMANN — **Installation view**, *Eden to Lima*, at neugerriemschneider, Berlin, 2007, courtesy neugerriemschneider, Berlin

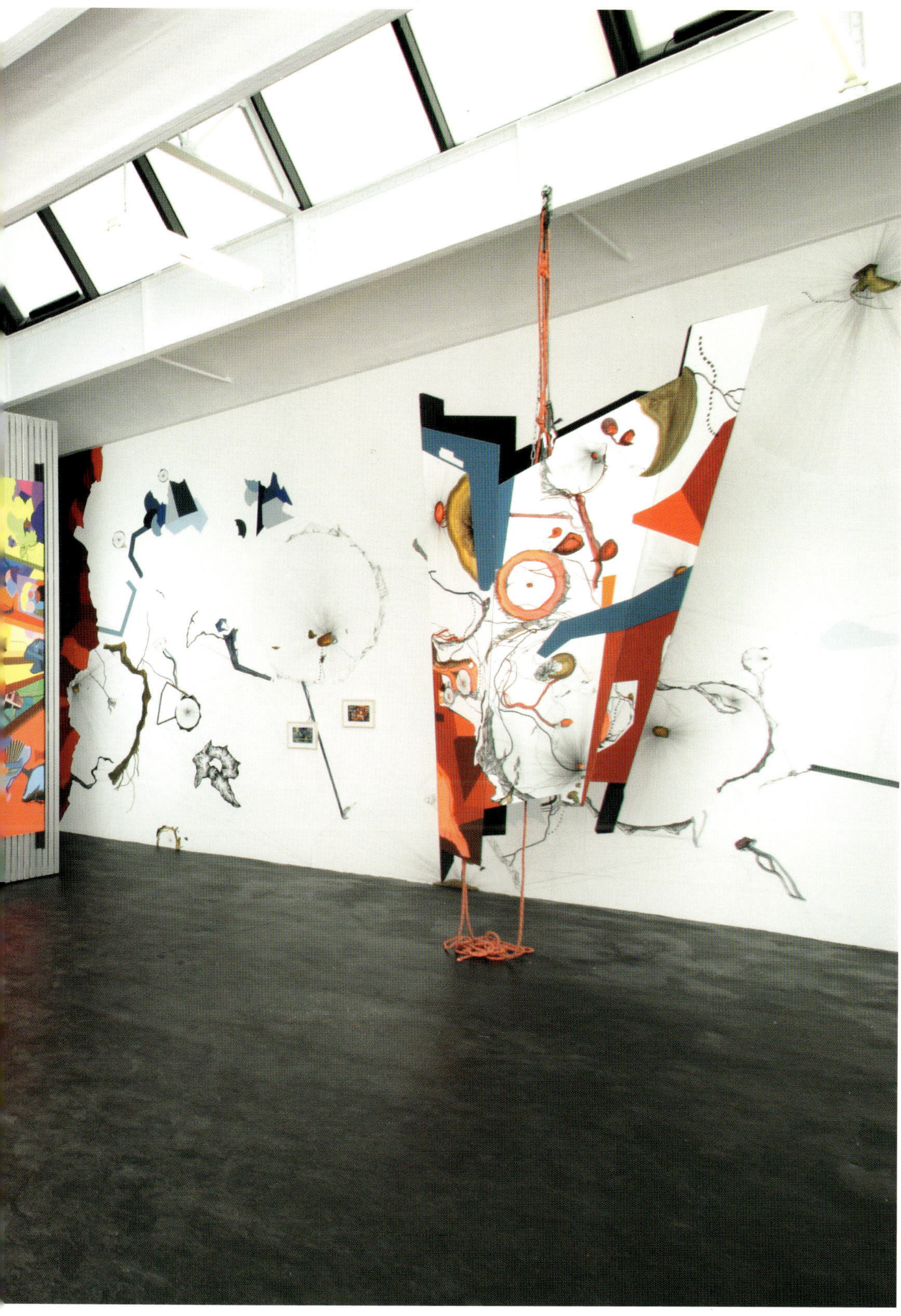

Darren
ALMOND

Out of range: Without network coverage – I am in Japan on a mountain to the northwest of Kyoto – It is 2AM. A very approachable and accommodating Tendi priest has arranged permission for me to meet, film and follow the path of a marathon monk. This has been a very long journey.

A couple of hours ago I was awakened in my small, business-type hotel by the familiar ring of my UK mobile – until then it hadn't rung on this trip. The caller quickly asked where I was – was I in London?

'No, Japan,' I replied.

'Then it's nine hours ahead – let me see ... you have a little time, it's just after 11PM.'

It was Nicolas asking if I could answer a couple of questions regarding the Triennial. I said I would oblige him but asked if he could mail them to me, explaining that I was on a shoot. 'Sure,' he said, 'I'll do that.' I tried to grab another hour but was unable, fearful of missing my early morning appointment.

The monks of Mt Hiei have seven years in which to complete their thousand-day trial, which ends in a staggering two-marathons-a-day run for a hundred consecutive days. Years ago, at the time of a London marathon, I read in the newspaper about the running monks of the sacred Mt Hiei. On average, every ten years one monk completes the full cycle. My monk was in year four.

Until now no collaboration with a cameraman has been granted such open access to the monks' practice, previously seen from afar. They begin around midnight and run through the high forest of the mountain by candlelight: 'Be aware of the wild boar – they can be career-ending. Also at this time of year it's mating season for the deer ... the stags can be aggressive.' Great! Perfect timing, I thought.

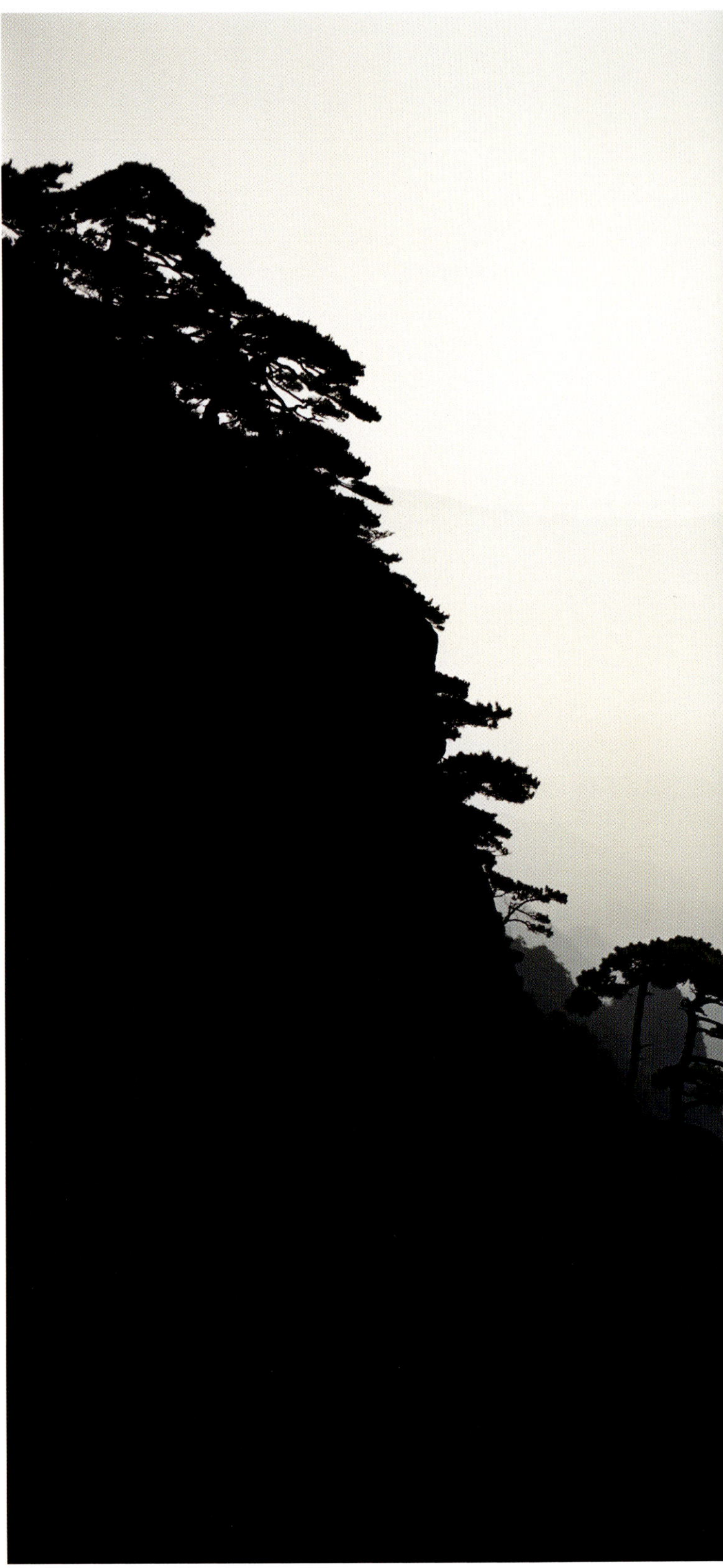

Along the track the monk stops at certain sites to chant. Some locations are gravesites, where those who had come before him, unable to complete the ritual, had taken their own lives by disembowelling themselves. At another spot by a sacred tree the monk times a pause from running to coincide with civil dawn, the time just before daybreak, when street lights diminish. From here the monk and I have an overview of the old city of Kyoto and I watch the lights go out one by one.

Then he is off again, and I still have no phone reception. It is at this point I realise that his practice traverses the same landscapes as the *Fullmoons*, the photographic practice I have been undertaking for the past ten years. Coincidently, the *Fullmoons* result in the same lack of coverage; occurring beyond the Web. They appear from the dark, lit only by the moon and their histories and historical associates. During the last moon I shot the Huangshan region of China, as first depicted in 1646 by Jiang Tao (who became the Zen monk Hongern). I have also shot the island of Rügen in the Baltic, as depicted by C.D.F. The *Fullmoons* are landscapes without surveillance cameras. In fact, in over ten years I have only bumped into one other photographer, despite visiting sites that by day can be simply overrun.

Some sites I return to time and again as it is not always possible to photograph – the clouds could be too thick or a downpour too strong. This affords me a longer, more seasonal view – in some ways similar to that of the monk on his mountain path.

As day has now taken hold I descend back down to the covered landscape to receive my messages. No questions arrive, just an email outlining the deadline for answers and a maximum word count.

Otsu, Japan, Sunday 9 November 2008

DARREN ALMOND — ***Fullmoon@The Sea of Clouds*, 2008,** C-print 183 × 183, courtesy the artist, Galerie Max Hetzler, Berlin and Jay Jopling/White Cube, London

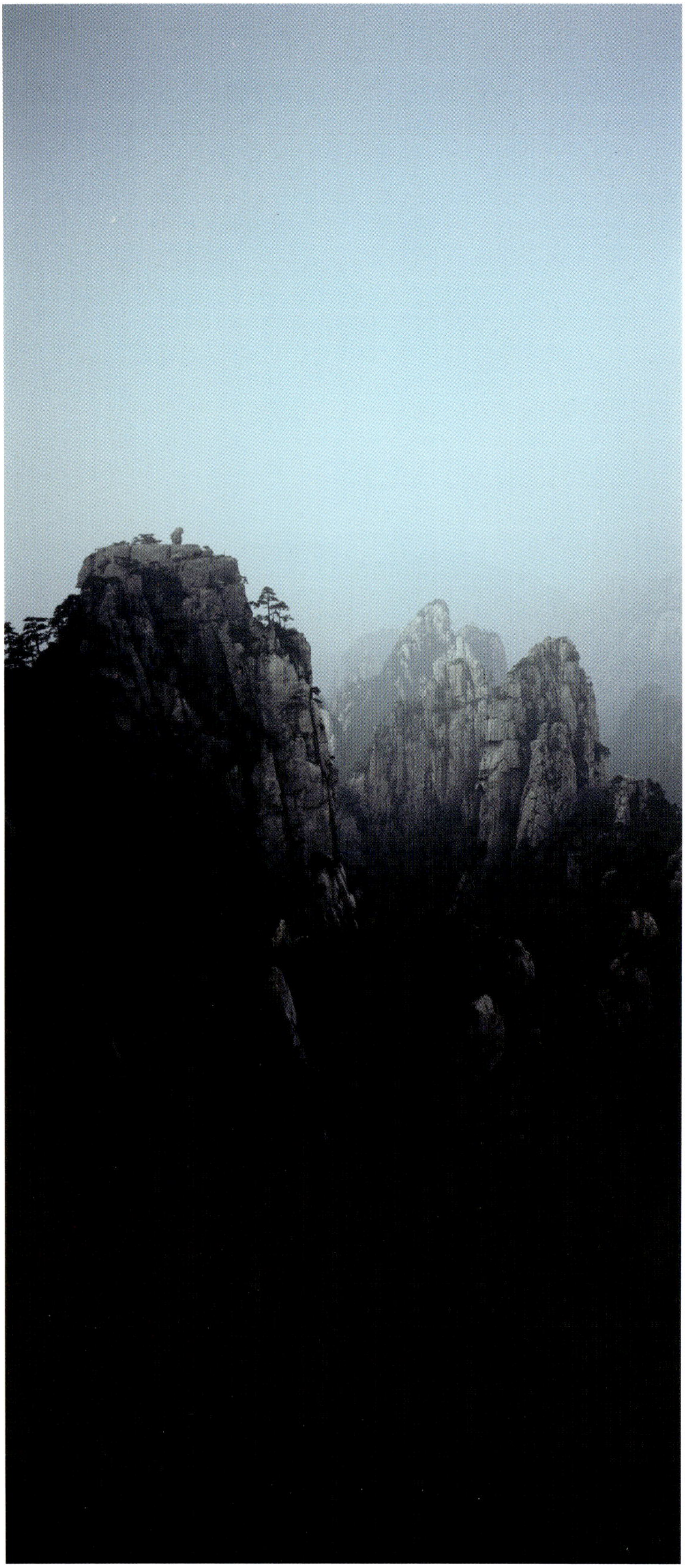

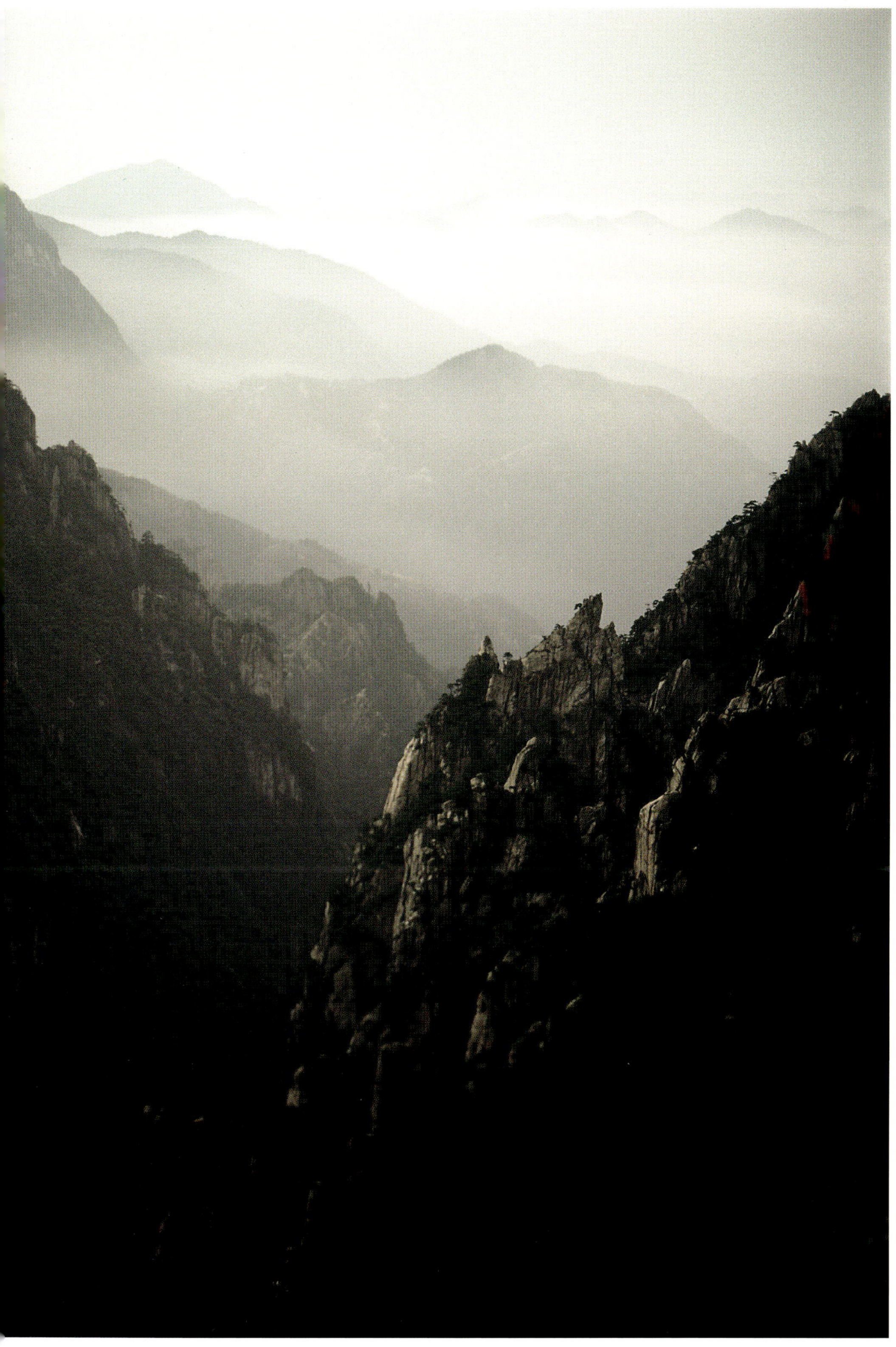

DARREN ALMOND — [LEFT] ***Fullmoon@Huangshan,* 2008,** C-print 276 × 127
[RIGHT] ***Dragon's Eye,* 2008,** C-print 180 × 180, courtesy the artist, Galerie Max Hetzler, Berlin and Jay Jopling/White Cube, London

Charles AVERY

NICOLAS BOURRIAUD *You define yourself, as an artist, through the figure of the explorer. What does this imply, and mean?*

CHARLES AVERY Before I was able to meaningfully assert myself as an artist I needed to define the 'art' I was supposedly trying to bring about by my actions. After much reflection I concluded that art must be defined and understood not as the totality of objects regarded as such according to a particular set of criteria, but as a quality, like, for example, the concept of size.

Size cannot be conceived independently of an object – one does not consider something to be a large, or a small. Nevertheless, we understand the term large because we know where to locate it within the structure of language: as the antonym of small.

Likewise, the term *art*, understood as being one extreme of a qualitative scale, need only be defined by its antonym. I propose it be located in opposition to meaning. (This is not to say that art is meaningless, rather that art is not meaning.) Accordingly, to say that art means or does not mean is akin to proposing that, for instance, large is small.

This qualitative definition accounts for the irresistible hunch that art is related to language, but it also draws a crucial distinction between the concepts of art – a quality that permeates the universe – and artwork, a made object, or expression that embodies this quality.

Much more needs to be said here, not least about how the concept of language fits into this structure – there is not the space to elaborate the full dialectic – rather I will define a few of the key concepts as clues to that thesis.

By art, therefore, I mean the opposite of meaning.

By artwork I mean a thing the meaning of which is to mean.

By thing I mean entity, phenomenon, object as opposed to subject.

By beauty I mean the unaccountable attractiveness of things.

By aesthetics I mean theories pertaining to the bringing about of this mysterious attraction, by action.

Having defined art as such I wondered what could be said about artists.

It can be said that an artist acts, and means their actions to have significance: they intend to intend. The artwork is the manifestation of this action, and may be the action itself.

I also thought about the sense of entitlement and conviction that an artist has. The right to profess the order independent of any higher appointment to it, and the sense of purpose/direction that seems essential to progression: the blind and subjective

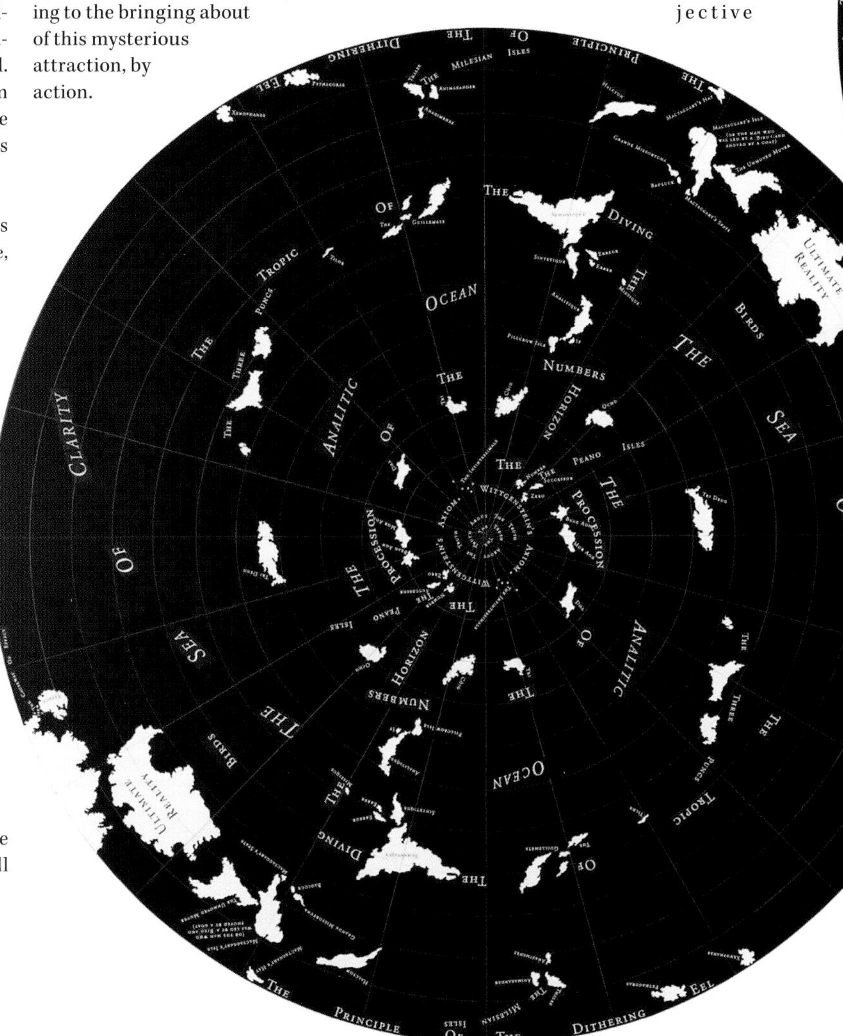

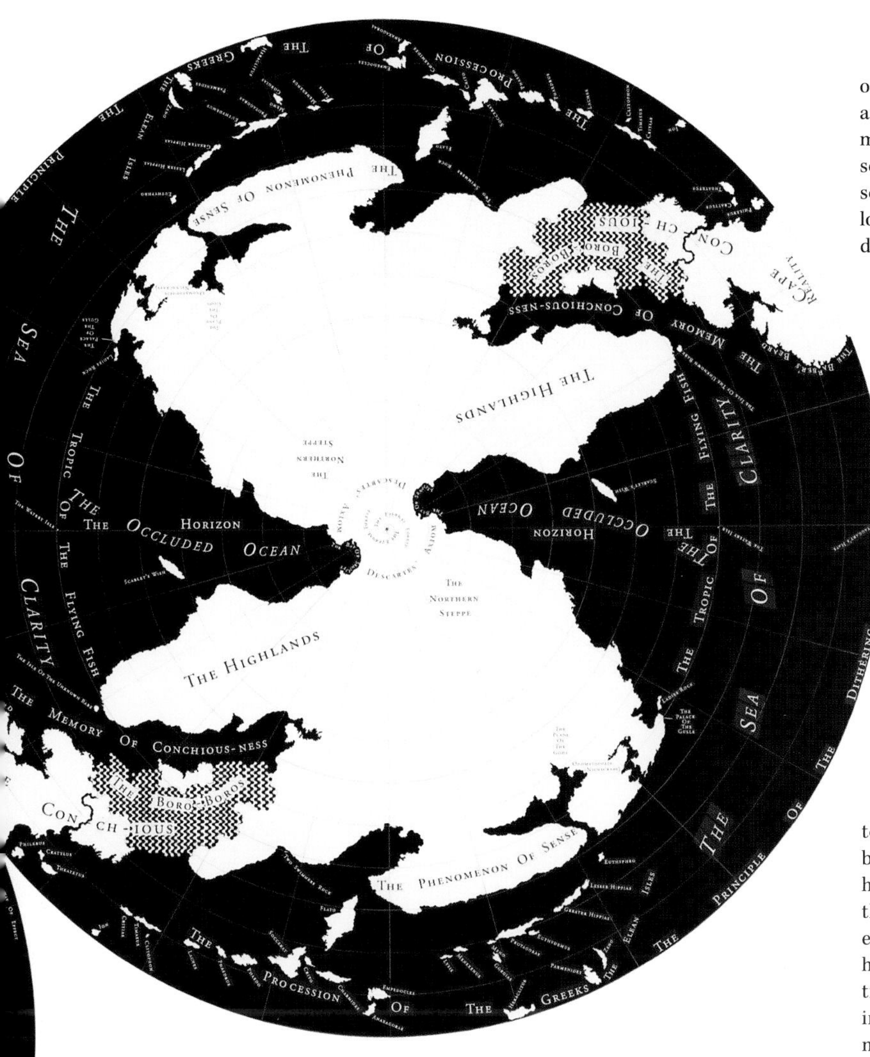

faith that is characterised by *Don Quixote de la Mancha.*

I decided that the ideal of the artist is shared with anyone engaged in the pursuit of truth: scientists, philosophers, mathematicians, explorers ... Such an individual may believe ultimate truth to be unattainable, nevertheless, if they believe there is a right way and a wrong way to go about their particular enquiry, to achieve that sense of purpose, they must uphold the existence of that ultimate destination, however transcendent.

The third defining characteristic which, surprisingly for me, validates the relentless output of the artist, is that of professionalism: the need to produce the artwork itself as hard evidence of the subjective realm through which one has been navigating. Not because of an irrepressible urge to create but, in a mercantile sense, the need to produce souvenirs of one's endeavour that can be sold in the marketplace, and thereby allow one to buy food, have a house, children, a collection of one's own, and most importantly so that one may conceive new and more intrepid explorations. The artwork, therefore, functions precisely as currency between the realms of the subjective and objective.

The role of the collector in this system is as patron, and that of the artwork is not as a masterpiece but as a reflection, map, or diagram of another system, a promise of future exploration, of untapped potential. The artwork should never be finished but always show promise.

It was these reflections that led me to the scenario of the explorer: a young man arrives on an island, a dark continent, believing himself to be its discoverer. He is soon disabused of this conceit by a young woman he meets on the shore. It transpires through talking to her that he is not even the first man to have gone there; he has been preceded by many generations of pioneers, prospectors, rushers, investors, industrialists, itinerants and mendicants, who inhabit a large town called Onomatopoeia. But the Island is also home to a mythical beast called the Noumenon, which has never been witnessed but is reputed to reside towards the dark interior. Time after time, the explorer returns to the Island with a view to apprehending this creature (even though history and reason seem to indicate its impossibility), funding his lengthy absences from objectivity through the sale of minor curiosities brought back from the Island.

CHARLES AVERY — ***Untitled (Flat Map)*, 2008**, 150 × 210, gouache, pencil and paper on card, courtesy the artist and Arquebuse, Geneva

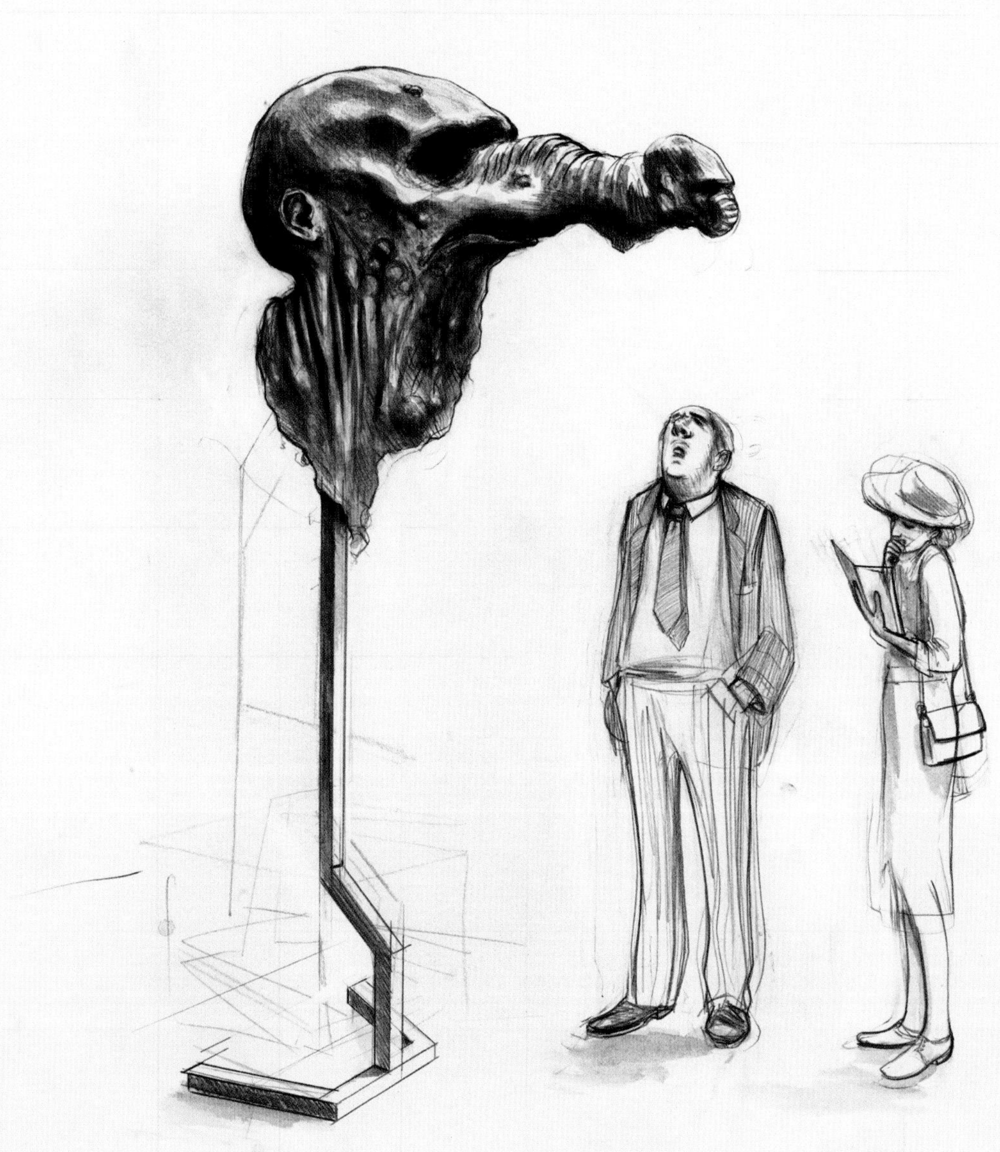

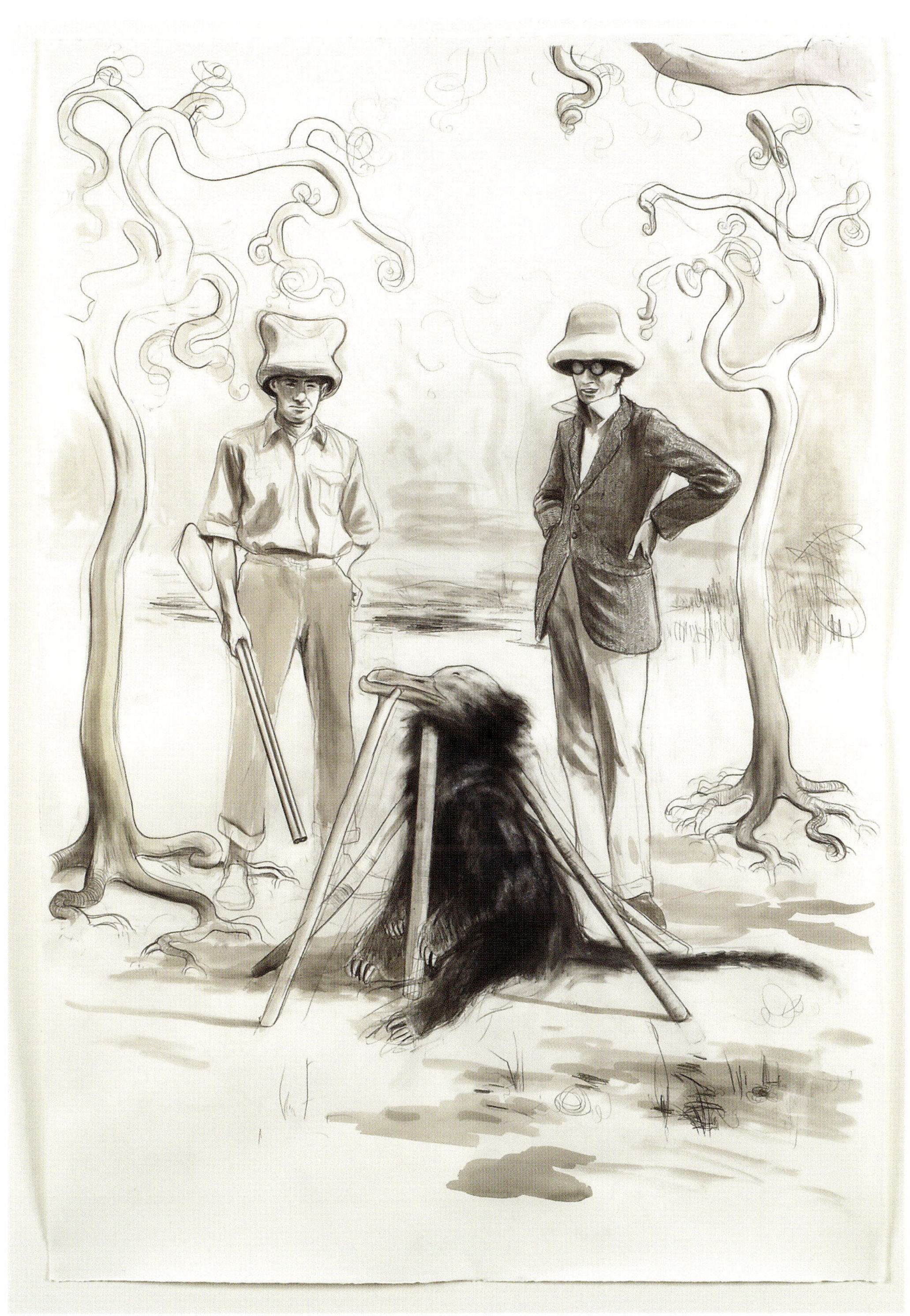

CHARLES AVERY — [LEFT] *Untitled (Two Triangleland Bourgeoisie studying the head of an Aleph)*, **2008**, 54 × 37, pencil on paper, courtesy the artist and Sonia Rosso, Torino
[RIGHT] *Untitled (Two Dilettantes)*, **2008**, 84.5 × 60, pencil and gouache on paper, courtesy the artist and doggerfisher, Edinburgh

Walead BESHTY

NICOLAS BOURRIAUD *Two questions. Firstly, how does travelling (and displacement) function in your work? Would you say that you are inscribing forms in space, rather than on paper or canvas? Secondly, in history, 'Modern' moments have always been linked to uprooting, nomadism, exodus. Do you think postmodernism is therefore coming to an end?*

WALEAD BESHTY In the airport, the airplane, in customs and security queues, abstraction is forced to reconcile itself with materiality, there the relation between the abstract rule of Law and the movement of bodies is realised with banally vulgar immediacy. I am not speaking in the classic sense of abstraction or materialism within art (especially not in the sense that the term 'abstract' is misused to mean 'non-figurative', or that materialism has come to be synonymous with a claim for ontological purity), but in how abstractions are manifest in compromised form within the quotidian, how they govern our experience of the 'real', or, more exactly, how they become concrete, and how this becoming produces moments of friction and error. In transit, concepts as amorphous as subjecthood (as constituted in the right to privacy, of personal property, free speech etc.) are rendered specific and given edges simply by their being momentarily subject to revision. In these marginal connective tissues, tacit hierarchies become spatial, physical: one's belongings are inspected, one's body relegated to queues, numbers, compartments, 'class'. Normally, the fragility of the state's guarantees manifest themselves only in moments of direct conflict and massive collapse (such as the recent credit crisis, or the revelations regarding the conditions at the American military prisons at Guantanamo bay or Abu Grahib), but in the case of air travel, the fragile malleability of social order is always close at hand, delineated by temporary post and rope stanchions, bracketed by pavilions and kiosks in linoleum topped chipboard, in colour-coded wall-to-wall carpeting, and the eye of the x-ray machine. It is a commonplace that the reason one is more likely to cry while watching a movie on an airplane is the implicit trauma of air travel, i.e. the fear of death, of crashing, which leaves us emotionally vulnerable. But the trauma of air travel is quite literally one's confrontation with one's tenuous grasp on autonomy, its little humiliations emphasising the conditional nature of self-hood: an alchemical transformation that allows inalienable rights to become suddenly alienable, subject to revocation.

In this constellation of forces, the x-ray has pride of place, delineating the edge between the 'real' world, and the siteless limbo of air travel. Its accidental discovery in the late 1800s fits seamlessly into modernity's fascination with transparency: the desire to capture the minutiae of movement (cinema), to turn objects into surface (photography), to see inside (x-ray). For me, these mechinations become palpable in moments of error, when there is a friction between modes of vision (i.e. organisational systems), as when enlightenment principles rub up against airport security, or x-rays damage vacation photos, or the distance an object travels results in damage.

Abstractions have reached the level of facticity. Financial markets, national sovereignty, the corporation as individual under the law, international airspace, property rights: all are interwoven ephemeral constellations that delineate the rights of the citizen subject and the conditions of the social sphere. The Bush Administration understood this fully, bending this abstract foundation to its whim. As a senior White House aide told a reporter for the *New York Times*: 'We're an empire now and when we act, we create our own reality. And while you're studying that reality – judiciously as you will – we'll act again, creating other new realities, which you can study too ...' (One is left with an image of former President George W. Bush as a character akin to Neo from 'The Matrix', able to reform the solid world – to which the unenlightened are subject – to his messianic whim.) Old notions of critique seem rather quaint in light of this formulation. The modernist transformation from the tangible to the intangible, from the object to the image, the haptic to the visual, is only half of the contemporary equation. With the passing of the last century and a half, these abstractions have been naturalised, entrenched, and built upon to such a degree that they have the quality of concreteness and stability. It makes no sense to claim either as 'real' or a 'fiction'. These have always been false oppositions; the actual circumstance is far less discrete. After all, the solidity of objects is as much an abstraction of the social systems that produced them, as the social systems are abstractions of these objects: a kind of capitalist realism. Classic critiques of power, some of which fall under the umbrella of the 'post-modern', rely on a 'reality principle', an idea that the real and fiction can be separated, that the revelation of power can threaten (not simply reify) dominance, that there is even something behind the curtain to be revealed, but these categorical delimiters are untenable. Monolithic expressions of power are simply an accumulation of compromise and negotiation, they all contain gaps; we, too are collaborators, even if we choose to relinquish this role. These momentary openings, the pockets between, their transitory spaces, ignored seams, and forgotten vistas, promise a site from which the either/or of utopian and apocalyptic thinking, or the political/formalist opposition can be dismantled, and production can be understood as embedded and at stake in all things, not at the level of grand abstraction, but as a bare fact evidenced in every moment of life. I think part of the problem is the search for 'endings', the desire to cleave the past from the present, to hope for libratory rupture. Abandoning this search might be the way to an affirmative proposition of critique, rather than a negative one. This is the choice between presence and absence, ascetic refusal and active negotiation. Perhaps, as the documentary filmmaker Hito Steyerl put it, 'the closer to reality we get, the less intelligible it becomes,' but still this 'reality' is what it seems like it is most important to confront, one that is camouflaged in plain view, the unintelligible that is everywhere around us.

WALEAD BESHTY — [LEFT] ***Transparency (Negative) [Kodak NC Color Film: August 17 – August 24, 2008 [LAX/IAD DCA/ORD ORD/LAX]*, 2008**, Epson Ultrachrome K3 archival inkjet print on museo silver rag paper, 150 × 112, courtesy Wallspace, New York and China Art Objects Galleries, Los Angeles

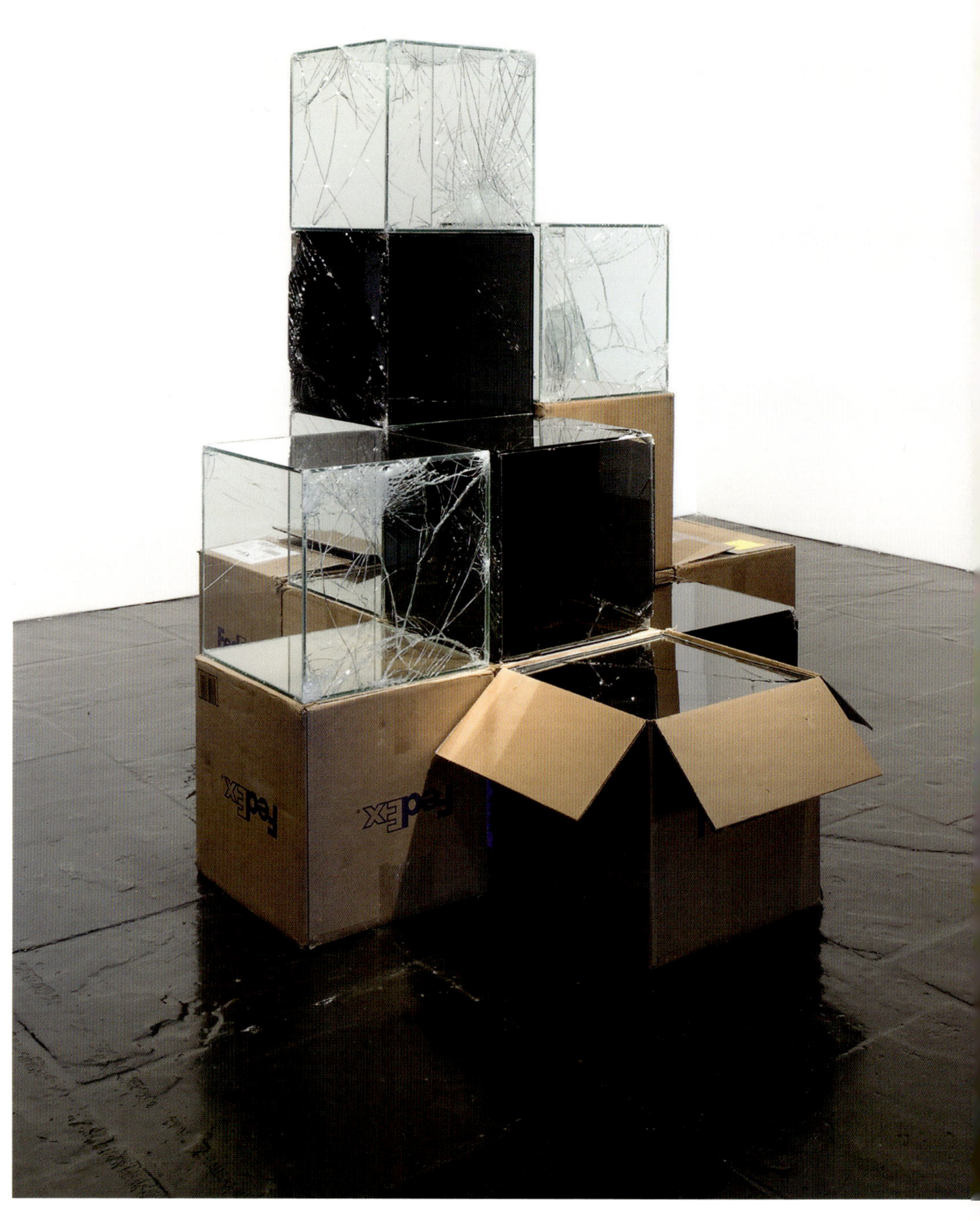

WALEAD BESHTY — [LEFT] **Installation view of *FedEx Sculptures*,** 2008 Whitney Biennial, Whitney Museum of American Art, New York [RIGHT] ***Travel Picture Mist (Tschaikowskistrasse 17 in multiple exposures [LAXFRATHF/TXLCPHSEALAX] March 27 – April 3, 2006),*** **2007–8,** Contax G-2, L-3 Communiations eXaminer 3DX 6000, and InVision Technologies CTX 5000, Chromogenic Print, 221 × 124.5, courtesy Wallspace, New York and China Art Objects Galleries, Los Angeles

Spartacus CHETWYND

NICOLAS BOURRIAUD *You are using 'historical' material in your work – signs or texts that pop up from the past (including your artist's name) – along with very specific elements of popular culture. When you mix Milton and Marx, you are connecting signs together. What is the nature of those connections?*

SPARTACUS CHETWYND Marx and Engels's *Division of Labor*, German ideology and Milton's *Paradise Lost* contain a longing for 'untainted existence'. My performance *The Fall of Man* at the 2006 Tate Triennial was an attempt to extract a moment from history in which Eden becomes a state of mind.

The same drive was behind my performance called *The Adamites* 2005/6. The Adamites were a sect that existed in Europe in the second century AD. Bosch depicts them in his painting *The Garden of Earthly Delights*. They wished to return to a state of innocence before the Fall of Man. Famously tried and tested, cults do not work out, they either end in murderous chaos or a strictly ruled protective up-tightness. I have been trying to maintain a moment of Utopia within the structure of a twenty-minute performance – no time for dissent!

An attempt to enter into moments of history through the use of invented ritual. By agreeing to regard yourself as an innocent (and to undertake to be naked and dance with others who are also are bound by this agreement), to enter into a state of trance, to play with a large strawberry or huge bluebell flower. By agreeing to achieve the unattainable within an agreement, a pact that only lasts twenty minutes.

NICOLAS BOURRIAUD *How do you see history – as a territory that your work is exploring? Could you say that you are a time explorer?*

SPARTACUS CHETWYND I see History as actually having happened, I understand that it is interpreted and rewritten but I believe it is not entirely fabricated. I enjoy the satisfaction of getting to know the answer, the benefit of hindsight, the intense pleasure in the laying out of 'facts', the making sense of and the problem solving, like doing a jigsaw puzzle. I guess it is like 'train spotting' but I like following up the historical context of art or material culture. Both the *Aeneid* and *Paradise Lost* were written after periods of civil war. When you read *Paradise Lost*, you recognise that the 'Eden' that sounds so familiar comes from Milton rather than the Bible. Another example is in the *Aeneid*, you assume the description of the Trojan horse comes from Homer's *Iliad* but it is instead from Virgil. The systematic narrative keeps on unravelling and holds your concentration.

NICOLAS BOURRIAUD *And how do you react to this concept of the 'altermodern'?*

SPARTACUS CHETWYND 'Altermodern' is exciting because it is auguring the future. It feels unusual to work with ideas that are spelled out – statements standing proud! But I don't feel uncomfortable by being so clearly labelled in being part of this show, instead it feels fun to be in described as a 'polyglot', to be seen as 'materialising trajectories' like Spiderman. Great! I'll start limbering up!

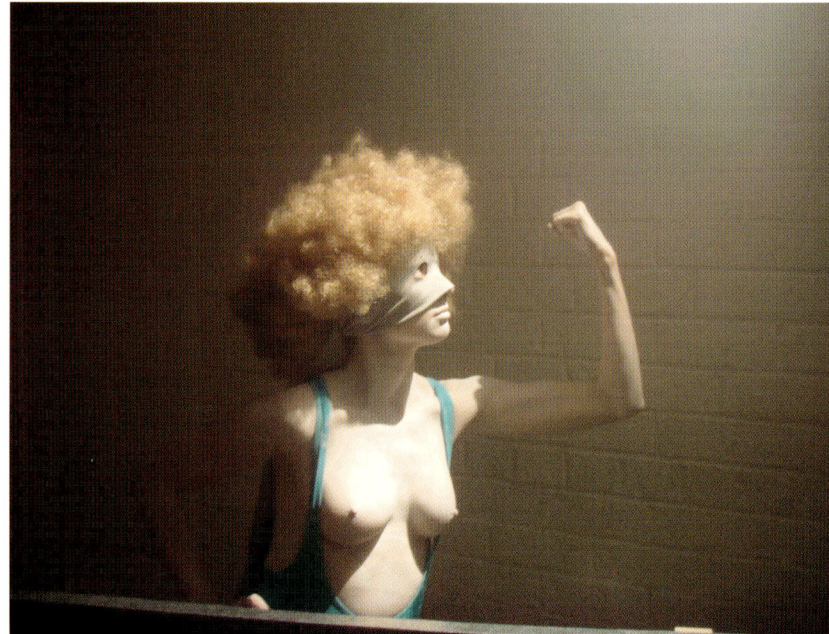

SPARTACUS CHETWYND — [LEFT AND RIGHT] ***Hermitos Children, The Dildo See-saw,*** **2008**, film still, courtesy Herald St, London

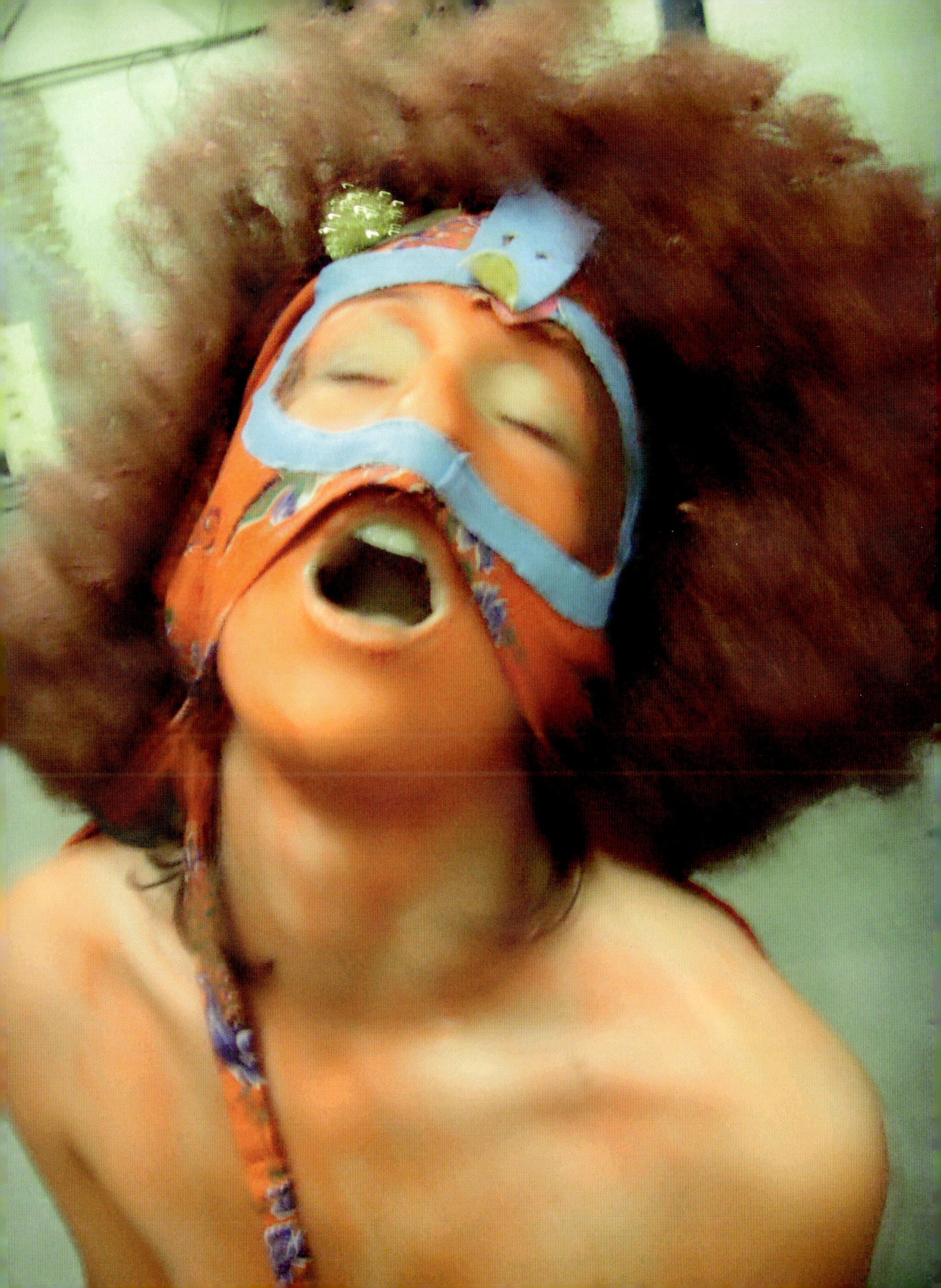

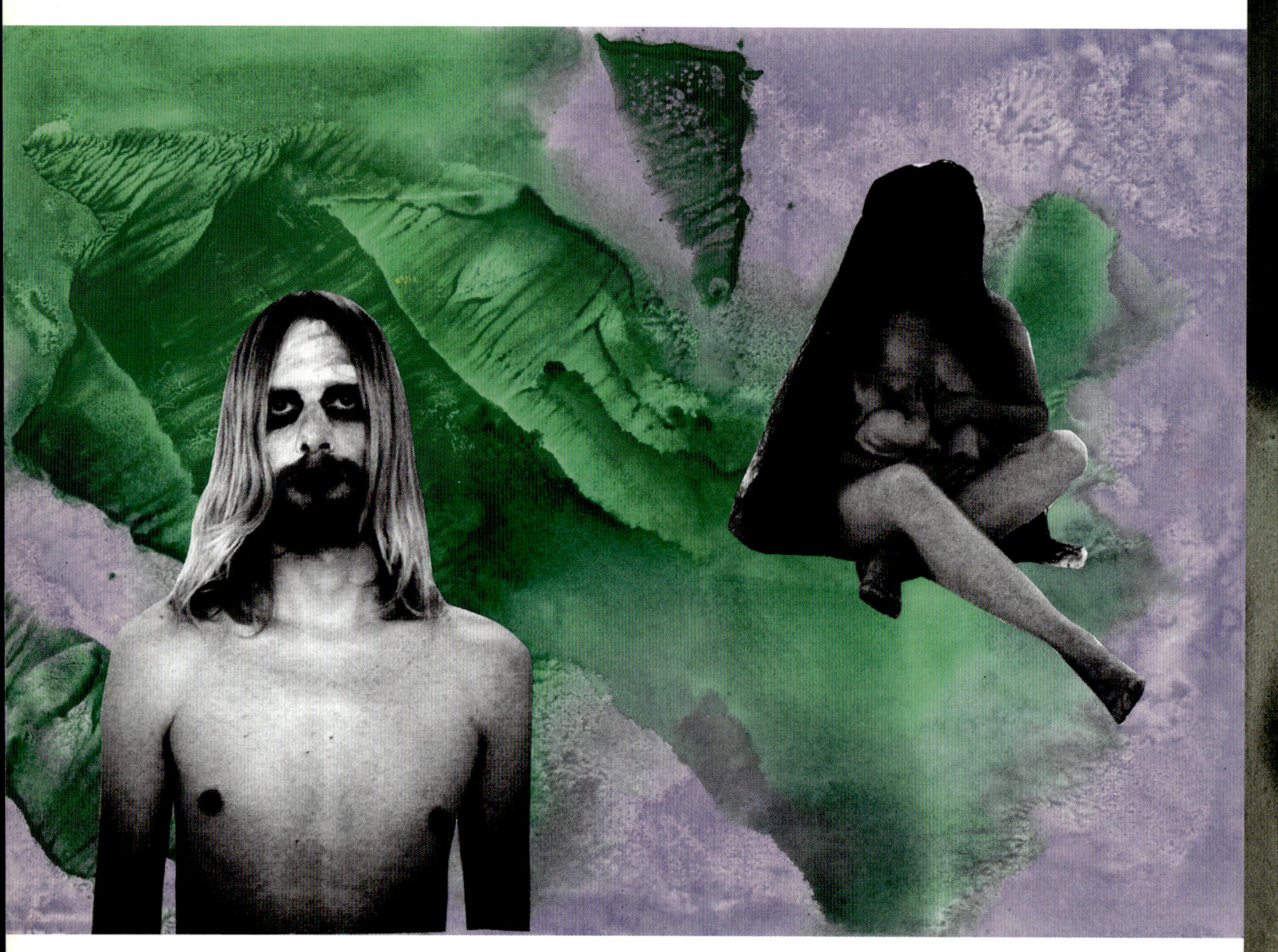

SPARTACUS CHETWYND — [ABOVE AND RIGHT] ***Hermitos Children,* 2008,** TV pilot (promotional material), courtesy Herald St, London

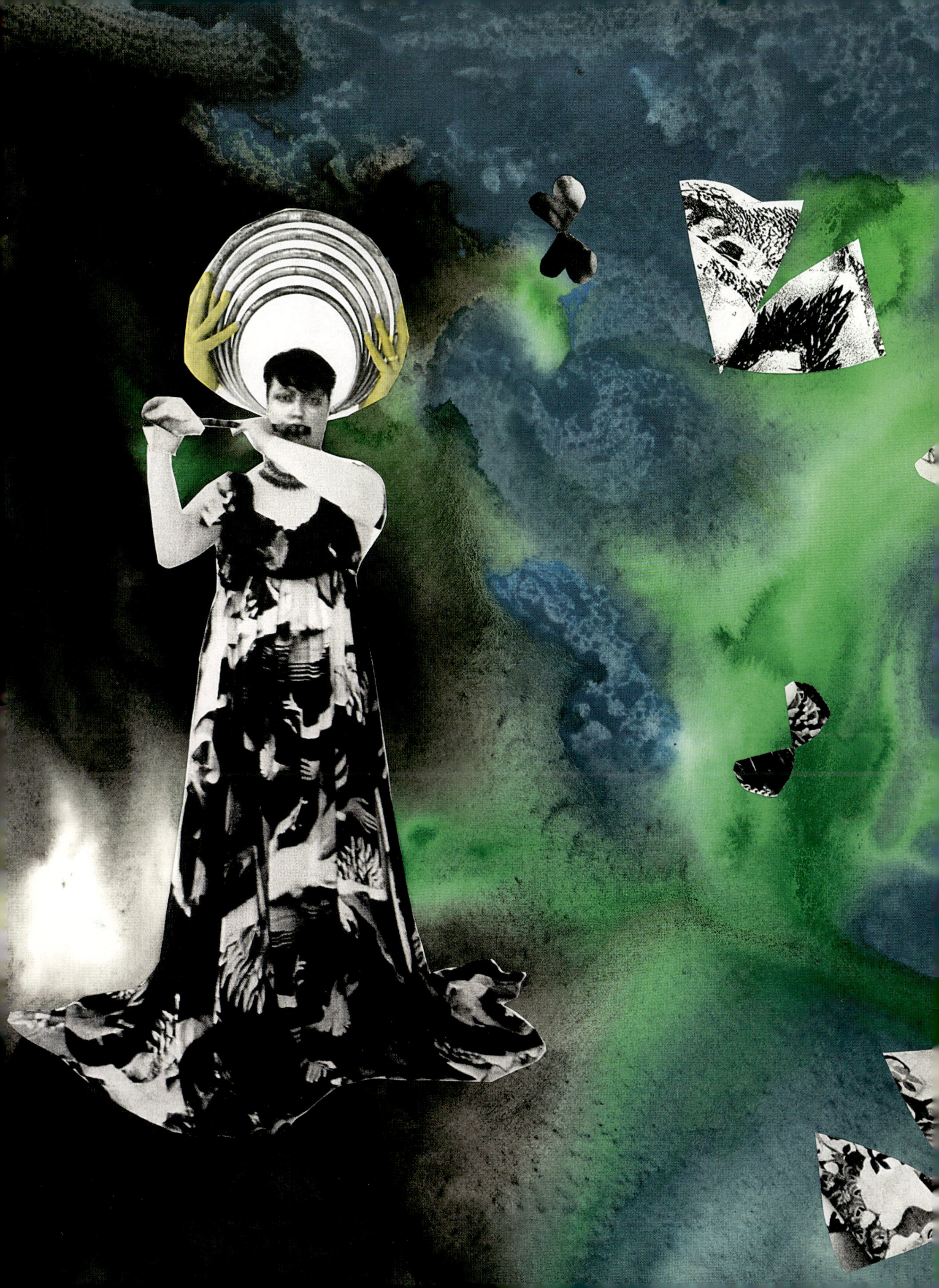

Marcus
COATES

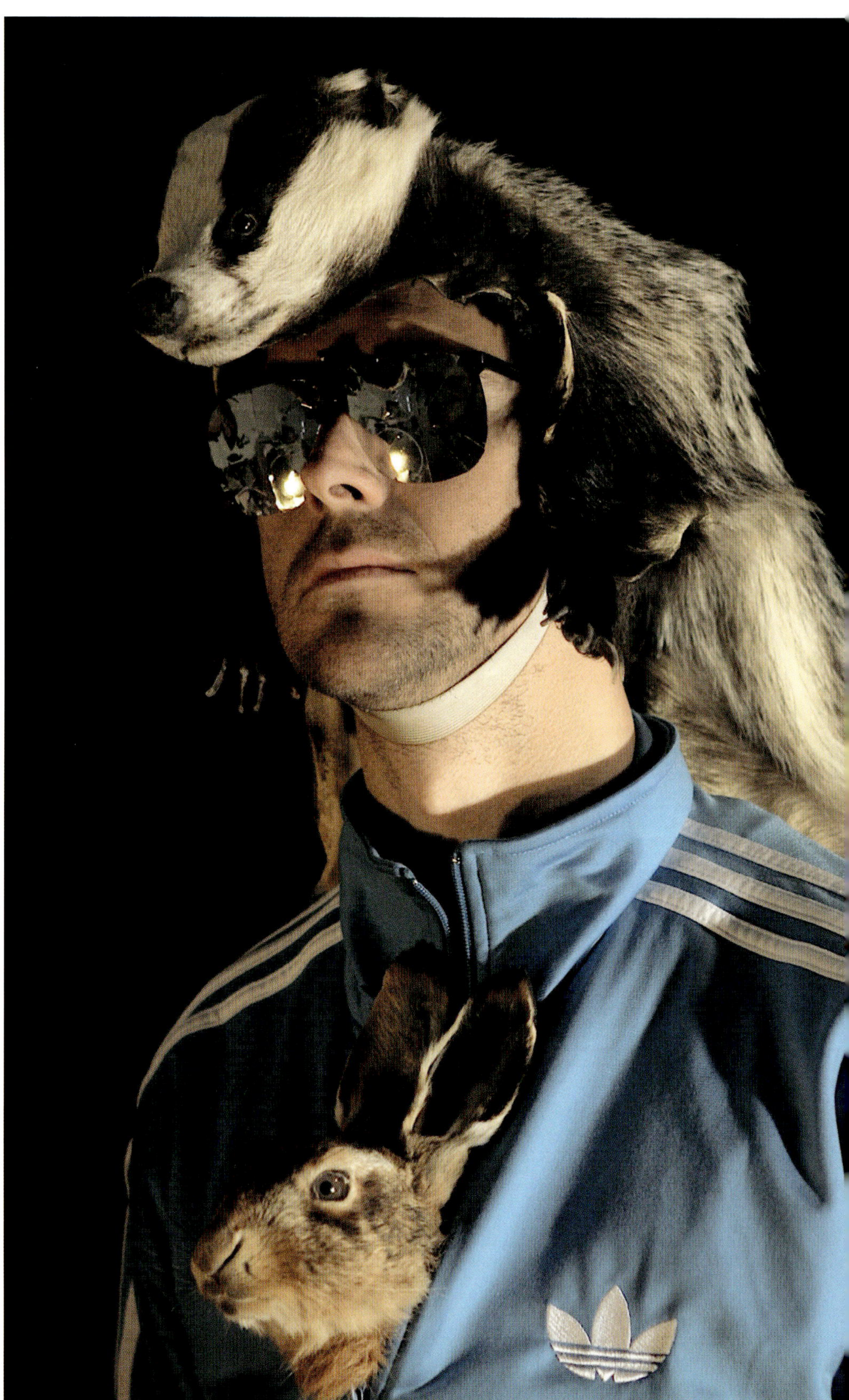

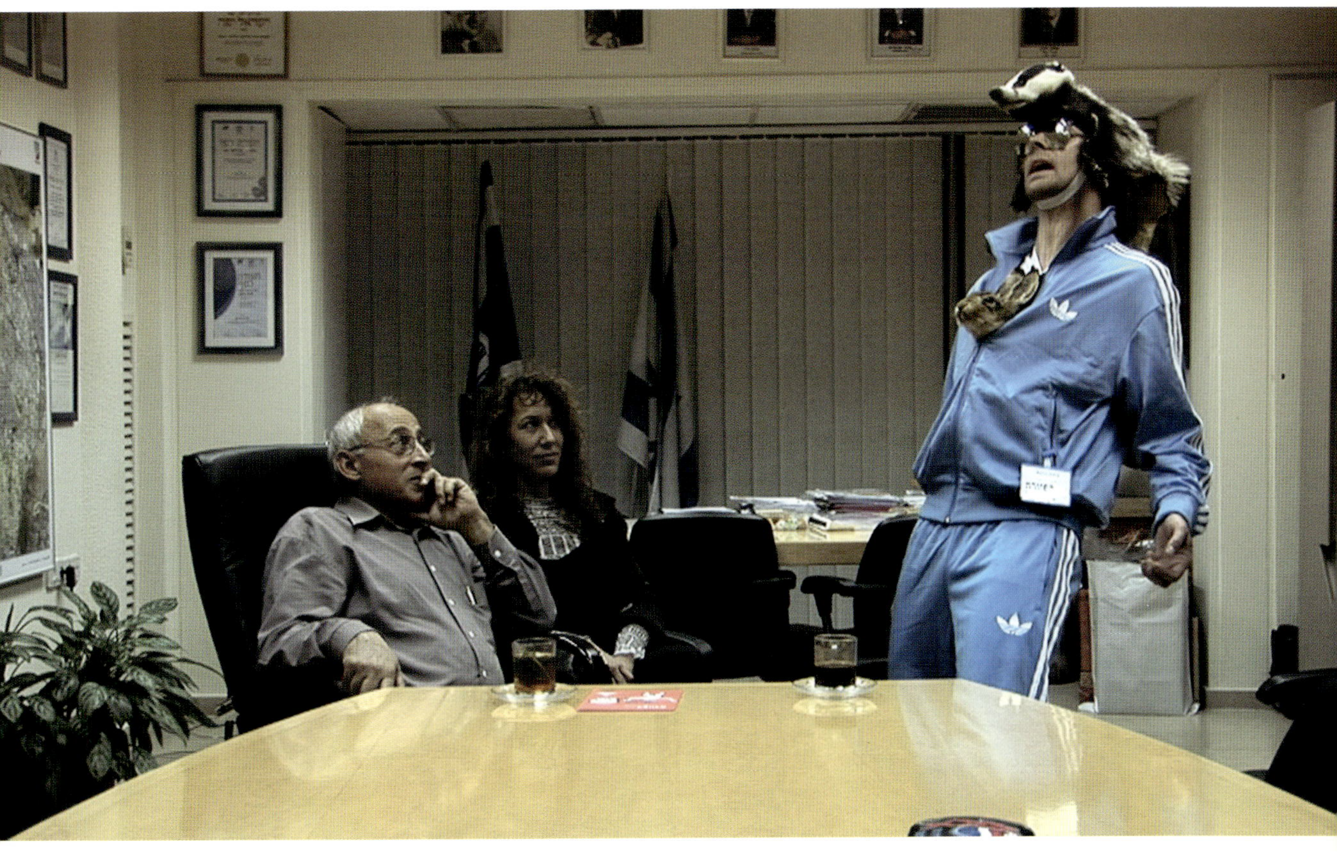

Nicolas Bourriaud *Is your shamanic method a way to travel throughout time and space?*

Marcus Coates Yes, it is a world that is initially generated by my imagination and ultimately becomes independent from my conscious self, a place that creates its own time and space.

I describe this reality and the occurrences within it to my clients, rationalising this place of subconscious understanding, enabling them to create significance and meaning.

Nicolas Bourriaud *Is this 'archaic' model a statement on our times and/or the role of the artist today?*

Marcus Coates I am using ancient techniques to answer modern-day questions, taking on a role that has ceased to be commonplace in Western society. This process is implicit in all traditional indigenous cultures and coincidently involves skills not dissimilar to those used by artists – to move at will between the conscious and subconscious, to articulate beyond language and to be visionary.

I am interested in the potential of the artist to:
— Use their unique skills on behalf of others.
— Be autonomous while having an immediate relevance to peoples lives.
— Be useful.
— Inspire a confidence in the power of collectivity and imaginative experience for practical purposes.
— Answer questions as well as ask them.
— Have a direct influence beyond a self-serving art market.
— Become effective and celebrated in society.
— Be practical visionaries.

Marcus Coates — [Left] ***Firebird, Rhebok, Badger and Hare,*** **2008**, archival inkjet print
[Right] ***The Plover's Wing (The Mayor of Holon, Israel),*** **2008**, video still, courtesy the artist and Workplace Gallery, Gateshead

MARCUS COATES — *Journey to the Lower World (Beryl)* 2004, archival ink jet, courtesy the artist and Workplace Gallery, Gateshead

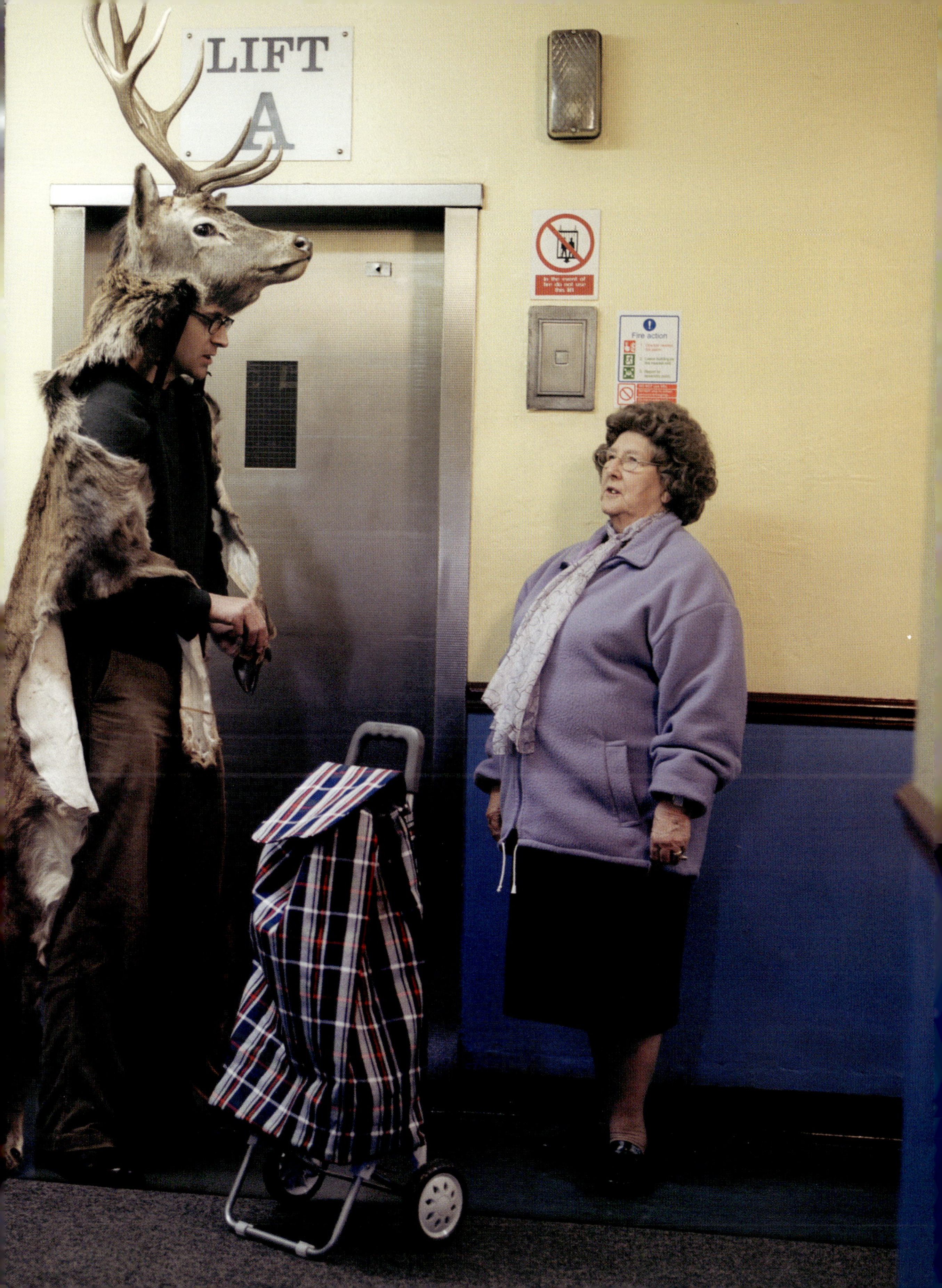
LIFT
A
Fire action

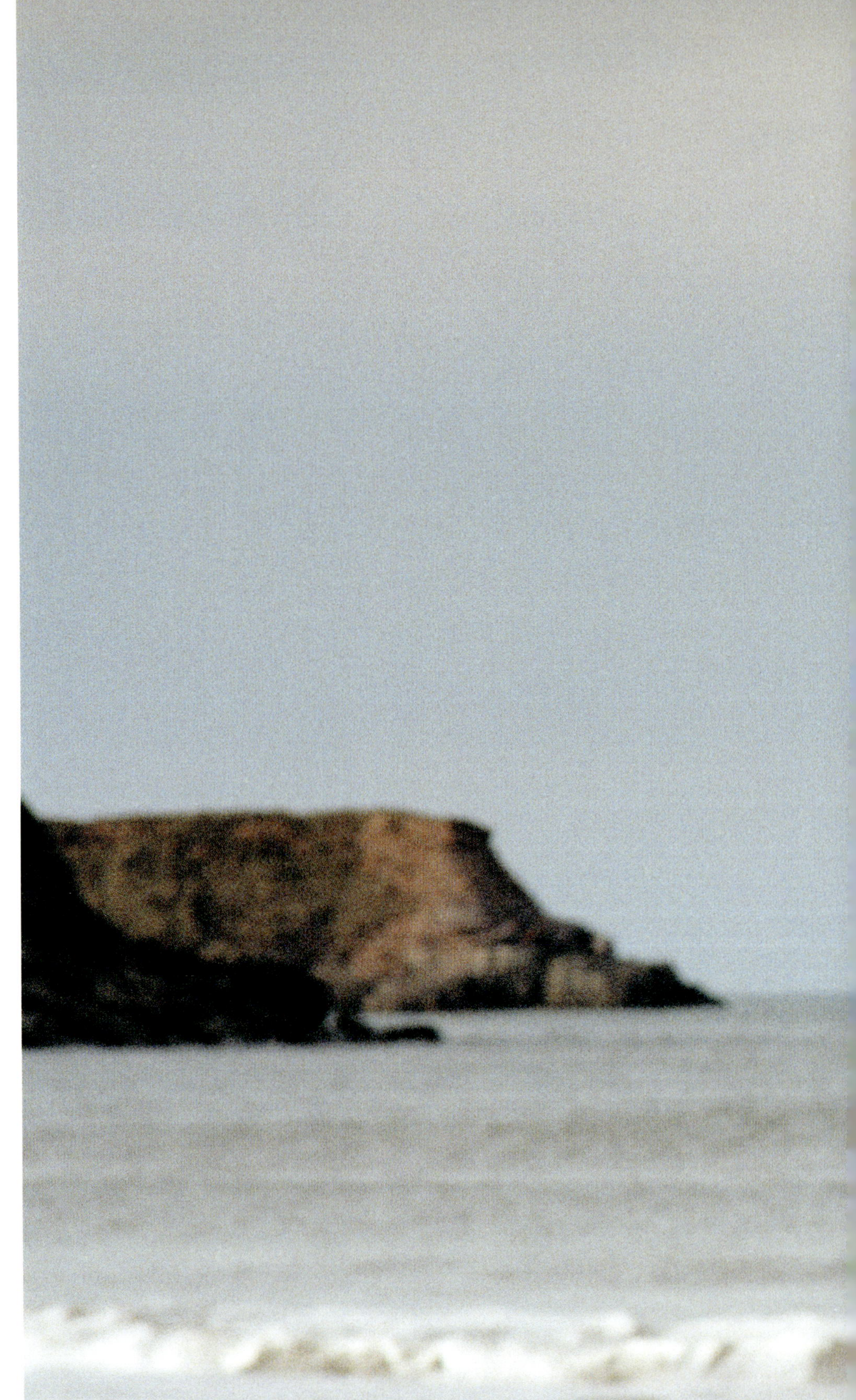

MARCUS COATES — *Sea Mammal, No.1,* 2003, archival ink jet, courtesy the artist and Workplace Gallery, Gateshead

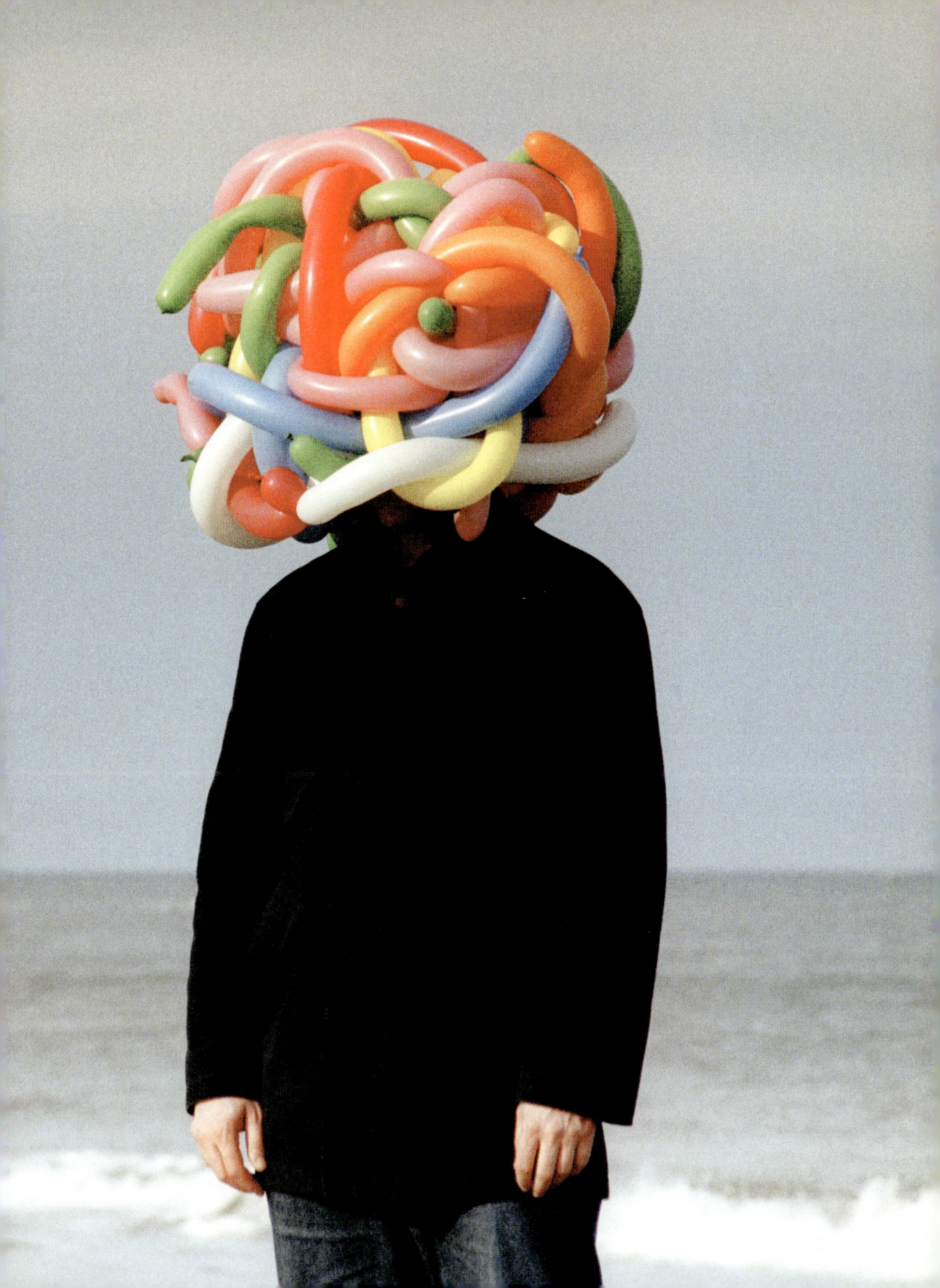

Peter
COFFIN

DEAR PETER COFFIN,

When you work on the myth of flying saucers or the movements of a whale, it is always through a movement of translation. How do you interpret reality through a shape? The essence of a piece like *Untitled (Bird in Space, Tropical Drink)* 2003, which creates a parallel between scientific research and the iconography of cocktails, resides in a formal analogy between two unrelated realities. I invented a word to describe the contemporary artist – the semionaut – someone who invents paths using signs. We can see this in such dissimilar artists as Rirkrit Tiravanija, Paul Chan, Francis Alÿs and Simon Starling: their work extends horizontally, in a wandering fashion, far from any predetermined formal identity. You – and they – invent paths among the signs, without limiting yourselves to a single type of space. In so doing, you have taken on an extraordinary challenge: to invent the visual culture of migrations. In *Around, About Expanded Field* 2007, iconic works are assembled on metal tripods and reduced to their shadows: these black silhouettes, which include those of Joseph Beuys and Max Ernst, seem ready for (movement). Portable, mobile, reduced to the essential: art in an era of fluidity, plunged into the 'expanded time field'.

Nicolas Bourriaud

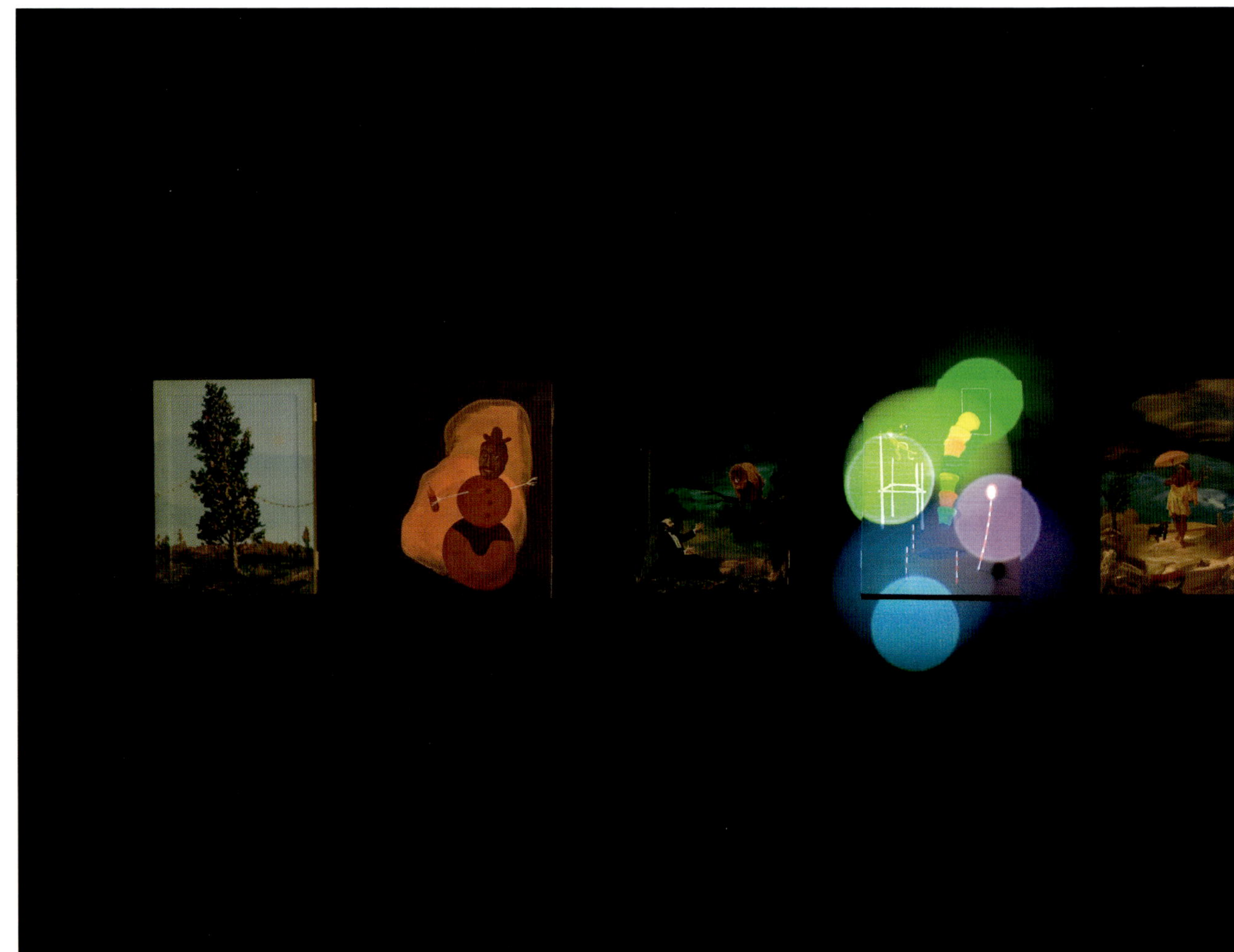

PETER COFFIN — ***Untitled (Djordje Ozbolt)*, 2008,** Flash animation video projection and 5 paintings (acrylic on board), dimensions variable, courtesy Herald St, London
[RIGHT] ***Untitled (Spiral Staircase)*, 2007,** powder-coated aluminium, 701.1 diameter, courtesy Andrew Kreps Gallery, New York; Galerie Emmanuel Perrotin, Miami/Paris; Herald St, London

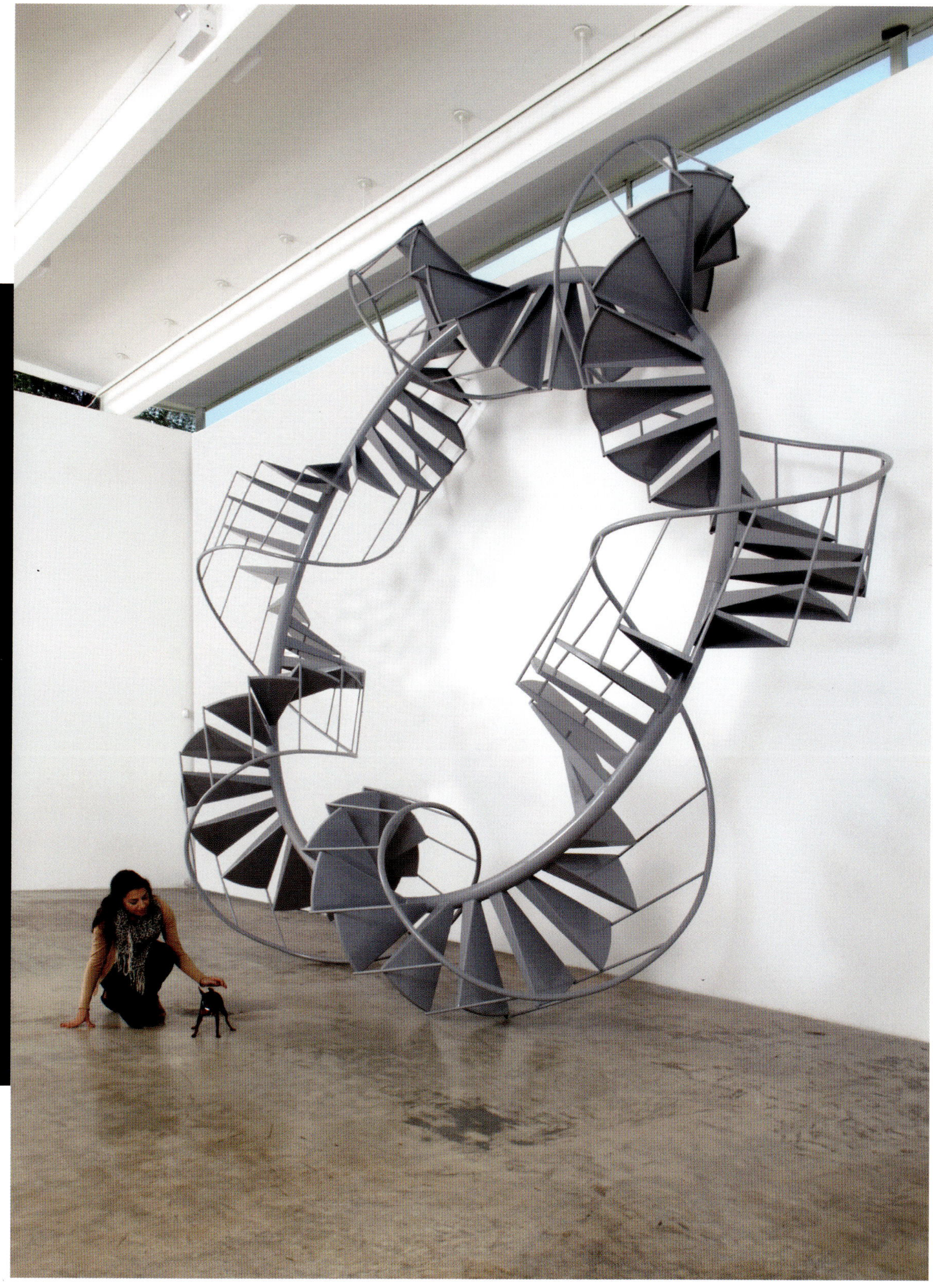

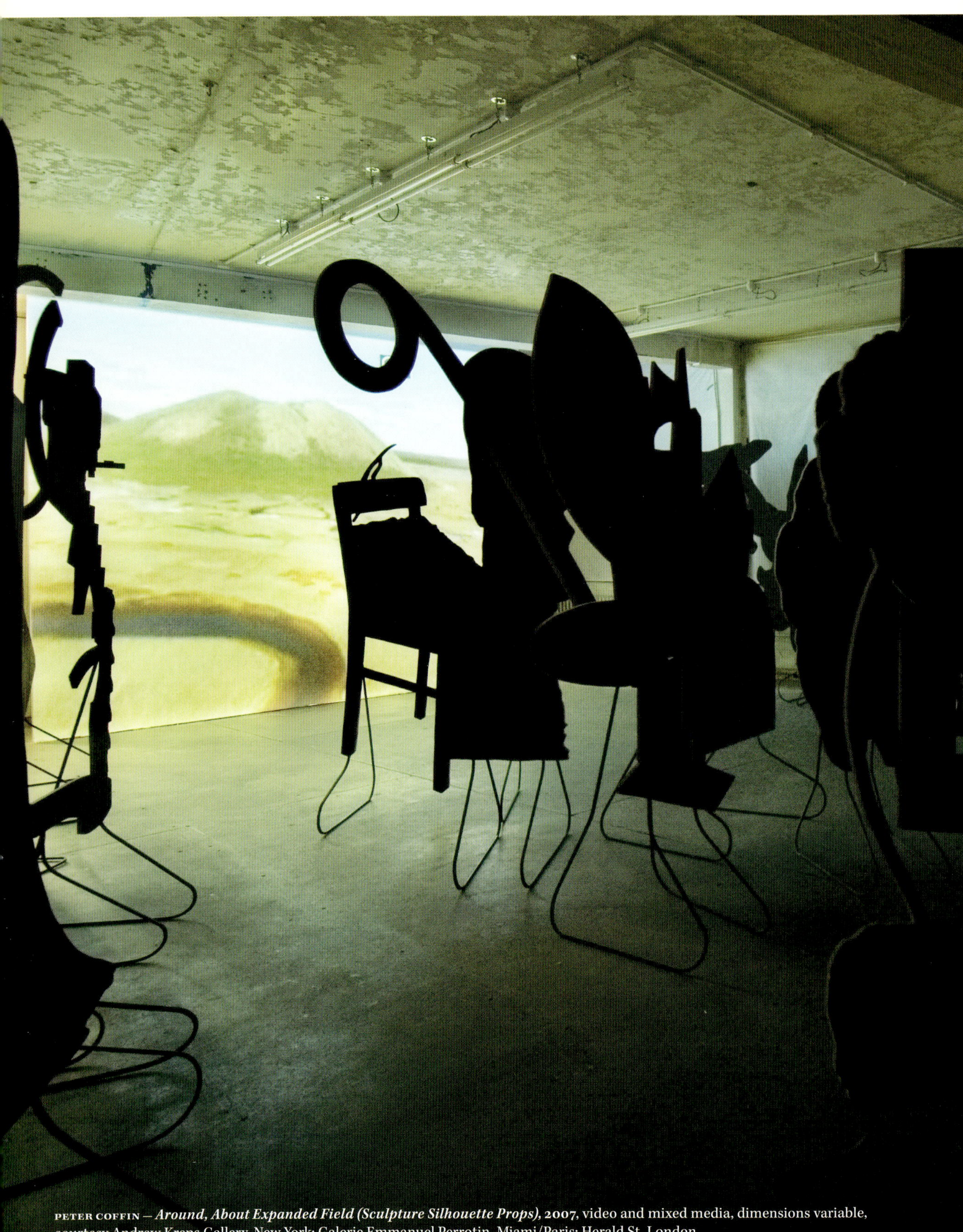

PETER COFFIN – *Around, About Expanded Field (Sculpture Silhouette Props)*, 2007, video and mixed media, dimensions variable, courtesy Andrew Kreps Gallery, New York; Galerie Emmanuel Perrotin, Miami/Paris; Herald St, London

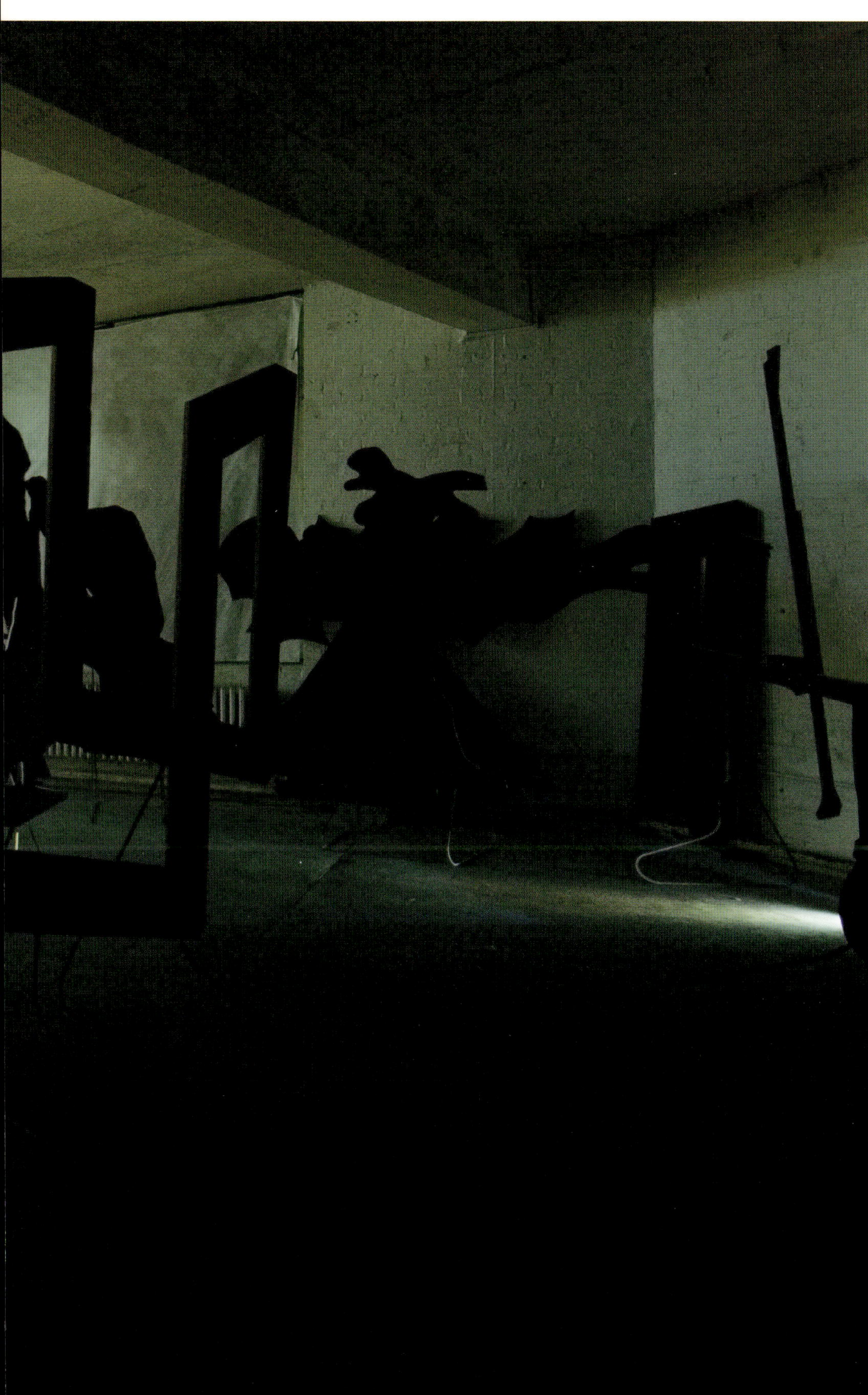

EXILES: 28 JUNE 2008

ULTRA-RED, Tania BRUGUERA, Flávia MÜLLER MEDEIROS and Nasrin TABATABAI, T. J. DEMOS, Eyal WEIZMAN

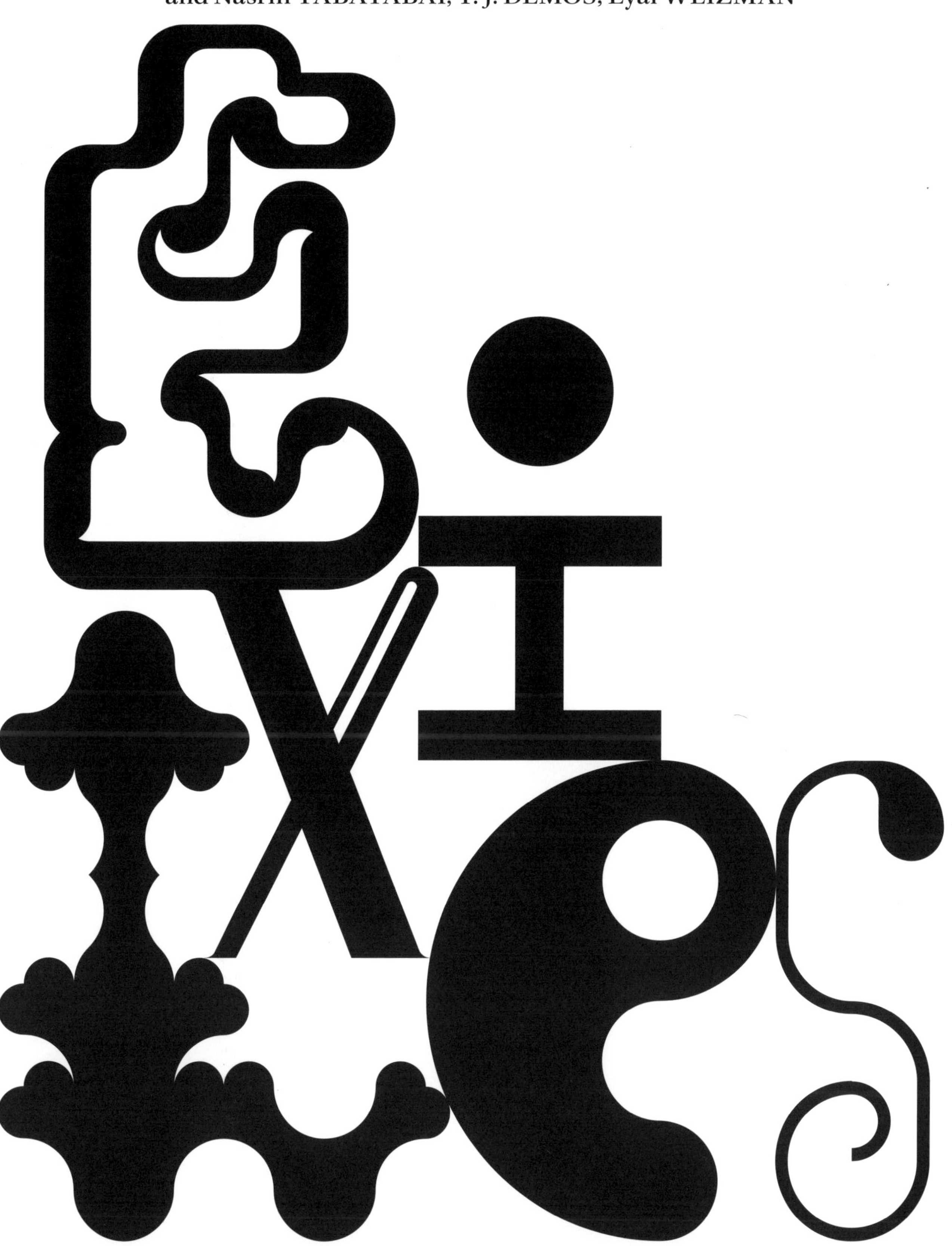

In 2002, according to the United Nations' International Migration Report, 175 million people were living in a country they were not born in. Rather than set one fixed root against another, a mythologised 'origin' against an integrating and homogenising 'soil', wouldn't it be wiser to assign other conceptual categories to the process of mutation? With about ten million more immigrants every year worldwide, increasing professional nomadism, the globalisation of goods and services and the formation of transnational political entities, isn't it about time to invent new ways of understanding what cultural identity is?

SATURDAY 28 JUNE 2008
TATE BRITAIN

from 10:00
DUFFIELD ROOM
ULTRA-RED
We Come from Your Future

14:00
AUDITORIUM
FLÁVIA MÜLLER MEDEIROS
and
NASRIN TABATABAI
A discussion on notions of exile

16:30
MODERN BRITISH ART
ROOMS 19, 20 AND 21
TANIA BRUGUERA
P6_TA-PROV(2008)029

16:30
AUDITORIUM
T.J. DEMOS
chaired by
EYAL WEIZMAN
Exiles

THE ENDS OF EXILE: TOWARDS A COMING UNIVERSALITY?

T. J. DEMOS

MODERNITY AS EXILE

VIEWED THROUGH THE LENS OF EXILE, modernity resembles a catastrophe, a storm of wreckage that propels redemption out of reach with implacable violence. Or so Walter Benjamin wrote about the storm from paradise that we call progress, as contemplated by the angel of history (he was thinking of Paul Klee's watercolour, *Angelus Novus* 1920). 'While the pile of debris before him grows skyward,' Benjamin famously wrote, he is cast backwards into the future as he views our present forlornly.[1] Gazing at that catastrophic modernity nearly fifty years later, the exiled Palestinian literary critic Edward Said rendered a verdict on the twentieth century that confirmed Benjamin's dark conclusion, written in the midst of an exile that ended in his suicide while attempting to escape the Nazis. 'Our age,' Said wrote, 'with its modern warfare, imperialism and the quasi-theological ambitions of totalitarian rulers – is indeed the age of the refugee, the displaced person, mass immigration.'[2]

Such is modernity as considered through the lens of exile, a period defined by the dislocating ravages and alienating effects of capitalism as much as by the psychic disequilibrium of traumatic *unheimlichkeit* – as it is comprehended in Marxist and Freudian thought. But modernity's darkness also intimates something more than what its mere political, economic and social circumstances suggest, which is clear in Benjamin's account of historical time that in effect leaves us all refugees in the present. Other philosophical diagnoses corroborate Benjamin's ontological account, defining our very epoch as one of 'transcendental homelessness',[3] according to Lukács; similarly Heidegger wrote that, 'Homelessness is coming to be the destiny of the world.'[4] But in Said's insistently political sense, modernity-as-exile – as glimpsed in Lamia Joreige's recent film, *A Journey* 2008, which shows a Palestinian refugee camp in 1948, the year of Israel's founding – identifies a counter-narrative and the repressed figure of the last century's otherwise celebrated glorious nationalisms, utopian political projects and vaunted technological achievements; for it reveals their failures, their human wreckage, the costs of their obscene audacity.[5]

I would like to open up that counter-narrative and that repressed figure here, yet avoid reading exile exclusively in the negative, as solely melancholic or chaotic, its identity metaphysically inscribed. As a wealth of literature, including personal and artistic testimonies, demonstrates, exile also unleashes a creative flight into the experience of multiplicity. Literally meaning 'to wander away',[6] its etymology possessing an ancient provenance – think of the epic biblical stories of wandering peoples and tragic banishments – exile suggests involuntary displacement as much as expatriation by choice, a harsh penal-like sentence as much as an earnest political commitment. Positioned adjacent to terms like diaspora (a geographical dispersal in the collective sense), refugee (the victim of persecution or forced expulsion) and migration (the traveller by choice, whether for economic necessity or, more recently, for ecological reasons), exile is both distinct and yet shares commonalities in its relation to the 'double consciousness' – in Paul Gilroy's terms – which is bestowed upon those who experience it. This 'double perspective' (in Said's words), a 'double frame' (in Homi K. Bhabha's), results from the bi-cultural knowledge it produces, generating in its positive expression a sensitivity towards difference (that of cultures, places and communities), and a newfound appreciation of the cultural character of one's origins when looking back from exile's awry vantage. In this sense, its transformative experience inspires both critical and creative energies, even among the existential vulnerability and material destitution it otherwise may bring.[7] Indeed, Hannah Arendt would write of 'refugees driven from country to country' in the midst of the unprecedented genocide of the Holocaust *not* as mere victims; rather, they 'represent the vanguard of their peoples'.[8] The reason, she explained, was that henceforth, these figures, shed of their national ties (at least in 1943, before the founding of Israel), would be the creators of their own destiny ('History is no longer a closed book to them and politics is no longer the privilege of Gentiles'). Likewise, Giorgio Agamben has recently proposed that in the present circumstances of massive demographic shifts – due to warfare and political repression, as much as emancipatory desire – the refugee represents 'the paradigm of a new historical consciousness', particularly because with that figure, we glimpse a future beyond the nation-state and its destructive exclusion of non-citizens.[9]

Keeping in mind, then, that exile designates a ruptured psycho-geography of fundamental ambivalence, calling up the longing for home and the embrace of elsewhere, and that it is antithetical to any unified meaning, let us consider some of the recent intersections of the geopolitical circumstances and the aesthetic negotiations of exile. These intersections in recent years have served multiple functions in contemporary art, oscillating between the calamitous and the creative: to find forms adequate to express the ravaging spatial and experiential effects of displacement; to invent archives capable of unleashing the hidden potential of historical consciousness; to discover innovative means to forge social bonds within transnational conditions that avoid sinking into regressive atavism or xenophobic hostility; to advance forms of life that reject the restrictive categories of identity and conventional modes of belonging; to direct the forces of mobility against the capture of commodification; and to resist the fundamentalist oppositions to, and equally the homogenising tendencies of globalisation – these are some of the various imperatives that have generated an aesthetics of exile over the last few decades.

THE DIASPORIC

MONA HATOUM'S *MEASURES OF DISTANCE* 1988, a video that relates the impossible intimacy of the London-based artist's long-distance relationship with her Lebanese-Palestinian mother living in Beirut; Isaac Julien's film *Territories* 1984, which mediates postcolonial subjectivity (that of British African-Caribbean-ness, in the context of London's Notting Hill Carnival) by opening up its fissures and fluctuating contours through the disjunctive textures of cinematic palimpsests; and Black Audio Film Collective's classic *Handsworth Songs* 1986, a film that deploys hybrid representations, both documentary and poetic, to reveal the diversity of local perspectives on the race riots against Thatcher's repressive measures in a working class area in Birmingham – these works demonstrate a powerful intertwining of the social and political facts of dislocation with the aesthetics of exile, which distinguishes British practices in the 1980s. Of course there have been earlier artistic engagements with exile, such as the historical avant-garde's, as in New York and Zurich Dada, and in the later displacements of European artists during WWII, in which modernist forms – decontextualised readymades, disjunctive montage, visual and textual fragmentations, disorienting spaces – expressed the experiential terms of geopolitical dislocation.[10] One could also cite the artistic dealings with travel – whether owing to personal desires, the commitments to internationalism or the political necessity of escaping repressive military regimes – encountered in the formations of CoBrA, the Situationist International and Fluxus, as well as in the global developments of abstraction and conceptualism (the work of Gego, Bas Jan Ader, Hans Haacke, Hélio Oiticica, Cildo Meireles, On Kawara, Yoko Ono, Yayoi Kusama and Tehching Hsieh comes to mind).[11] However, it was in the British context that exile was poignantly and uniquely negotiated both thematically and formally, correlating with decolonisation struggles, the experience of diaspora in the wake of the crumbling of empire, and the engagement with the discourses of identity politics and multiculturalism.

Considering the way Hatoum has directed her experience of geopolitical displacement into a post-minimalist sculptural phenomenology of disjointed everyday spaces and uncanny domestic objects, Edward Said writes how in her work 'exile [is] figured and plotted'. Born into a displaced Palestinian family in Beirut, she was studying art in London and found herself stranded there when the Lebanese civil war broke out in 1975. By enacting 'the paradox of dispossession as it takes possession of its place in the world', Said writes, Hatoum's projects draw out the 'irreconcilability' of strangeness and familiarity that defines the experience of living away from one's homeland.[12] Said's reading bears directly on *Measures of Distance*, which shows Hatoum's mother in the intimacy of her shower, while Arabic fragments of her correspondence with her daughter form a barrier over the image, expressing simultaneously the painful distance and the longings for closeness that mark the artist's experience. Kobena Mercer focuses similarly on the subversive aspects of related filmic disjunctions in Isaac Julien's *Territories*, for instance, in which he mounts a 'cultural struggle to decolonise and deterritorialise cinema as a site of political intervention'. By provoking a carnivalising of cinema as much as a cinema of carnival, Julien unleashes a 'dialogical tendency' appropriate to a 'diasporic people'. For Mercer, artists such as Julien and Black Audio Film Collective developed the techniques of montage, which, drawing on Bakhtin's notion of 'multi-accentuality' and 'inner dialectical quality' of the ideological sign, were posed against what Franz Fanon called the 'ideological fixity of the signs of colonial authority'.[13]

'If the exile was the figure of early modernity,' write Jean Fisher and Gerardo Mosquera, then 'the diasporean or immigrant was the figure of postmodernity with its decentered and deterritorialised subject'.[14] Yet while such a historical distinction accurately situates the diasporic within the context of postcolonial uprooting, the projects of artists such as Hatoum, Julien and Black Audio Film Collective (as well as Ceddo and Sankofa collectives in Britain) acted more as an oppositional force *against* the postmodern, in my view, than an affirmative expression of it. According to Fredric Jameson's now classic model, postmodernism – as both a periodising term and a cultural logic – designates the schizophrenic disorientation and debilitating amnesia of the subject in the state of advanced multinational capitalism.[15] The geographical homogeneity of built space and the ahistorical imagery of the culture industry were seen by him to compromise the ability to situate oneself in time and space. Jameson's is surely a still relevant account for an expanded history of exile (one that views it as a signifier for a variety of forms of displacement in recent history), particularly in view of the forces of dislocation in the now global capitalist economy.[16] But rather than viewing the diasporic position within critical art practices as an expression of that immobilisation, a work like Black Audio Film Collective's *Signs of Empire* 1984 precisely resisted that culture of simulacral vacuity and mindless consumerism. It did so by determinedly recovering the historical conditions and examining the alienating effects of the legacy of imperial dominance, as found in the visual archive of exoticised and colonised peoples, juxtaposing these images with views of London's now-worn public monuments to imperialism. Given its plural sensitivities, the diasporic was uniquely situated to address the politics of difference, connecting with civil rights, feminist and anti-imperialist struggles, and resurrecting historical, political and cultural figures, like Harlem Renaissance writer Langston Hughes in Julien's *Looking for Langston* 1988, in order to animate and empower current political engagements, thereby defying postmodernism's debilitating image regime.[17]

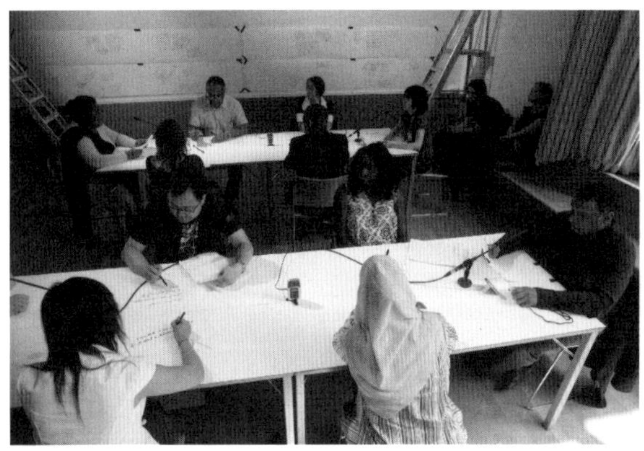

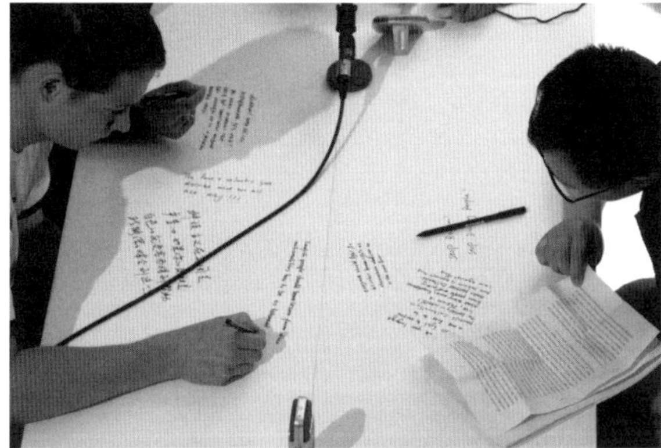

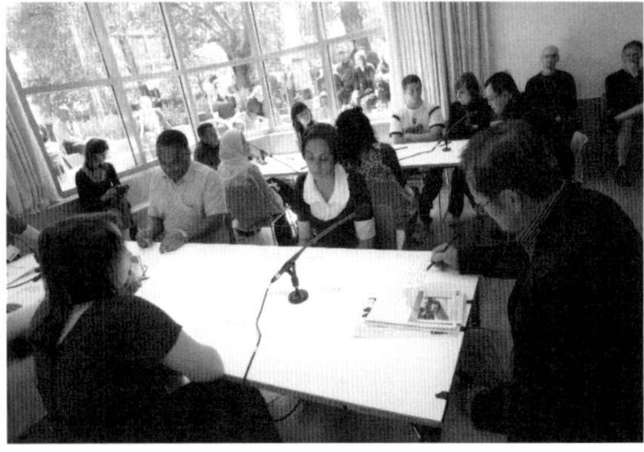

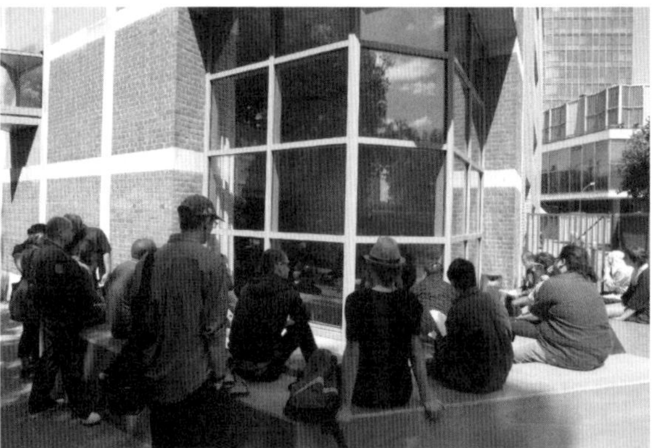

FOR THEIR PERFORMANCE, *We Come From Your Future*, sound art and activist collective **ULTRA-RED** collaborated with the anti-racist organisation The Monitoring Group to present a sound investigation into the future of anti-racism in the UK. The audience had the opportunity to contribute statements and to listen to invited speakers, including people who have been involved in the anti-racism movement for many years and those who have recently experienced racist violence, as well as participants in The Monitoring Group's 'Rural Racism' project, based in southwest Britain. The statements, written in the participants' different languages, were mounted on the wall after the discussions, forming a multilingual collage.

If the practices of Julien and Black Audio – and one could add Hatoum here as well – propose a 'critical dialogism', then it is, according to Mercer, one that challenges 'the monologic exclusivity on which dominant versions of national identity and collective belonging are based'.[18] They do so by eliciting the 'disjunctive time' and 'internal liminality' of the marginal and the migrant, as Homi Bhabha has noted.[19] At stake here is not only the defiant retort that diasporic practices made to postmodernist amnesia and spatial perplexity, but also the critical vantage point they established on earlier and even contemporary, competing modes of identity defined within the multicultural and feminist formations of the time – particularly those that attempted to assert a branding of identity (whether in terms of race, gender, sexuality or nationality) as a ground from which to counteract the forces of political and social exclusion.[20] As is now well established, because diasporic experience 'is defined, not by essence or purity, but by the recognition of a necessary heterogeneity and diversity', in the words of Stuart Hall, it models 'a conception of identity which lives in and through, not despite, difference'.[21] Black Audio Film Collective's *Signs of Empire* proposes just this hybridity in terms of its complex tapestry of still images, texts and sounds – as does Hatoum's *Measures of Distance* – proposing structures that disrupt the purity of film and language alike. As a result, the categories of the visual, the auditory and the scriptural are rendered insufficient on their own, as necessarily dialogical and stranded in their incompleteness and therefore contingent on contextual determinations for their meanings. In other words, this work defeats essentialism through formal means, even while it commits to the particularities of ethnicity, race and gender that define the lived circumstances of the subject within a heterogeneous cultural frame.

Still, despite these highly nuanced artistic treatments of the effects of displacement on subjectivity, by the mid 1990s came the gradual institutionalisation of multiculturalism in Europe and North America – meaning the emergence of the pervasive administration of identity-based and minority-directed policies within dominant governmental, civil and educational institutions, contributing to a veritable 'race industry' of managerial practices.[22] As Chandra Mohanty wrote presciently, 'In a post-Communist, post-national era, multiculturalism has been theorised as a paternalistic, top-down solution to the "problem" of minorities, a dangerous reification of "culture", or a new way forward to a politics of "recognition" and "authenticity". But is multiculturalism simply a novel project of social engineering, devised for the twenty-first century by well-meaning liberals or communitarians?'[23] Yet despite challenges such as Mohanty's to these developments, the result has been the fixing of cultural, racial and sexual signs within the discourse of political correctness, which correlated in the 1990s both to the social divisiveness of identity politics and to the commodification of ethnic and racial difference within neo-liberal globalisation. For theorists like Slavoj Zizek, as well as Michael Hardt and Tony Negri, 'multiculturalism' has been instrumentalised as 'the cultural logic of multinational capitalism';[24] for others, such as Paul Gilroy, the imperative for critical intellectuals consequently becomes one of writing 'against race'.[25] In other words, against the institutionalisation of multiculturalism – and its radically simplified notions of difference and cultural identity – we must continue to challenge static categories of subjectivity, whether those tied to geographical place – such as calls for a return to the local in order to resist the homogenising forces of globalisation[26]

– or those that continue the commitment, however fraught, to sexual and racial classes as a basis for a cultural politics of recognition.[27]

THE NOMADIC

IT WAS IMPERATIVES such as these that contributed to the development in the 1990s of nomadism, which presents us with a second formation in this genealogy of contemporary art and exile. Rirkrit Tiravanija's installation of nomad kitchens in which the New York, Berlin- and Thailand-based artist would cook free Thai food for guests, as in *Untitled (free)* at New York's 303 Gallery in 1992; Gabriel Orozco's *Yielding Stone* 1992, a ball representing the artist's weight in plasticine, rolled around New York City by the Mexican artist; and Francis Alÿs's *Paradox of Praxis* 1997, for which the Belgian artist moved a block of ice around the streets of his adopted Mexico City for nine hours until it disappeared – these projects exemplify the poetic lyricism and romantic sensibility of the nomadic. Freed from the constrains of fixed identity and detached from the postcolonial burdens of the struggle for minority recognition that sometimes reinforced those static conceptions of race, ethnicity and nationality, 'artistic nomadism' represents a new model of 'cosmopolitanism', according to critic Jean-Pierre Criqui. While the nomad is 'always carrying along ... a part of one's native country', he or she remains 'independent of the melancholy one ordinarily associates with uprooting', notes Criqui: the nomad is 'a mobile and polymorphous entity'.[28]

Unlike exile, then – whose 'essential sadness', for Said, 'can never be surmounted'[29] – nomadism embraces dislocation as a permanent home with lightness and joy. Indeed, positioned by Hardt and Negri as precisely a 'resistance to bondage', the nomadic represents a 'struggle against the slavery of belonging to a nation, an identity, and a people,' and a 'desertion from sovereignty and the limits it places on subjectivity', a desertion they see as 'entirely positive'.[30] In this regard, nomadism advances a critical strategy for resisting the double tendencies of globalisation: on the one hand, its creative mobility challenges the homogenising aspect of capitalism that renders all places and things alike[31]; on the other, nomadism defies the regressive returns to localism, tribalisation and essentialist identities that the backlash against cultural and economic globalisation sometimes inspires. As Achille Oliva puts it, 'nomadic artists exercise their right to diaspora, their freedom to wander across the boundaries of various cultures, nations and media forms ... They adopt a tactic marked by cultural nomadism to escape the perverse consequence of tribal identity and, at the same time, claim the creation of what is symbol[ic] against the commoditisation of global economy.'[32]

Yet how critical is this strategy? One could ask, first of all, what means of social commonality or solidarity is available to this class of itinerant individuals? How does the nomadic avoid collapsing into the same debilitating loss of collective solidarity, the splintering of which plagued identity politics? For instance, even postcolonial critic Gayatri Spivak has proposed – *pace* nomadism's anti-identitarian posture – the 'strategic' use of an opportunistic and temporary 'essentialism' to unite people in order to achieve specific political goals.[33]

Critics have also pointed out that nomadism's lyrical and romantic tendency is a non-critical one, where the poetic flight of fancy – which tends to dramatise first and foremost the artist's own privileged peripatetic existence – fails to reflexively consider the institutional, historical and geographical parameters in which the nomadic is inhabited, and ends up typically 'veiling the specific material circumstances of the gallery'.[34] In addition, despite the nomad's purported escape from identity, the art market's star system tends to reward individuals with widespread name recognition; consequently when the promoters of discursive sites and relational scenarios are marketed as exemplary artistic personalities, we encounter what Miwon Kwon describes as 'a hermetic implosion of (auto)biographical and subjectivist indulgences', which may be 'misrepresented as self-reflexivity'.[35] These tensions become particularly apparent when mid-career retrospectives are organised for artists like Tiravanija, exhibitions that deploy a monographic format that reaffirms authorial identity despite the artist's attempts to variously problematise that logic via collaborative procedures, the elimination of art objects and non-autobiographical projects.[36]

Still, one could argue that these dangers are more the results of the institutionalisation of the nomadic as an art world and mainstream cultural fashion rather than the unavoidable outcomes of artistic practices, and moreover that the nomadic nevertheless retains its radical potential when it comes to the critique of identity and belonging in a period marked by the troubling reassertion of nationalism, ethnicity, and religious fundamentalism. Perhaps the nomadic holds within itself a similar resistance to traditionalism as that one encounters in the expatriate avant-garde, the critical necessity of which has once again gained ground. In this regard, the shifts of emphases in the cultural expressions of exile over the course of modernity – from anti-nationalist exile, to postcolonial diaspora, to global nomadism – are not so clear cut, nor is their periodisation punctual or definitive. It is not surprising that Edward Said and Homi Bhabha, for instance, return to Theodor Adorno and Walter Benjamin in their discussions of the cultural and political effects of displacement; similarly Kobena Mercer, in his own theorisation of dialogism, revisits the Russian formalist Mikhail

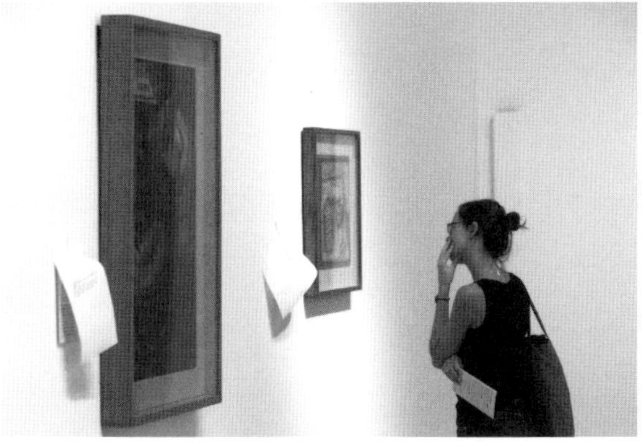

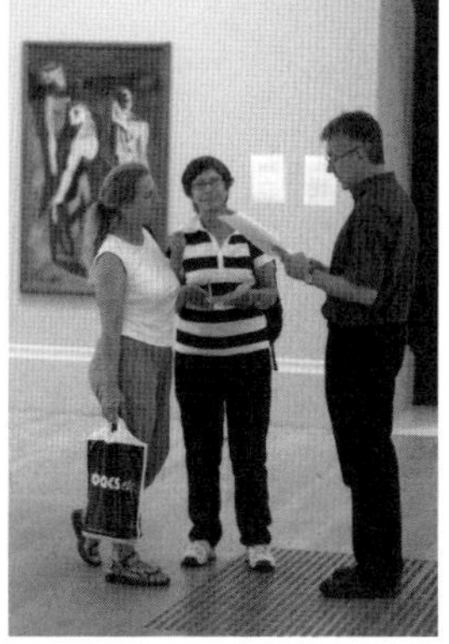

TANIA BRUGUERA is a Cuban artist who divides her time between Havana and Chicago. Her interdisciplinary work focuses on the relationship between art, politics and life. Since 2002 she has been working on a series of projects in which she appropriates structures of power, creating political situations rather than just representing them. Here, **BRUGUERA** instructed the curators to 'fly post' the Tate Britain galleries with pages from the directive on the return policy for illegal immigrants (*P6_TA-PROV(2008)0293* – the title of the intervention), approved by the European parliament just a few days before the Prologue. In the manner of a protest, the pages covered the rooms and obscured interpretation panels. The intervention was 'activated by' a gallery attendant, employed by **BRUGUERA**, who read out loud passages from the directive whenever visitors asked questions, whether relevant to the intervention or not. By obstructing the usual appearance and function of the gallery and humorously blurring intended participation with the confusion of those taken by surprise, the artist encouraged the audience to engage with issues of migration and exile. **BRUGUERA** was invited to participate in Exiles but was unable to obtain a visa to enter the UK. Her absence, though unfortunate, resonated with the themes of the day.

Bakhtin, and one can trace the nomadic back to Gilles Deleuze and Félix Guattari's 'nomadology,' and from there, to Kafka and Duchamp. Rather, as competing articulations and schematic descriptions, the contours of these formations sometimes overlap, at other times operate in tandem. But what of the fate of the nomadic today, in a context where globalisation more than ever threatens to erase difference and particularity, and where the market's voracious appetite for mobility, flux and expansion makes the nomad an exemplary role-model for the trans-national capitalist? And given the resurgence of the nation-state in our post-9/11 environment, with the current governmental obsession with terrorism and security, what is the status of the nomadic in this new political environment animated by the fear and paranoia of migrants?

In view of this now pervasive geopolitical framework, a further risk of the nomadic is to naively romanticise the privileges of borderless travel while overlooking how the less-privileged are excluded from that same freedom. In 1993, for example, Christian Philipp Müller performed *Green Border*, a project included in the Venice Biennale's Austrian pavilion, for which the Swiss artist was photographed crossing Austria's eight national borders, including those of the former Eastern-block countries of the Czech Republic, Slovakia, Hungary and Slovenia as well as the others shared with the Western states of Italy, Switzerland, Liechtenstein and Germany. Along with his installation at the Austrian pavilion, which interrogated the architecture's historical relation to spatial partitioning and territorial divisions, Müller's was a complex symbolic act: it not only retrieved the historical connections between Austria and Nazi Germany (in 1938 the country had been annexed and its newly built Venice pavilion was formally associated with Germany), but also contested the remaining forms of geographical exclusion in the post-Wall era by transgressing Austria's borders in the fictional persona of that nation's representative artist.[37]

Yet against Müller's implication that Europe was becoming a free, borderless zone, the reality in the EU, conversely, was shifting towards the political imperative of stemming the tide of migration from North Africa and Eastern Europe. The Schengen Agreement, instituted in 1990, is key to this history, for it created an open region within Europe but simultaneously acted to reinforce Europe's borders with its neighbouring areas. It did so, moreover, by exacerbating the impoverishment and oppressive political circumstances of nearby African countries by conditioning economic aid upon strict population control achieved through militarised border security.[38] As refugee camps and detainment centres for illegal immigrants have since proliferated across the European continent – as shown in various maps by migrant rights groups, such as Migreurop[39] – it seems increasingly problematic to celebrate the nomadic today. Doing so once expressed the radical hope of global citizenship, situated in the period of the waning of the nation-state and its social-political hierarchies, particularly in the jubilant years immediately following the dissolution of the Soviet Union, which was the historical context for Müller's project. And while this hope may survive in current struggles – for instance, one reads in the pages of *Empire*: 'circulation must become freedom ... In other words, the mobile multitude must achieve a global citizenship'[40] – to sing the praises of nomadism today within the narrow scope of the European framework without that radical political demand – as is so often done in contemporary art discourse –

appears self-congratulatory, even narcissistic. In such cases, nomadism suggests a contemporary 'primitivism,' one that subscribes to a fantasy of freedom from all attachments, but which cruelly operates in a system that denies that freedom to the very people from whom it borrows its name.

WE REFUGEES

THE IMPERATIVE TO AVOID perpetuating the separation of citizen and refugee, and to contest the withdrawal of political rights from the migrant, has led to further modellings of exile within contemporary art, which build on the above-mentioned critical antecedents and yet are still in the process of emergence today. Consider Christoph Schlingensief's sardonic reality-TV event *Please Love Austria (Foreigners Out!)* 2000, which offers a compelling dramatisation of the current limits of nomadism. For that project, the German theatre director and provocateur invited a group of immigrants to live in a shipping container in Vienna's main square for a week. During that time, Austrians could monitor their existence online in real time and vote out – Big Brother style – two asylum-seekers per day for deportation. The longest to survive was designated the winner, and he or she could 'look forward to a cash prize and the prospect, depending on the availability of volunteers, of Austrian citizenship through marriage'.[42] The biting sarcasm of the event was that in performing the ideological truth of Jorg Haider's recently elected extreme-right party (the FPÖ, or Austrian Freedom Party), the event pitted the spectacle of xenophobia against itself, inviting Austrians – in Schlingensief's words – to get in touch with their 'inner Nazi'.

A related response to Europe's geopolitics of exclusion has been to relinquish the false universality of the nomadic and turn instead to ethnographic procedures and documentary tactics to expose the often far from romantic living conditions of actual refugees. Multiplicity's *Solid Sea 03* 2003, for instance, compares two parallel voyages of the same 70-kilometre distance through the West Bank, one travelled by a Palestinian from Hebron to Nablus via checkpoints and gravel roads, and another travelled by an Israeli from Kiryat Arba to Kdumin on special Israeli-built highways. Whereas the distance was roughly identical, the Palestinian's trip took five hours, compared to the Israeli's hour-long journey. The divergence between the two dramatises the significant disparities of mobility today, which depend on the identity of the traveller. Or take Ursula Biemann's video-essays, such as *Sahara Chronicle* 2006–7, which investigates northward transmigration in the Sahara, with Biemann interviewing and documenting people desperately and daringly making their way from Niger to Libya or Algeria, with hopes of eventually gaining illegal access to Europe. This critical exposure has also been the goal of various recent exhibitions on migration, such as *Port City: On Mobility and Exchange*, at Bristol's Arnolfini, 2007;[43] and *No Place – Like Home: Perspectives on Migration in Europe* at Argos in Brussels, 2008, which organisers described as an investigation into the status of 'illegal refugees who are today's modern nomads'. Both exhibitions explored the 'variegated tale of migration networks and refugee trafficking, cartography and geographical military data, migration management and border infiltrations, international rights, lack of rights and lawlessness'.[44] These shows – and others like them – are salutary in that they reject the superficial romance of the nomadic in favour of exposing the circumstances of those excluded from its privileged realm; as well, they contest media stereotypes and governmental spin regarding migrants as so many criminals and terrorists, which tend to polarise camps, drawing citizens and refugees ever apart. The challenge of the documentary treatments found commonly in such shows is therefore to avoid reaffirming the excluded as victimised objects of representation, ironically reiterating the relations of inequality they are otherwise trying to contest. It is not surprising that these problems have inspired the creative reinvention of documentary strategies of representation in order to avoid such objectifications, leading to the disavowal of truth claims in favour of subjectively reflexive narrative approaches, and the installation of multiple screens and projections that construct a participatory physical mobility on behalf of the viewer, as in Multiplicity's and Biemann's work. Inevitably, these artists employ deracinating presentations to disavow objectifying representations, which suggest a correspondence with nomadic tendencies, even while these documentarists would disavow the fashionable celebration of nomadism as a form of artistic identity.

These models not only bear witness to the deeply ambivalent experiences of displacement, relaying both the hardships and pleasures, the pathetic indigence and the productive possibility; they also generate powerful aesthetic constructions that dislocate the viewers' space and time of perception and self-positioning. In doing so, exile becomes a shared experience between artist and viewer alike, suggesting the basis of an emergent political construction. Think of Emily Jacir's performative, installation-based investigations into the everyday lives of those caught in the Palestinian diaspora, such as her *Material for a Film* 2007; Yto Barrada's *A Life Full of Holes – The Strait Project* 1998–2004, comprising a photographic cycle depicting Moroccan migrants on the Strait of Gibraltar; Steve McQueen's cinematic treatments of migrant labourers that liberate them from the bondage of representation, as in *Gravesend* 2007; and the Otolith Group's films that destabilise the temporality of nationality and empower the potentiality of historical oppositional struggles, as in *Otolith* 2003 – in these cases, the viewer is placed in proximity to what Edward Said has called 'permanent exile', a term that draws on exile's metaphorical sense to describe a protean state of being, rather than a local reality defined by specific social and political circumstances. Said's notion comes close to what Giorgio Agamben calls 'being in exodus', that is, a perpetual state of revolution.[45] This positioning declines an ultimate redemption, a deferred homecoming, a naturalisation or national independence; instead, the deconstructive force of this conceptualisation of exile suggests, finally, a form of 'singularity' that is more about infinite becoming than static existence, and which is posed against citizen and nation-state alike – an existential exile without state, nation or identity.[46] While this articulation reaffirms the nomadic surpassing of identity, it nevertheless insistently invents new criteria for the specificity of lived reality and collective association – whether it be territorial-based (for instance, using urban space as a site of connection and transit for ephemeral communities of displaced persons); or transnational political affiliations (as in global movements for social justice and environmental sustainability); or again they might be communities of sense (as in the building of social connections through artistic participation and discourse); or what Okwui Enwezor calls the 'diasporic public sphere' of international biennial exhibitions (where participants reflexively problematise their economic and social position, as well as the exclusions of the location, even while they create the terms of cross-cultural interaction).[47] Most importantly, these models represent forms of sociability that remain open to foreignness, mobility and flux – in distinction to the potentially generic nomadic set, and to the biological and ethnic ties of familial and regional bonds.

Consider Emily Jacir's project *Where We Come From* 2002–3, which assembles a series of some thirty photograph and text diptychs that narrate the stories of Palestinians unable to travel due to Israeli restrictions. Jacir asked her invited participants, 'If I could do something for you, anywhere in Palestine, what would it be?' The texts present the various responses in Arabic and English: 'Visit my mother, hug and kiss her and tell her that these are from her son'; or, 'Go to Haifa and play soccer with the first Palestinian boy you see on the street'; or, 'Go on a date with a girl from East Jerusalem whom I have only spoken to on the phone.' The photographs portray the artist carrying out those requests, as Jacir could move about Israel and the Occupied Territories at the time with her US passport (although this would no longer be possible today, due to the worsened political situation). With this project, Jacir constructs a Palestinian diasporic community, one based on, even constituted by, the conditions of dislocation. What these participants share is the occupation of a position of exclusion from national belonging, and this relation touches the viewer as well. When we view the piece, we become displaced, owing to the ambiguity of representation, to the divisions between text and image, and to the multiple stories and fragmented structures of identification. Munir, for instance, who was born in Jerusalem, lives in Bethlehem, and has a Palestinian passport and a West Bank ID, writes: 'Go to my mother's grave in Jerusalem on her birthday and put flowers and pray. I need permission to go to Jerusalem. On the occasion of my mother's birthday, I was denied an entry permit.' When we look at the image, we see the artist's shadow cast over the grave. But that shadow also becomes ours as we gaze at the picture. Owing to the ambiguity of pronouns, for a fleeting moment, Munir's 'I' becomes ours as we share a proximity with the excluded. What if this form of sociability – one based on occupying a position of exile – was held in suspension, posed against the de-

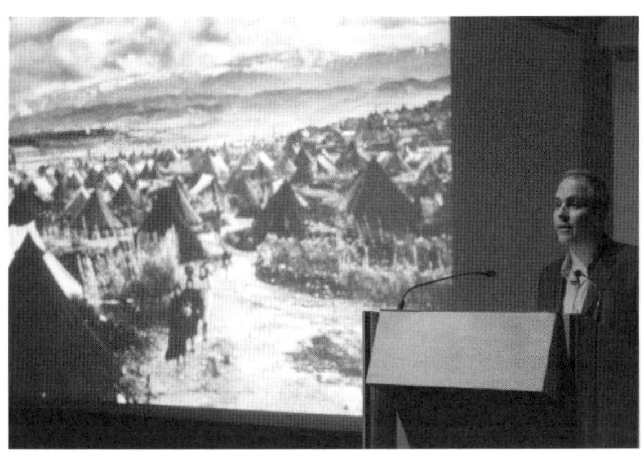

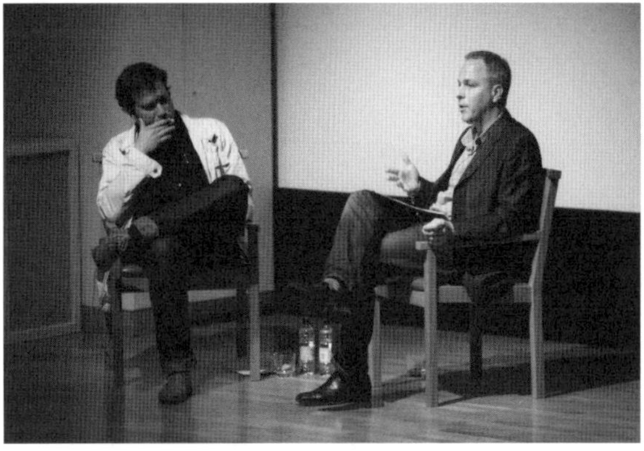

T.J. DEMOS, writer, critic and lecturer, investigates the ways in which artists operate in the context of an emerging global co-existence of political sovereignty and statelessness, and the relationship of contemporary art to the experience of social dislocation and political crisis. For the prologue **DEMOS** explored concepts of exile with reference to contemporary art in the context of the 'altermodern'. The talk was followed by a discussion, chaired by Israeli architect **EYAL WEIZMAN**.

sires for nationality, channelled against xenophobic communities, against the cycles of fear and violence that have torn the world apart? What if this community of the displaced was put to task against the desires for a national home, against the nationalism of Israelis and Palestinians alike, which violently divides all, geographically, socially and politically?

EXILE AS THE COMING UNIVERSALITY?

AGAMBEN HAS SUGGESTED that only when 'the citizen has been able to recognise the refugee that he or she is – only in such a world is the political survival of humankind today thinkable'.[48] The radical nature of this proposal is that the recognition of one's fundamentally dislocated self dissolves the division between citizen and refugee, proposing a space 'where exterior and interior in-determine each other', where one is placed in 'a relation of reciprocal extraterritoriality' to the other.[49] In opposition to the regime of social and political separation that constitutes what Étienne Balibar has identified as a 'virtual European apartheid'[50] – by which he means the undemocratic and exclusionary policies of the EU in regard to its non-citizen residents – this 'relation of reciprocal extraterritoriality' breaks the seemingly inextricable bonds between nation, state and territory, and severs the ostensibly natural links between citizen, nationality and human rights. What opens up, according to Agamben, is the possibility of a 'refuge of the singular', where rights are reinvented on the basis of residency rather than citizenship, and where nationality can no longer operate as the logic of segregation and discriminatory justice.

From this abstract theoretical speculation, it is hard to grasp what such a 'refuge of the singular' would actually be or look like in reality. What post-national institutions, political infrastructure and administrative mechanisms would guarantee its protection? Who would

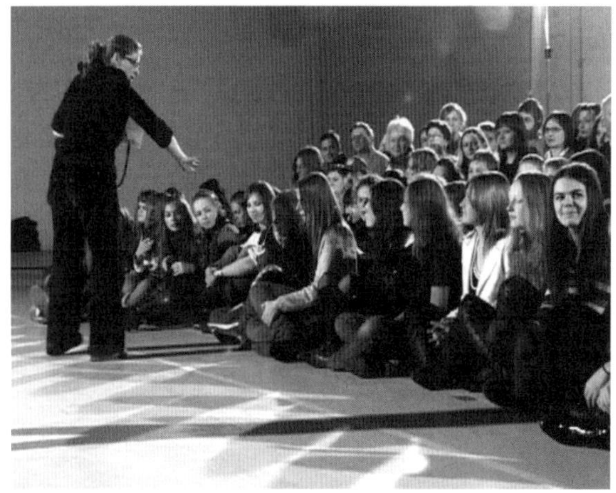

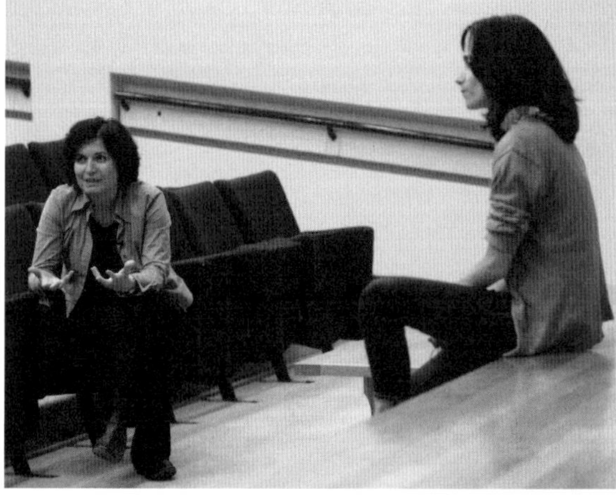

FLÁVIA MÜLLER MEDEIROS invited artist **NASRIN TABATABAI** for a discussion during which they each took one of their previous works as the starting point to question and reflect on notions of exile. In 2007 **FLÁVIA MÜLLER MEDEIROS** spent time in the capital cities of the Baltic region as part of a 'Holiday in' residency, and became interested in the European Humanities University, a Belarusian university which relocated to Vilnius, Lithuania after its forced closure by the Belarusian government in 2004. Her video *Untitled* 2007 documents the making of the first group portrait (see above left) of the politically displaced EHU students at the Contemporary Art Centre Vilnius. **NASRIN TABATABAI** in her video *Passage* 2005 presented a portrait of an immigrant performing her daily life while selling magazines at a shopping mall in the city of Rotterdam.

protect the rights of those within it? What would it mean to transvalue statelessness and universalise it as a condition of political equality and radical democracy? These questions have yet to be answered. In this regard, exile still promises a future redemption that seems out of grasp, just as it did in Benjamin's apocalyptic time. That future redemption might designate, following Zizek, a 'universality to come' – specifically an age of the universality of the singular. *To recognize oneself as the refugee:* this means that the relation to the shadowy figure of the exile defines the way one relates to oneself; in other words, it demands, paradoxically, 'identifying universality with the point of exclusion'.[51] For Zizek, this manoeuvre is the converse of the standard one of deconstructing universality as false, by revealing, for instance, the hidden interests behind some abstract universal idea – such as the 'his' of history that exposes the traditional patriarchal construction of the past as presented in supposedly 'objective' accounts. Similarly, it is easy to show how the segregation of citizens and migrants creates the terms of social and political inequality. But to merely criticise that system remains a reactive response, which fails to provide alternatives other than further reforms that potentially leave the structures of division intact. Far more radical is to universalise exile as the condition of being human, and to determine a politics of equality on that basis. It may currently be unlikely to conceive of this eventuality in today's political environment. But perhaps this is exactly where artistic practice may assume its most radical role: to imagine alternatives otherwise impossible to contemplate, unleashing an imagination that may produce material effects in turn.

NOTES

1. **WALTER BENJAMIN**, 'Theses on the Philosophy of History', (1940) in *Illuminations*, ed. Hannah Arendt, trans. Harry Zohn, New York 1968, p.258.

2. **EDWARD SAID**, 'Reflections on Exile', in *Granta* no.13, Autumn 1984, p.159.

3. **GYÖRGY LUKÁCS**, *The Theory of the Novel: A Historico-philosophical Essay on the Forms of Great Epic Literature*, trans. Anna Bostock, London 1971, p.41.

4. **MARTIN HEIDEGGER**, *Basic Writings*, ed. and trans. David Farrell Krell, Routledge 1993, p.243.

5. See **NIKOS PAPASTERGIADIS**, *Dialogues in the Diasporas: Essays and Conversations on Cultural Identity*, London 1998, p.1: 'Does modernity still promise to be the home of enlightenment, progress and reason, or is it an exilic state shrouded by techno-mystification, sliding deeper into chaos, committed to inequality, a shabby justification for ecological and cultural upheaval?' See also **NIKOS PAPASTERGIADIS**, *Modernity as Exile: The Stranger in John Berger's Writing*, Manchester and New York 1993.

6. The etymology of exile dates from c.1300, from the Old French *exillier*, and from the Latin *exilare* and *exilium*, meaning 'banishment', and *exul*, meaning 'banished person', combining *ex-* 'away' and *al-* 'to wander' (cf. the Greek *alasthai* 'I wander'). According to the *Oxford English Dictionary*, exile variously signifies penal expatriation, banishment and voluntary expatriation for any purpose.

7. **PAUL GILROY**, *The Black Atlantic: Modernity and Double Consciousness*, Cambridge, Mass. 1993; **HOMI BHABHA**, *The Location of Culture*, London 1995; **EDWARD SAID**, 'Intellectual Exile: Expatriates and Marginals', in *Grand Street*, Autumn 1993, p.121. This double frame also implies a space of aporia, as Gayatri Spivak suggests, in 'Asked to Talk About Myself…', in *Third Text*, no.19, Summer 1992. Still, we must keep in mind Said's warning that to think of the literature of exile as solely 'beneficially humanistic is to banalize its mutilations'. 'Reflections on Exile', p.160.

8. **HANNAH ARENDT**, 'We Refugees', in *Menorah Journal*, no.1, 1943, p.77.

9. **GIORGIO AGAMBEN**, 'Beyond Human Rights' (1993), in *Means Without Ends: Notes on Politics*, Minneapolis 2000, p.16.

10. I have written about these contexts elsewhere. See **T.J. DEMOS**, 'Zurich Dada: The Aesthetics of Exile', *The Dada Seminars*, ed. Leah Dickerman, Washington DC 2005, pp.7–30; and **T.J. DEMOS** *The Exiles of Marcel Duchamp*, Cambridge, Massachusetts 2007. See also **STEPHANIE BARRON**, *Exiles + Emigrés: The Flight of European Artists from Hitler*, Los Angeles 1997.

11. See *Global Conceptualism: Points of Origin, 1950s-1980s*, ed. L. Camnitzer et al., exh. cat., Queens Museum of Art, New York 1999; **MONICA AMOR**, 'Gego: Exploding the Field', in *Art Journal*, Winter 2007; and **FRAZER WARD**, 'Alien Duration: Tehching Hsieh, 1978–99', in *Art Journal*, Autumn 2006.

12. **EDWARD SAID**, 'The Art of Displacement: Mona Hatoum's Logic of Irreconcilables', in *Mona Hatoum: The Entire World as a Foreign Land*, exh. cat., Tate, London 2000, p.17.

13. **KOBENA MERCER**, 'Diaspora Culture and the Dialogic Imagination: the Aesthetics of Black Independent Film in Britain', *Welcome to the Jungle: New Positions in Black Cultural Studies*, London 1994, pp.253–4.

14. **JEAN FISHER** and **GERARDO MOSQUERA**, 'Introduction', *Over Here: International Perspectives on Art and Culture*, Cambridge, Massachusetts 2003, p.3.

15. **FREDRIC JAMESON**, 'The Cultural Logic of Late Capitalism', in *Postmodernism, or The Cultural Logic of Late Capitalism*, Durham, North Carolina 1992.

16. **FREDRIC JAMESON**, 'Notes on Globalization as a Philosophical Issue', in *The Cultures of Globalization*, ed. F. Jameson and Masao Miyoshi, Durham, North Carolina 1998.

17. On this general development, see **AMNA MALIK**, 'Conceptualising "Black" British Art Through the Lens of Exile', in *Exiles, Diasporas & Strangers*, ed. Kobena Mercer, London 2008. On the diasporic, see **JANA EVANS BRAZIEL** and **ANITA MANNUR** (eds.), *Theorizing Diaspora: A Reader*, Malden, Massachusetts 2003.

18. **MERCER 1994**, p.62.

19. **HOMI BHABHA**, 'Dissemination: Time Narrative and the Margins of the Modern Nation', *Nation and Narration*, London, 1990; also see, **HOMI BHABHA**, *The Location of Culture*, London 1994.

20. One such formation was the YBA phenomenon, inaugurated in 1988 with its notorious *Freeze* exhibition organized by Damien Hirst, the reception of which made claims for a resurgence of British identity. For a critique of that resurgence, see **KOBENA MERCER**, 'Ethnicity and Internationality: New British Art and Diaspora-Based Blackness', in *Third Text* 49, Winter 1999–2000, pp.15–26.

21. **STUART HALL**, 'Cultural Identity and Diaspora' (1990), in *Theorizing Diaspora: A Reader*, ed. Jana Evans Braziel and Anita Mannur, Malden, Massachusetts 2003, p.244.

22. On the 'race industry' see **CHANDRA MOHANTY**, 'On Race and Voice: Challenges for Liberal Education in the 1990s', in *Cultural Critique* 2, 1990.

23. Mohanty, pp.179–208. See also **TARIQ MODOOD**, ed., *The Politics of Multiculturalism in the New Europe: Racism, Identity and Community*, London 1996.

24. **SLAVOJ ZIZEK**, 'Multiculturalism, Or, the Cultural Logic of Multinational Capitalism', in *The Universal Exception*, London 2006, pp.151–182. See also Hardt and Negri in *Empire*, who query: 'What if a new paradigm of power, a postmodern sovereignty, has come to replace the modern paradigm and rule through differential hierarchies of the hybrid and fragmentary subjectivities that these [postcolonial] theorists celebrate? In this case, modern forms of sovereignty would no longer be at issue, and the postmodernist and postcolonialist strategies that appear to be liberatory would not challenge but in fact coincide with and even unwittingly reinforce the new strategies of rule!' **MICHAEL HARDT AND ANTONIO NEGRI**, *Empire*, Harvard 2000, p.138.

25. **PAUL GILROY**, *Against Race: Imagining Political Culture Beyond the Color Line*, Cambridge, Massachusetts 2000; see also **ERIC HOBSBAWM**, 'Identity Politics and the Left', in *New Left Review*, May/June, 1996; and on the question of post-black aesthetics in the United States, see **DARBY ENGLISH**, *How To See a Work of Art in Total Darkness*, Cambridge, Massachusetts 2007.

26. See **LUCY LIPPARD**, *The Lure of the Local: Senses of Place in a Multicentered Society*, New York 1997.

27. For instance, in **MAURA REILLY**, ed., *Global Feminisms: New Directions in Contemporary Art*, London 2007.

28. **JEAN-PIERRE CRIQUI**, 'Like a Roling Stone: Gabriel Orozco', in *Artforum*, April 1996.

29. **SAID** 1984, p.159.

30. **HARDT** and **NEGRI** 2000, pp.360–1.

31. For further consideration of this development, see **MIWON KWON**, 'One Place After Another: Notes on Site Specificity', *October* no.80, Spring 1997.

32. **ACHILLE BONITO OLIVA**, 'The Globalisation of Art', in *Belonging and Globalisation: Critical Essays in Contemporary Art and Culture*, ed. Kamal Boullata, London 2008, pp.43–4.

33. Spivak proposed 'a strategic use of positivist essentialism in a scrupulously visible political interest' – yet not without a controversial reception. See **DONNA LANDRY** and **GERALD MACLEAN** (eds.), *The Spivak Reader: Selected Works of Gayatri Chakravorty Spivak*, New York 1996, p.214.

34. **JAMES MEYER**, 'Nomads', in *Parkett* no.35, May 1997, p.207. Meyer differentiates 'lyrical nomads' (such as Tiravanija and Orozco), who practice 'a mobility thematized as a random and poetic interaction with the objects and spaces of everyday life', from 'critical nomads' (including Andrea Fraser, Christian Philipp Müller, Renee Green and Mark Dion), designating those who work out of the tradition of institutional critique. The latter model 'does not so much enact and record a discrete action or movement as locate the structures of mobility within specific historical, geographical, and institutional frameworks' (p.206).

35. **KWON** 1997, p.104.

36. Exemplary is **RIRKRIT TIRAVANIJA**, *A Retrospective (Tomorrow is Another Fine Day)* in 2005 at Musée d'art moderne de la Ville de Paris/ARC at the Couvent des Cordeliers, Paris.

37. Müller exemplifies one of Meyer's 'critical nomads'. Also see: **GEORGE BAKER**, 'Lies, Damn Lies, and Statistics. The Art of Christian Philipp Müller', in *Artforum*, February 1997, pp.74–7, 109.

38. See **ALI BENSAÂD**, 'The Militarization of Migration Frontiers in the Mediterranean', in *The Maghreb Connection: Movements of Life Across North Africa*, ed. Ursula Biemann and Brian Holmes, Barcelona 2006. Also see **T.J. DEMOS**, 'Europe of the Camps', in *Manifesta 7: Companion: The European Biennial of Contemporary Art, 19 July – 2 November 2008, Trentino, South Tyrol, Italy*, ed. Adam Budak and Nina Möntmann, et al., Milan 2008.

39. See www.migreurop.org/. See also **CLAIRE RODIER**, 'The Migreurop Network and Europe's Foreigner Camps', in *Non-Governmental Politics*, ed. Michel Feher et al., New York 2007.

40. **HARDT** and **NEGRI** 2000, p.361.

41. It also suggests a logic whereby the excluded are necessary to the self-constitution of the nomad's position of freedom – which is similar to the mutually constitutive logic of minority and majority, and subaltern and hegemon, as developed in **HOMI BHABHA**, 'Unsatisfied: Notes on Vernacular Cosmopolitanism', in *Text and Nation: Cross-Disciplinary Essays on Cultural and National Identities*, ed. Laura Garcia-Moreno and Peter C. Pfeiffer, Columbia, South Carolina 1996, pp.191–207.

42. http://www.schlingensief.com/projekt_eng.php?id=t033.

43. **TOM TREVOR** (ed.), *Port City: On Mobility & Exchange*, exh. cat., Arnolfini, Bristol 2007.

44. Argos's description on its website: http://www.argosarts.org/articles.do?id=431. Other relevant recent exhibitions include *B-ZONE: Becoming Europe and Beyond* at Berlin's Kunstwerke in 2005–06; and *Be(com)ing Dutch*, Charles Esche's 2007–08 project at Eindhoven's Vanabbemuseum.

45. **SAID** 1993, pp.116, 119; **AGAMBEN 1993**, p.25.

46. **SAID** 2000, p.17: 'Better disparity and dislocation than reconciliation under duress of subject and object; better a lucid exile than sloppy, sentimental homecomings; better the logic of dissociation than an assembly of compliant dunce. A belligerent intelligence is always to be preferred over what conformity offers, no matter how unfriendly the circumstances and unfavourable the outcome.' Not surprisingly, before his death Said came to favour a binational – and distinctly anti-nationalist– solution to the Israeli-Palestinian conflict. See **EDWARD SAID**, 'The One-State Solution', in *New York Times*, 10 January 1999.

47. **OKWUI ENWEZOR**, 'Mega-Exhibitions and the Antinomies of a Transnational Global Form', in *Manifesta Journal*, no.2, 2004.

48. **AGAMBEN** 1993, p.26.

49. Ibid., p.25.

50. **ÉTIENNE BALIBAR**, '*Droit de cité* or Apartheid?', *We, the people of Europe? Reflections on Transnational Citizenship*, trans. James Swenson, Princeton 2004.

51. According to **ZIZEK**, in 'Multiculturalism', 'this, perhaps, is how one should read Rancière's notion of *singulier universel* [as developed in his book *La Mésentente*, 1995]: the assertion of the singular exception as the locus of universality which affirms and subverts the universality in question', note 27.

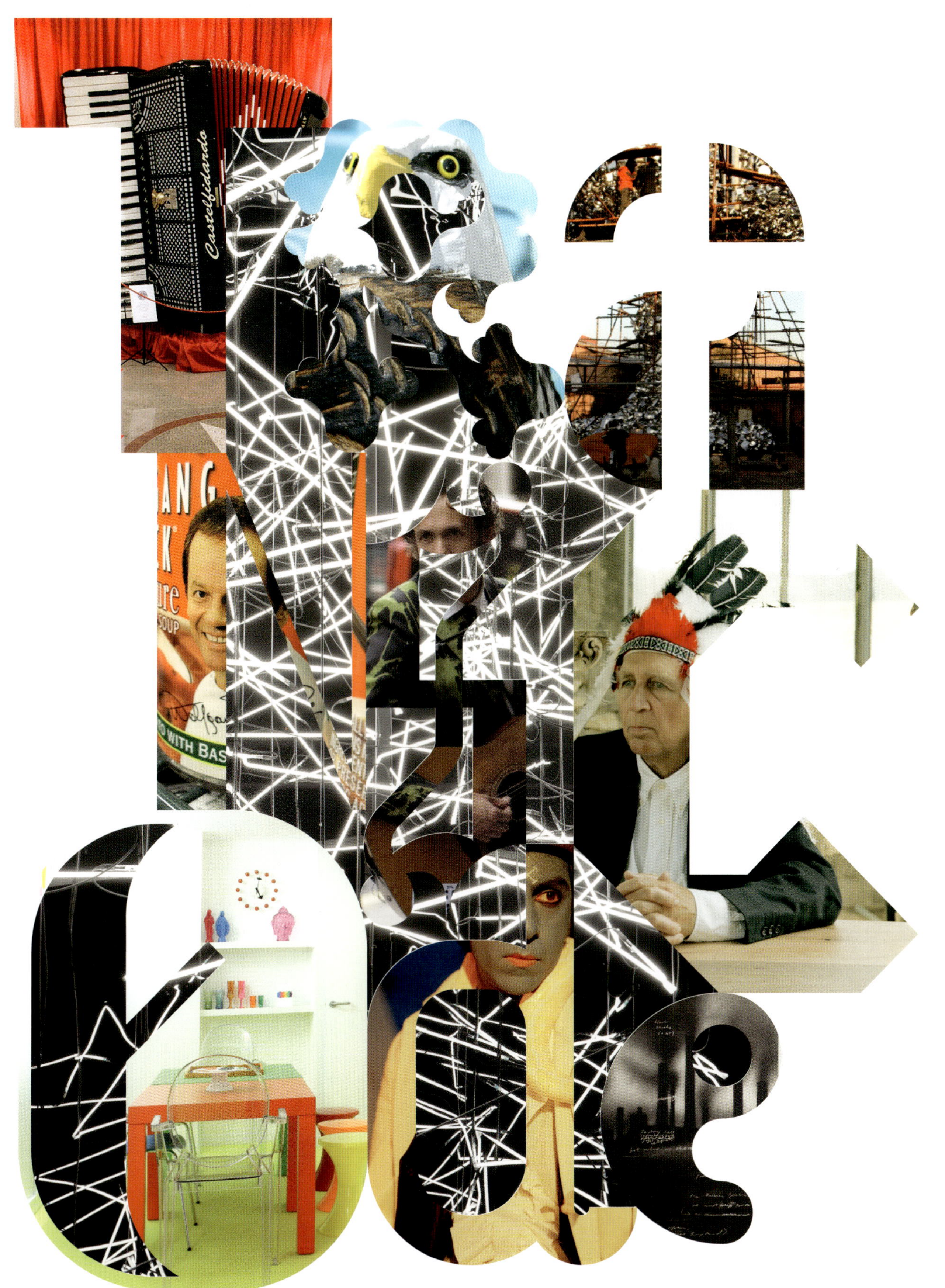
Castelfidardo
SOUP

Matthew DARBYSHIRE

***PALAC*: A HYPOTHETICAL FACE-LIFT INSPIRED BY THE PUBLIC, WEST BROMWICH, ON THE PALACE OF CULTURE AND SCIENCE, WARSAW, HERE IN TATE BRITAIN, LONDON**

A BRIEF DESCRIPTION: Combining the shared architectural languages of Tate Britain's Duveens sculpture hall from 1937 with the Soviet monumental 'classicism' of Russian born architect Lev Rudnev's Palace of Culture and Science in Warsaw (PCS) of eighteen years later, I aim to achieve a convincing representation of the Warsaw building here in London. This would then serve as a backdrop for me to conduct stage two of the installation; a hypothetical face-lift on the Palace of Culture and Science, inspired by The Public in West Bromwich: a Community Arts Centre designed by one of the UK's most popular avant-garde modernist regeneration architects, Will Alsop.

Palac compares Soviet Socialist Realism (SSR) with 'New Labour', the policies of both as realised publicly in their respective built environments. These periods of change are highlighted via examples of their respective architectures: the Palace of Culture and Science, Warsaw and The Public, West Bromwich. I state both as archetypes of their ruling parties and proffer their failings. For example has the Palace of Culture and Science confirmed and realised its aspirations?

In *Palac* the SSR- and New Labour-tinged building projects are deemed architecturally arrogant as they presuppose interlacing the cohesive metaphor of architectural construction with that of social construction; the governments steering public urbanisation and the specified buildings are concerned with advancing social policy. *Palac* realises a version or versions of this policy as erected around us in our built environment, and as an installation it is a hotchpotch of controlling ideologies. Privy to the failings of Soviet Socialist Realism thanks to history, the blemishes marking our urbanscape in the twenty-first century, overt aestheticisation in the public sphere, and buildings like that of The Public can now be questioned alongside the social policy that directs it.

Palac asks what function these buildings serve. A comparison of the two enlightens the contemporary by using the past as critique – the before butts up against the now, East Europe folds into West Europe, and architectural multiplexes are still looking to attract and identify a multicultural citizen. By dismantling and re-erecting the two buildings, I am questioning architectural domination, its effect on the public and the people it seeks to enlist.

Caroline Levines's *Provoking Democracy* proposes the artist as closely allied with a 'minority' position: their task to antagonise the public sphere and hence save it from majoritarianism. Our public spaces are increasingly undifferentiated because of a generalised aesthetic conception; 'homogenisation' is viewed as the result of a structurally aligned democracy. The Public, through its appropriation of a design language so readily available in our built environment – colour palettes, visual motifs, interactive tendencies etc. is a good example. What we see there, we see everywhere. Is it the case that present design culture saturation in our public sphere – seen in centralised projects like The Public – is linked with the one-sided tendencies of democracy and the grip of the majority? Citizens navigating our public sphere, participating in culture and the places that support cultural and public engagement, assimilate a false democratic togetherness through a forced cultural sameness. Levine's 'artist as provoker of democracy' is a valid and valued political position and in this context mis-representation in the public sphere is questioned. What might derail the artist as antagoniser today are the places where their individual projects are realised and supported: our institutions and public access buildings. Places of this nature risk being co-opted through a need for sameness in our democratic society, a need assigned by a higher ground majority. Centrally funded arts spaces adhering to government policy may run the risk of supporting a centralised democratic sameness, and sameness in our built environment could well be a lid to structural democracy.

Seen as a gift from the UK to Poland, a reinterpretation of Stalin's fifty years earlier, *Palac* would be a timely face-lift on a former SSR structure, given the worsening diplomatic relations between Poland and Russia today, due largely to Poland's alliance with the UK and the USA. It would mark the country's successful economic re-integration with the West and further its pro-business climate with yet another Western intervention, in synch with a string of other cultural venues being constructed by the likes of celebrity architects Zaha Hadid and Daniel Libeskind.

Palac also coincides with the Polish Season in the UK, which is being prepared by the Adam Mickiewicz Institute and has the objective of presenting Polish contemporary culture as one of the most influential and opinion-forming within our affluent European Union. Shaped by the needs and expectations of the British side, it has received criticism in Poland for its ignorance of alternative activities within the tradition, culture and history less agreeable to Western preferences. *Palac* therefore not only brings out firmly from the shadows a history of Socialist Realism as a reminder of our betrayal of Poland, which we'd prefer to forget, but also raises questions around the very issue of Western cultural influence. Through subjecting Polish culture to the exact failures that we ourselves are witnessing here in the UK, I hope to prompt, on both sides, contemplation for an alternative.

A RESPONSE TO THE ALTERMODERN MANIFESTO

I've been feeling quite misunderstood lately when attempting to talk about this observed globalised perception on the one hand and specific context on the other, probably owing to my misuse of the ingrained abstract colonial western vocabulary you mention and all the historical associations it calls to mind, which I suppose against today's backdrop inevitably creates confusion and contradiction. Suddenly your notion of 'global altermodernity' puts paid to such problems and as you say, programmes and chains of heterogeneous elements can articulate one another without slipping into the outmoded pit of modernist universalism (or postmodernity).

I think the text applies to my works in that they seem to be at once disparate and uniform in their composition; all incorporate heterogeneous design elements from the past, present, here and elsewhere, and all at first glance appear unified by aesthetics which upon further contemplation hopefully unfold into explanation, critique and analysis of both their own personal attributes and each others.

The shared globalised perception that you speak of is articulated through a collapse of boundaries and a merging of different origins, histories and contexts. Each individual component is deliberately played off against its counterpart and it is through these similarities, comparisons, repetitions and alliances that I hope questions can be raised and, at times, warnings implied.

Regarding a more objective commentary on altermodern, I feel that much of the text deliberately prompts questions in its refusal to explain itself fully, questions that the reader is compelled to consider independently but also, I suspect, that are hoped to be expanded upon by the actions of those participating within the exhibition. Perhaps only then, and via the voices of others, can a global altermodernity be initiated and in turn its viability determined or challenged.

Having been privy to the text from the beginning, I have almost had to make it my project to resist and ignore it, and to carry on regardless in the hope of resolving some of the questions it has raised through my continued activities rather than through any self-conscious desire to correspond.

Some of the questions that I hope might be confronted, expanded upon and resolved are: how are our travel, cultural exchange and examination of history any different to that of previous centuries? What are the signs that suggest that the historical period defined by postmodernism is coming to an end? Who today is the Far Right and, perhaps most importantly, who is the reader of this text? In a locale of all sorts where cultural relativism and the project of multiculturalism has failed, where does this leave difference and how does society protect the interest of the minority subject? Is language the problem and has modernity and universalism, followed by a fragmented and self-reflexive postmodernity, left us in a state of no return? Is it only the everyday citizen going through a process of creolisation or is it also being translated at government or state level? Is altermodern a global art discourse?

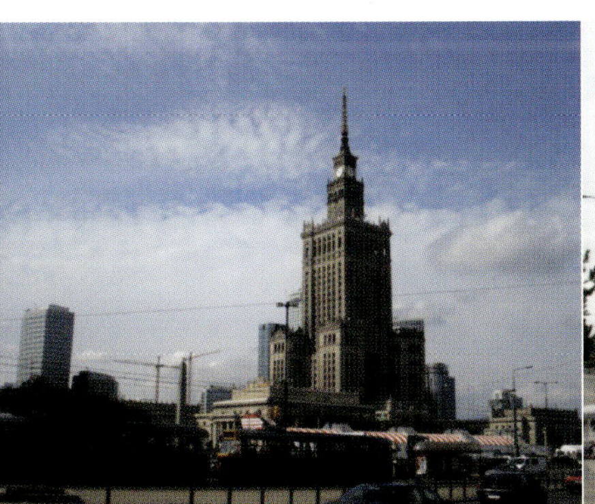

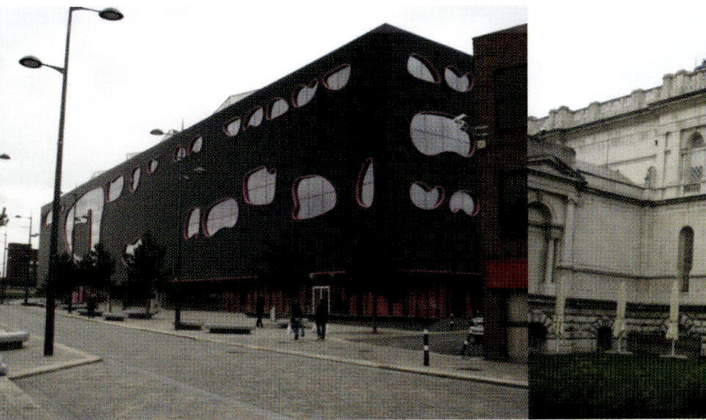

From left: Palace of Culture and Science, Warsaw; The Public, West Bromwich; Tate Britain, London

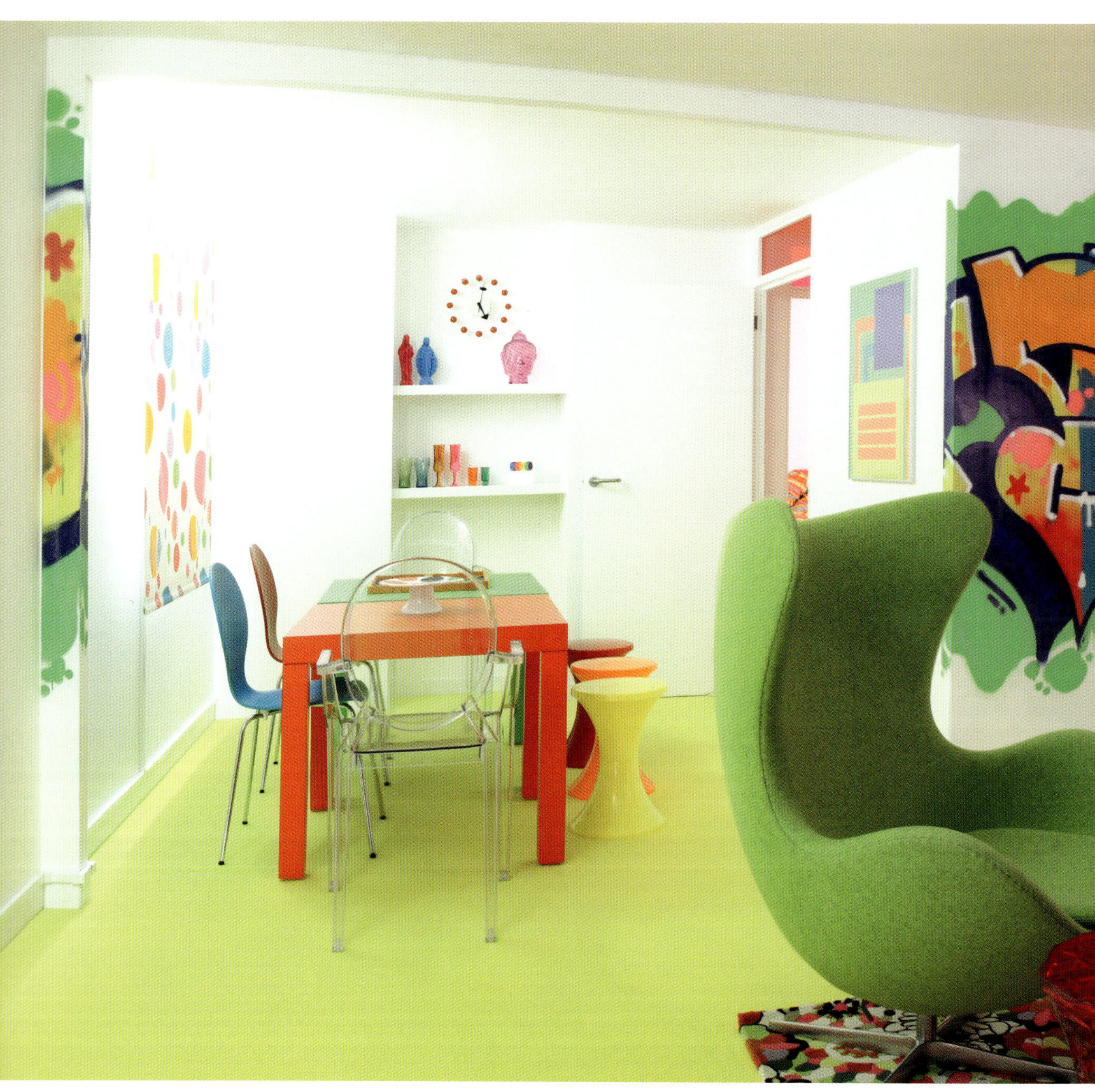

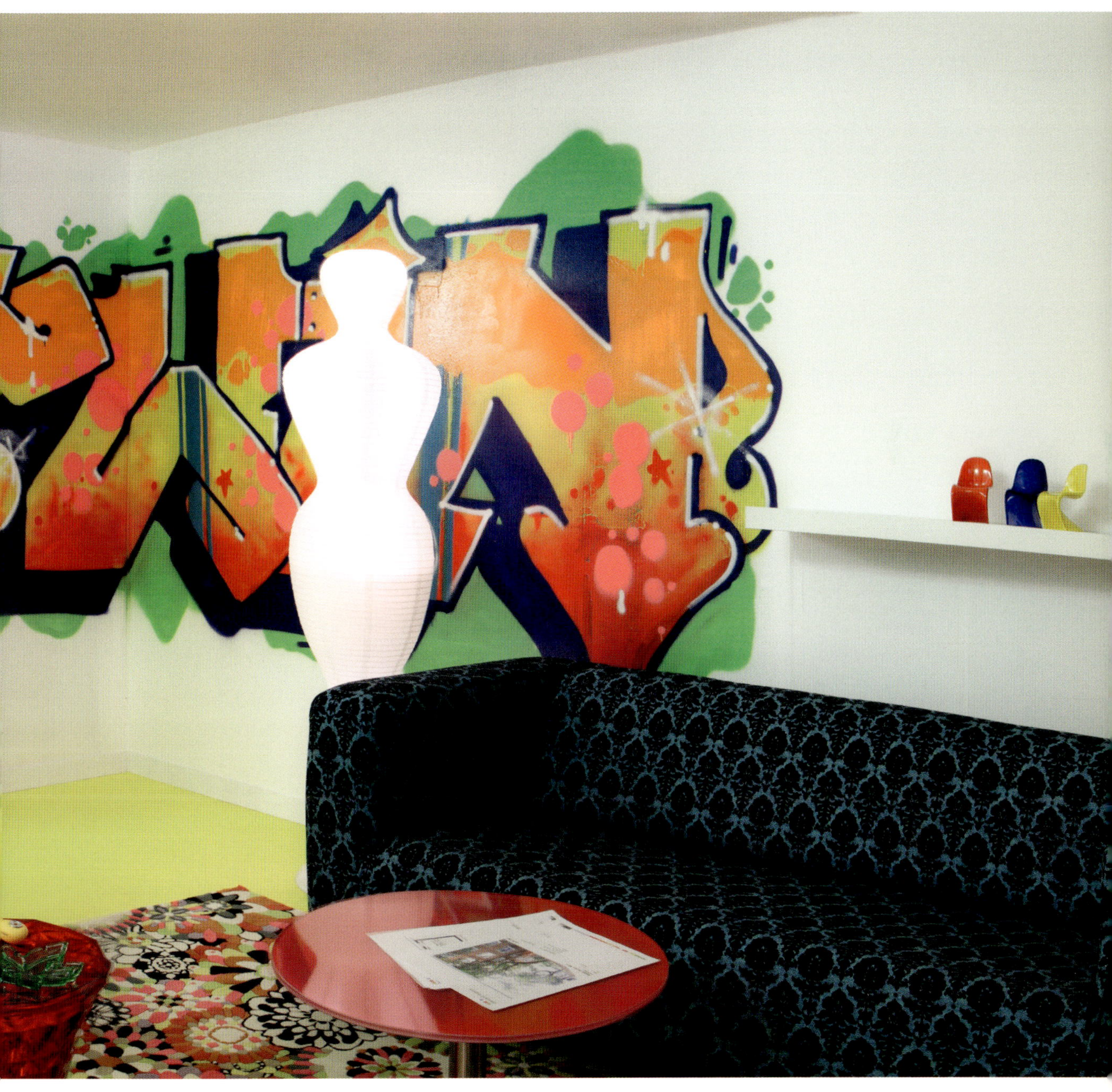

MATTHEW DARBYSHIRE – *Blades House*, 2008, installation view, Gasworks, London, courtesy Herald St, London

Shezad DAWOOD

THE ABILITY TO work with signs becomes a crucial understanding of what you might call the structure of things. The current crisis of perception makes this all the more evident: that our failure to understand the multiple sign, rather than its concrete appearance is the source of both anxiety and auto-destruct.

By stepping into this circulation of signs with multiple meanings, I guess I arrive at a halfway point – an intermediary you might say. On a superficial level one might talk about culture and relativism, but if that is merely understood as narrative, one has failed to step into an idea of the nodal connections that underlie even the symbols themselves. Whether one takes a skull, Norse mythology, Krishna, Wagner, they are in truth not relative but part of a horizontal field, which once understood will pave the way for new systems of governance, religion and nomadic community... God is in the detail, but perhaps that is already saying too much.

These constant iterations of the modern themselves become a kind of narrative of anxiety – perhaps what one might call the pathology of otherness or separation anxiety. As we are less able to relate to others and to ourselves, we feel the need to exhume new systems, that ultimately are approximations of the bones of previous systems. Like a city within a novel that begins to virally infect the world as it self-replicates – a philosophical construct that spins out of control, and starts to tear reality apart as it mutates, so that as people go steadily, shriekingly, insane, the last 'sane' person left is forced to ask themselves: 'Is this how it has always been, or is this a new proposition?'

I suppose what I try to do is play with varying elements to reflect the absurdity and hidden meanings in the structure of the city (the world as perceived construct) in order to attempt a kind of Brechtian wake-up call, or at least have some fun and invite others to join.

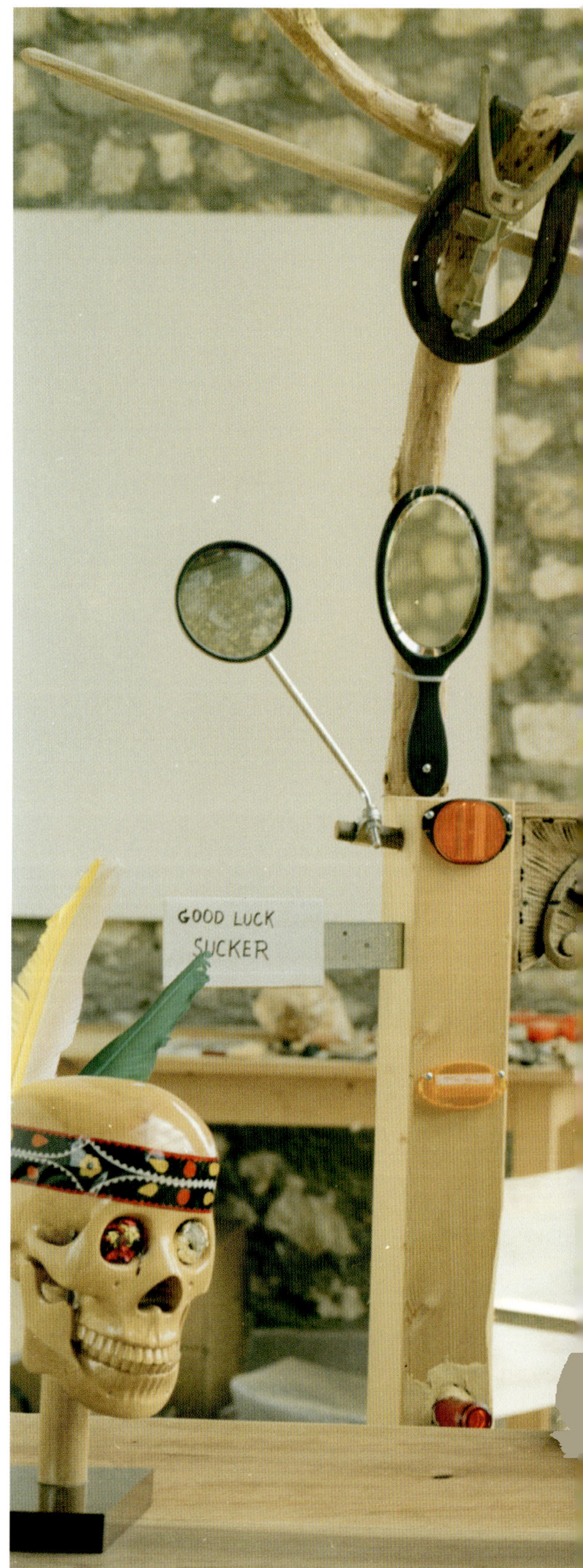

SHEZAD DAWOOD – *Feature*, 2008, production still, courtesy the artist and Paradise Row, London

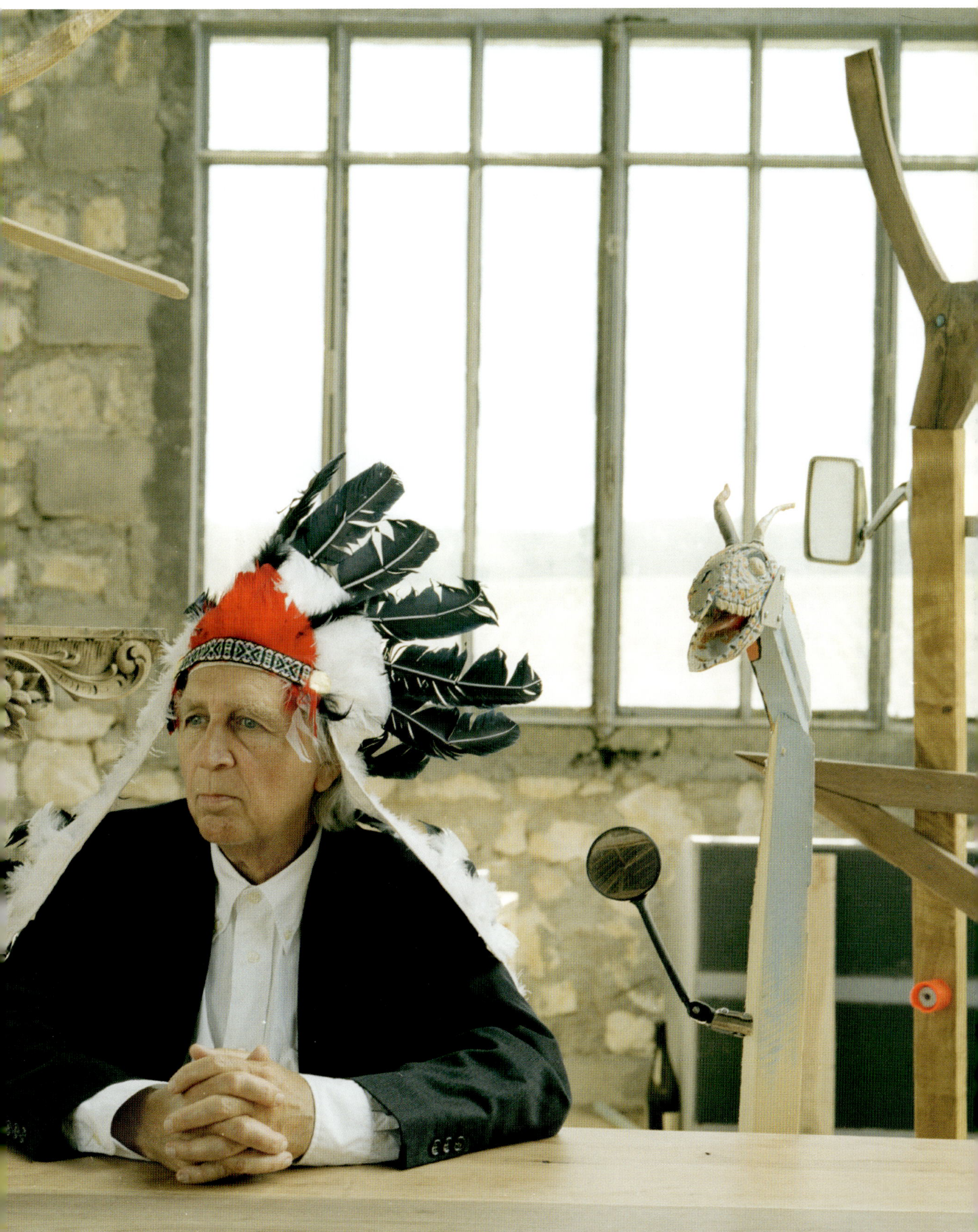

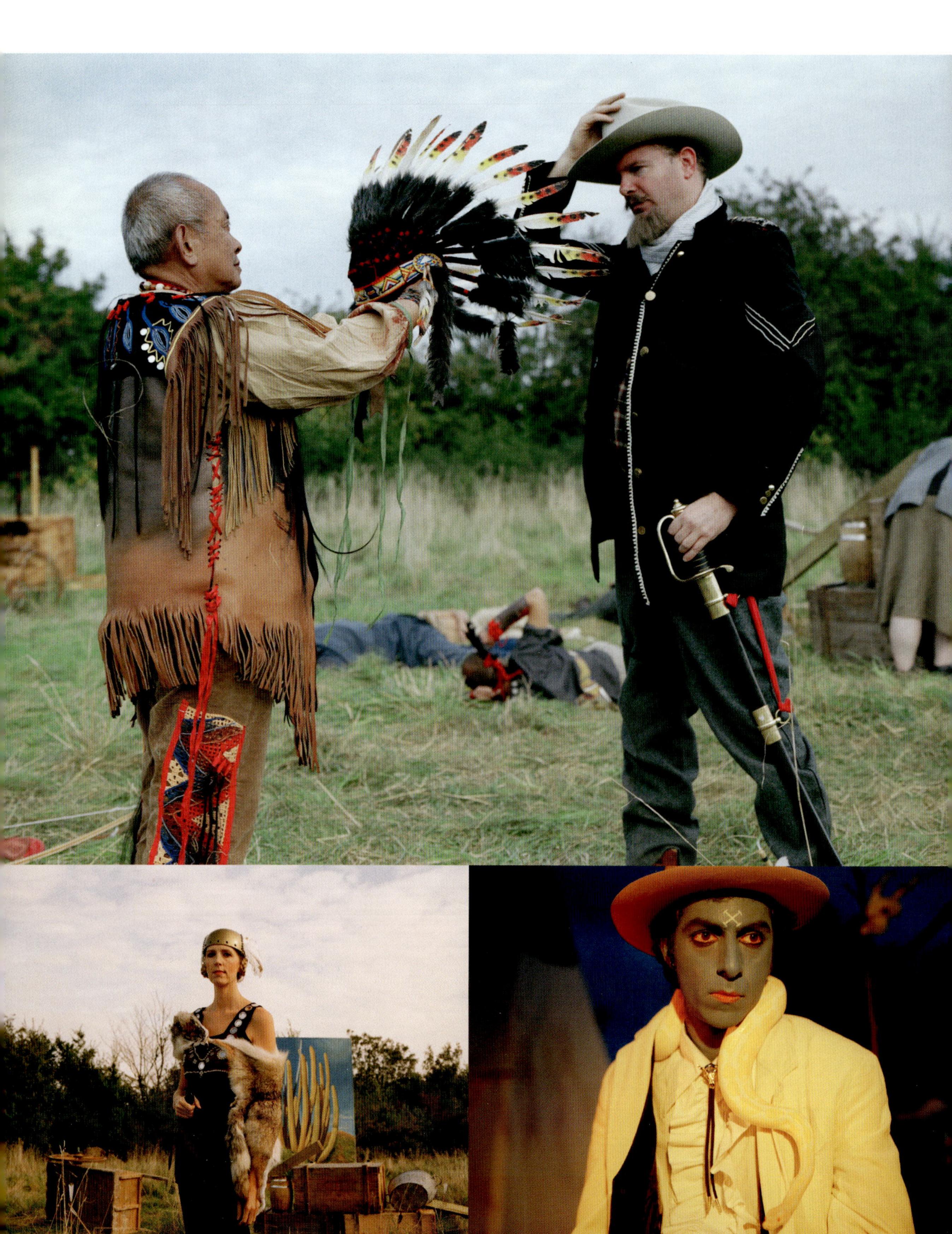

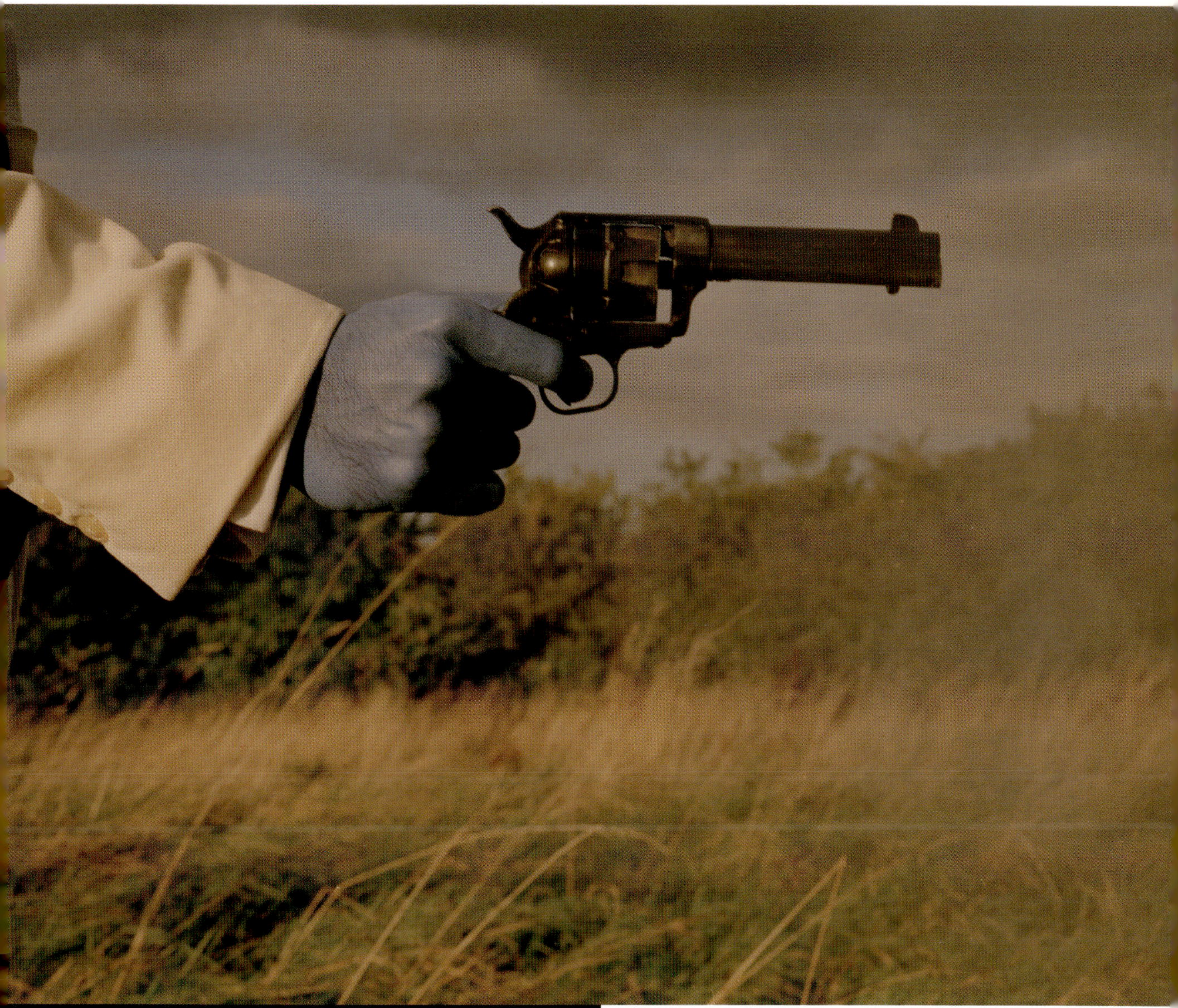

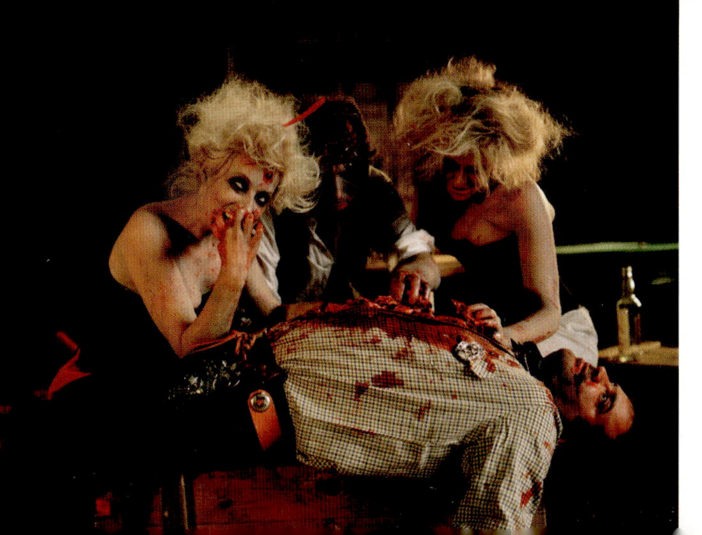

SHEZAD DAWOOD — *Feature,* 2008,
production stills, courtesy the artist and Paradise Row, London

Tacita DEAN

HOW THAT WHOLE story began was I found a photograph of this girl stowaway in a second-hand book at a flea market, *The Last of the Wind Ships*. She stowed away in 1928 on a ship called the Herzogin Cecilie, which was sailing from Australia to Falmouth in England, Cornwall. I was instantly attracted to this image of her so I bought the book. It was actually my first relevant flea-market purchase. Then I took it with me on a trip to Glasgow, Scotland, and in Heathrow Airport I put my bag, which had the book in it, through the hand-luggage x-ray machine, walked through the security arch, and then went to collect it, and the bag had just disappeared. It was extraordinary. Then quite mysteriously and strangely, a week later I got a phone call, while I was still in Glasgow, saying that my bag had been found going around and around the Aer Lingus luggage belt in Dublin Airport. (...)

I picked it up at the airport on my way back to London, and at first I was trying to get some press attention on how unsafe it can be to put all your best belongings into that x-ray machine. But then I decided to write the newspaper article myself, telling the story of how my stolen bag containing the stowaway's picture had made its way to Dublin by this strange circuitous route. I made and printed it in the style of the British newspaper The Guardian. At the same time I wanted to make a parallel article in the style of the period that I imagined she had stowed away in. I had studied at Falmouth School of Art, so I already had a relationship to that town. I rang up the Falmouth Packet, the local newspaper, and told them I wanted to fabricate an article about the stowaway, and they actually had a record of her arriving in Falmouth on the Herzogin Cecilie in 1928; her name was Jean Jeinnie and she stowed away from Port Lincoln in Australia. So in my fake 1928 article, I had her stowing away in order to try to get to Dublin. So when you first encounter these two newspaper articles, you read that she was trying to get to Dublin but you don't know if she made it or not, but you do know her photographic self made it there nearly seventy years later.

After that, I decided to take it even further and I fabricated a film with a windup Kodak camera of her, I mean of somebody who looked a bit like her, aboard my version of the Herzogin Cecilie. She'd stowed away in 1928, and I found out the ship had wrecked in 1936. At that point I decided to go on a sort of pilgrimage to find the place where the real Herzogin Cecilie sank, off Bolt Head in Devon, the county up from Cornwall. It had been a calm night, but the ship hit a rock and let in a lot of water, and in its hold was grain, and grain when it meets salt water goes rotten very, very quickly. At that point the boat could still have been salvaged, but Salcombe harbor, which is protected on all sides by the wind, refused to let her in because the local council were afraid the stench of rotten grain might scare off their tourists, so they towed her into this little bay called Starehole Bay, which is exposed from the southeast, and the wind changed and the boat was immediately wrecked.

I went to Starehole Bay with a friend and camped above the wreck (which you can still see) which you're technically not supposed to do. We filmed the wreck of the Herzogin Cecilie the next morning on this beautiful July day, and then left. Then a day or two later, we saw that on the very day we were there, hours or even minutes after we left, a young woman had been raped and murdered in daylight. The whole thing became sort of uncanny and unpleasant because we became the last people who – the friend I was with in fact turned out to be the last person who had seen her alive and he also saw her murderer.

In interview with Jeffrey Eugenides talking about Girl Stowaway *1994*, Bomb, *no.95, Spring 2006*

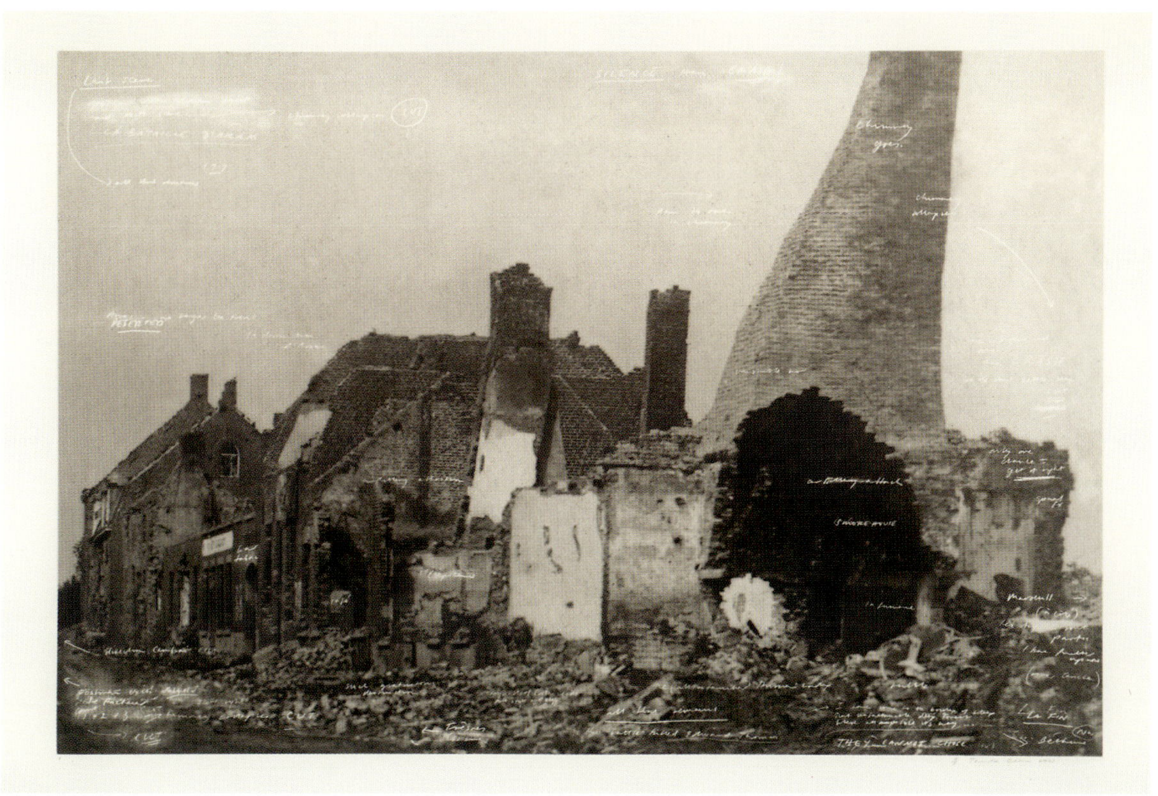

TACITA DEAN — *La Bataille d'Arras* (from *The Russian Ending*), 2001, photogravure on paper 45 × 68.5, Tate. Presented by the artist 2002.

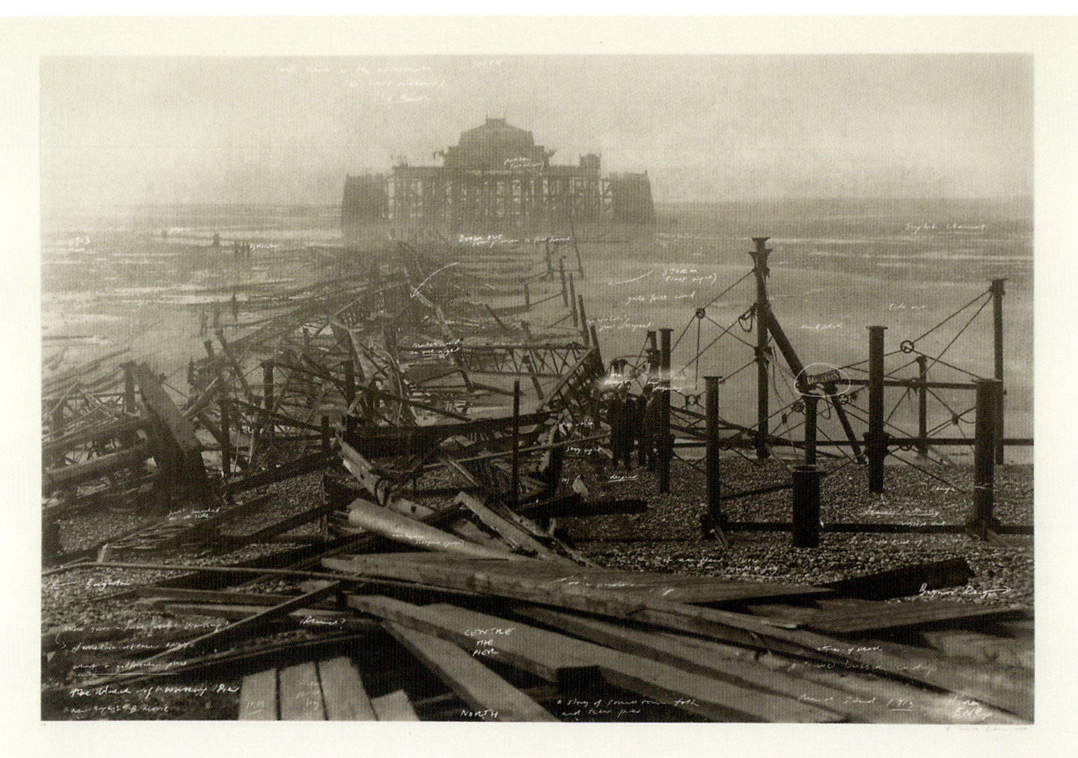

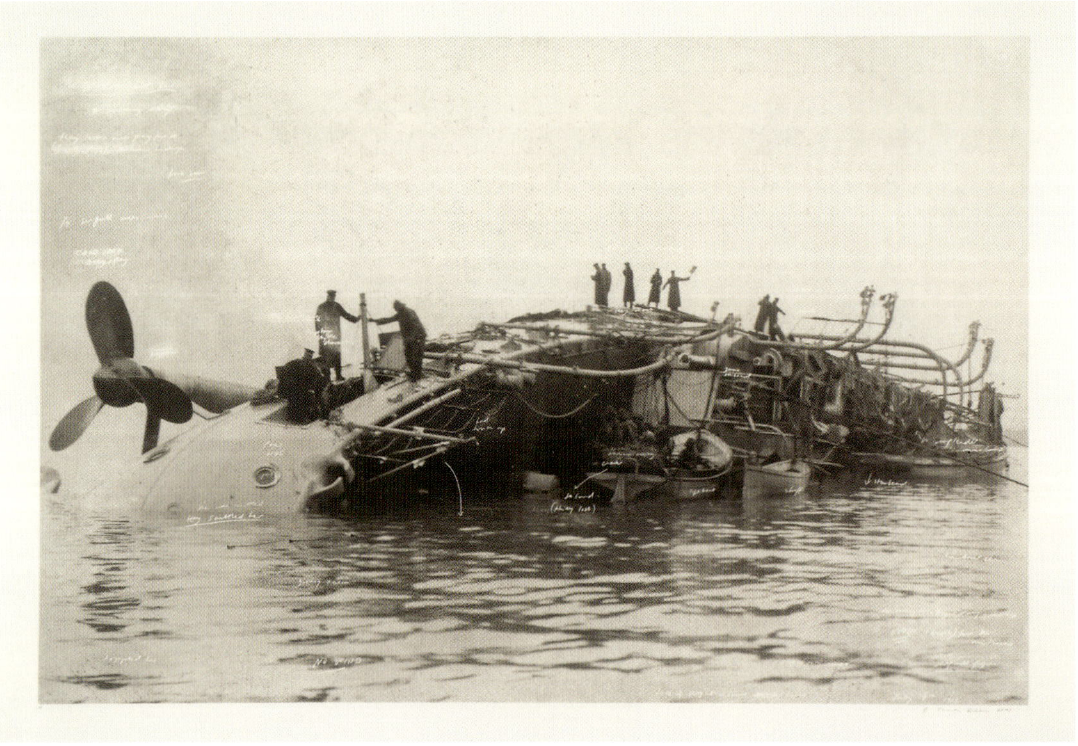

TACITA DEAN — [TOP] *The Wreck of Worthing Pier* and [BOTTOM] *So They Sank Her!* (from *The Russian Ending*), 2001, photogravure on paper 45 × 68.5, Tate. Presented by the artist 2002.

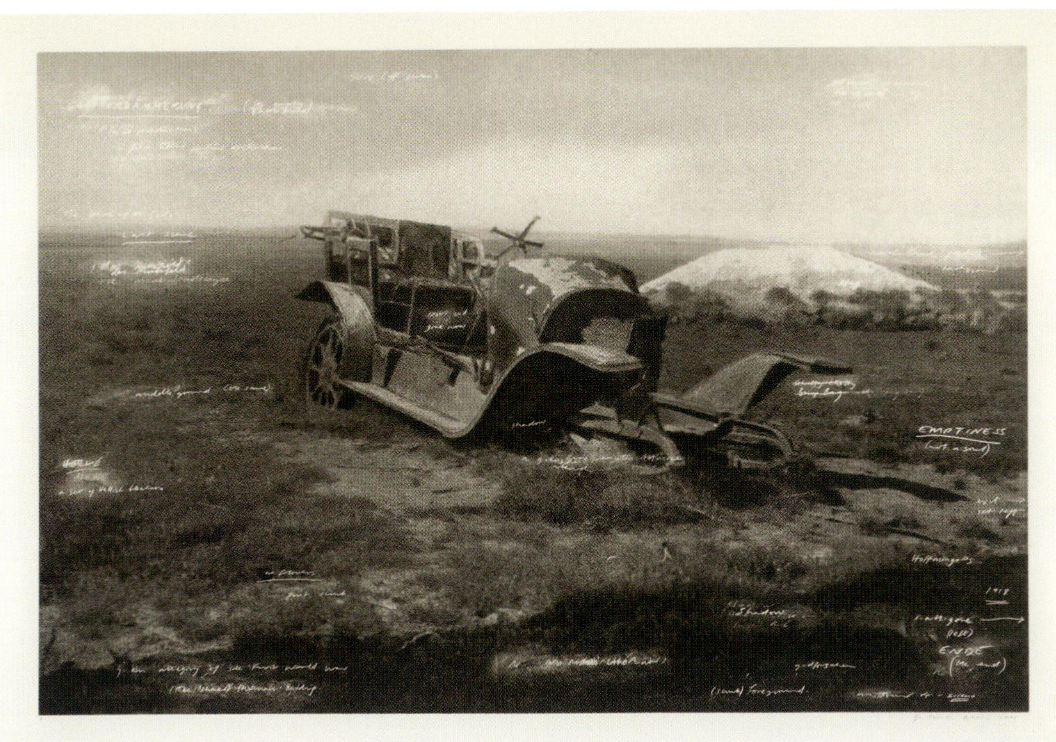

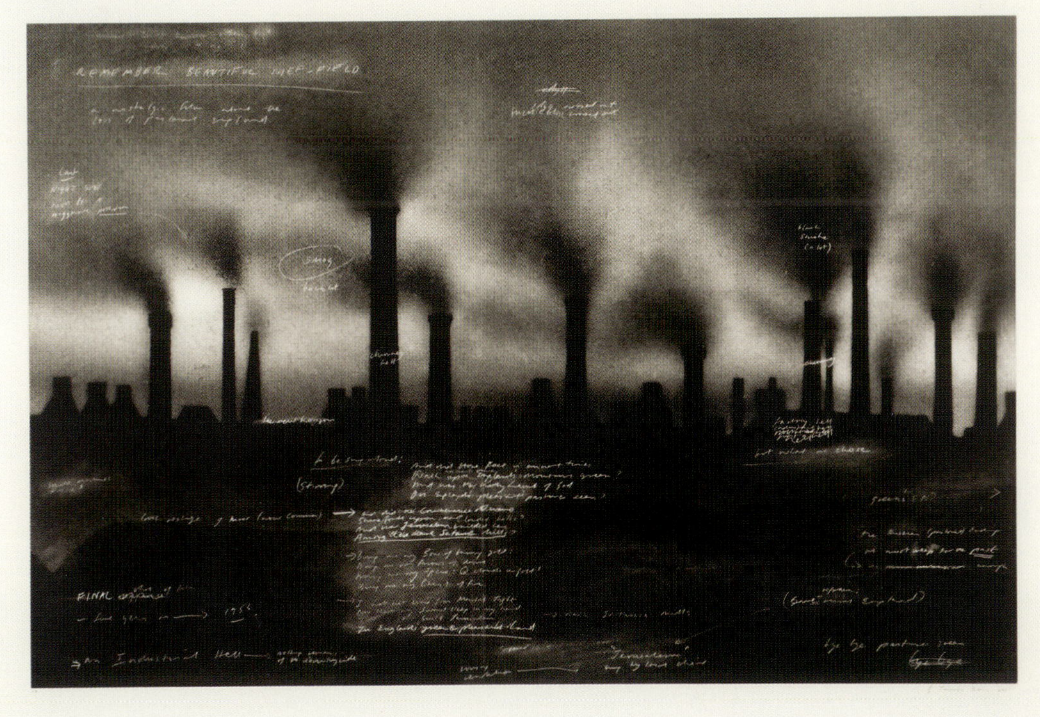

[TOP] ***Götterdämmerun*** **and** [BOTTOM] ***Beautiful Sheffield*** **(from *The Russian Ending*), 2001,** photogravure on paper, 45 × 68.5, Tate. Presented by the artist 2002.

Ruth EWAN

MY WORK references anecdotes from both recent and distant cultural and social history, excavating specific elements so that when they appear in the final work in the form of performances, drawings or events, they have a resonance in the present. In basic terms, I am interested in viewing history not as remote past but as alive and potentially relevant to the present; in seeing how ideas circulate through 'unofficial' channels, such as oral history, songs or myths; in how a movement, event or cultural product from the past may produce ripples in the present; and in how those ripples can be controlled, transferred or tampered with in order to produce new meanings and interpretations.

'Squeezebox Jukebox' is a development of an ongoing project started in 2003 called 'A Jukebox of People Trying to Change the World', a music archive housed in a CD Sound Leisure Jukebox, the kind regularly found in pubs. This project came about because of an interest in the perceived absence of Left ideology within popular culture – I started to map and collect recordings from diverse genres and periods, varying in sincerity and popularity, but with a notion of 'progress' or a utopian vision at their core.

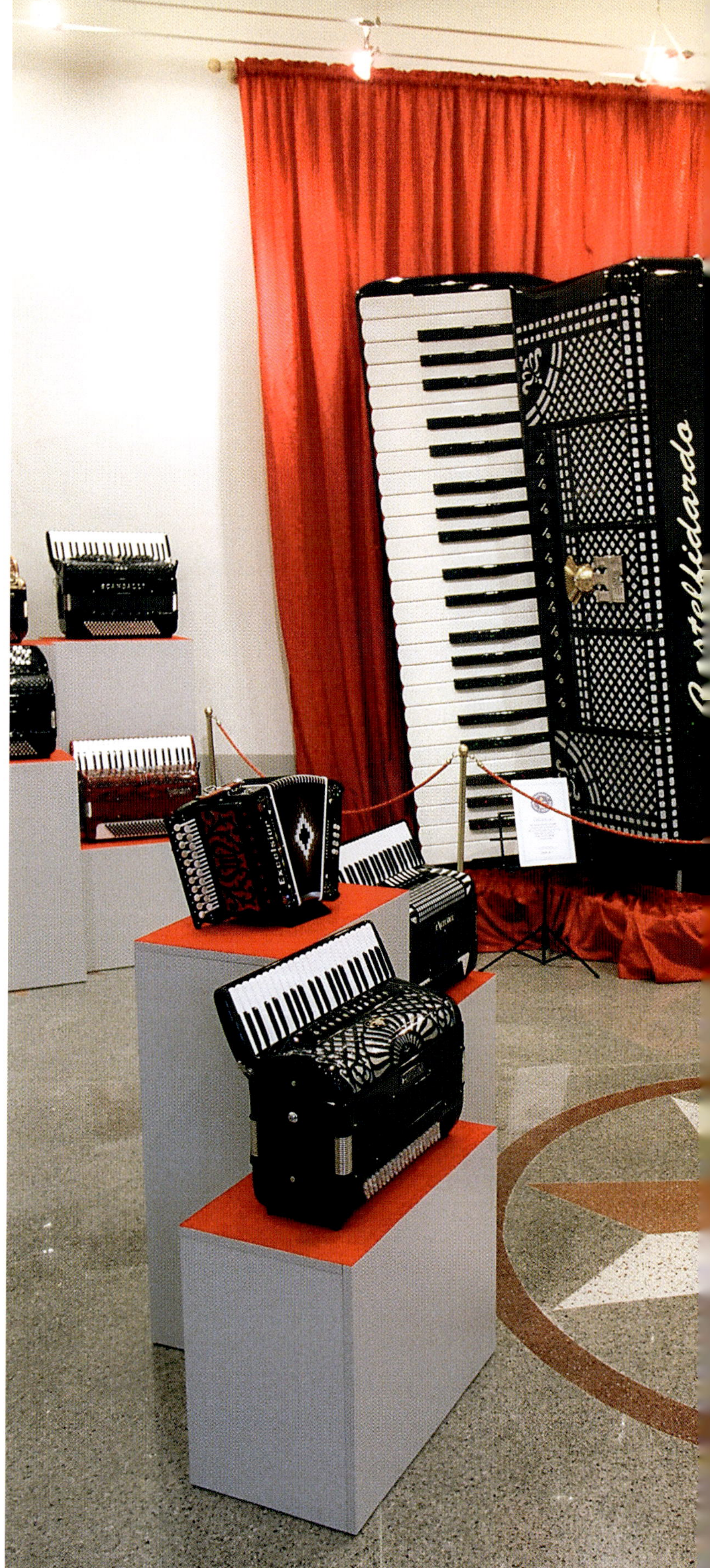

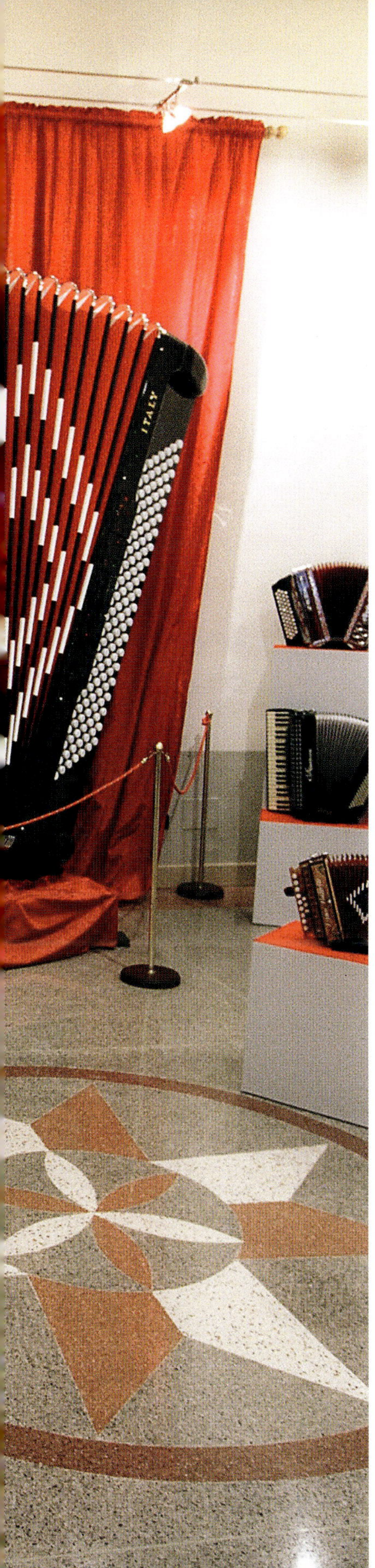

I chose the accordion specifically as a channel for a selection of these songs not only because of its immense scale but also because it intrigued me as some sort of cultural bastard. Within Western popular culture it is an unfashionable and outdated instrument. Although it was not invented until the nineteenth century – it is an unlikely instrument of the post-industrial age – making anachronistic appearances in fictional works, including Disney's recent *Pirates of the Caribbean* film franchise, where it appears against a seventeenth-century backdrop. There is a fake authenticity to this nomadic instrument, first patented in Vienna in 1829 and then adopted by Gypsy and Jewish musicians from Eastern Europe, it still plays a central role in the folk music of many countries outside of Europe including Mexico, Colombia, Russia, and North and South Korea.

The accordion has long been the butt of many jokes. From a cartoon by French artist Honoré Daumier published in *Le Journal Amusant*, 1866, where one man says to the other 'one does not yet have the right to kill the people who play this instrument, but there is hope that we will soon get it' to a popular definition of a gentleman as 'someone who can play the accordion, but doesn't'.

The gargantuan accordion magnifies its own unpopularity; the instrument, although exquisitely crafted, becomes an awkward and graceless object, difficult to co-ordinate and play. The scale becomes a signifier for exteriority, an unmanageable, massive instrument that transforms its performers into miniature people trying to grapple with a tune. The series of songs can be seen as citations that invite re-engagement with the specific social movements to which they belong. However, rather than being straightforward recitals, the performance will expose the gulf between the historic desire for social change and the difficulty in resuscitating and reasserting that desire today.

RUTH EWAN — Giancarlo Francenella's 'Giant Accordion', used by Ruth Ewan in ***Squeezebox Jukebox*, 2009**

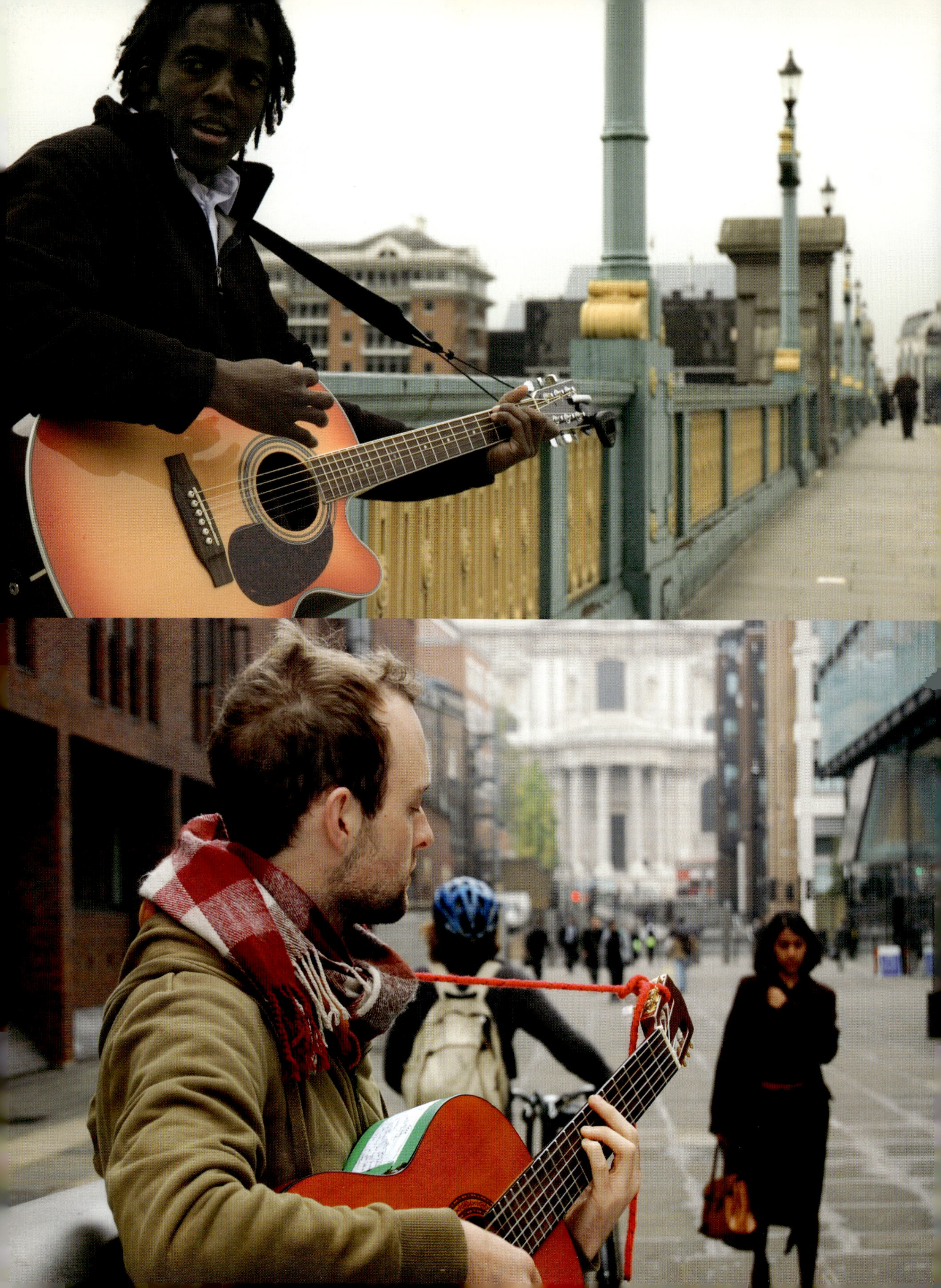

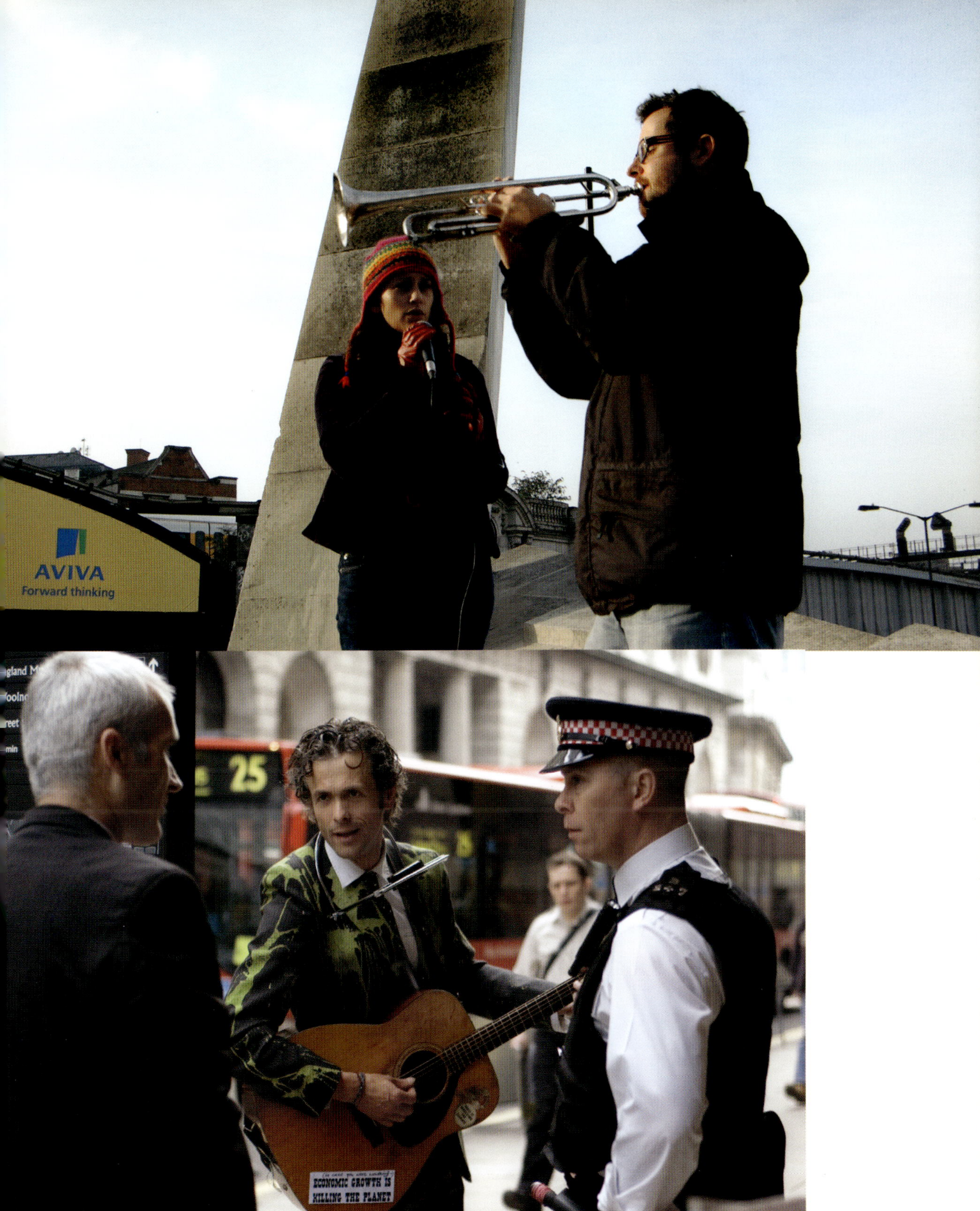

RUTH EWAN — *Did you kiss the foot that kicked you?* 2007,
public performance, various sites across London, courtesy the artist and commissioned by Artangel

Loris GRÉAUD

DEAR NICOLAS,
'That which invented the boat, also invented the shipwreck.'[1]

Let's go back over this failure: 'As you know, classic experiments are meant to stay in the laboratory. If they reach the outside they become reality and fail as experiments.'[2] The experiment conducted with the neurologist aimed to record the activity of my brain while conceiving the exhibition and translate it into a new form. Form, in the field we're considering, might just be the balance sheet of a thinking process, 'materialising trajectories rather than destinations'[3] as you put it. This experiment is all about achieving a physiological process and then translating it into a representation based on frequencies of images, of ideas, that can be embodied by graphics, lights, sounds, language and eventually vibrations.

Here, form is but the outline of its function; form follows ideas, there is no accident. It's no accident that the aesthetic result refers to a circuit and conveys the image of the network. It's no accident that my note begins *in medias res*, and takes the form of a letter ... 'there is no singular or absolute truth but multiple "truths" and "notions". The task of explanation therefore becomes one of discourse analysis and deconstruction, of revealing the discursive structures, ideological beliefs and textual strategies that we use, consciously or unconsciously to establish the context and persuasiveness of our different knowledge claims.'[4]

What's to be blamed? The 'tool' for its failure or the complexity of the object that escapes the interpretive net because of it?

The recurring contrast among post moderns between a relevant diagnosis on state changes of the phenomena they examine and their difficulties in producing new concepts and new interpretive theories to comprehend those phenomena, justifies the fact one questions the final failure of their practice. Those figures of an end are very peculiar because they don't show the way for a new start, but for a new altermodernity.

Bien à toi

Loris

1. LAO TSEU
2. R. MALASAUKAS, A. SCHUSTER, L. GRÉAUD, *Cellar Door*
3. N. BOURRIAUD
4. R. MARTIN 1994

Transcription of a handwritten letter, 11 November 2008

LORIS GRÉAUD — ***Tremors Where Forever (Frequency of an Image, White Edit)*, 2008,** modified micro vibrators, specific electronic development, plexiglass console, white paint, courtesy GréaudStudio and Yvon Lambert, Paris/New York

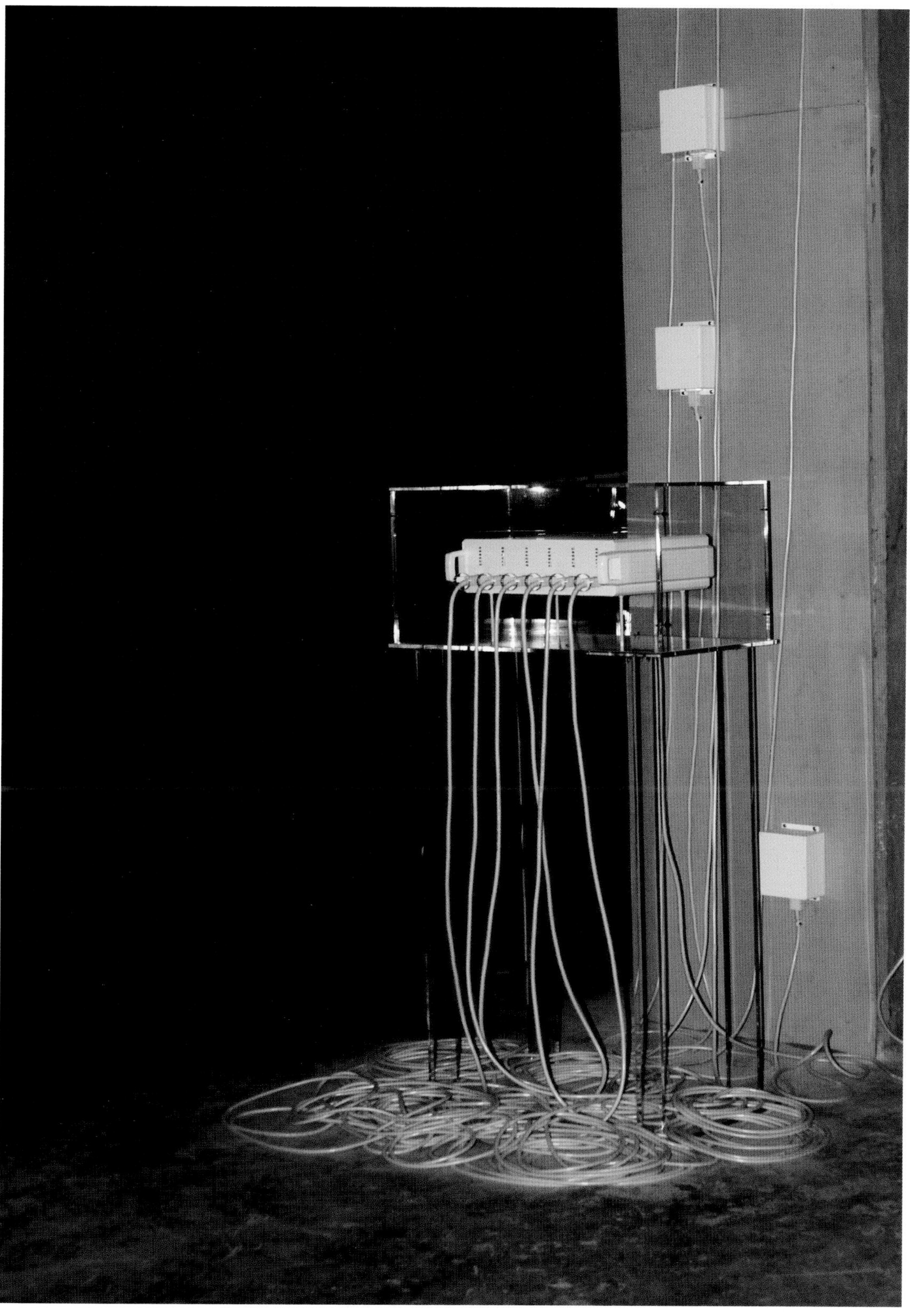

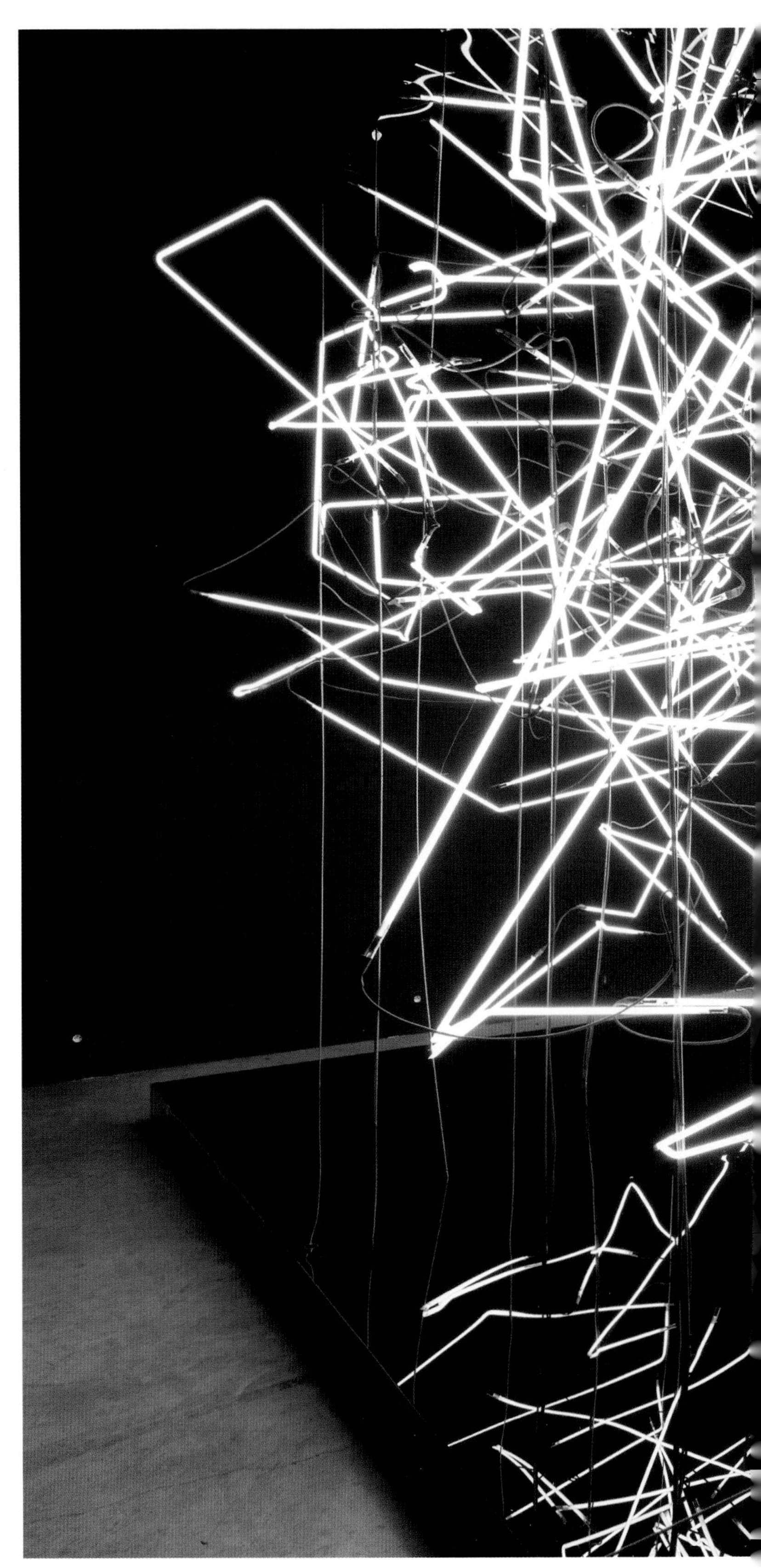

LORIS GRÉAUD AND DGZ RESEARCH
— ***Neon Ball Bubble,* 2007–8,** Neon lights, inox structure, black altuglass, 400 × 400 × 400, François Pinault Collection, courtesy Yvon Lambert, Paris/New York and DGZ research

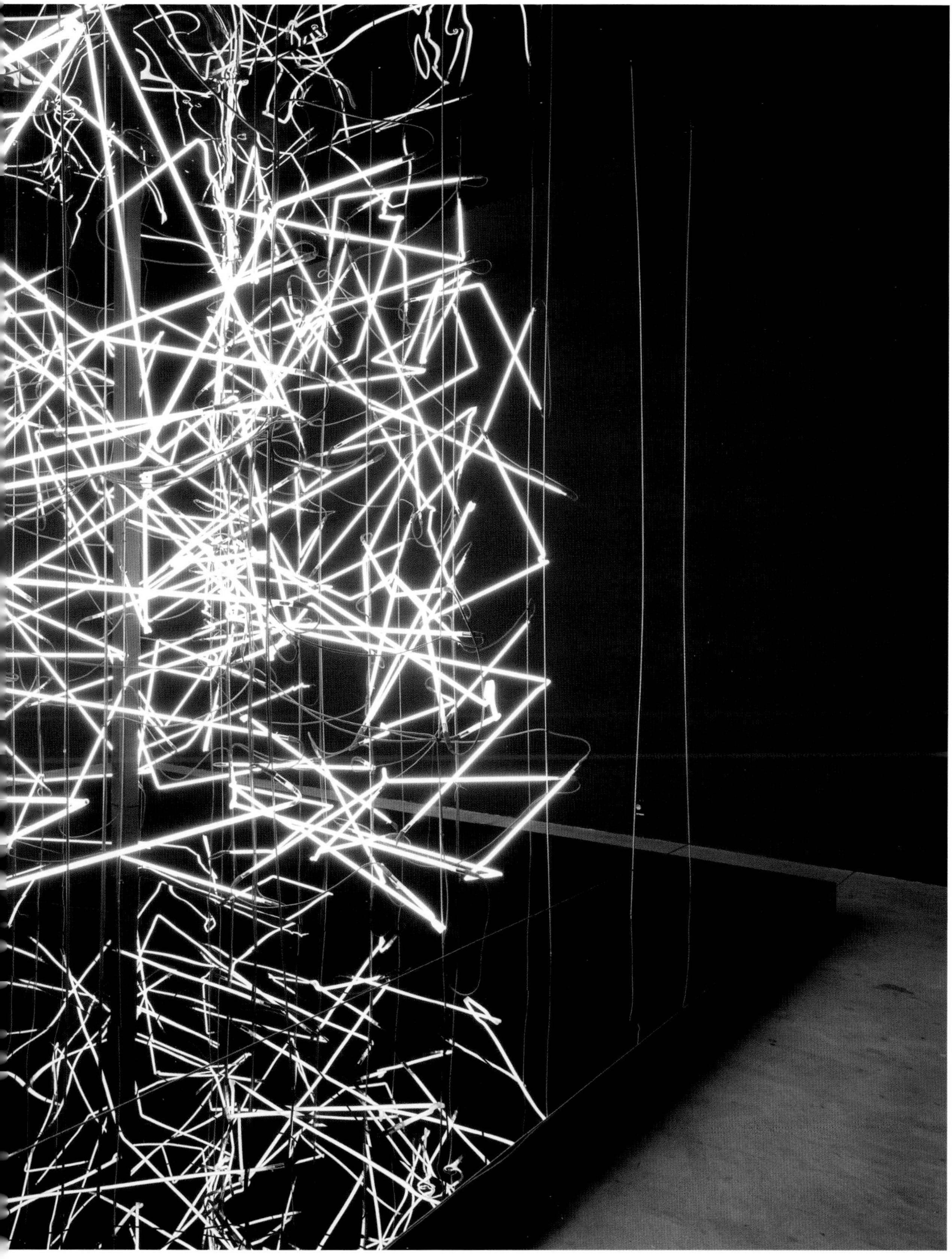

Subodh GUPTA

DEAR SUBODH GUPTA,

Your work links pop art with Indian visual culture, and with his own baggage Tiravanija operates in a similar way. It would be a mistake to consider this a mere highlighting of 'cultural differences' as such. At a time when uniformity has never been stronger, it is of little consequence for art to give itself the task of noting the distinctions between languages and visions of the world. It is the divergence that is productive; the differences merely rise from bland appraisals that make a fetish of folklore and particularities placed in context. Postmodernism and postcolonialism are not as synonymous as one would have us think: the postmodern cult of differences is a subtle Trojan horse of neocolonialism, the economic one.

Artistic practices that explore cultural digressions create new connections and scrutinise basic principles of differences which produce creative potential: what can be generated from Hinduism? What happens when it's linked to contemporary forms, if it's remixed with ways of thinking and doing that are foreign to it? *Giant Leap of Faith* 2006 evokes Brancusi's *Endless Column* as much as it does the multiplication of figures in certain Hindu images.

Thinking by short circuit... as an artist you think by translating bits of messages, lines of text, from one language to another. This act of translation is fundamental: without doubt, it signifies today's emerging modernity, a new modern and global gesture based on volatility and inherent resistance to the action of translation.

Nicolas Bourriaud, extract from 'A Letter to Subodh Gupta about Cultural Precarity', in Subodh Gupta, *exh. cat., Jack Shainman Gallery, New York 2008.*

SUBODH GUPTA — *Line of Control*, 2008, 1000 × 1000 × 1000, stainless steel and steel structure, stainless steel utensils, courtesy the artist, Arario Gallery, Beijing and Hauser & Wirth Zurich/London

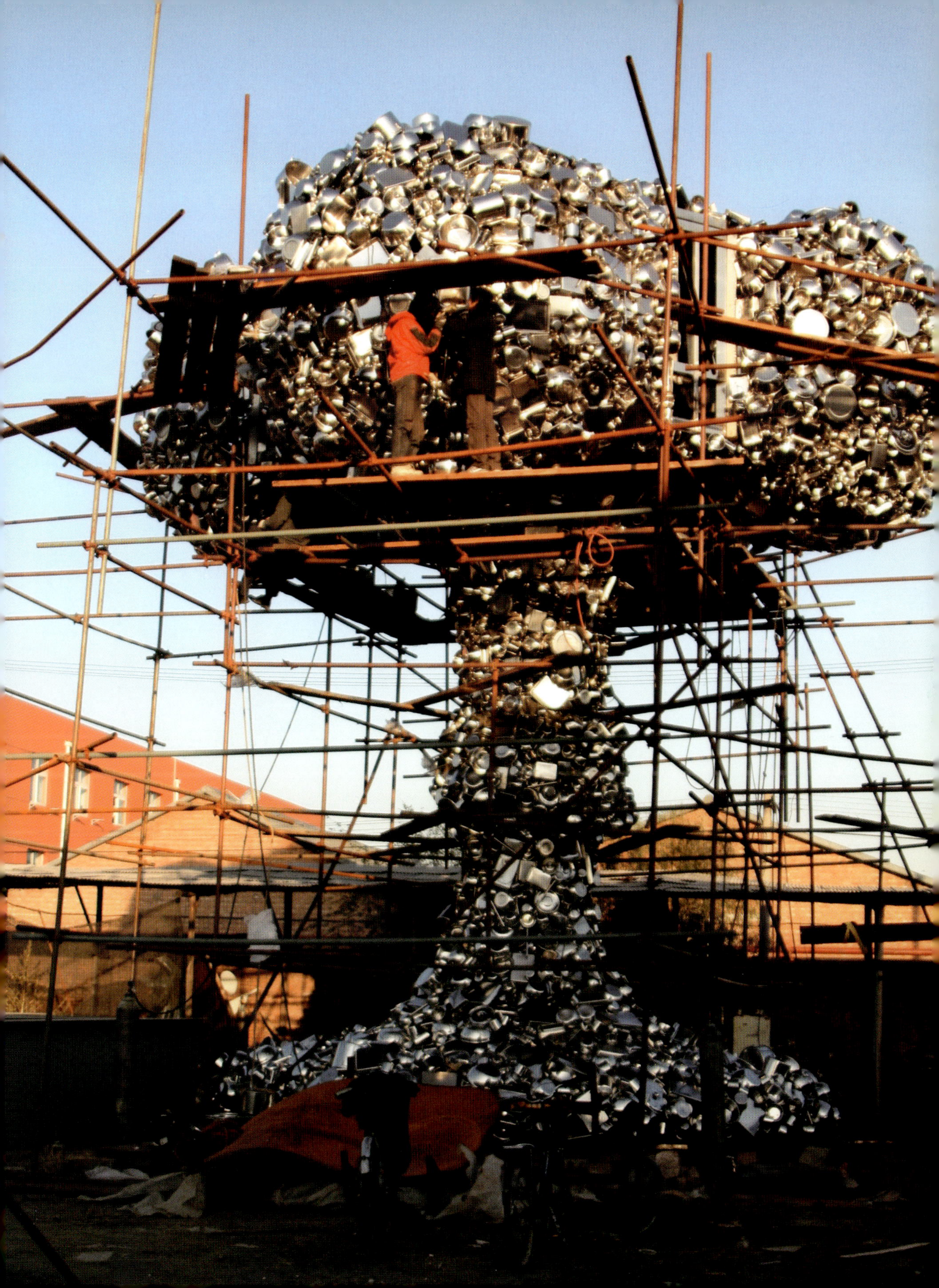

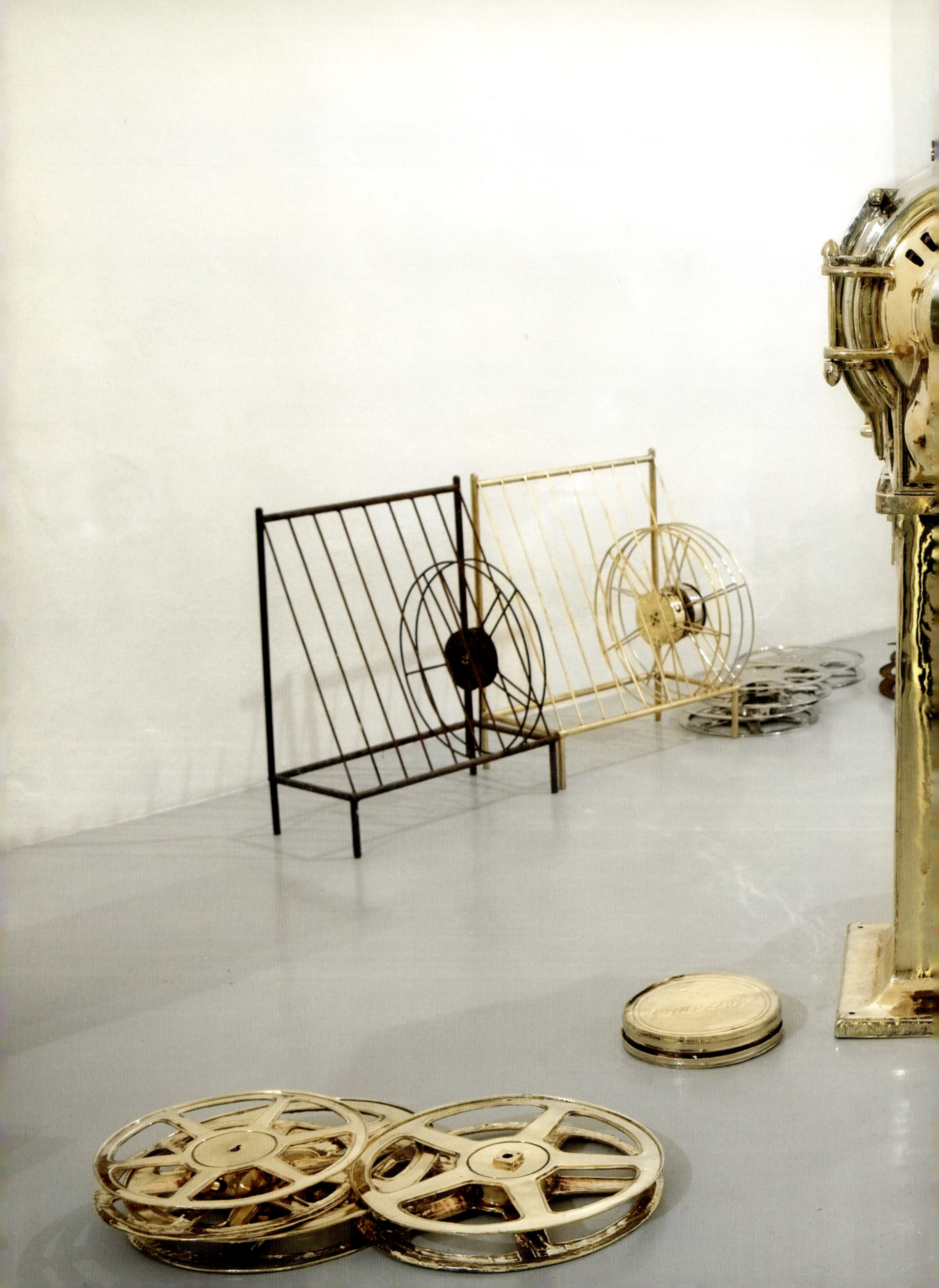

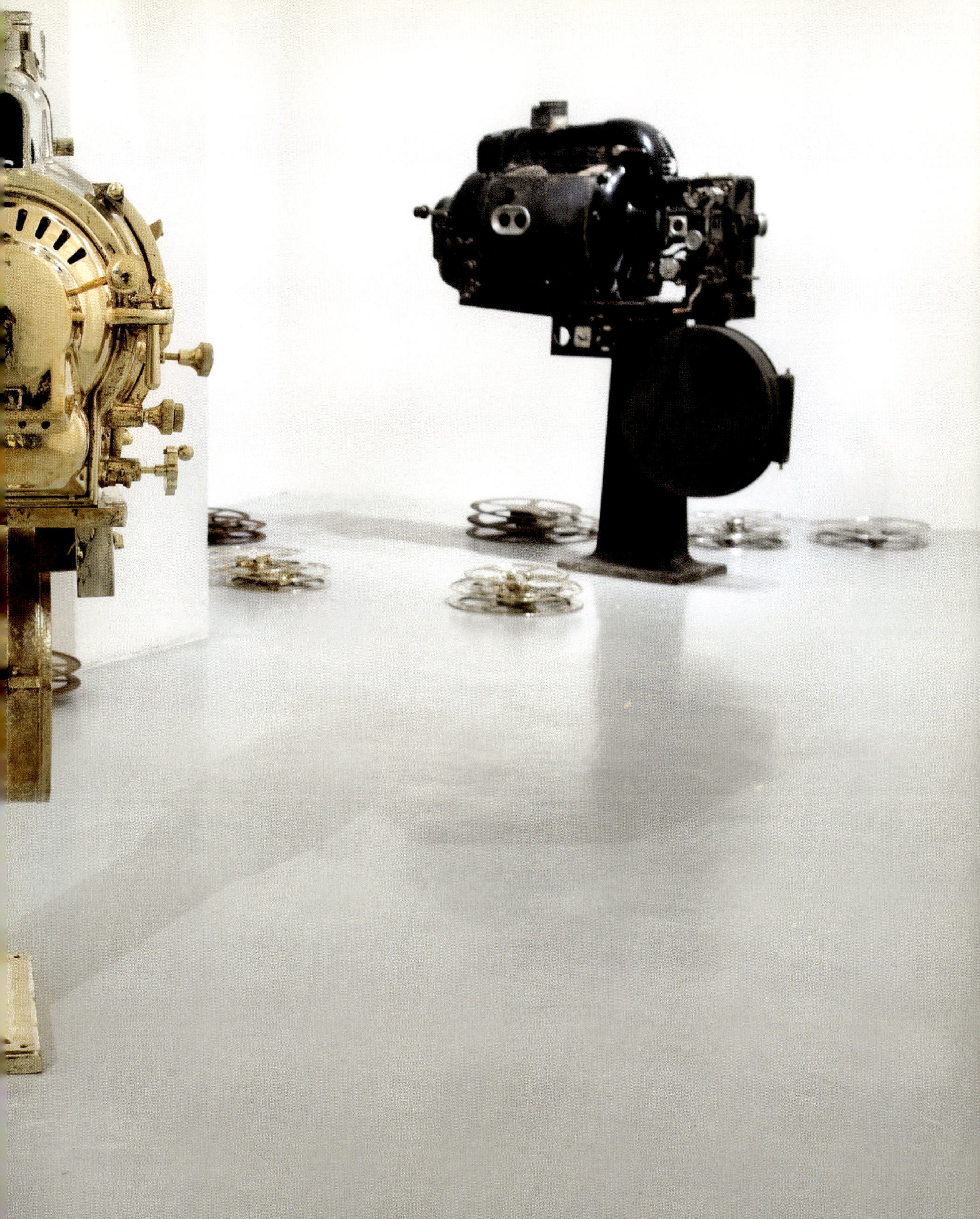

SUBODH GUPTA — *There is Always Cinema (1)*, 2008, found objects, nickel, brass, dimensions variable, courtesy Galleria Continua, San Gimignano/Beijing/Le Moulin

Rachel
HARRISON

SCULPTURE GOES FOR A WALK: Forming a horizon line [...] is *Voyage of the Beagle*, Harrison's series of fifty-seven digital photographs. A row read horizontally from left to right and back again, these ink-jetted *headshots* are taken from mannequins, menhirs, bronzes, Brancusis, hunting trophies, posters, record covers, and magazines. Beginning and ending with close-ups of Corsican menhirs, the series, like the voyage it was named after, is a sort of quest for the origins of sculpture, but in this case a comically circular one. The menhirs are now put on equal footing with a Buddha-like statue of Gertrude Stein and a stuffed beaver, for example, and Harrison's democratic and horizontal photographic embrace takes in many others too: Stryofoam wig displays, Kevin Bacon, a detail of a Giacometti, Beyoncé, etc. Sculpture (and identification), it seems, begins and ends everywhere: in the park, the street, shop windows, yard sales, magazines, the internet, etc. And the lateral arrangement of these images reminds us that standing up is only one possible trajectory for a work that is sculptural. Another takes the form of a *walk*, as the artist – a sort of bee in this garden of forms – goes camera in hand through everyday life, collecting sculptures wherever they turn up. If elsewhere in Harrison's work the photograph is put into play as sculptural material, here it continues its work by other means. To produce sculpture is sometimes merely to notice it, to find it, and usually not in the museum.

John Kelsey, from the catalogue essay, 'Sculpture in an Abandoned Field' published in Rachel Harrison: if i did it, *Zurich 2007*

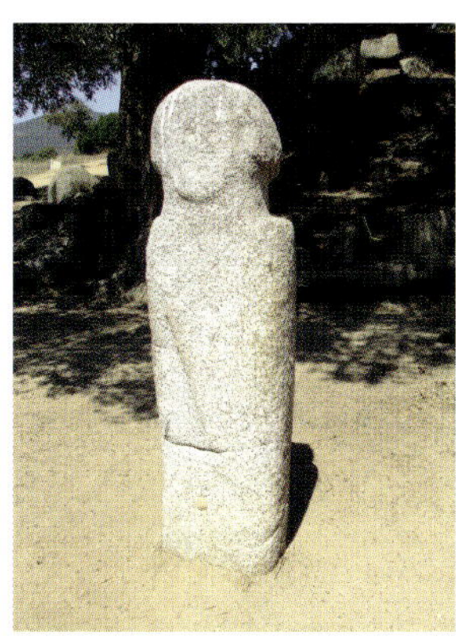

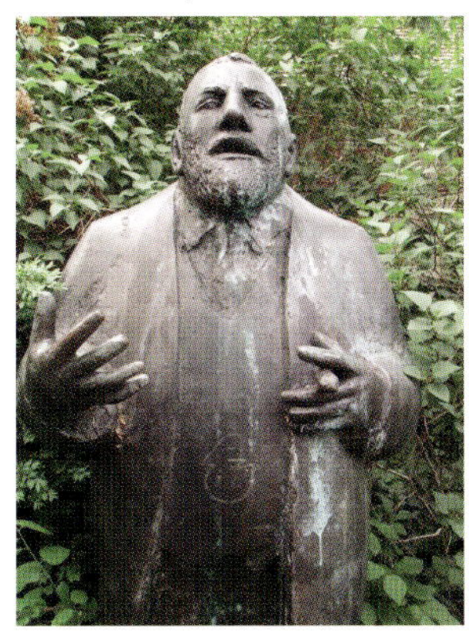

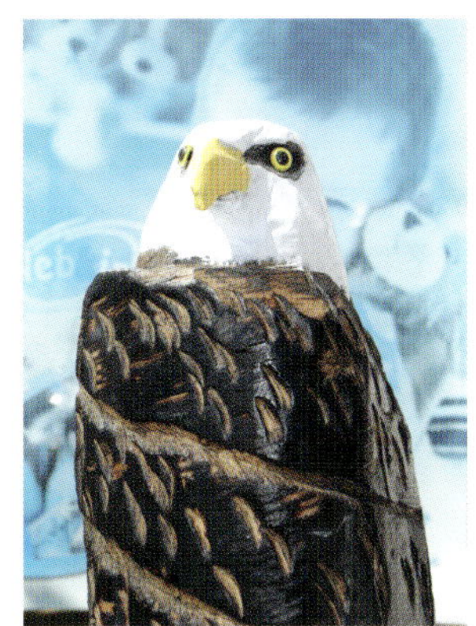

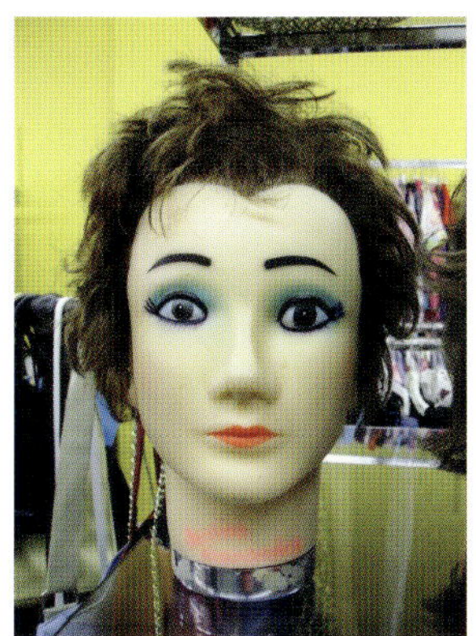

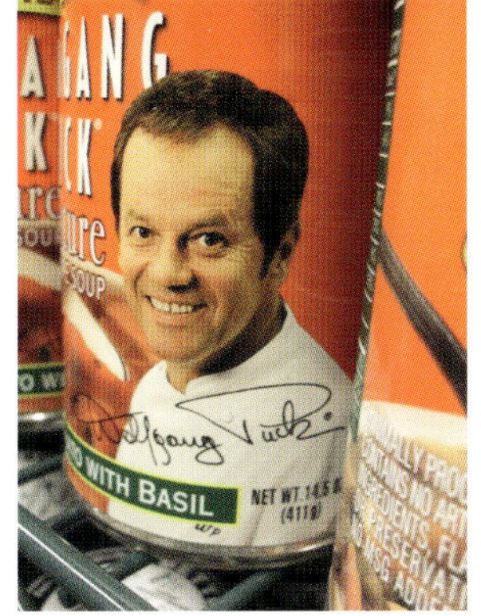
WITH BASIL

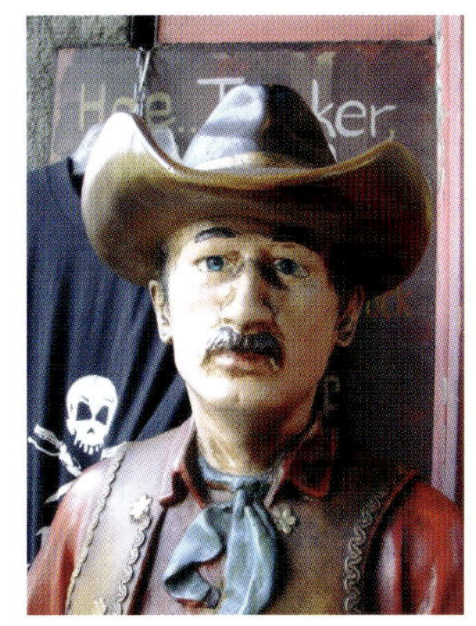

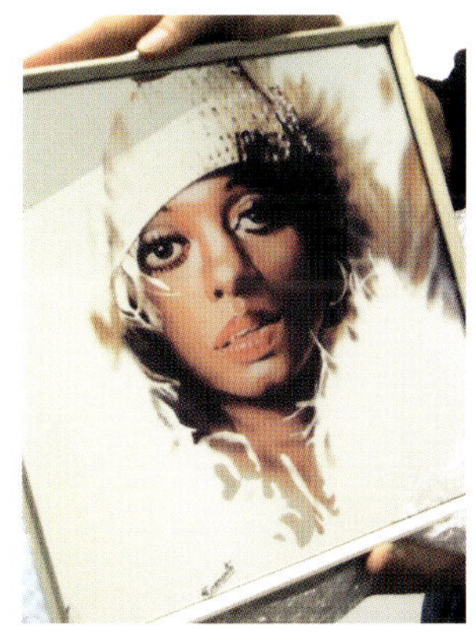

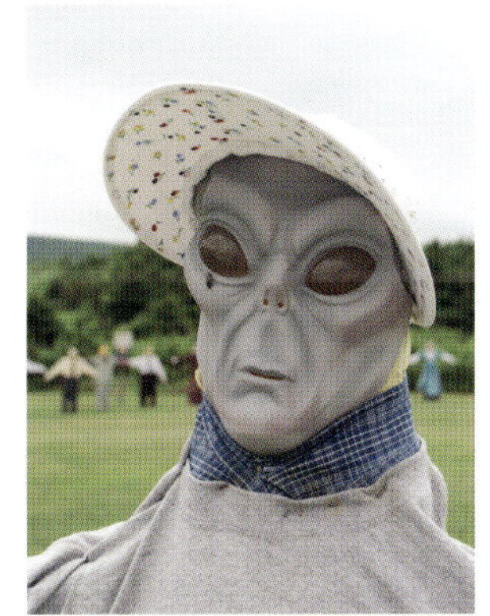

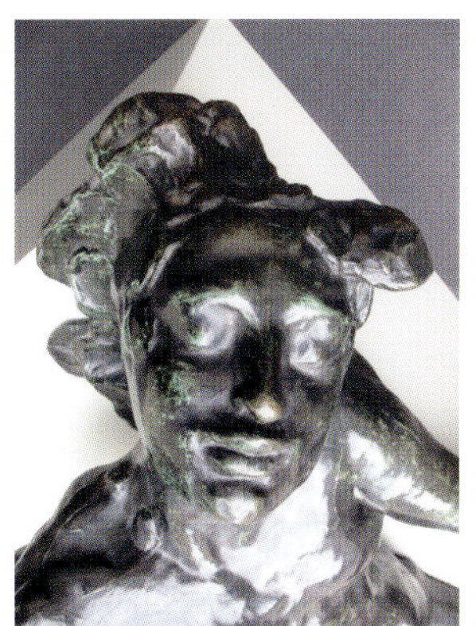

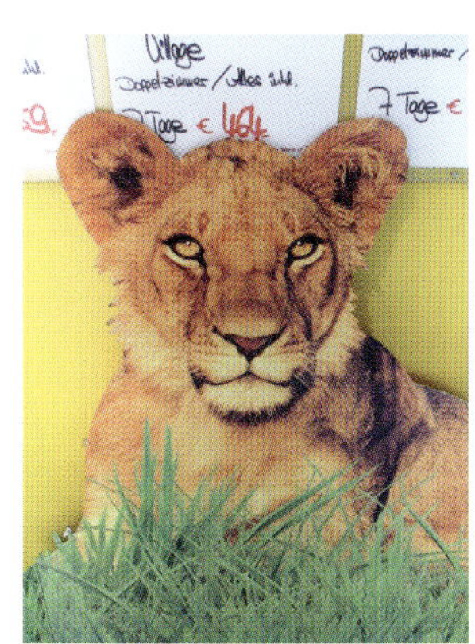
7 Tage €

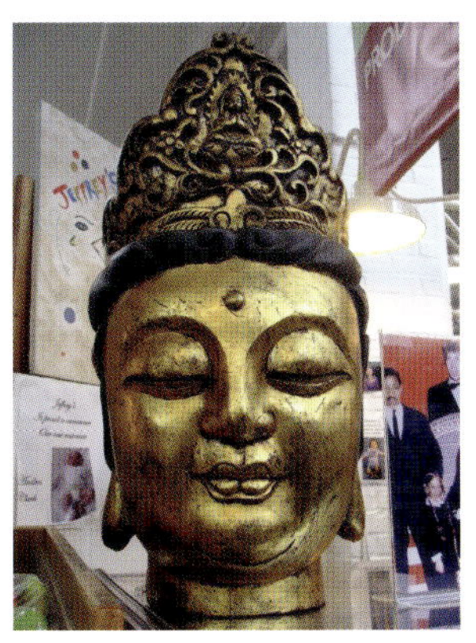

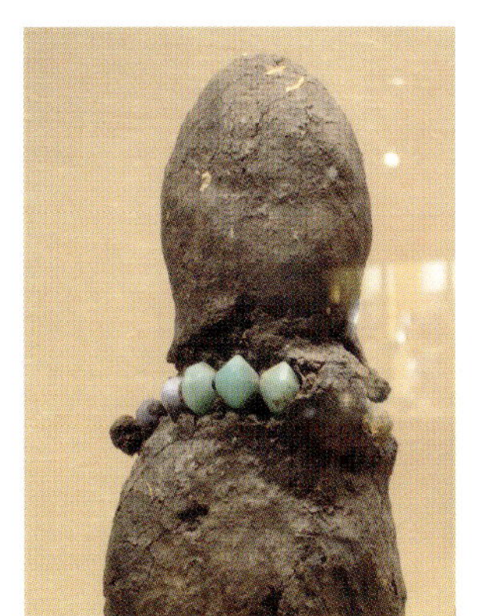

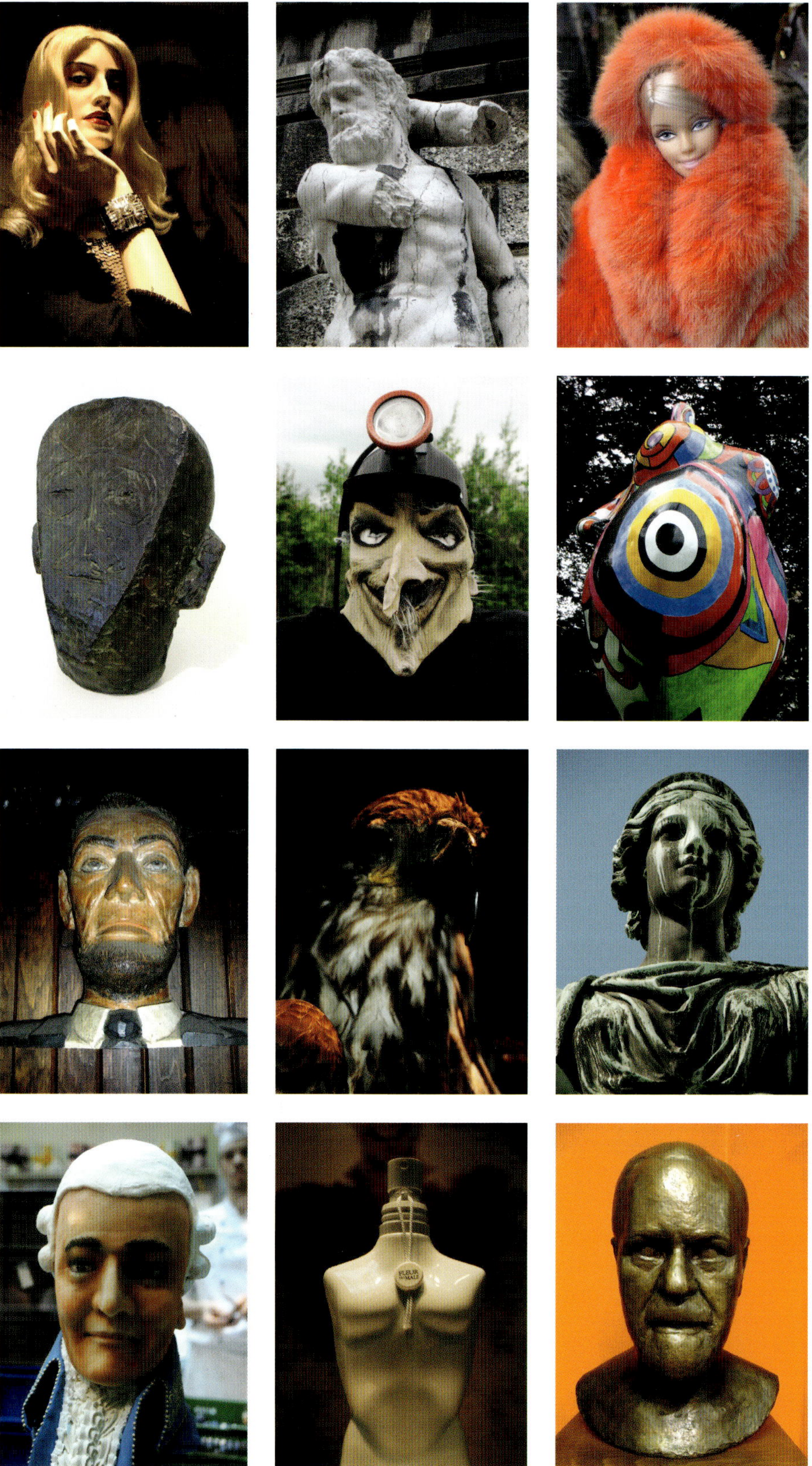
FLEUR

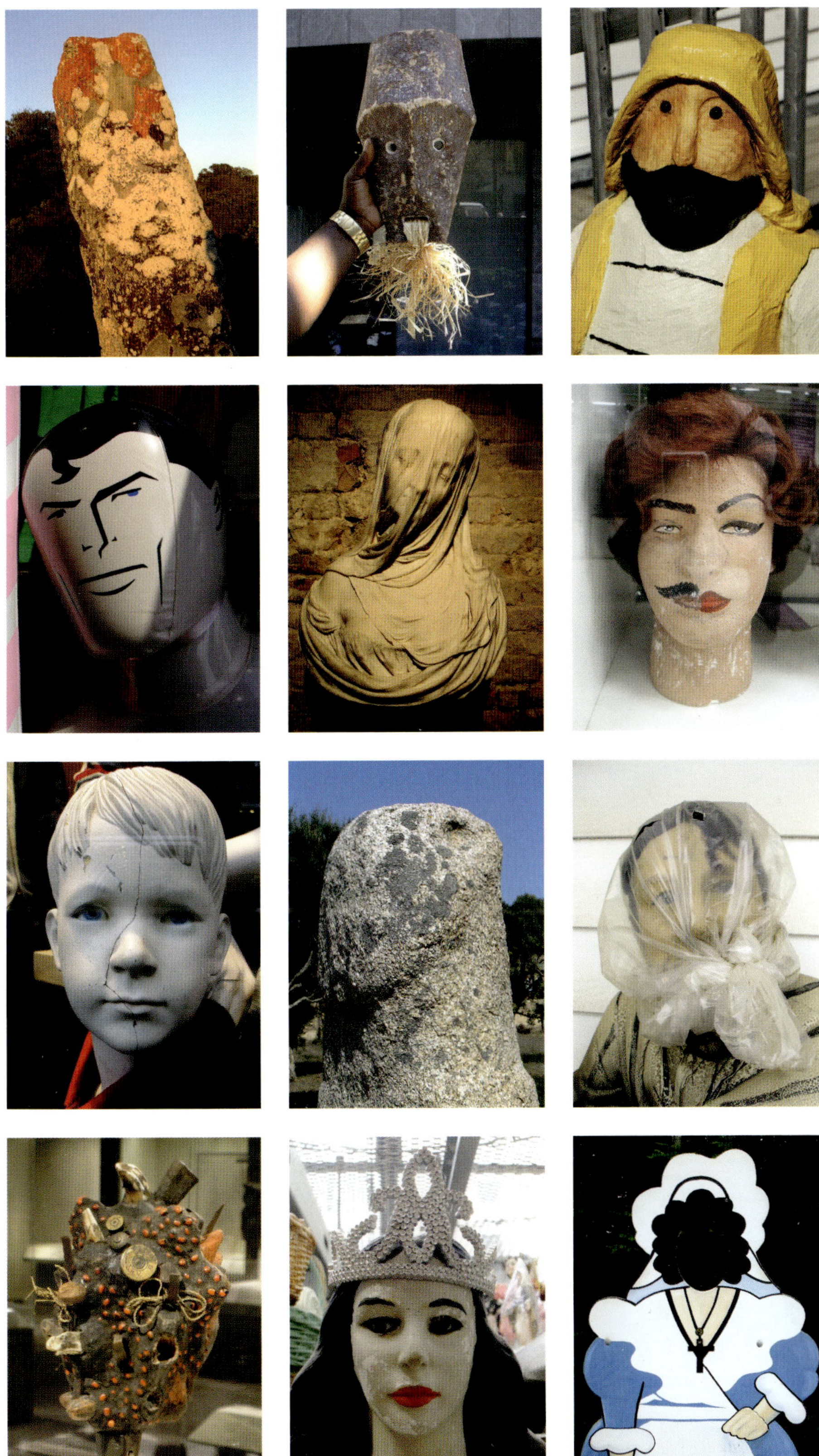

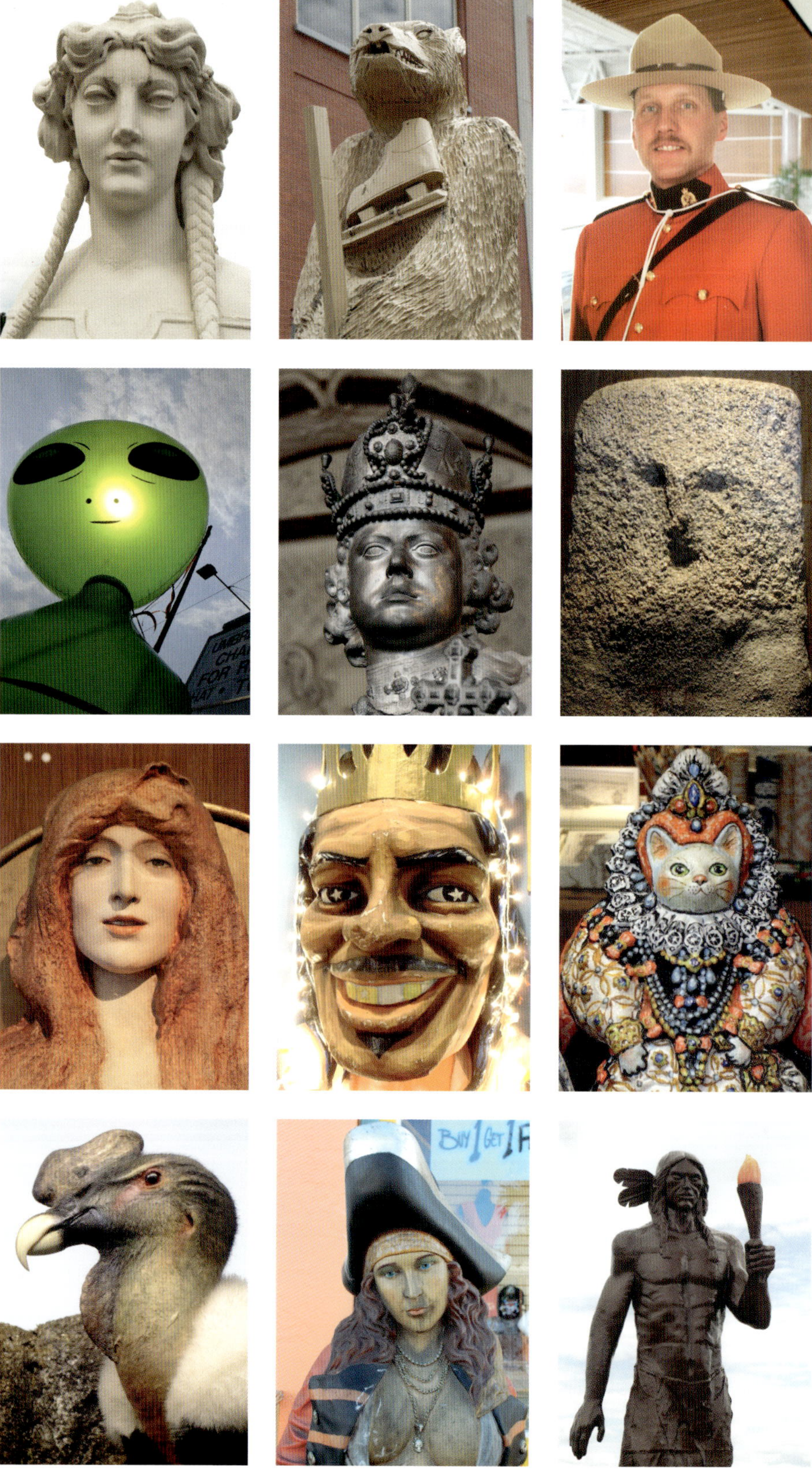
BUY 1 GET 1

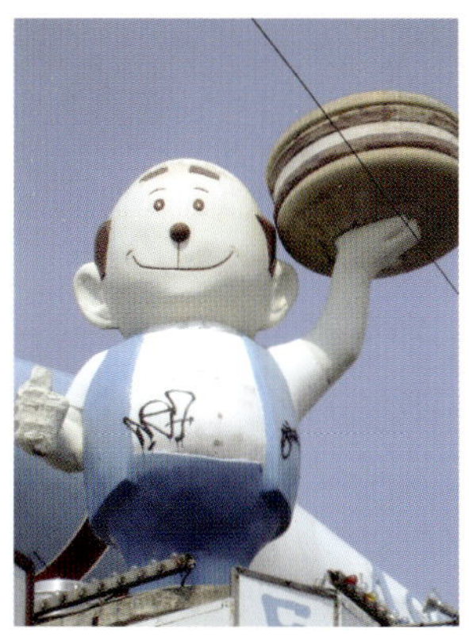

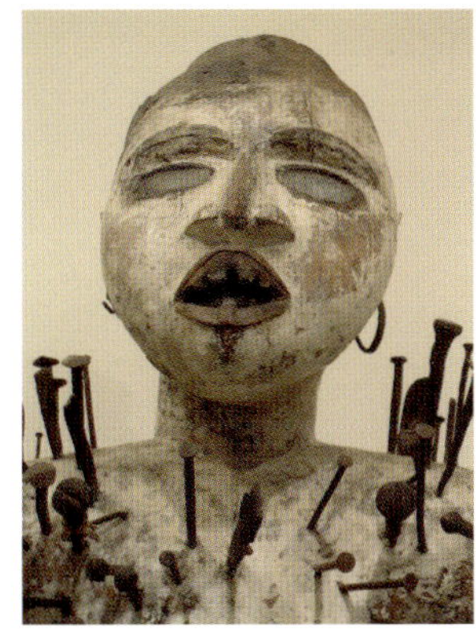

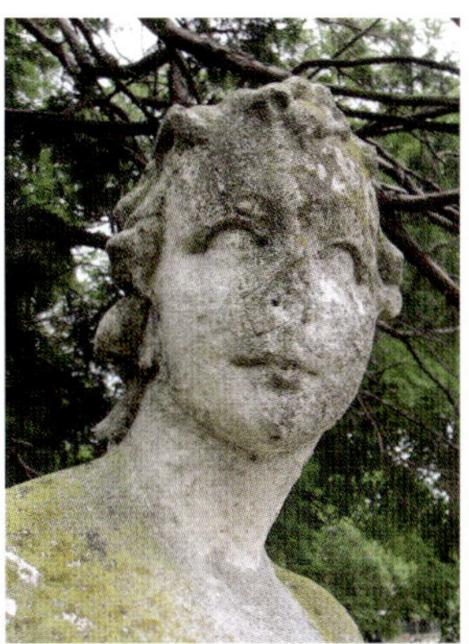

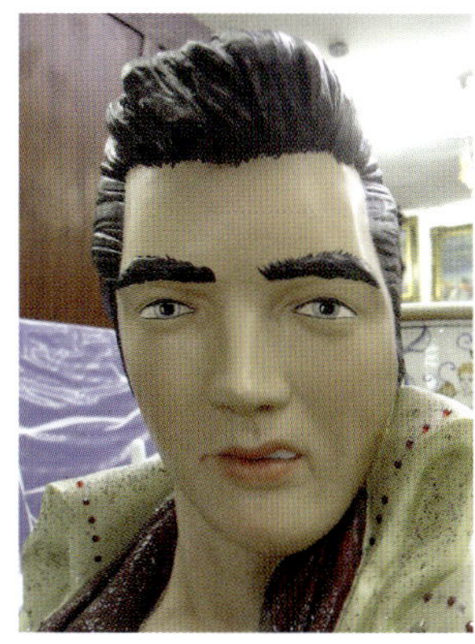

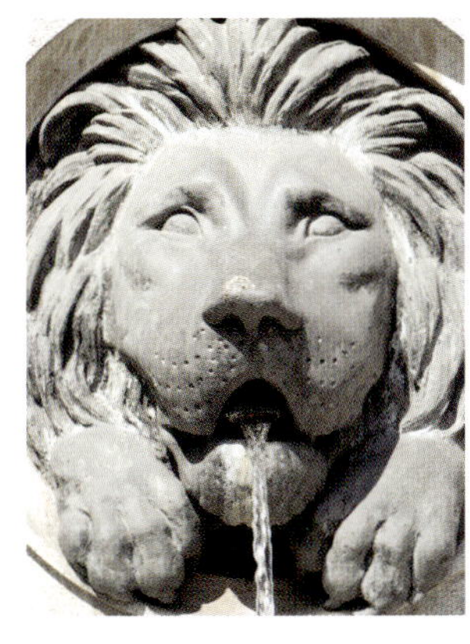

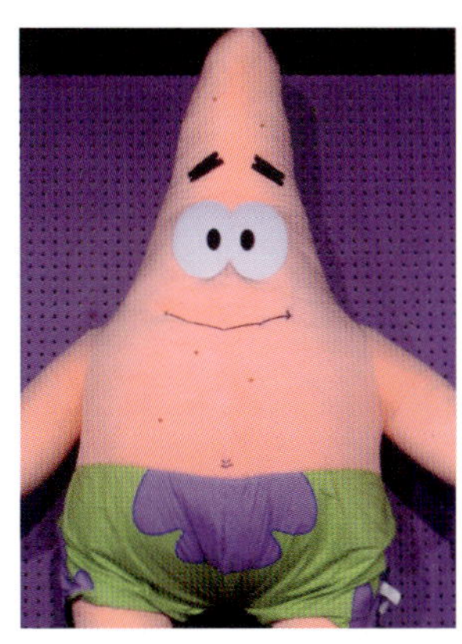

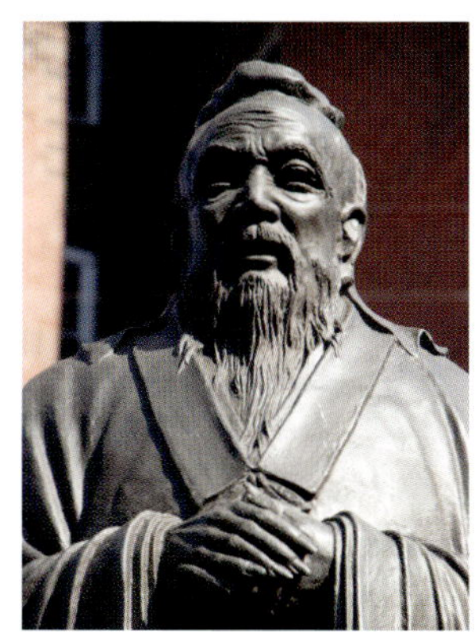

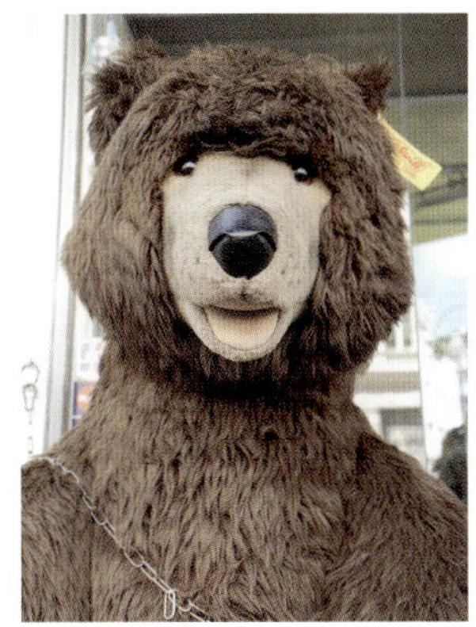

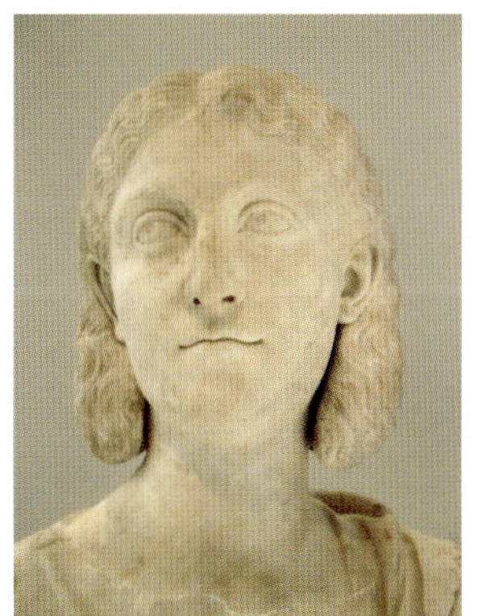

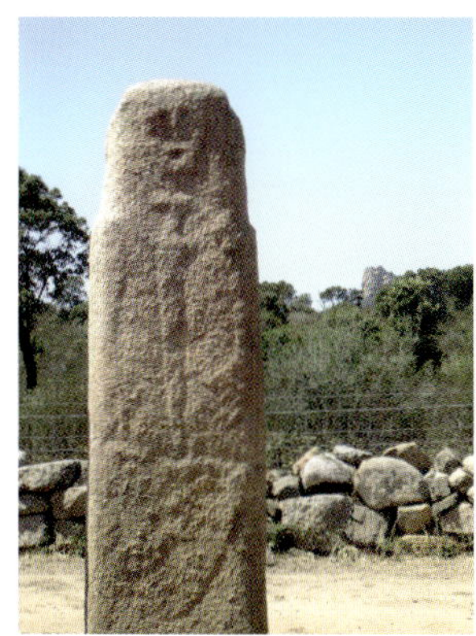

RACHEL HARRISON — [PP.116–19] ***Second Voyage,* 2008,**
suite of 58 digital inkjet prints, 40.6 × 29.2 each, courtesy Greene Naftali, New York

TRAVELS: 18 OCTOBER 2008

John SMITH, Carsten HÖLLER, Zoran NASKOVSKI

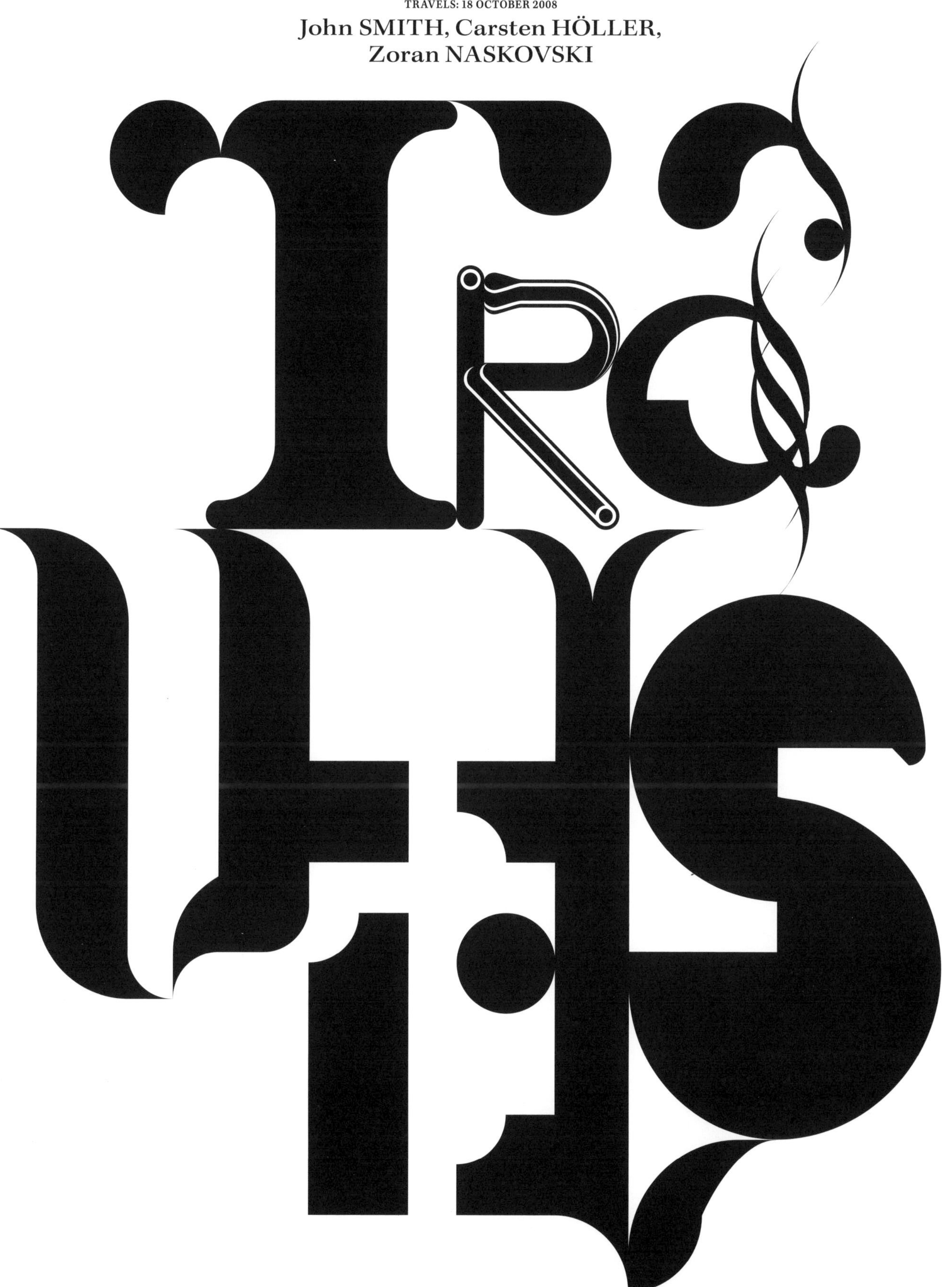

TRAVELS

For the first time in the history of mankind there are no terrae incognitae, no unknown lands. Satellite images have filled in the last voids on the world map. This situation challenges today's art. Artists organise expeditions to the Antartic or the Amazon, searching for the unseen or the unknown among the most hostile or remote lands on the globe. Geography and history have become intertwined and time appears to be the last territory to explore. In other words, travel is now a medium in itself. Furthermore, it brings into art practice some of its patterns: translation, displacements, diaries and the exoticisation of familiar events.

SATURDAY 18 OCTOBER 2008
TATE BRITAIN

14:00
AUDITORIUM
JOHN SMITH
Hotel Diaries 2001–7

14:00
DUFFIELD ROOM
ZORAN NASKOVSKI
Death in Dallas 2001

16:30
AUDITORIUM
CARSTEN HÖLLER
Kinshasa Rumba Brazzaville

KINSHASA RUMBA BRAZZAVILLE

For the Travels *Prologue, German artist Carsten Höller presented an informal slide lecture stemming from his travels in the Congo. Whilst acknowledging the troubles that have beset the country both historically and today, on this occasion Höller chose to emphasise aspects of Congolese culture that those outside the country are rarely exposed to. Focusing on the capital, Kinshasa, he ranged over topics such as food and street-life, adverts and architecture, but his primary focus was the music that drew him to the country in the first place. The talk was followed by a discussion with Nicolas Bourriaud and audience members.*

NICOLAS BOURRIAUD What is the position of this investigation of Kinshasa within your work? Does it have any impact on your art?

CARSTEN HÖLLER At the end of the day, it's basically an interest I have – 'obsession' is probably too strong a word – in the music. But then, you wonder if you really want to make work about it. In this case, I do it only when I reach the point where I can turn it into something else. It's not interesting for me to document it and show it. This talk I just gave was not a work, it was really like when you go and see somebody talking about Majorca or some other travel destination. But I'm actually finding this a good substrate to work with – Kinshasa I mean. I've been doing an experimental film project with Congolese music, which I've been showing in London at the Gagosian Gallery: bits of film flickering onto a wall, not synchronised with the music, but where the sound enhances a visual phenomenon known as the Phi Phenomenon, where you start to see the image jumping in-between two projection sites. Imagine you have one light source here, one light source there, going on and off at a very fast speed. When you look at it, you see something moving between the two. I wanted to see, using concert footage that we filmed in Kinshasa, whether it's possible to create a situation where you would see the people not only in the frame of the image, but literally flying, over the wall to the different places of projection and, in this sense, introducing a moment of instability. But there are also a few other projects that came out of this interest, like The Double Club that is opening in London in November, and a documentary film about Congolese music, which is a project made in collaboration with the Swedish filmmaker Måns Månsson.

NICOLAS BOURRIAUD This is the film you're working on at the moment?

CARSTEN HÖLLER Yes. I found another place on this planet where something is going on that is so different from what we are doing, and so beautiful in its own terms, that it stimulates me to think about other possibilities. A lot of my work is based on this frustration: I cannot believe that reality is limited to all that we have access to; there must be more to it.

NICOLAS BOURRIAUD I was thinking about a text which I'm really fascinated by: Victor Segalen's, 'Essay on Exoticism'. There's a kind of balance that you have to find as a traveller: not negating yourself

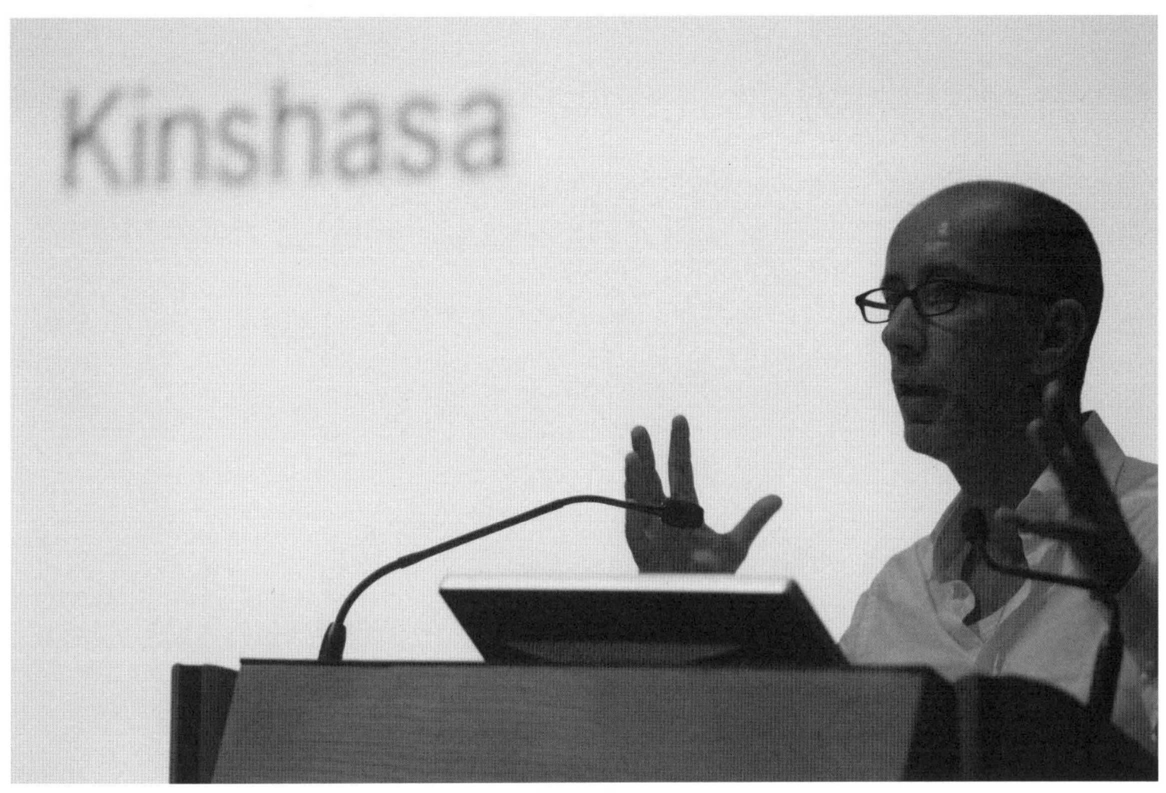

'KINSHASA IS EXTREMELY INTENSE, but it has a certain beauty to it, and it is this beauty I want to speak about now. You have the expression 'country in freefall', to describe something that is lost. The Congo is rich in minerals, in coal, in gold, it even has oil, it has timber, it has everything: but nothing works, everything is corruption. *Heart of Darkness*, Joseph Conrad's book, has elicited so many fantasies that we've developed a culture in the media where we speak badly about the Congo. I want to show you what's nice about it.'

and your own culture, and not falling into a kind of fascination either.

CARSTEN HÖLLER I would say I can only see it through my self: it's my own personal experience. I feel different in Belgium as compared to being in London. I really believe there is a certain personality of a place, a psychology. I don't think this is just a place in which we are all individuals that communicate with each other; I think we form, in some way, and it may sound a bit strange, a body on its own, like a larger body. It's like the human body, which is composed out of different cells; we are the cells of this city, London, where we are now, and we make up one big body. If another cell/

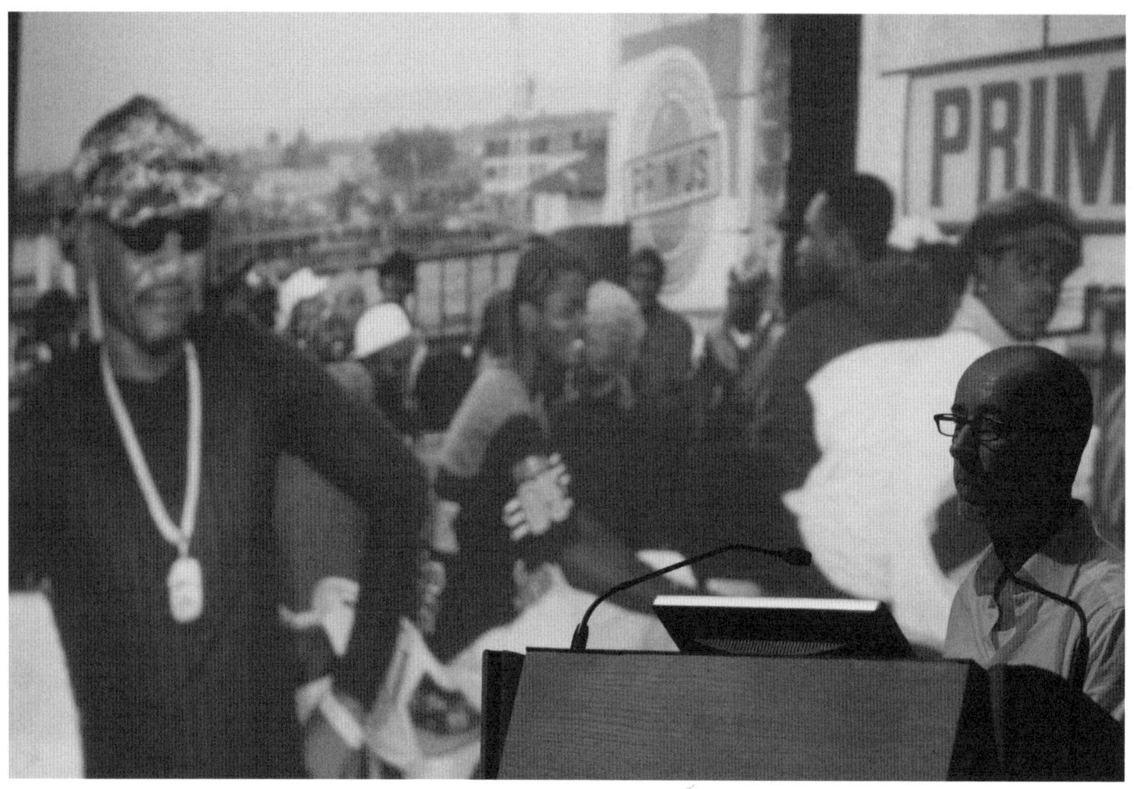

'The main thing in Kinshasa is the very vibrant music scene: there are probably more musicians playing live, from Wednesdays to Sundays, than any other place on earth. It typically starts on Wednesday, sometimes Thursday. The concerts get longer and longer, and there are more and more of them in one evening until Sunday night, which is just completely crazy.'

traveller comes into this body, he/she becomes part of the body and his/her own intellectual metabolism changes. I think this is how I would look at it. There are places that almost push you out; and there are places that suck you in. There are places, like Kinshasa, which pull me in first and push me out after ten days because I can't handle it anymore. But it's really like exposing yourself to some kind of outer influence – and that is an exotic influence – but you are exposing yourself and you just see what the result of it is.

Audience member 1 This is going to come out rather oddly formed, inevitably. However, if you go back a step and think about who Kurtz

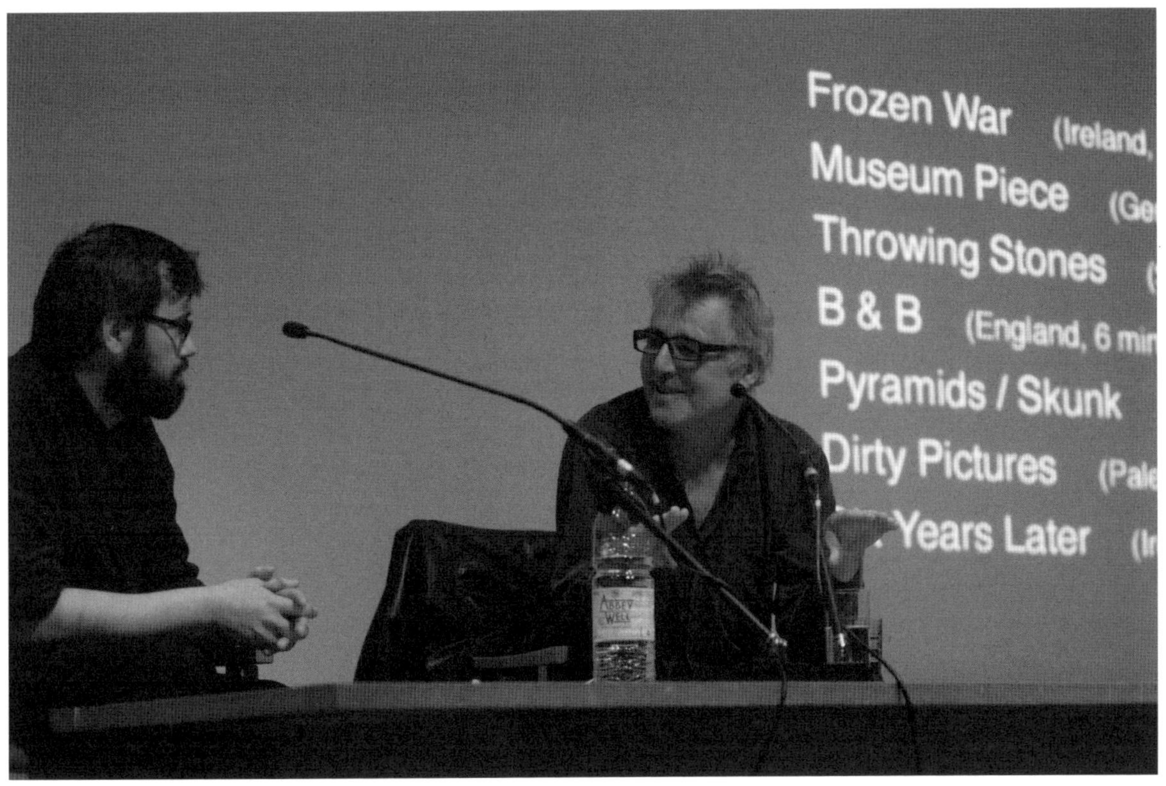

JOHN SMITH's *Hotel Diaries* is a series of video recordings made in hotel rooms around the world between 2001 and 2007, all of which relate the artist's personal experiences to the current conflicts in the Middle East in the 'found' film set of a hotel room. Selections of videos from the series were screened, followed by a discussion between Smith and Tate Britain curator **ANDREW WILSON**. The entirety of the *Hotel Diaries* was also screened throughout the day in the Clore Foyer.

is, this fictional character, and the fact that you know Chinua Achebe has written a seminal text about whether Conrad was a racist and to use this as a basis for a talk about the Congo which chooses to ignore the historical realities which have brought about what is being presented and, also, to fall into the sort of familiar trope that Africa is a place of music and nothing else – and I would choose to isolate cultural representations from the realities of everyday existence – becomes quite difficult for me, who am of African origin, and also becomes quite difficult for me as an artist who has to engage in the everyday realities of my presence here and in other parts of the world.

CARSTEN HÖLLER Yes, but the point is: do you only want to talk about the difficulties, as we are doing all the time when it comes to 'the Congo', or do you want to talk about something else too? My position is that I don't want to talk about only the difficulties. I think it's very harmful, actually. I wanted to do something else, to show something that you hadn't seen before because this culture is not reaching us. I wanted to present it from a personal point of view and show the beauty of it. So, of course, there's a history of 'the Congo' but it is not the topic of my talk; not today. Though it's not something I want to neglect, of course. I'm not talking about Conrad, really. I just think it's interesting to consider Conrad's book, especially the title, and the whole story of Mr Kurtz and *The Horror*, as well as *Apocalypse Now*, and everything that is constructed on the basis of this book and has entered into our culture. This can be a very damaging or productive element for a country and its culture. There are probably many examples other than the Congo. For instance, you know, I live in Sweden, and there was a book written about the country by a German author in the middle of the nineteenth century, describing the Swedish people as being stiff, not having any sense of humour, and introverted. I wonder how much a book like this, or Conrad's book, or Madame de Staël speaking about Germany, is actually influencing the character of a place because there is possibly a whole chain reaction going on. Something may stick in your mind about this, a view you have about the place. You're looking at it from this perspective; it gets more and more cemented and then it produces exactly what has been described from what I think is not a very objective point of view.

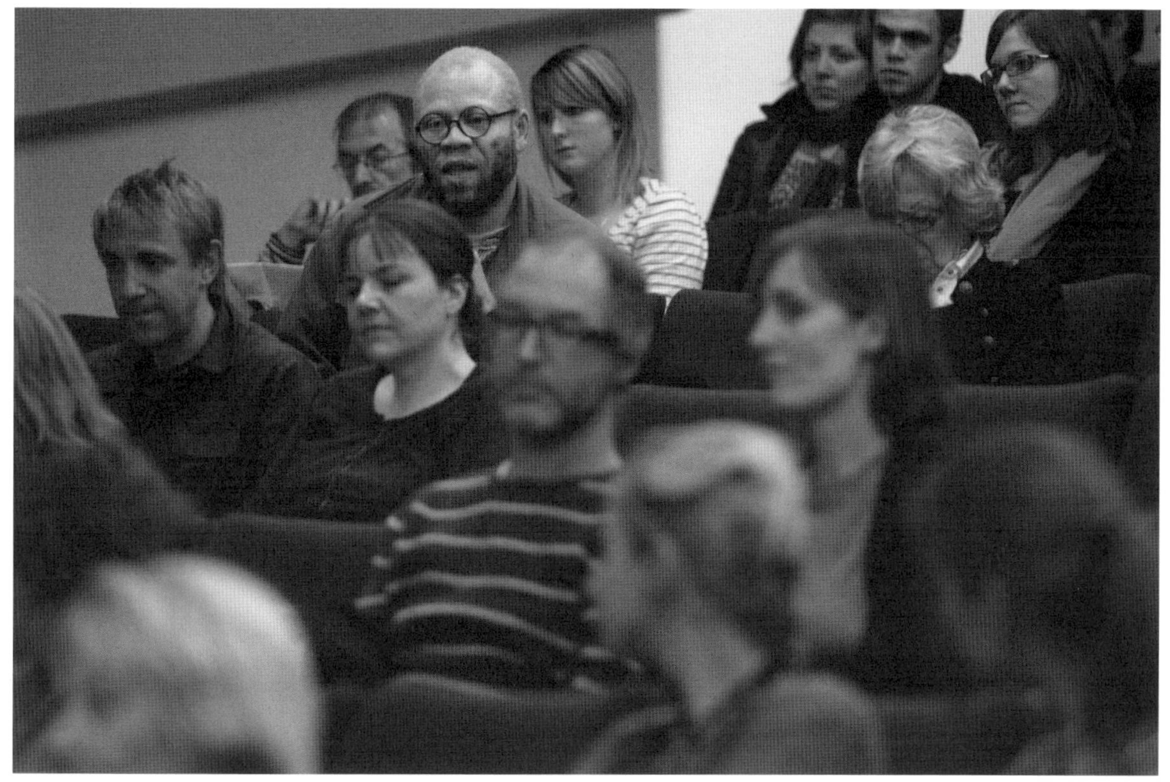

Audience members responding to issues raised in **CARSTEN HÖLLER**'s slide lecture.

AUDIENCE MEMBER 1 If what you're saying is true, that the world doesn't know about those aspects of cultural life in Kinshasa, then it is incumbent on you to present these realities because, in your own words, this is an ignorant audience: if they're ignorant, then enlighten them.

CARSTEN HÖLLER I don't want to enlighten them; I want to enlighten us. I mean, it's a very big difference. I'm not speaking for them; I'm speaking for me and from my cultural background. I think there's a lot to learn from this. It's something that I want to look at because it's incredible, it's beautiful, it's something amazing and it's not something of which I should say 'we should enlighten them'.

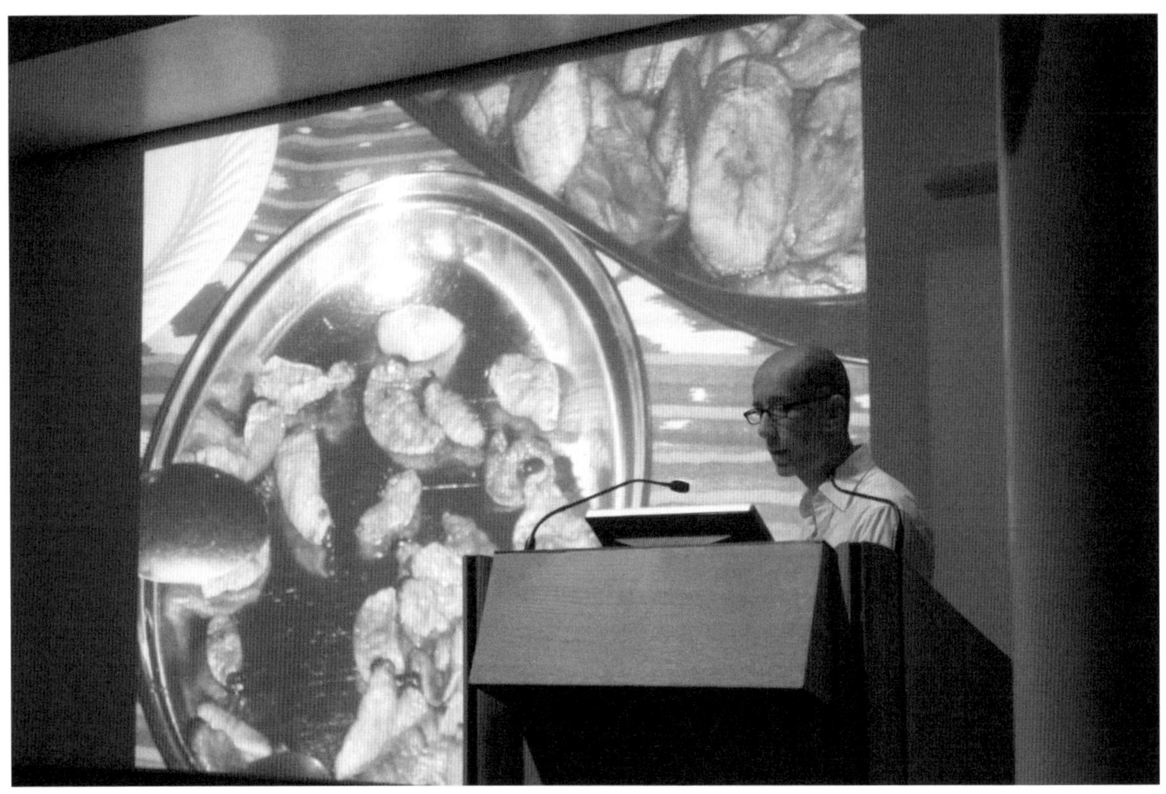

'The food is very good in Kinshasa. There's no wine, but there's a lot of beer. The beer's excellent: it comes in very big bottles. They eat some things that we might find a bit strange, like larvae. The first time you have this in your mouth, you might think it's disgusting but, actually, it's a bit like when you eat a shrimp for the first time: you want to have it again. It is actually delicious; all the friends that I've travelled with to Kinshasa, we all like to eat these larvae.'

But I guess you meant 'them' not 'us', so I gave you the wrong answer.

audience member 2 I find quite interesting that you used the word 'instability' at one stage, how you go to a place and every single place has a certain beauty about it. How much does that sense of instability relate to your art?

carsten höller Yes, now we are back to something that I thought, maybe, we were not going to speak about today because I didn't want to speak about my art in this context. But it is an interest of mine to introduce a certain moment of instability or confusion into my life and to use this confusion as a basis for feeling 'different', and trying to reset the order that I have been constructing all my life. I would like to know if it's possible to reorganise my mind, and to start from another position. I don't know who I really am but I would like to know if I could be somebody else. I have done this once in my life before: I used to be a scientist, working in a university. I didn't know anything about this whole art world and, at some point, I found a certain frustration at being a scientist because I could see the rest of my life just in front of me, being clear to me, all the things that would happen all enjoyable or not to a certain degree. And that made me stop. Now, being an artist, I actually have quite a similar feeling: I have a feeling that I'm not as interested as before, or at least, not interested in the same way in the whole notion of being an artist, producing artworks and showing them. My Congo fascination, or fascination with Congolese music, certainly has something to do with the fact that I'm looking for a way to become another person again. The figure of the artist is good for me, it works well, I know how to do it, I have learnt the techniques, I can do it – but, you know, now that I have done it I want to be born again and start another time. And this explains my fascination for being two things at the same time: a double specialist, if you want, but in the sense of two specialists at the same time. I want to become schizophrenic – but not in a medical way – and try to bring two lives into my one body. I have a strong interest in this and my recent artworks have to do with it. So, there has been a gradual shift in my artistic career from somebody who is producing objects that can be shown in the context of a museum or gallery, into somebody who's producing experiences. My objects are not really meaningful without the viewer having a personal experience with them. Actually, the object I'm trying to produce is the personal experience. That is something you can take home and do something with, instead of some kind of constructed meaning extractable from the art object. It is a very significant shift, and I think I am going in the right direction here. Now my interest is to bring this out of the pure art context into a more real-life context: try these ideas of double identities in a situation that is closer to life, not purely representational but really based on experience. What we are doing here in London at The Double Club is to bring these ideas to life, into the entertainment world if you like, by opening a bar, a discotheque and a restaurant. The main idea behind this project is to gather two different cultural worlds, or ways of being, into one single space, without fusing them. I keep them apart, but present at the same moment in the same space. It doesn't take the representational level way, but it adds something on top of it. That's also a Double.

NICOLAS BOURRIAUD Can you develop this idea of entertainment?

CARSTEN HÖLLER I'm interested in the idea of entertainment and fun from a theoretical viewpoint: I believe it is something that we tend to underrate. It is a very, very strong driving force in our lives, and I have an almost dictatorial relationship with my desire for fun. I think this is interesting enough to go into a more research approach towards this and to manipulate my own desire for fun and try to bring it on another level, more conceptual. Because the

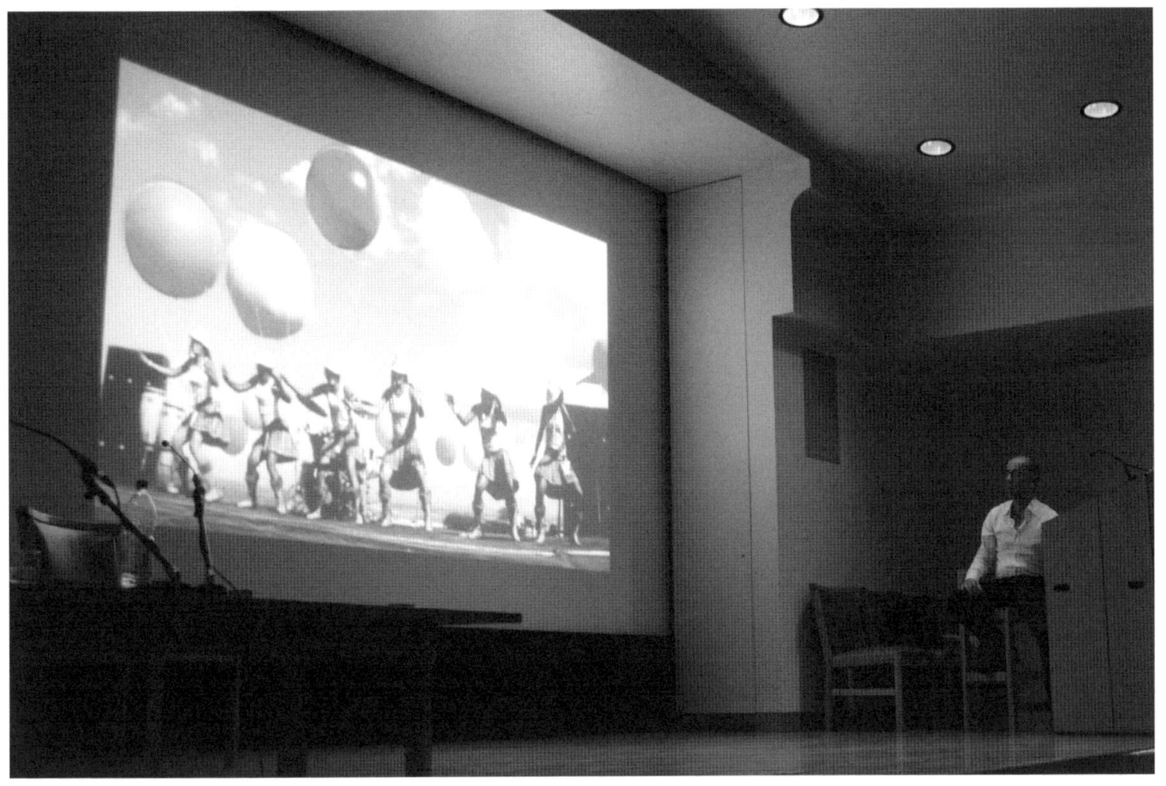

'IT'S A VERY INTERESTING THING: big-name musicians playing their best songs for one of the beer brands in Kinshasa. There's great competition not only between musicians but also between the two main beer brands, Skol and Primus. The musicians need the beer brand because the beer brand sponsors their concerts; they transport all the equipment, they make sure it's working, and they pay for everything. So it's a very strange, mutual relationship between the musicians and beer brands.'

eerie aspect about fun, in my opinion, is that it is invisible: it is something that doesn't have any form at all. In order to materialise it, it could be interesting to have two different kinds of fun competing against each other, in the same space at the same time. How do they make each other up? How does it function with the people that go there? How does it affect you when you get this information in stereo without one element coming together with the other?

AUDIENCE MEMBER 3 Did you dance when you were there?

CARSTEN HÖLLER Did I dance? Not really. It's hard because these songs, the new songs, often come with a new dance and I know how

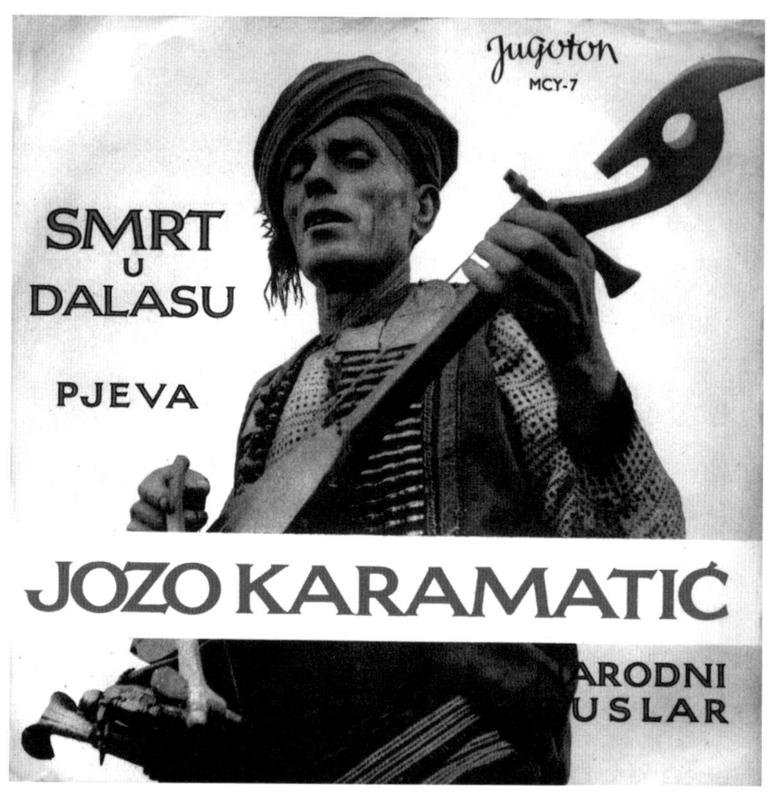

ridiculous it looks if somebody who comes from a different cultural background tries to imitate that. But, you know, that's only when you're alone. I've organised two concerts with big Congolese bands in Stockholm and that's another situation because you have a lot of Swedish people and then there's a lot of dancing and it works very well. Dance is another fun thing to do. It has the potential of bringing you into some kind of other spirit, like travelling.

AUDIENCE MEMBER 4 You seemed to have a very distanced relationship with the images you brought back from Kinshasa, and from the real ity you describe. How do you explain that?

CARSTEN HÖLLER I probably would have been able to give a better talk to you if I was talking about something I really know. I performed

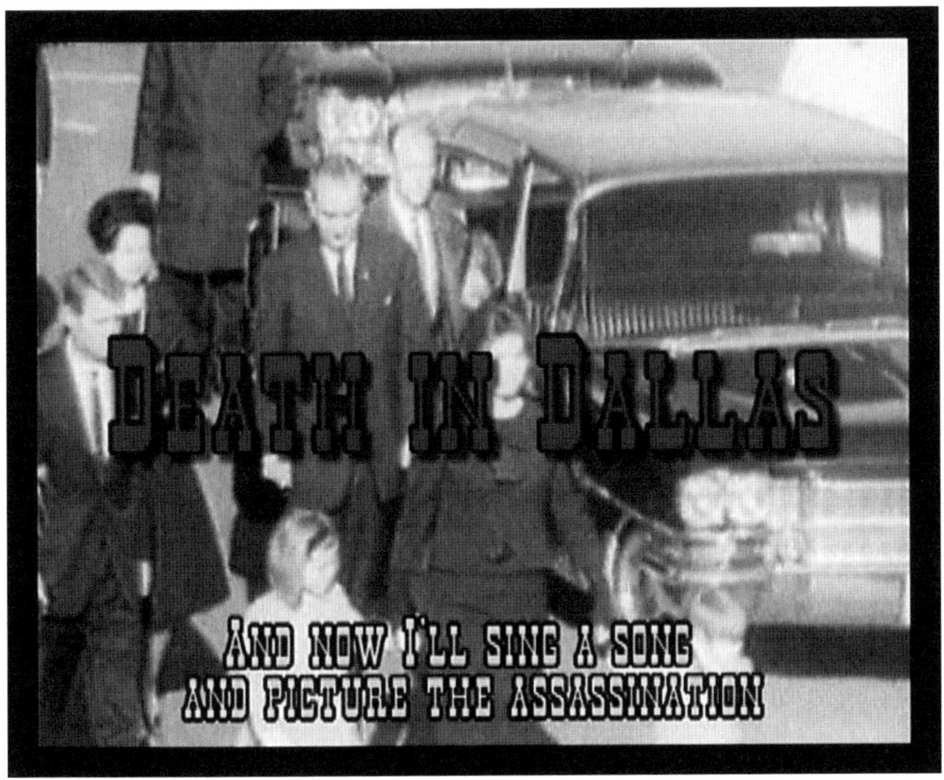

IN HIS VIDEO *Death in Dallas* 2001 (17 mins) Serbian artist **ZORAN NASKOVSKI** presented a reinterpretation of the events surrounding the assassination of John F. Kennedy in 1963. **NASKOVSKI** sets iconic archive footage to a ballad recounting the news in the Slavic tradition of oral history. Based on a recording the artist found in a Serbian flea market, the song is performed by **JOZO KARAMATIC** accompanied by a gusle, an ancient single-stringed Balkan instrument.

this lecture almost naked, because I didn't know what would really happen, what I would really say. That's how I often work. It's a deliberately naive approach but it's about trial and error and seeing what comes out of it. If it's good, I continue; if not, I stop. I often work with different possibilities at the same time. I also have a hard time deciding, almost to a medical-problem degree, and I don't know what I should do in front of an infinite number of possibilities. So, my way of approaching the matter is to pin it down to a few of them and try to keep them alive, both, or three or four, or however many you can handle, instead of taking any decision. But it is about my personality: I'm not really there, I'm out of it; but that's only really because I have no idea who I am.

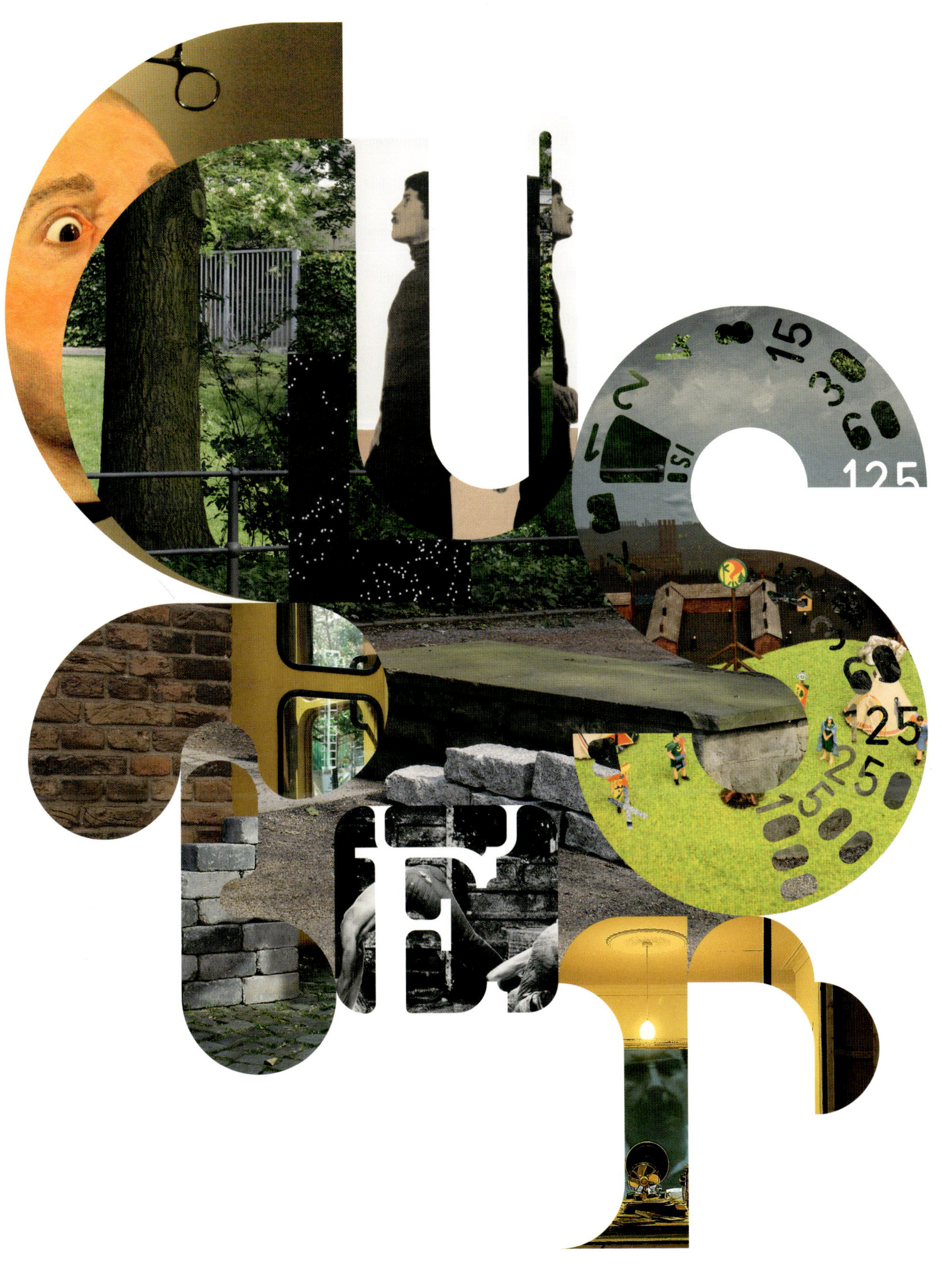

Joachim KOESTER

THERE IS 'TRUTH' in the legends – but not the 'truth' of history. 'What really happened' in this case took place (as hashish smokers might say) on another plane. And that plane is accessible.

From Hakim Bey, 'The Bhang Nama: Hemp as a Sacrament', in Hakim Bey and Abel Zug (eds.), Orgies of the Hemp Eaters: Cuisine, Slang, Literature and Ritual of Cannabis Culture, *New York 2004.*

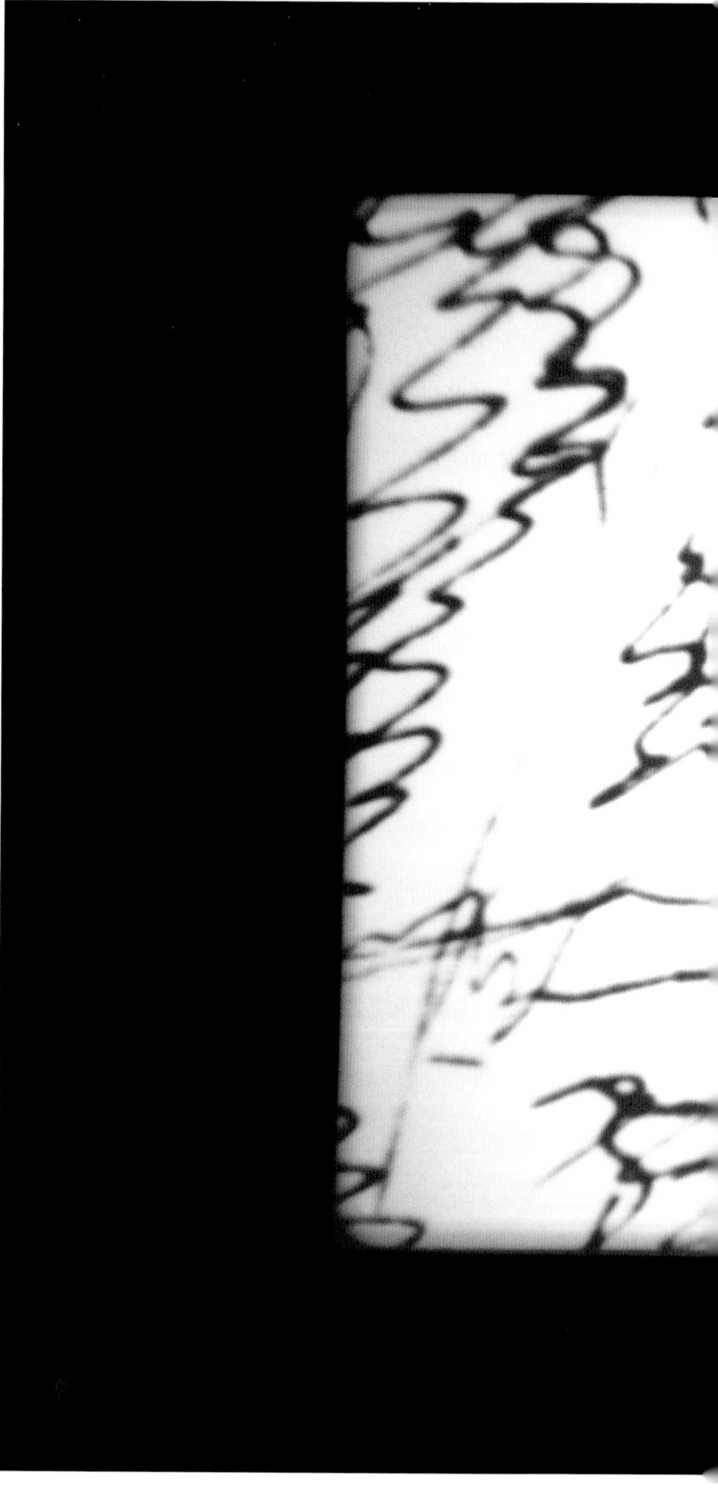

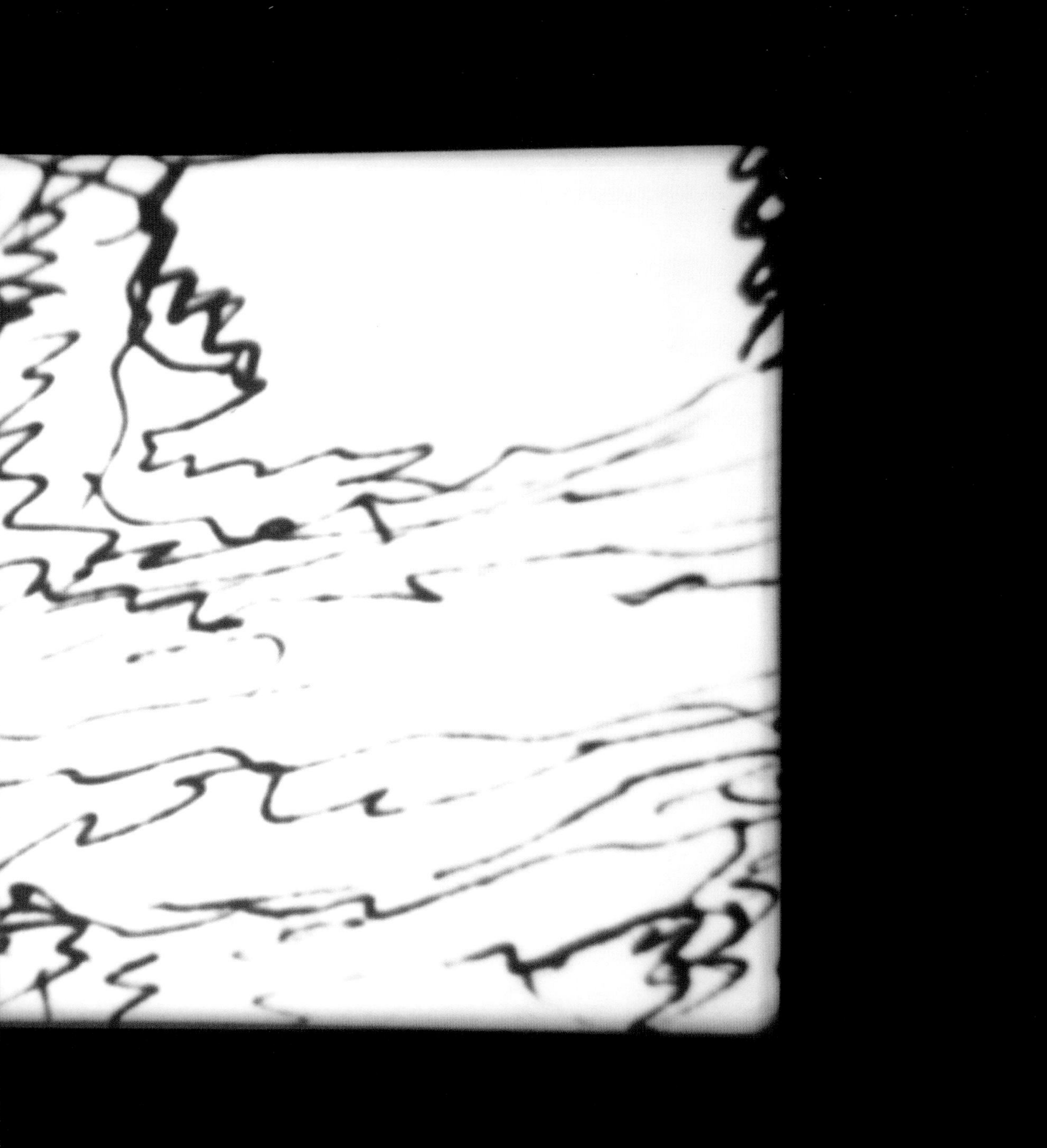

JOACHIM KOESTER – *My Frontier is an Endless Wall of Points (After the Mescaline Drawings of Henri Michaux)*, 2007, 16mm film animation, courtesy Gallerie Jan Mot, Brussels/Galleri Nicolai Wallner, Copenhagen

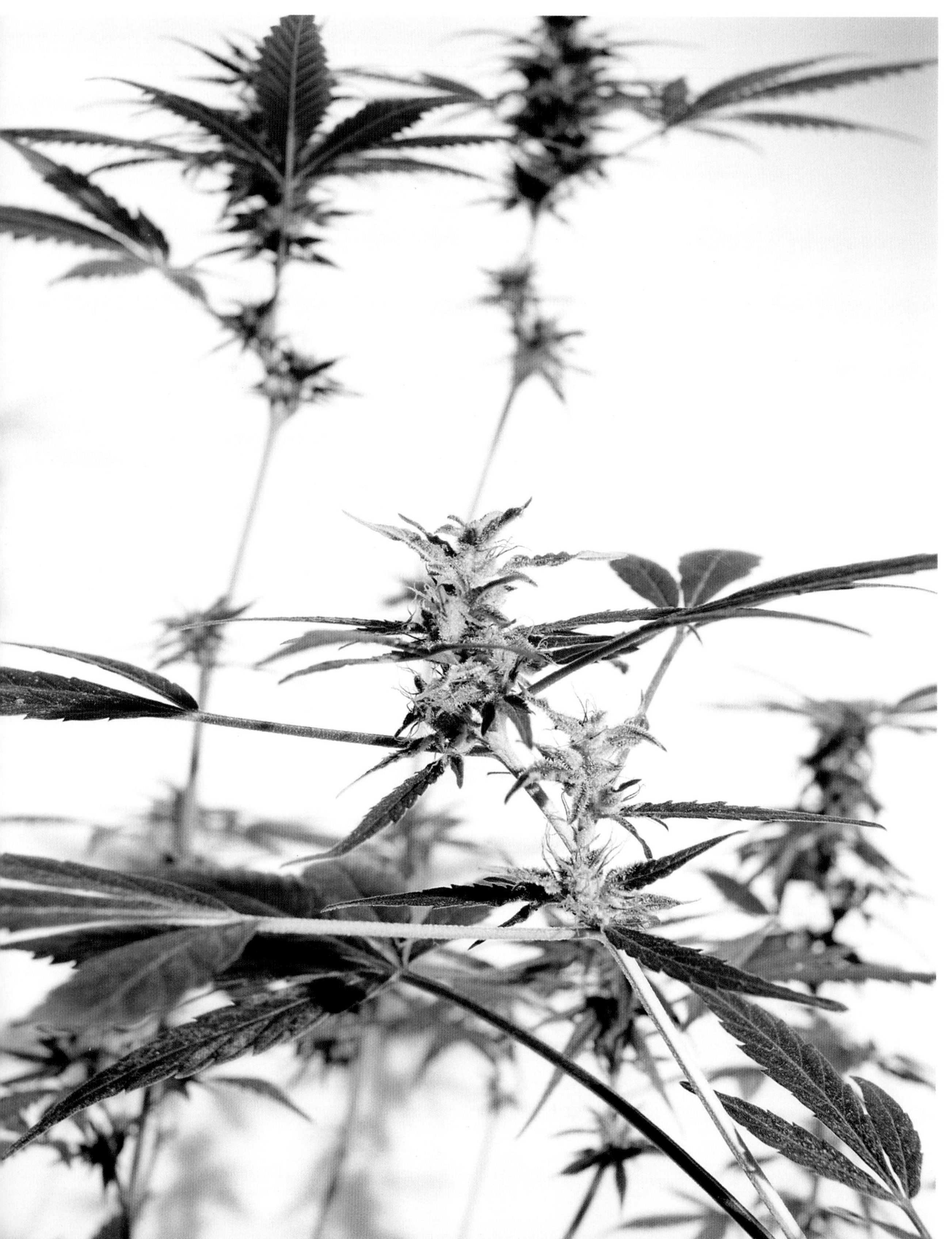

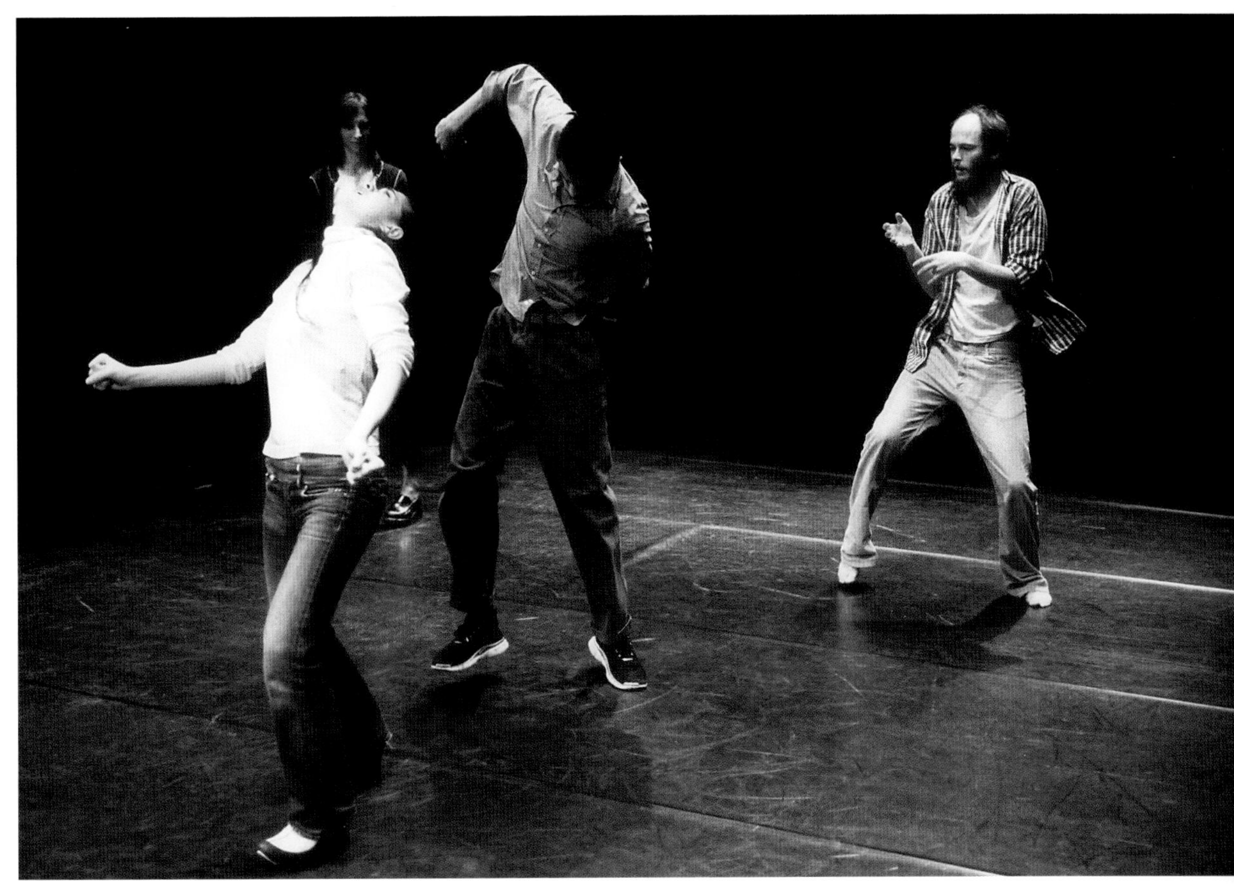

JOACHIM KOESTER — [LEFT] *The Hashish Club*, 2007, still from 16mm film installation, [RIGHT] *Tarantism*, 2007, still from 16mm film installation, courtesy Gallerie Jan Mot, Brussels/Galleri Nicolai Wallner, Copenhagen

Nathaniel MELLORS

NICOLAS BOURRIAUD *The other day I was in Madrid, visiting the Prado and I was struck by the fact that I was aware of the subtext of most of the paintings, which were all, let us say, leaning over a text, sheltering under a text, developing a text (mainly the Bible) – an infinite storytelling, paintings to be read as much as 'felt'. How do you see your work within this problematic, and what is its relation to text, narratives or scenarios?*

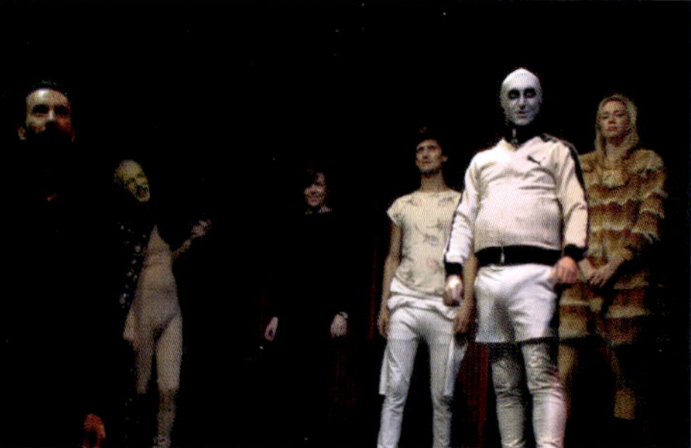

NATHANIEL MELLORS At the moment the words come first – I write my own scripts and direct and film their performance in different and deliberately conflicting ways. Increasingly, the visual aspects of my work seem to be fashioned or improvised within a primarily linguistic arena – this liberates my approach to the visuals, it opens up lots of possibilities. I love absurdism and satire and I am fascinated by the range of effect that words can have. A particular concern is with the potential and 'use value' of language; that is to say, how it is being deployed, by whom and with what ambitions.

To be more specific, my own narratives are played out in scenarios where the relationship between word and external reality has often slipped, or is in the process of slipping further away from sense. The characters wrestle with this confusion. There can be control issues – like in *The Time Surgeon* 2007 – the narrative of which is essentially a battle for the control of language. My very basic idea was to make an absurdist version of *La Jetée* (Chris Marker, 1962), in which one character experiences the other's verbal descriptions of torture as physical reality. It is possible, within these scenarios, to use humour in different ways, to pitch things so that they're funny in parts, then not entirely funny, or suddenly not funny at all. I like these shifts in register.

NICOLAS BOURRIAUD *Why are you developing the theme of cannibalism in this work? How is it related to our times – especially to the conditions of culture?*

NATHANIEL MELLORS Well, I found out that it is traditional to invoke cannibalism to distract attention from your own appalling behaviour! I have to summarise the new work to answer this clearly. In my script *Giantbum* 2008 a group of explorers are lost inside the body of a giant and are trying to find a way out. They are starving to death. They send their spiritual leader, The Father, down into the giant's bowels in search of an exit. On returning it appears that The Father has failed to find the exit, and in fact has gained weight, resorting to shit-eating to survive. He invokes cannibalism – initially as an excuse. He claims that a group of 'half-human half-faecal' cannibals are guarding the exit and prevented him from finding a way out of the giant's body. Furthermore, these cannibal-zombies – who he refers to as The Ploppen – engendered his survival by coprophilia. He implies that *these things did not happen of his own free will.* I was specifically interested in the idea of cannibalism and coprophilia as extreme illustrations of a hermetic situation in which the action has become reflexive – *a feedback loop.* Coprophilia is presented as an advanced, looping form of cannibalism. The Father becomes infinite through his 'regeneration', developing from scatological to eschatological. He eats himself, shits himself and can be 'born again' and again. The situation starts to refer to itself, and the words start to refer to themselves. It becomes a closed circuit. The feedback loop enables the possibility of total manipulation of the environment by The Father, and as he becomes more confident in his claims he evolves into a sort of absurd but dangerous suicide-cult leader. Ultimately he leads the entire group (apart from the rational 'Sir Boss' and the naïve 'Truthcurator') to 'redemption' – 'digestion' into 'heaven' via what he claims is the stomach of God. I am working on a series of different manifestations of the *Giantbum* script, each moving further away from a straight performance of the written word – getting more fragmented and abstracted. I've got this idea for the Triennial installation – that it should be as if the script is digesting itself. That you can walk through the stages of digestion.

With the idea of cannibalism and the use of coprophilia I've taken considerable influence from Pasolini: *Porcile* (1969) and *Salò* (1974) respectively. I think *Salo* is a masterpiece, quite unlike any other film I've seen. It has a heightened sense of realism despite its lack of naturalism. Pasolini demonstrates the worst possible outcome within an environment where 'the rules have changed' – there has been a deliberate disconnection from any comparative measure of reality – and he shows this as a precondition for torture and total abuse. You see this progression in *Salo*. First, people are abducted from their normal lives – the beginning of the slippage but it gets worse and worse. On the island-state where they are taken, the languages of art and power refer only to their own art and power. Horror becomes normalised; the environment is degraded. There are many parallels that can be made between that manipulation of 'the rules' and trends in our social and political environment post 9/11. I am particularly interested in the systematic disconnection of a collective and consensual measure of reality through language. To my mind, it is no coincidence that inside the house in *Salo* there is so much avant-garde-looking art reduced to mere decoration. It looks like something but it isn't that thing. Its new function is to demonstrate the power of its owners through its appearance.

The reconfiguration of the relationship between what something looks like and how it is being used is a base characteristic of cultural recycling. You can read cannibalism and coprophilia as crude metaphor for cultural recycling. Over the last fifteen years in the UK there has been a nostalgic recycling of almost all forms of pop music; it feels like those bands that aren't completely dead have reformed. There have been similar tendencies in art making, a growth of sentiment for the past – this trend has been quite dominant. My concern is that this can betray a responsibility to the present. I think it is about evoking the reassurance of group consensus precisely where there is none in the present – we can all feel nostalgia for the radicalism of the past, but that doesn't necessarily empower our engagement with the present; you can dope people with familiarity, regurgitation and re-styling. To bring it back to the first question – there is a conflation of what is 'felt' and what is 'read', in that the discussion it engenders is primarily about the content of the (twenty-five-year-old) music, not about the sentiment of its present day usage.

I love artists that work inside, outside and against their form. François Rabelais (an inspiration for the basic *Giantbum* scenario) is the greatest writer I have found who can question a form and simultaneously dance an amazing dance with it – as he does in every chapter of *Gargantua & Pantagruel* (1532–64). That book feels like it contains the whole world. And it seems like in many chapters he's deploying different parodic forms – it is not homogenous. I would extrapolate that if you choose to work as an artist you have an implicit critical, even moral, responsibility to the form in which you work – and that the form or language does not mean much in itself, outside of how and why it is used, even though it may appear to.

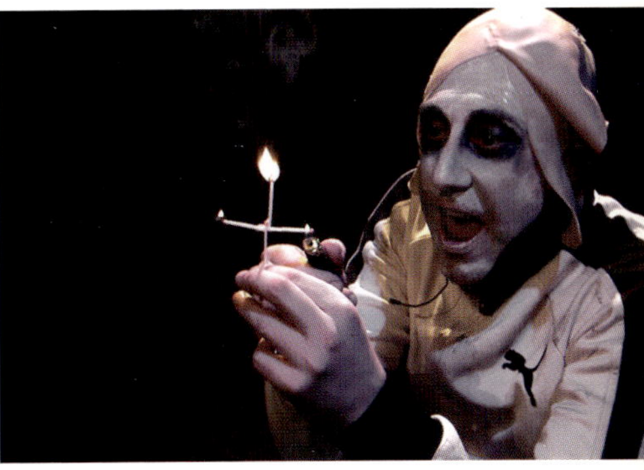

Because we can all be seduced by special effects. I just saw *The Dark Knight* and enjoyed the first hour. There is mass agreement on various websites (it is August 2008 as I write) that it is an 'edgy', 'complex' 'masterpiece' – which it may be, but certainly not in the (filmic) terms presented there. To me it feels like an emotionally comforting film for anyone feeling guilty about Western 'terror' policy. Again, there is this conflation of what is 'felt' and what is 'read'. It is so easy to be manipulated! I think artists have to work with an awareness of this stuff, and resist deploying the 'hollowed out' languages unknowingly, not putting the Fall album on the wall unless there is a really convincing reason for it. There are alternatives – many artists are showing that it is possible to assemble their own, strange language, from left, right and centre – something of and for the present. Even if it looks unsuccessful, seems clunky, confusing and/or is relatively unpopular, in the long term I think this is of great value. I feel that the primary responsibility for contemporary art at the moment is to develop a contemporary vernacular. I want to see art that works for and against the idea of art, rather than within its image.

NATHANIEL MELLORS – *Giantbum*, 2008, video stills, courtesy the artist and Matt's Gallery, London

NATHANIEL MELLORS – *Giantbum,* 2008, (work in progress), animatronic sculpture, courtesy the artist and Matt's Gallery, London

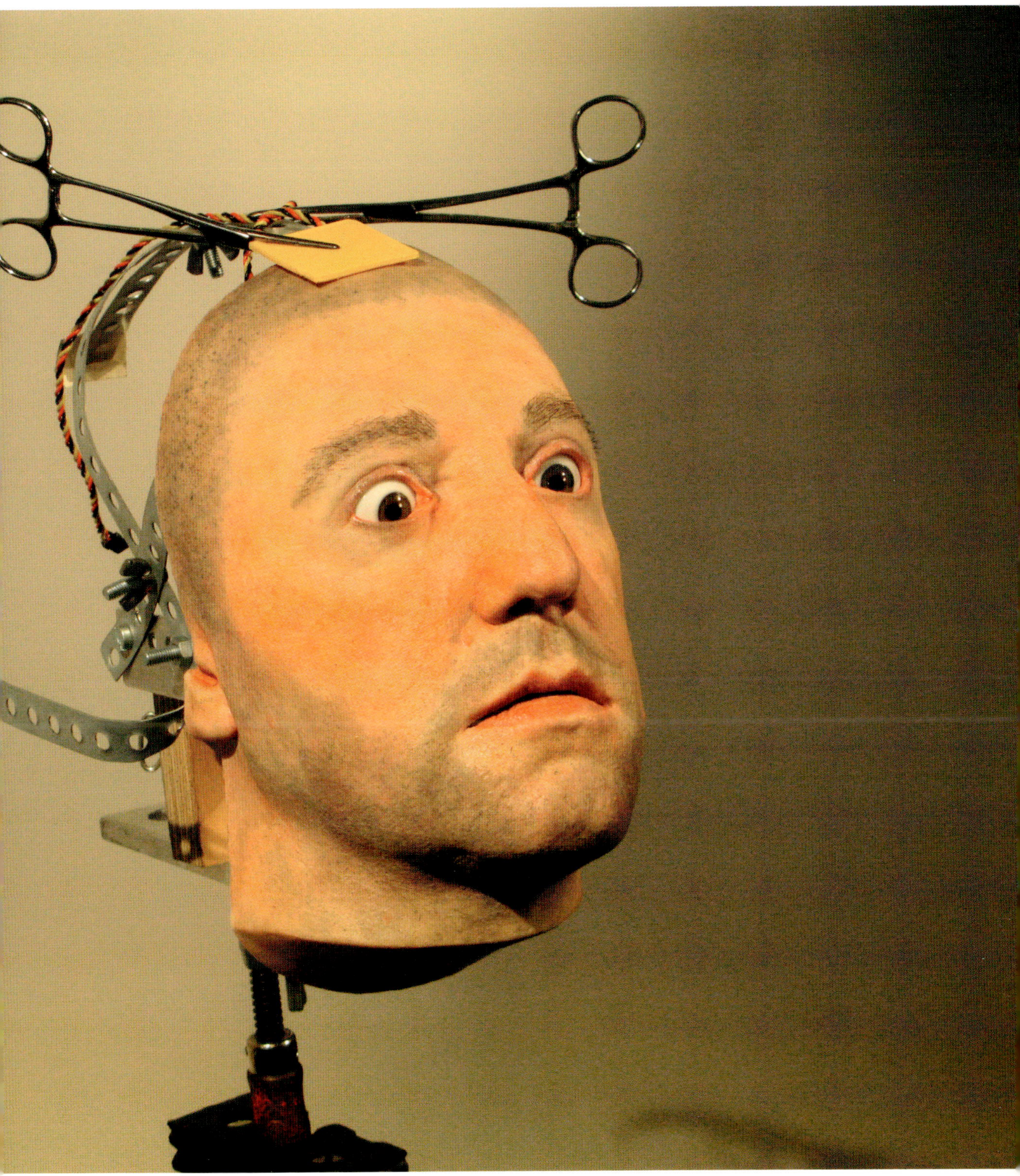

Gustav
METZGER

THE SPACE THAT surrounds disintegrating or growing art is as important as the visible material. The peeling or expanding fragments of matter carve, burn or tear their way through the adjacent space. There occur chemical-electrical interactions, fusions, explosions, implosions – between the work and space. The artist seeks the most direct contact with advanced ideas and forms of life. Time reversal, anti-matter, exploding galaxies. Annihilation of men through self-destructive mechanisms. Research into the creation of all forms of life. The art forms are a form of *realism*.

Art is a carrier of information. It is necessary to constantly invent new arts forms to carry the available information – expanding at an exponential rate. It is through a maximum use of random forms and motions that art can begin to convey available information. The random in art is also a powerful catalyst in social change.

We need to initiate the most comprehensive analysis ever undertaken on the history and pre-history of man. We must unravel step by step, over a period of 100,000 years, the manner in which mental and physical activity has related with social activity and scientific and technical invention.

From 'Auto Destructive Art', in Granta, *Cambridge, 6 November 1965*

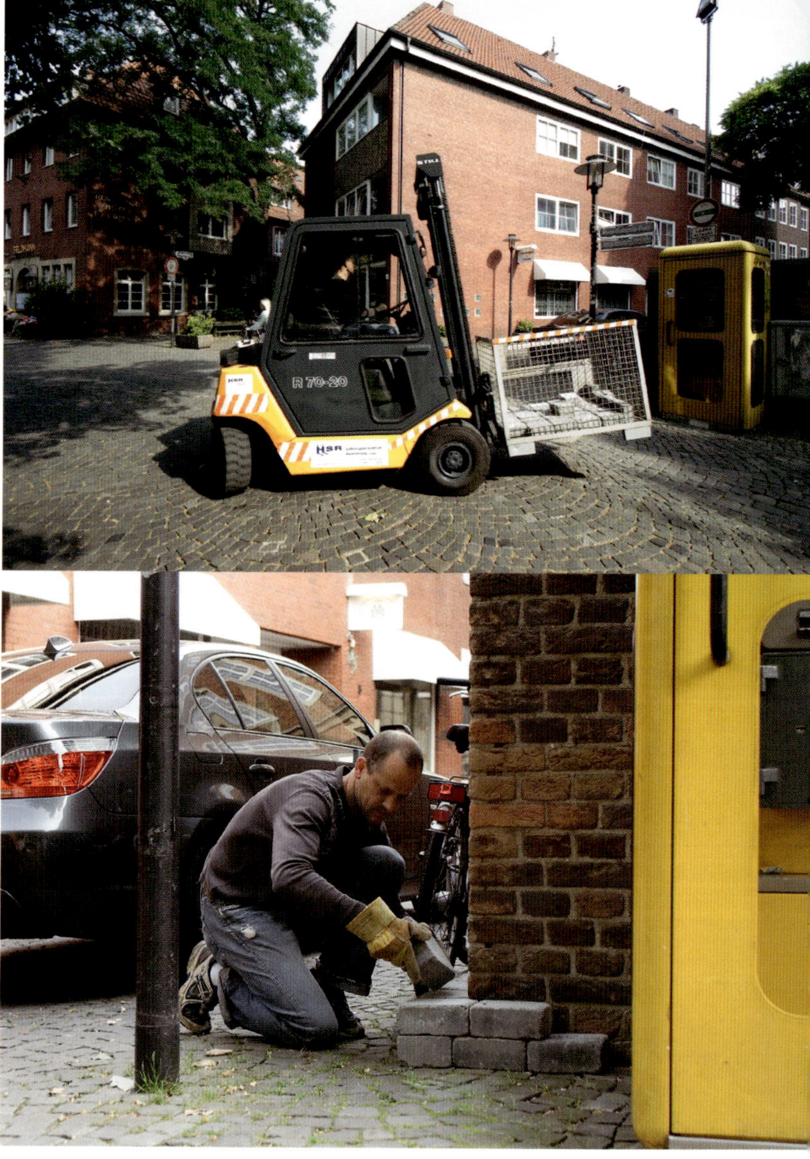

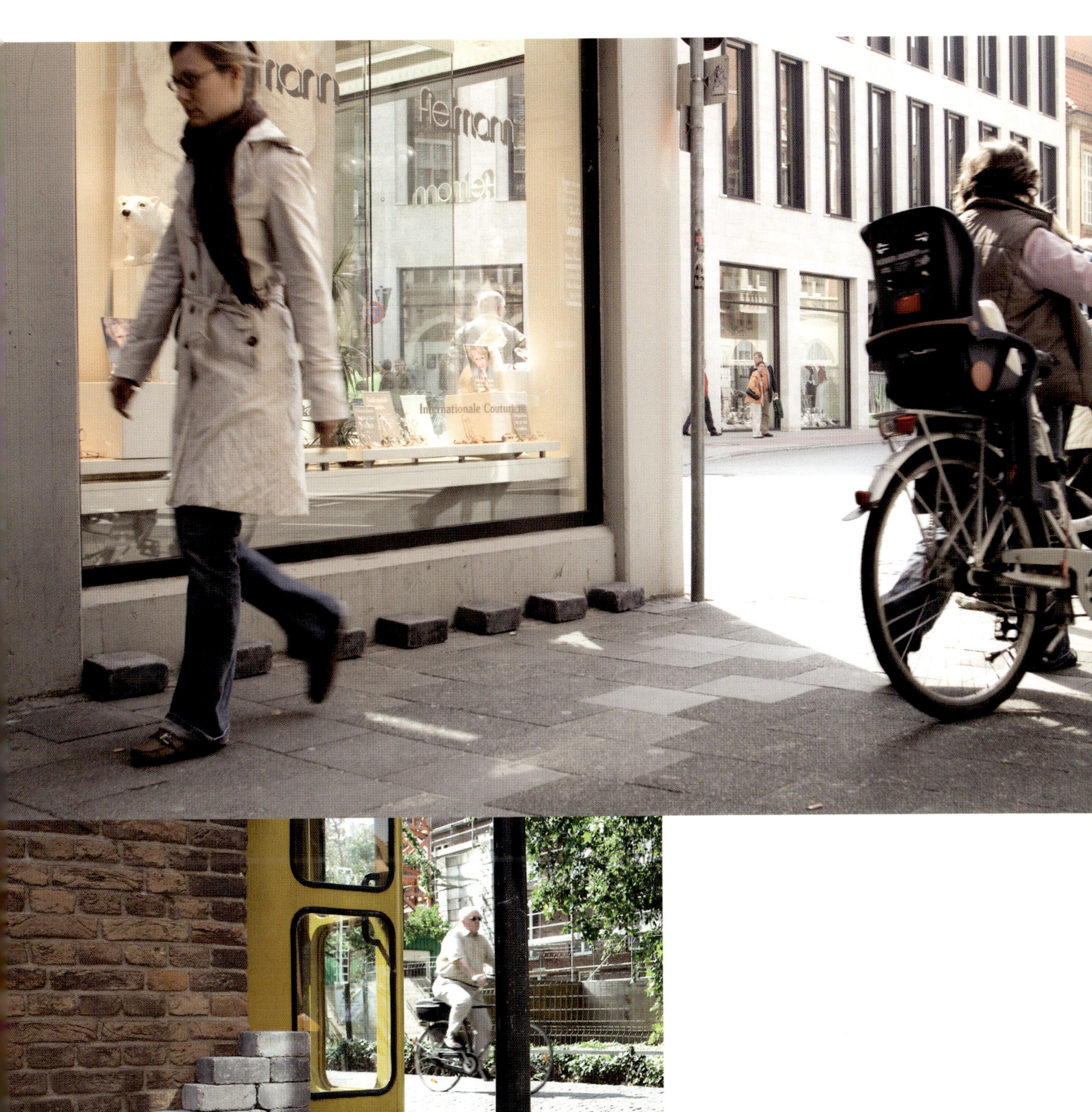

GUSTAV METZGER — [OPPOSITE AND BOTTOM RIGHT] ***Shattered Stones, Maria-Euthymia-Platz 22.07.2007***
[TOP RIGHT] ***Shattered Stones, Rothenburg/Geisburgweg 30.07.2007***, Münster Sculpture Project 2007

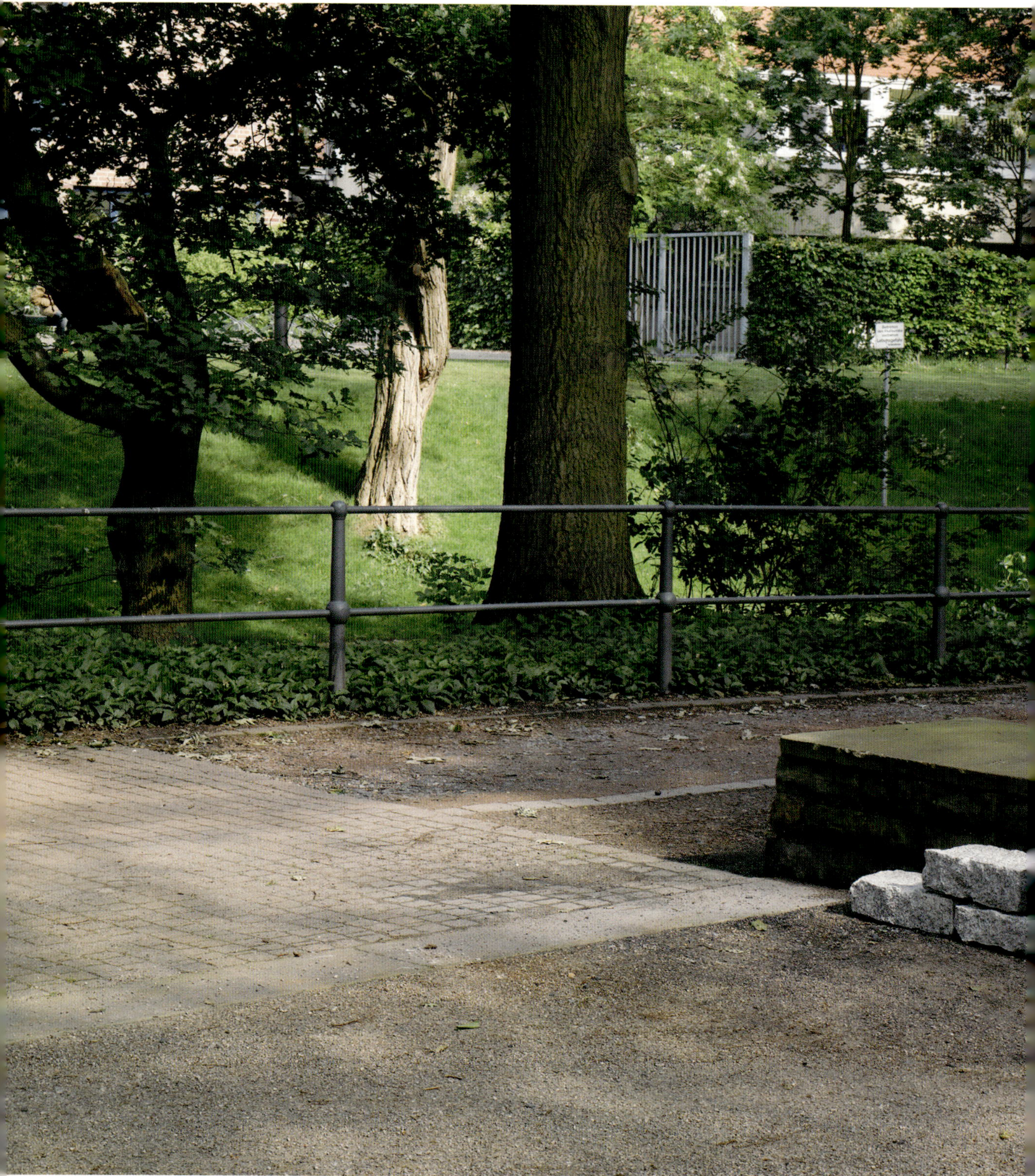

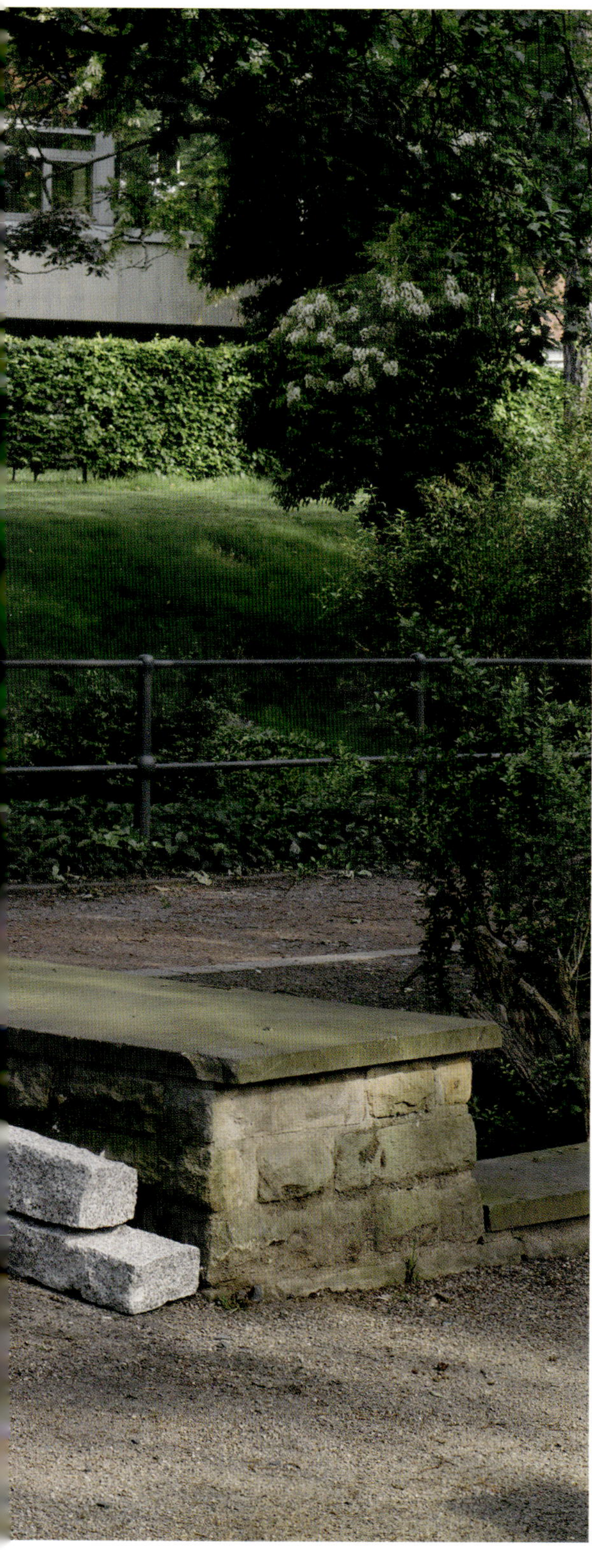

GUSTAV METZGER — *Shattered Stones, Aa/Mauer 22.09.2007*, Münster Sculpture Project 2007

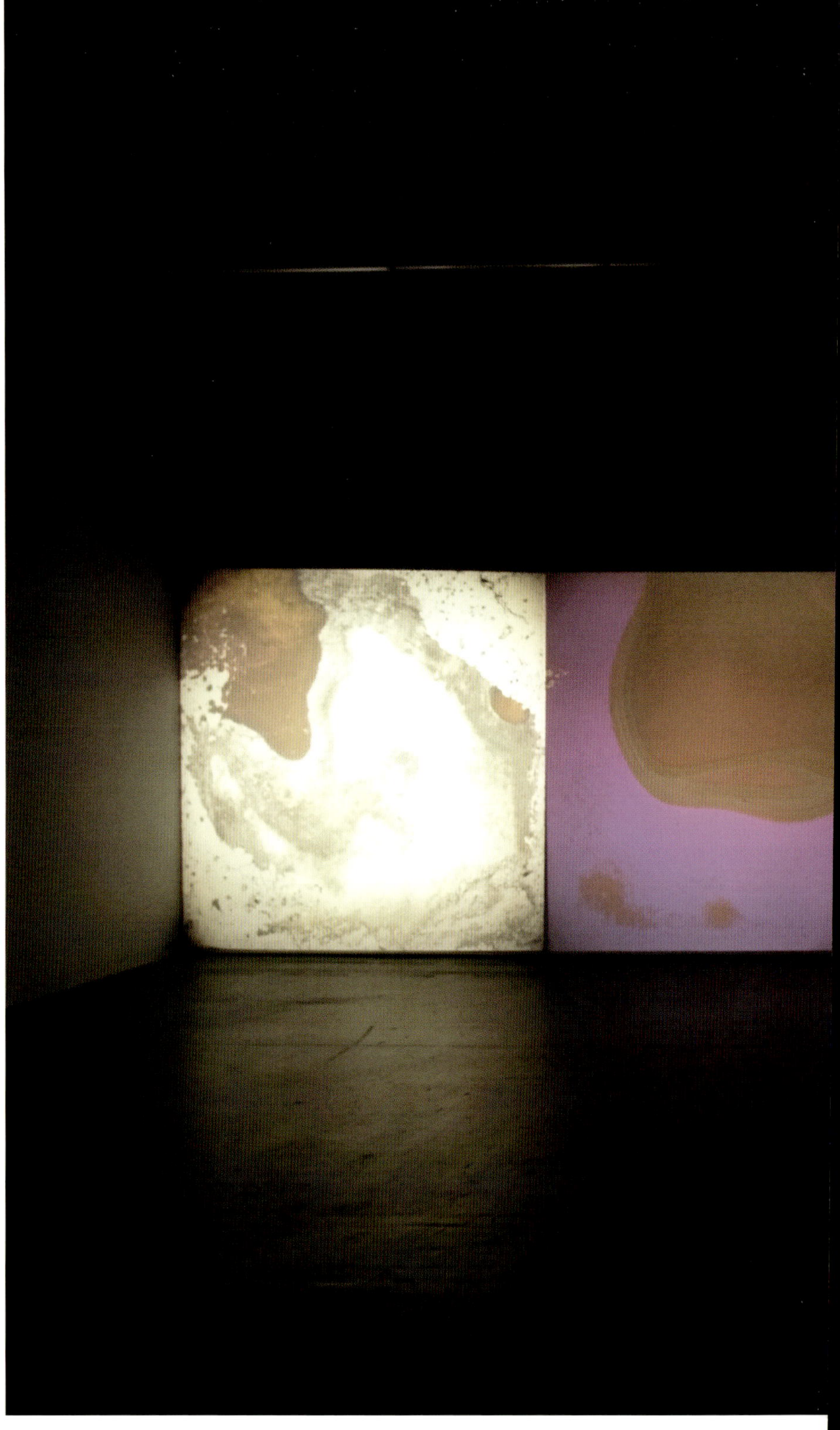

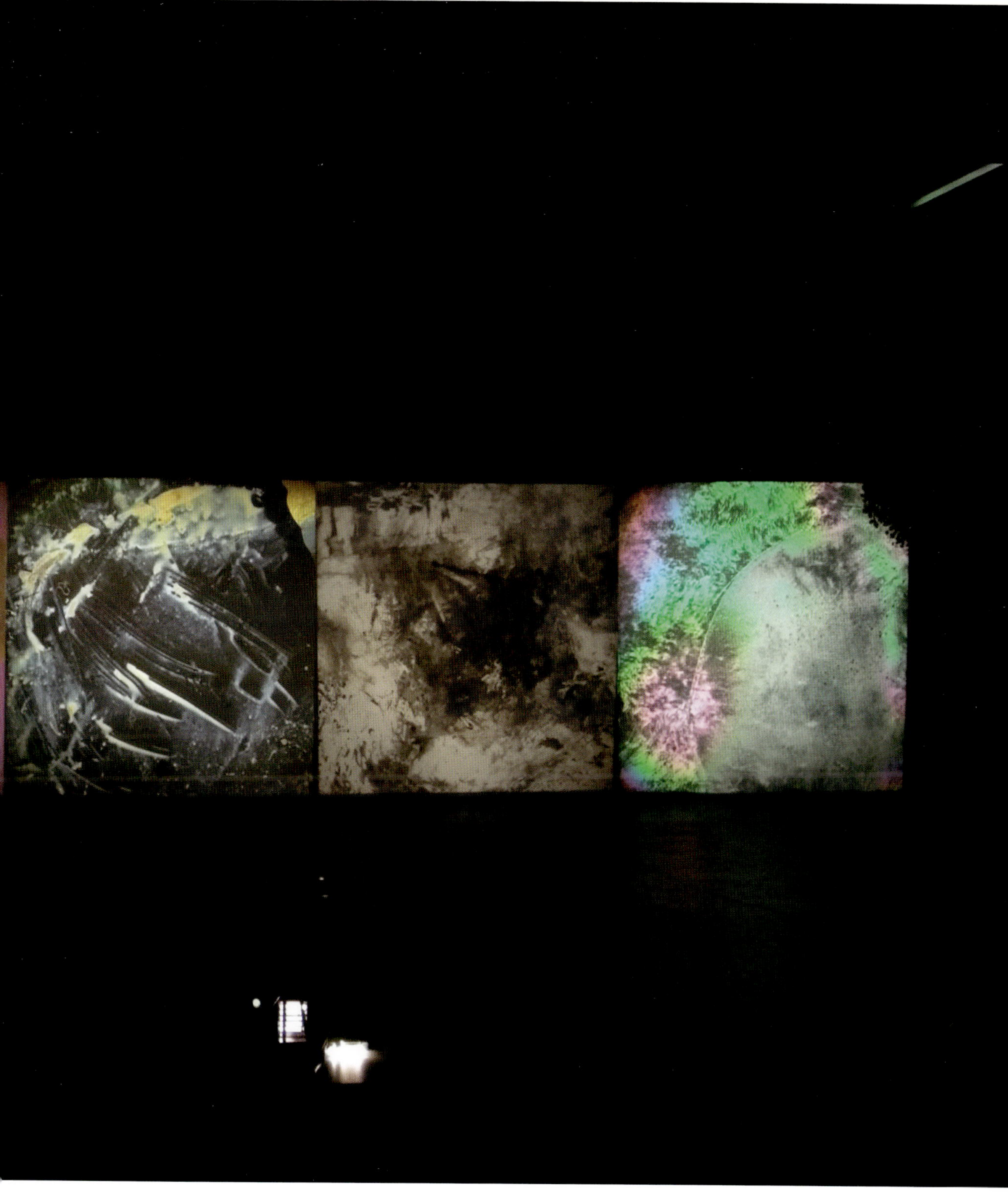

GUSTAV METZGER – *Liquid Crystal Environment*, 5 slide projectors, liquid crystals, glass slides, mechanical control, dimensions variable, installation at Sammlung migros museum für gegenwartskunst, 1998, permanent loan by the artist

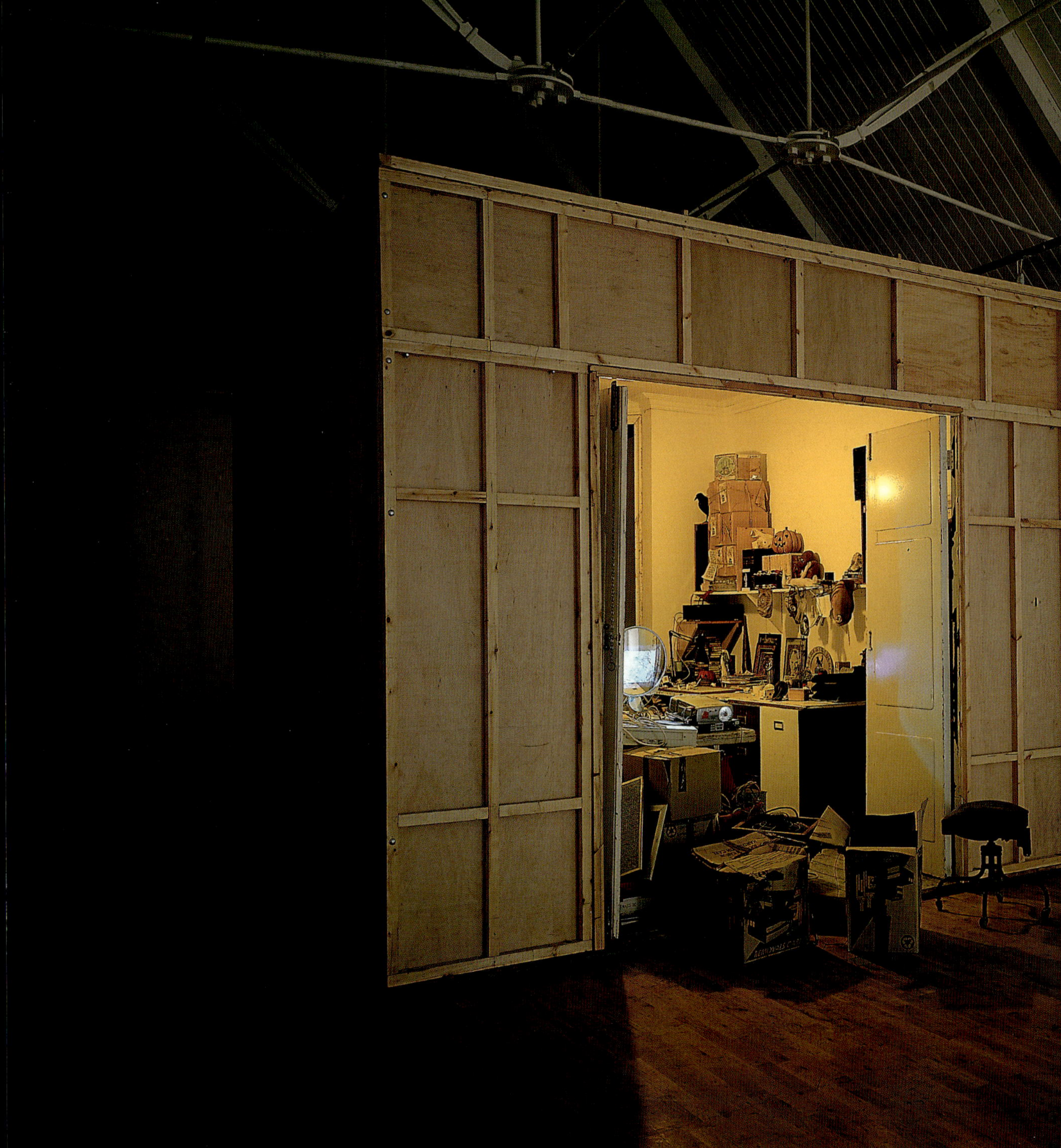

MIKE NELSON — *The projection room (Triple Bluff Canyon)*, 2004, originally commissioned by Modern Art Oxford, courtesy the artist, Franco Noero Gallery, Turin, Matt's Gallery, London and 303 Gallery, New York

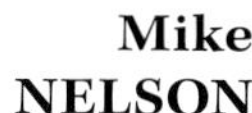

Mike NELSON

PATRICIA BICKERS Triple Bluff Canyon *works very differently from the installations that preceded it. As in* The Deliverance *and* The Patience, *you have chosen to reveal the artifice behind some of its construction, but in this case, the characteristic 'transit space' of the foyer only leads us back into the gallery. Instead of the immersive experience of earlier work, there are three separate but connected elements.*

MIKE NELSON Yes, it kind of forces you to stay outside it. This piece came on the back of Magazin; *Buyuk Valide Han* for the Istanbul Biennale and *The Pumpkin Palace* for Capp St Projects in San Francisco. In a way I was very aware that I'd not shown in Britain since 2001, so there would be certain expectations. Also I was working within the constraints of a museum – although they were very generous with time, I was given six weeks to construct the piece. My original idea for the piece was to build a multiplex cinema featuring the foyer downstairs but with locked doors. You'd then have to turn back and work you way up the staircase to the back of the cinema where you would have found all these theatres, projection rooms and receptions, each with their own identities and narratives going on. There would also have been a sequence of films running so that in a sense it would have been a narrative or journey with a jump cut of space aggravated by a jump cut of film, so there would have been a doubling of the narrative. I would still like to build this cinema one day and people will enter the foyer and perhaps experience a sense of déjà vu. In the present installation the foyer functions almost like a trailer, intended to build up the suspense, the sense of expectation, yet you step outside it into the empty space of the gallery, and I am sure that after raising so much expectation a lot of people were disappointed. I will build sequential rooms again one day, but it is nice to stop that in its tracks just now.

PATRICIA BICKERS *The identification of the artist with the obsessive is perhaps not so surprising when the installation includes Jordan Maxwell's 'Basic Slide Presentation' demonstrating his paranoid vision of the world 'bounced off and distorted through a convex mirror', as you put it, and projected on to the gallery wall.*

MIKE NELSON For me *Triple Bluff Canyon* came about partly through an interest in magic, and alchemy that I have referred to in other works. The studio desk and shelf, for instance, had earlier been replicated in 1998 for a piece entitled *The Black Art Barbecue, San Antonio, August 1961*, based on Dürer's *St Jerome in his Study*. The idea of replacing the replica with the real complemented the cyclical structure of the Robert Smithson rebuild and the Brian Aldiss short story that he wrote for the catalogue, and added to the alchemy that turned an earthwork into politicised icon, and finally into a re-politicised art work.

PATRICIA BICKERS *That represents another sense in which* Triple Bluff Canyon *is a departure in that is directly references the work of another artist.*

MIKE NELSON The reference to Smithson was not meant to be a homage. Although I knew of *Partially Buried Woodshed*, which he made for Kent State University, Ohio, in 1970, I'd never fixated upon it till I found a copy of the 1978 *Arts Magazine* special Smithson issue, with a photo of the work on the cover, in a pile of magazines I bought for £10.00. As an image on a magazine cover it somehow became more distanced, yet more tangible. I don't know if that sounds odd, but it almost became the reason, the most absurd and banal reason, to rebuild it. Also, I kept coming back to the final scenes in *Stalker*, and to *Roadside Picnic*, which has been a constant reference point in my work over the years. The strange, almost desert-like terrain kept coming back to me and that, combined with the references to magic, alchemy and geometry, especially in the form of the foyer, together with land art reference represented the three different trains of though that went into the building of the show. There are also references to the work of artists I'd been interested in as a student like Walter de Maria, most obviously to *Earth Room*, 1968, but also to the geometry of pieces such as *Broken Kilometer*, 1979. These, combined with J.G. Ballard's The Crystal World, a seminal text for Smithson, with its shifting planes of perception in the fractured crystalline forms of the jewelled jungle, underpinned the idea re-articulating *Partially Buried Woodshed.*

Extract from an interview first published in Art Monthly, *no.278, July – August 2004*

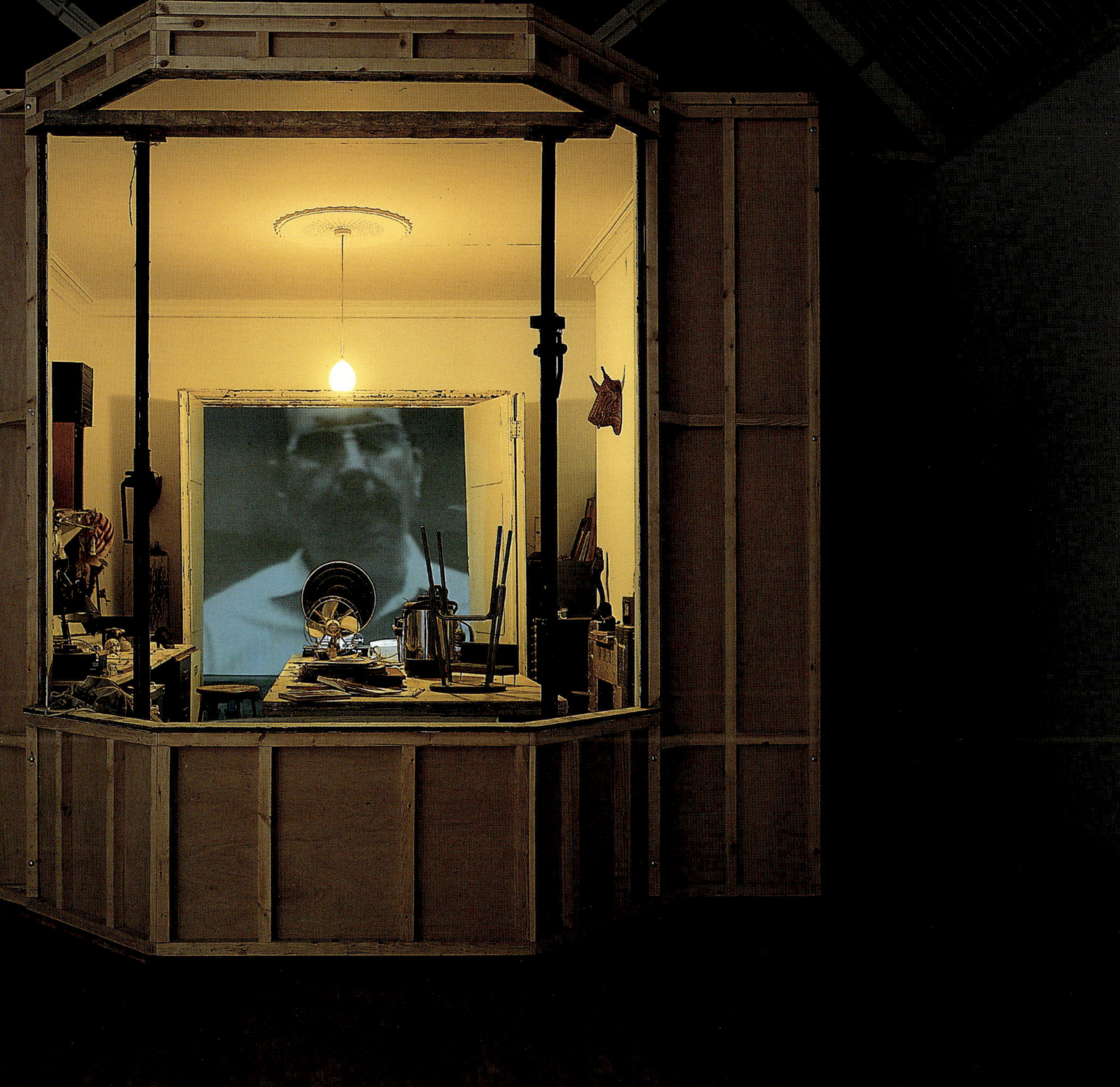

MIKE NELSON — *The projection room (Triple Bluff Canyon)*, 2004, originally commissioned by Modern Art Oxford, courtesy the artist, Franco Noero Gallery, Turin, Matt's Gallery, London and 303 Gallery, New York

David NOONAN

EVERY PIECE is different. I look for images from various sources. It can be a very random process but I look for images with potential – an image that may activate another image.

I have an archive that I have been gathering for years that I draw upon; I think of it as a kind of library of possibilities.

When I make images they are almost always a combination of two elements, for instance a figurative and an abstract element. Combining them is an intuitive process. To me the provenance of the images is not important; it is the new relationship formed between them that matters. The meanings of my images and sculptures are fluid and often ambiguous; I do not believe that my work should necessarily follow a linguistic logic.

I relate to the idea that 'the form of the work expresses a course, a wandering, rather than a fixed-space time'. I think of the content of my work as time travel to some extent, taking things from different eras and bringing them together to form new temporal scenarios.

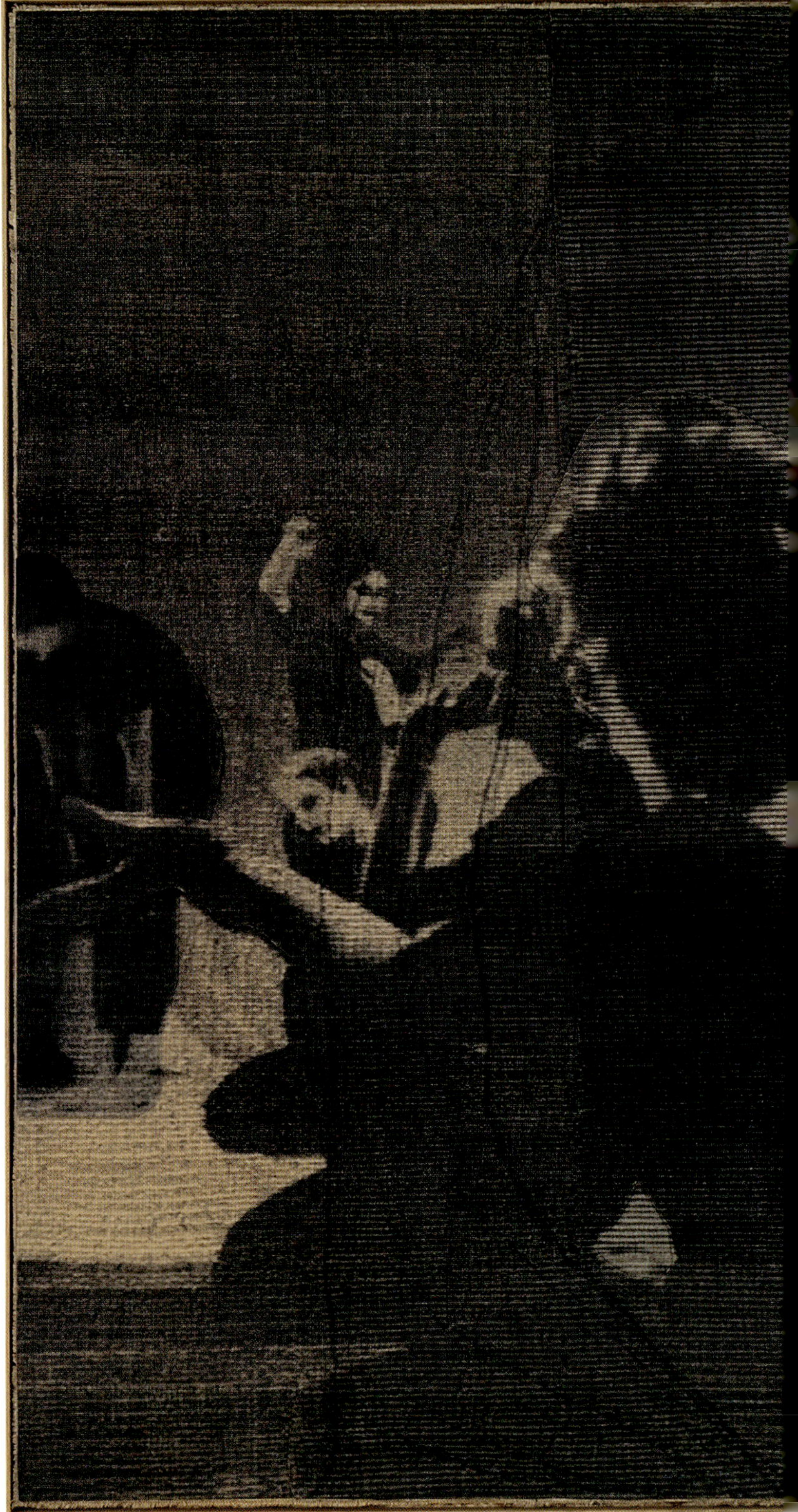

DAVID NOONAN – *Untitled,* 2008, silkscreen on jute and lined collage, 210 × 300, courtesy HOTEL, London

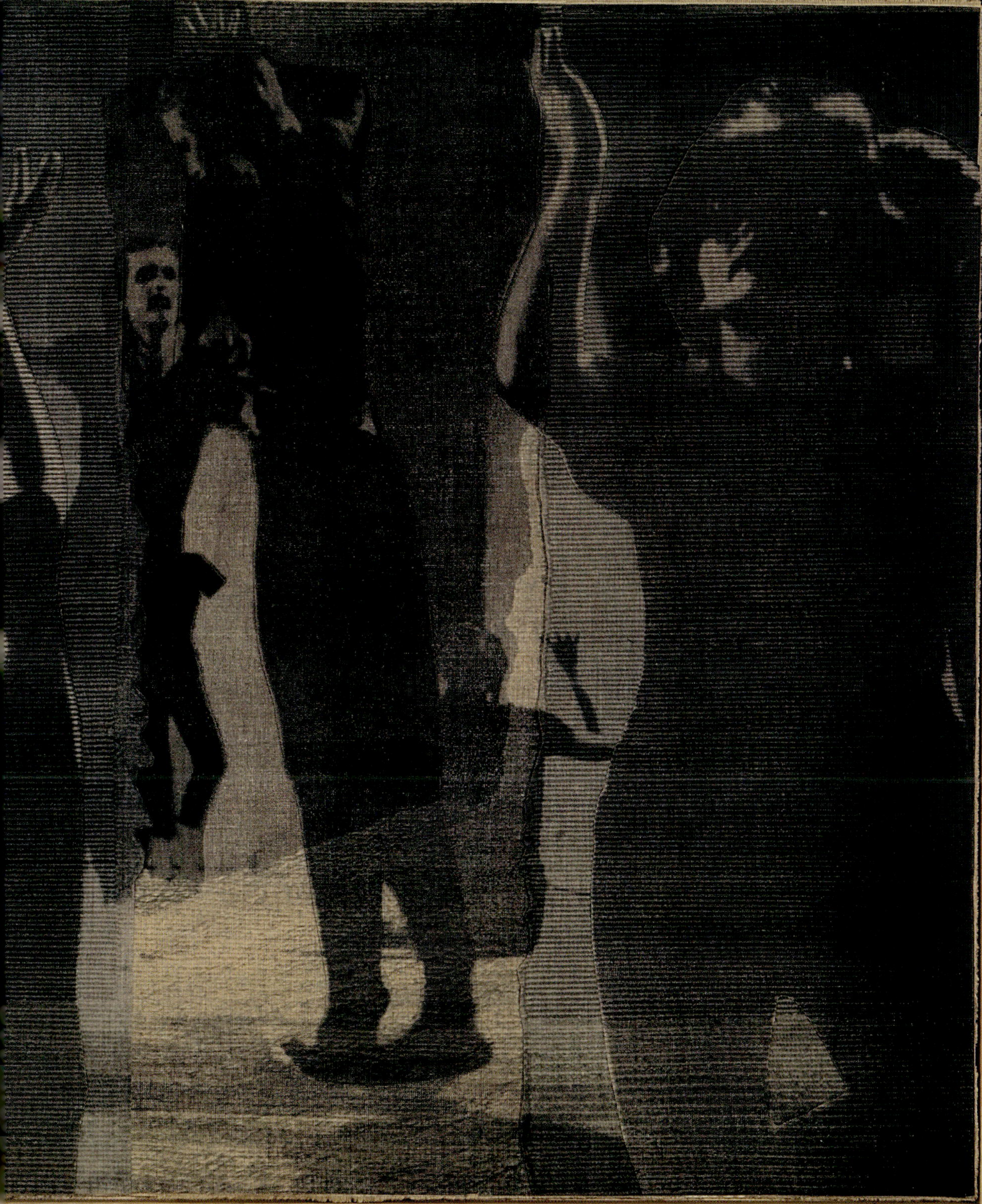

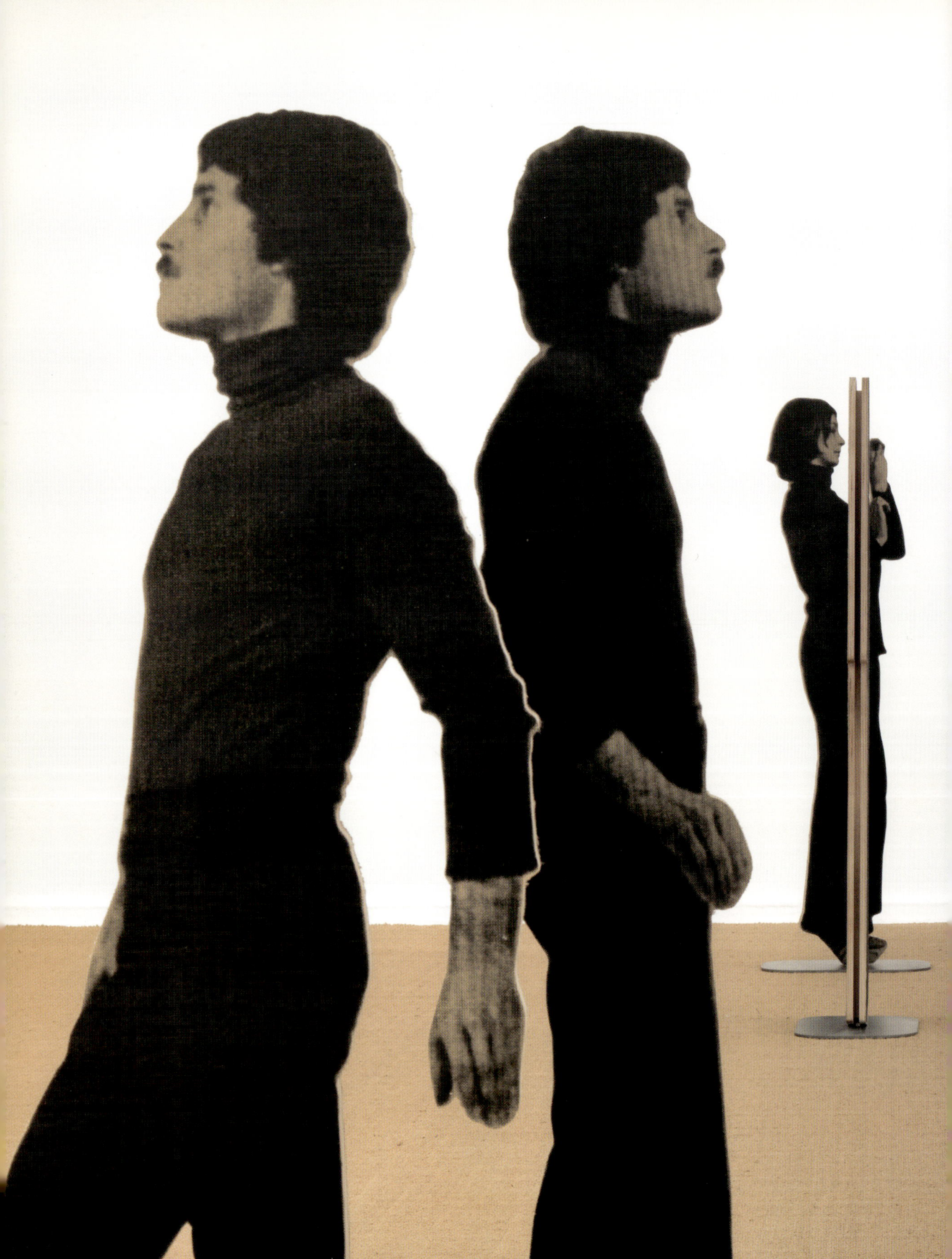

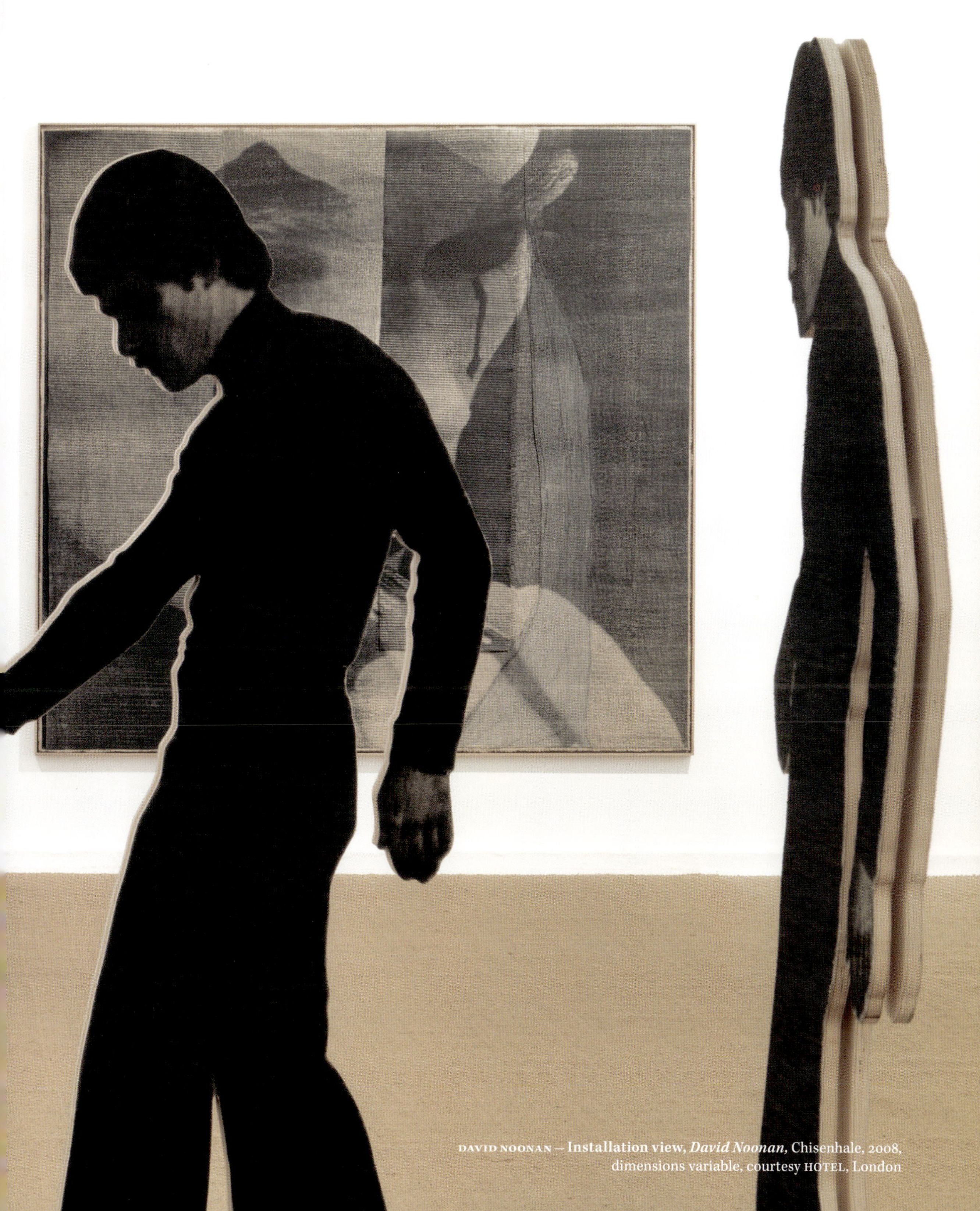

DAVID NOONAN — **Installation view, *David Noonan*,** Chisenhale, 2008, dimensions variable, courtesy HOTEL, London

Katie
PATERSON

IT SEEMS THAT over time all the energy of the big bang is being converted into mass by E=mc2 – first forming particles, then atoms, stars, planets, life – and overall the entropy of the universe continues to increase. If the universe keeps expanding then the entropy will just increase and everything will slowly die and there will be no free energy left. (Isaac Asimov wrote a short story about that.) But maybe it will collapse, and in effect all the black holes will merge together into one massive black hole, and explode again into a new Big Bang? Sometimes I think of life as the localised reversal of entropy. When we grow we make matter more organised, but of course that is at the expense of increasing the entropy of other matter: the food we eat being converted into something less... pretty, you could say, haha. Well, enough rambling.

Email to Paterson from Alex Gibbs, Astronomer, 16 September 2008

KATIE PATERSON — ***All the Dead Stars,*** **2009,** etched metal, 200 × 300, courtesy the artist and Albion, London

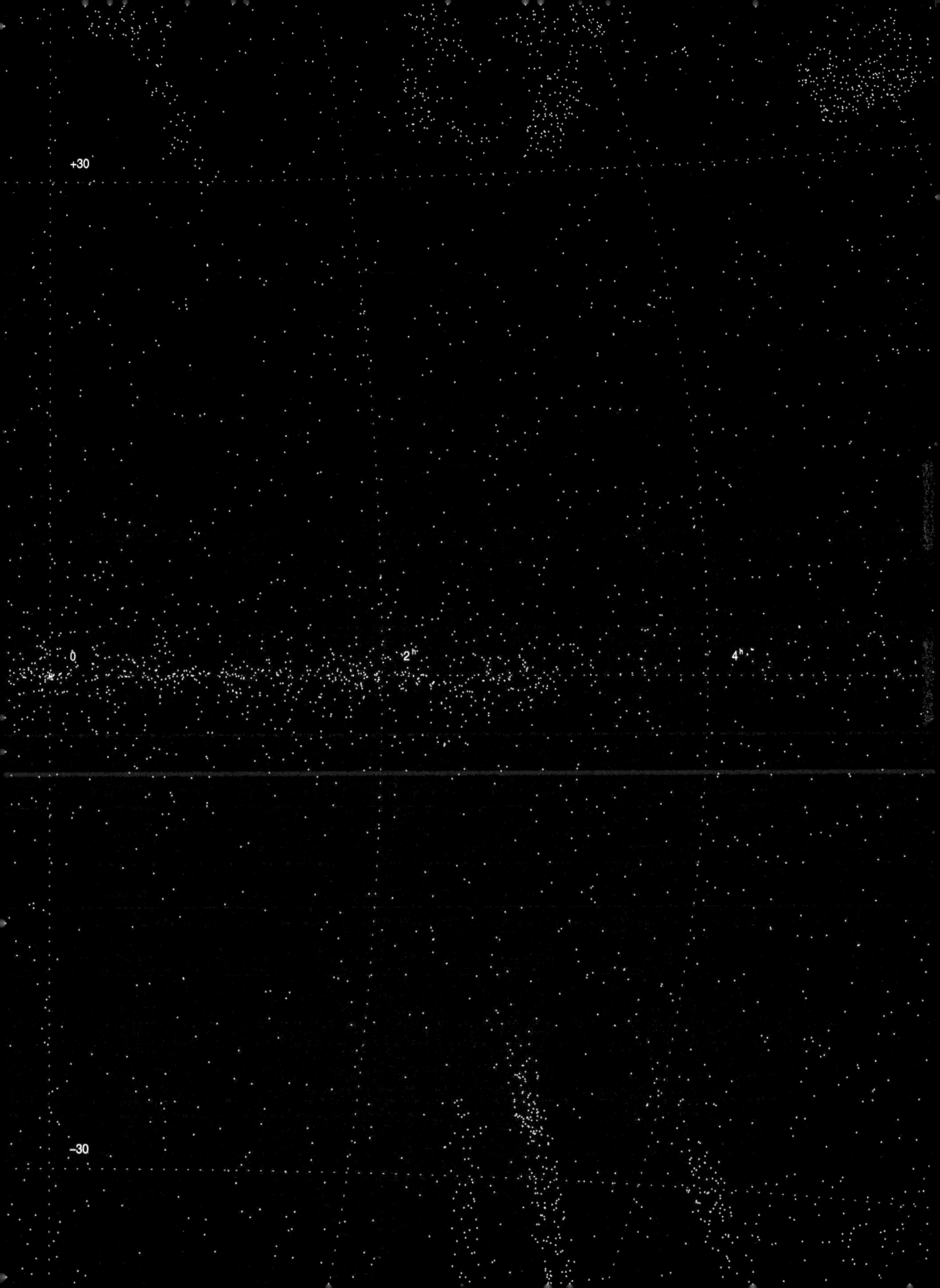

+30

0

2^h

4^h

−30

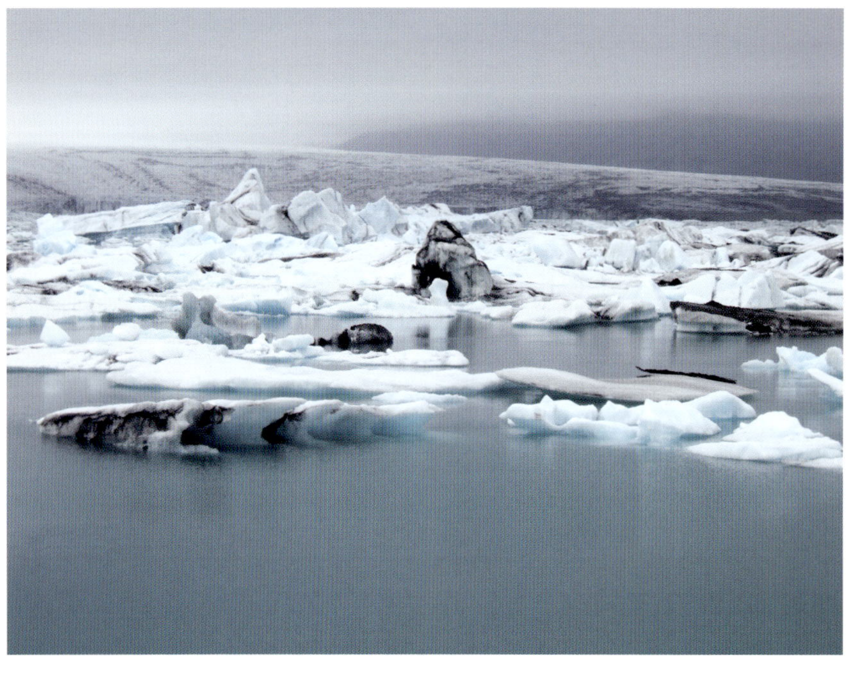

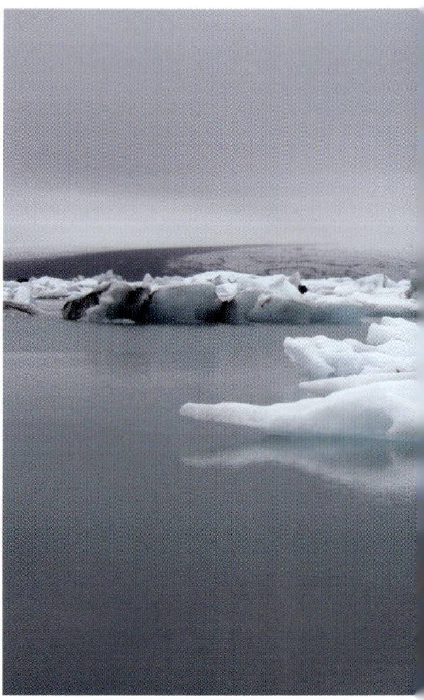

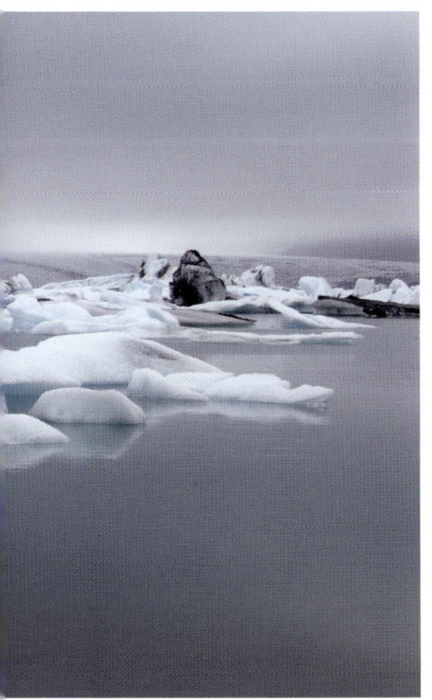

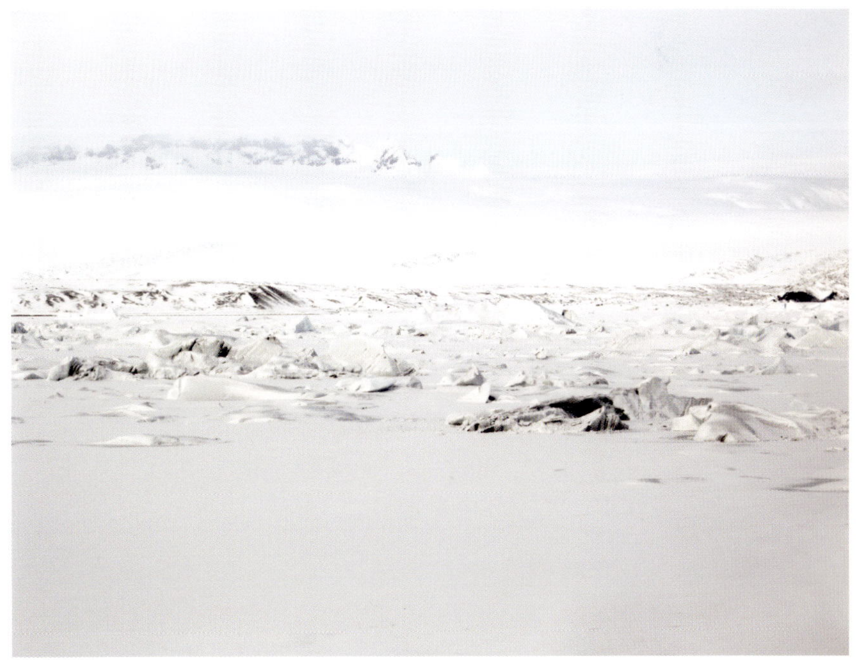

KATIE PATERSON — *Vatnajökull (the sound of)*, 2007/8, hydrophone, mobile phone, DE500, courtesy the artist and Albion, London

Olivia PLENDER

MACHINE Shall be the Slave of Man, But We Will Not Slave for the Machine is based on my research into the Kibbo Kift Kindred, a British youth movement established in the 1920s by artist and novelist John Hargrave that lasted up until the 1950s. The installation functions like an authoritative historical museum display, complete with diorama and reconstructions of the Kibbo Kift's costumes and banners, alongside a narrative video. Titled *Bring Back Robin Hood* and written as a travel log of sorts, the video details my search for material relating to the Kibbo Kift Kindred, including attempts to access archives and contact former members and academic historians, each of whom perpetuate a different view of this movement. Originally part of the Boy Scouts, the Kibbo Kift split from Baden Powell's conservative organisation in order to establish a socialist youth movement, in collaboration with veterans of the Campaign for Women's Suffrage and the Co-operative Movement. They were initially involved with such emancipatory causes as clothes reform, pacifism, vegetarianism and the democratisation of the arts, but following a second split (from the Co-operators), Hargrave established himself as a charismatic leader, and camping was elevated to a ritualised spiritual activity.

As a response to the economic crisis of 1931 Kibbo Kift became the Green Shirt Movement for Social Credit, a uniformed group who marched through the streets of London advocating a now discredited monetary reform theory. Parallels can be drawn with the German *Lebensreform* movement, and in part the video considers the

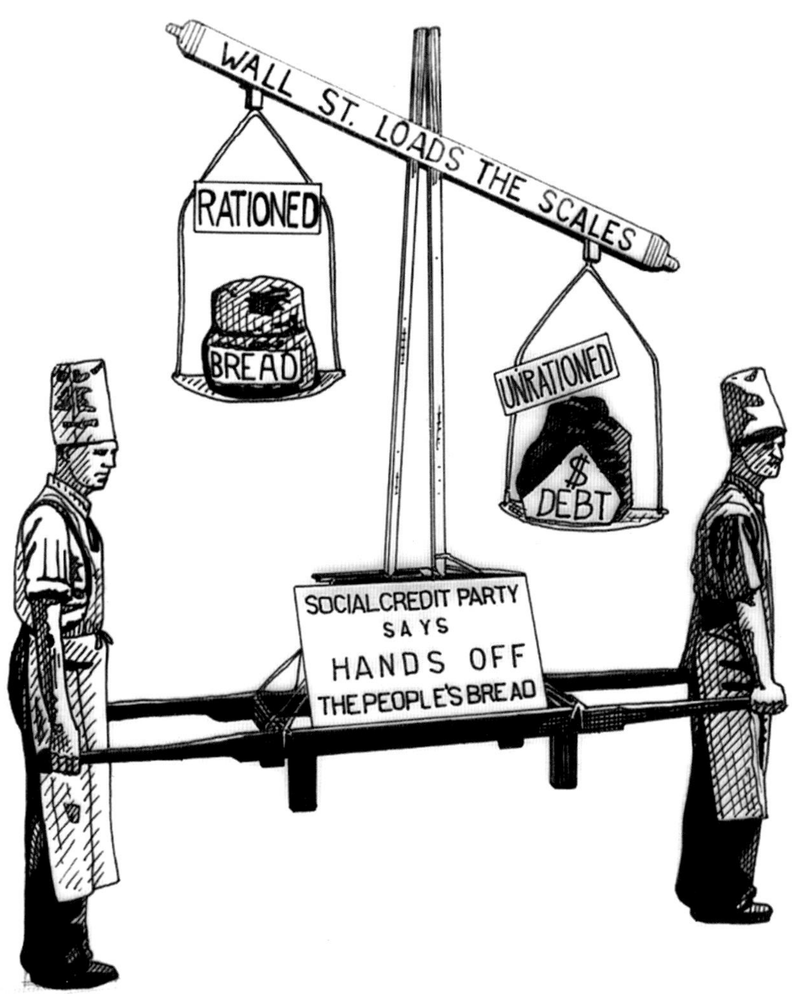

OLIVIA PLENDER — Video stills from *Bring Back Robin Hood: Notes on an Imagined Community*, **2008**, courtesy the artist

recurring dream of returning to a pre-industrial golden age: a romantic and potentially nationalistic idealisation of the past, especially in the face of economic and social crisis, which is personified by figures like Robin Hood. As the circular story weaves back and forth in time the Kibbo Kift are situated in relation to parallel texts both personal and historical: observations on life in London since the beginning of the current global economic crisis, a trip to Argentina in the period after that countries economic collapse in 2001, the rise of nationalism and neo-colonialism in the nineteenth century and the origins of the current financial system in the period after the British revolution. As a tale with no beginning, middle or end, the story mirrors the narrative pattern of events since the start of the modern period, the features of our financial system such as the recurrence of economic crisis, (neo) colonialism and the attendant dangers such as the rise of nationalism. By using a first person mode of address, in direct contrast with the academic didactic mode of presentation used within the traditional lecture format or museum display, I put the veracity of the information (historical or otherwise) presented in question, as a subjective voice telling a history lacks authority. This is part of a wider body of work in which I question both the ideological framework around the narration of history and the legitimacy of knowledge produced within an academic context versus 'illegitimate' knowledge, often produced within a religious framework by amateurs and auto-didacts.

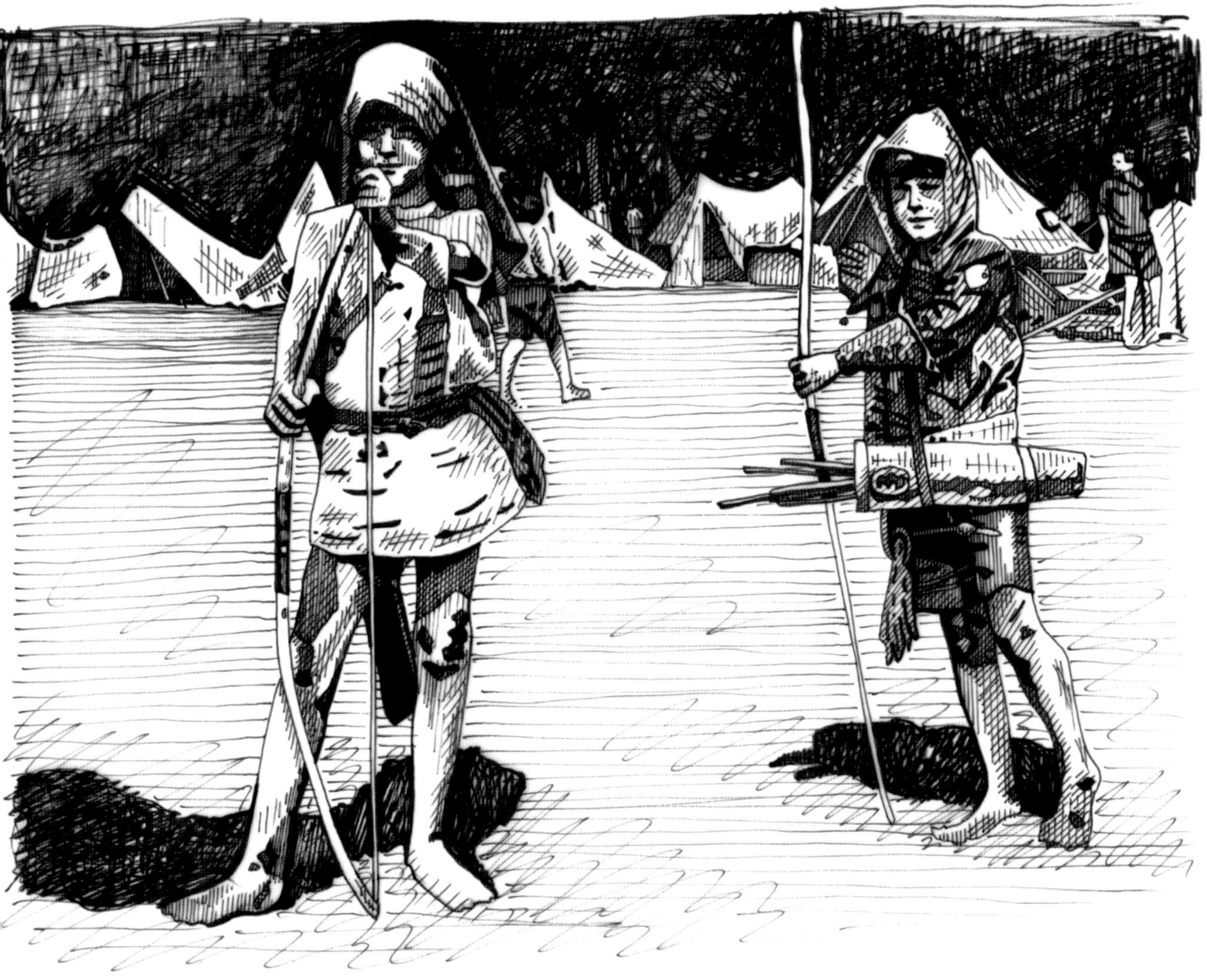

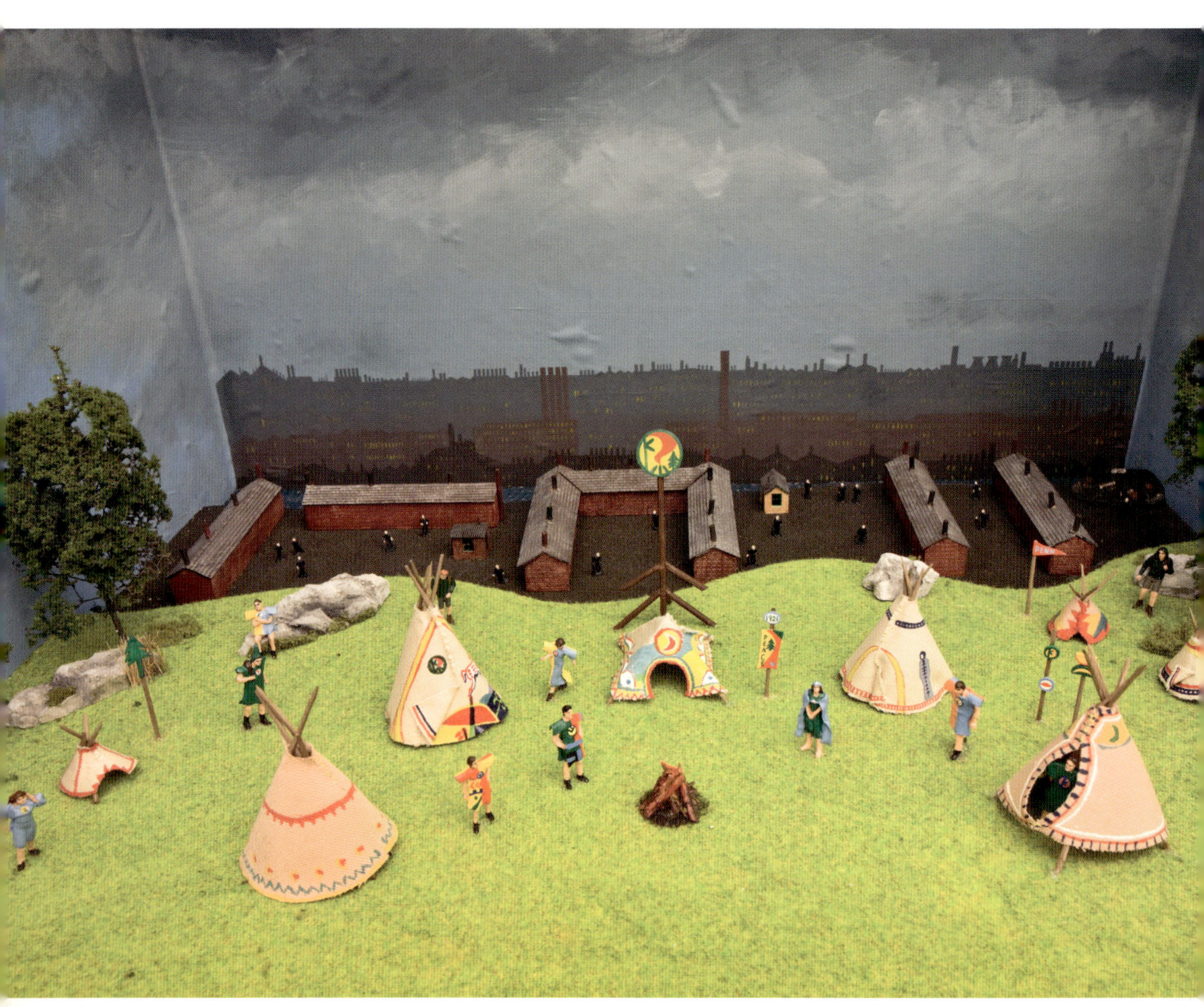

OLIVIA PLENDER — [LEFT] ***Machine Shall be the Slave of Man, but We Will Not Slave for the Machine,* 2005–8**, mixed media, dimensions variable, from the exhibition ***The Great Transformation: Art and Tactical Magic,*** Frankfurter Kunstverein, 2008. [RIGHT] ***Machine Shall be the Slave of Man, but We Will Not Slave for the Machine,* 2005–8**, view of the installation at MARCO, Museo de Arte Contemporánea de Vigo, 2008

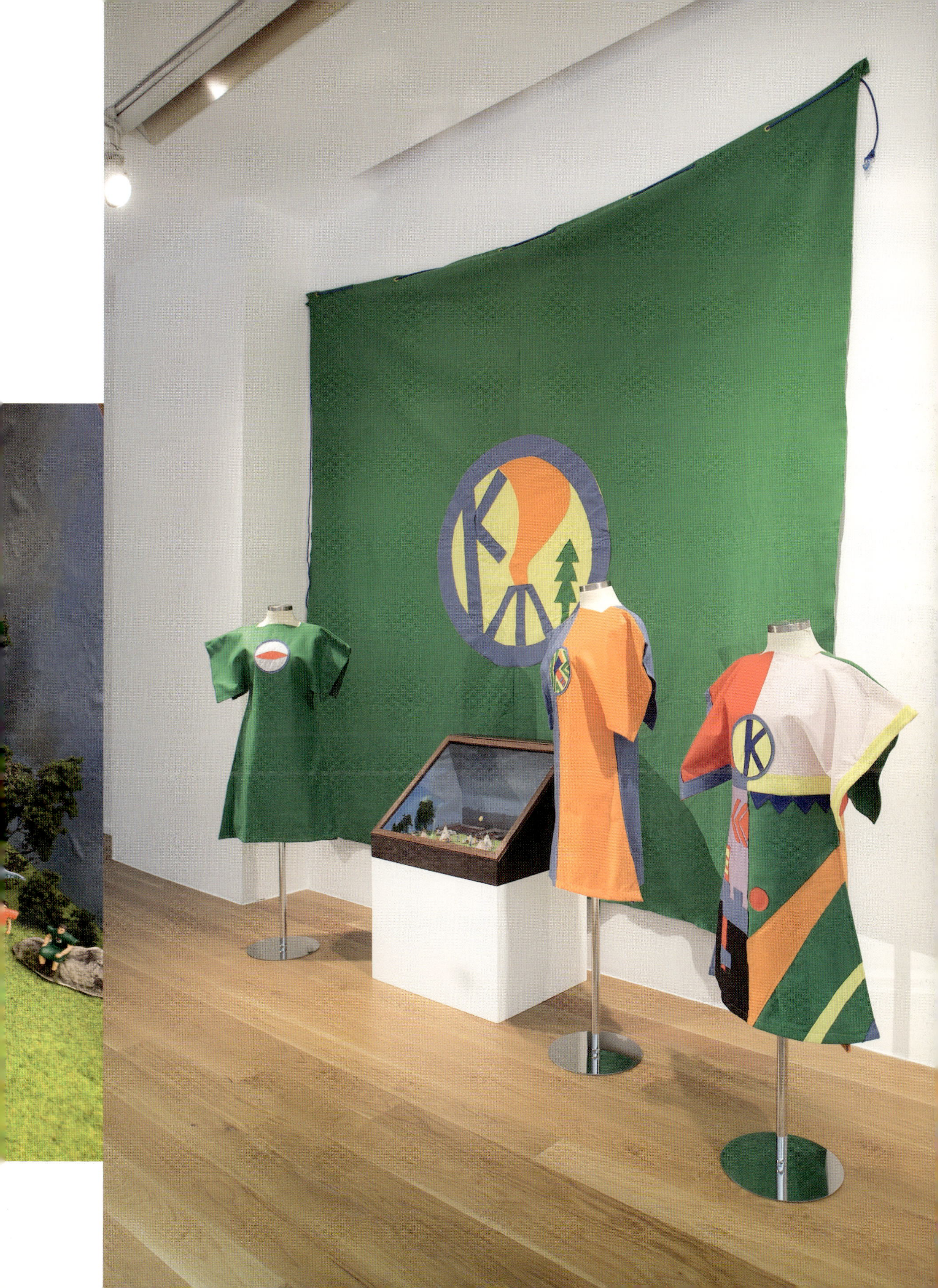

The INTERNATIONAL NECRONAUTICAL SOCIETY, GENERAL IDEA, J.J. CHARLESWORTH, T.J. DEMOS, Matthew DARBYSHIRE, Tom MORTON, Bob & Roberta SMITH

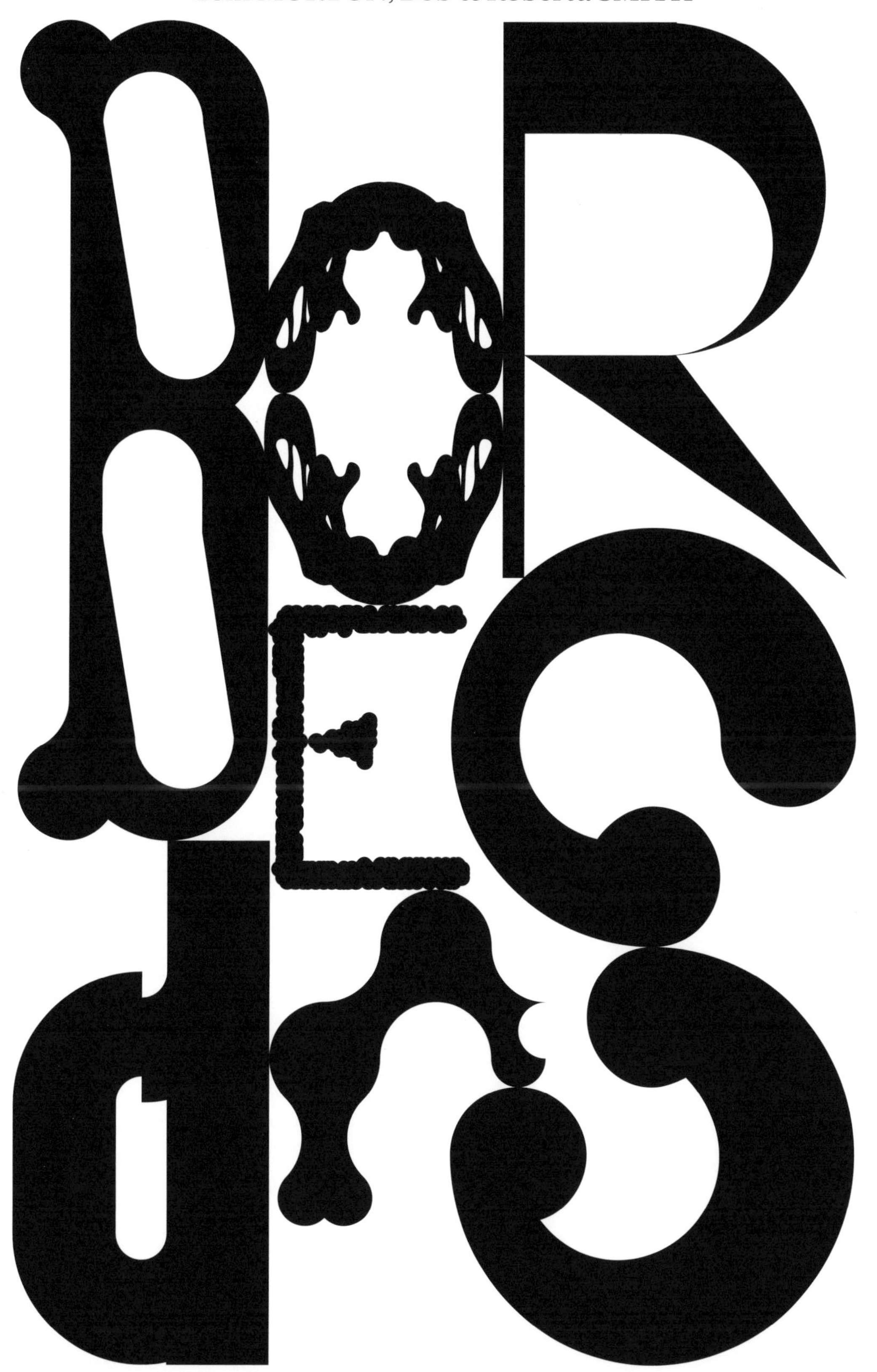

BORDERS

Twenty-first-century culture has become an archipelago: no longer an entire continent, but islands of thoughts and forms; no longer a totality but separated fragments connected by unusual circuits. The fourth Prologue, Borders, centred around the idea that the artist is now a traveller who constantly trespasses the ancient borders existing between disciplines and formats. Passing from one linguistic system to another, decoding and recoding: cornerstones of an emerging altermodernity.

SATURDAY 17 JANUARY 2009
TATE BRITAIN

12:30
AUDITORIUM
GENERAL IDEA
Pilot 1997
Test Tube 1979
Cornucopia 1982
Loco 1982
Shut the Fuck Up 1992

14:30
AUDITORIUM
INTERNATIONAL NECRONAUTICAL SOCIETY
Tate Declaration on Inauthenticity

16:30
AUDITORIUM
J.J. CHARLESWORTH, MATTHEW DARBYSHIRE, T.J. DEMOS, TOM MORTON, BOB & ROBERTA SMITH
Round Table Discussion: Borders

INTERNATIONAL NECRONAUTICAL SOCIETY
TATE DECLARATION OF INAUTHENTICITY

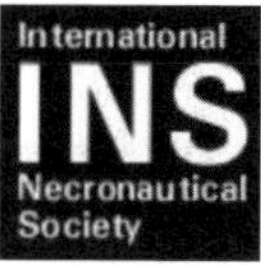

http://www.necronauts.org

Official Document

Title:	Tate Declaration on Inauthenticity
Type:	INS Declaration
Authorised:	First Committee, INS
Authorisation Code:	TMcC290907

Document follows

The Tate Declaration: INS Statement on Inauthenticity

Delivered by INS Chief Philosopher Simon Critchley and INS General Secretary Tom McCarthy at Tate Britain, London, 17th January 2009.

We start by thanking Tate Triennial curator Nicolas Bourriaud – firstly for his provision of a platform for the delivery of this joint statement on inauthenticity for the first time in the UK; and, equally importantly, for placing at our disposal this piece of conceptual hardware, 'the altermodern'. As a notion, it resonates loudly with the INS's own concerns. As an organisation, we have always resisted the catchall term 'postmodernism' – and particularly when it is used to designate a historical or cultural period that follows 'modernism'. This is a misuse, plain and simple. Jean-François Lyotard himself, the term's first proponent, was at pains to point out that, far from naming an epoch, the postmodern describes a rupture and eruption within the modern, and an attitude of incredulity towards grand narratives, be these aesthetic, ideological or metaphysical. *This* definition we celebrate, while recognising that the nomenclature in which it originally came wrapped is beyond recycling.

But we want to go further, interrogating even the term 'modern'. For us, all forms of periodisation suck. We have no idea when modernity is meant to have started and no clue when it might end. Sometimes we think that maybe it never happened. And if the postmodern is defined in terms of incredulity towards meta-narratives, then when does that begin? In Aeschylus' *Agamemnon*? In Socrates' endless irony? In Paul's rejection of the Old Law? With Averroes' implicit separation of rationality from the authority of faith? With Copernicus' rejection of the Ptolemaic universe? This list could be extended. The point is that the possibilities are infinite. There has always been incredulity towards grand narratives and there have always been cracks in the historical stories any social group tells itself. What the INS is interested in are the breaks, fissures and shadows that the modern has always had within it; we are interested in the way that the modern has always, and very self-consciously, been devoted to failure, to its failure and the failure of any attempt to circumvent it in an idea of the postmodern. To put it in the outdated Heideggerese of the deconstruction business, the modern has always already been altermodern.

Bourriaud's altermodern chimes with the INS's own project further still. In his vision, the artist becomes a 'homo viator' who travels and transpasses, drawing lines in space and time, materialising trajectories. The words could be taken from the INS's own First Manifesto, which, behind the signifier 'death', envisaged space: a space of transit and transition, marks and traces, a provocation to cartography. Beneath the manifesto's talk of 'craft' laboured allusions not only to technologies and vehicles of transport – and, by extension, to technology itself – but also to 'craft' in its wider sense of practice, know-how, skill; and, through this, to the philosophical notion of *techné* as revealing or unfolding. The General Secretary's First Report to the First Committee, *Navigation Was Always a Difficult Art* (delivered in the Map Room of the Royal Geographical Society in London in 2001), took as its symbolic protagonist the figure of Melville's Queequeg: epitome of homo viator, a displaced third-world labourer endlessly transported along the vectors of the global enterprise of whaling. The vehicle on which he finds himself, the Pequod, is given over to a grand project: Captain Ahab's revenge. But Queequeg has his own *petit projet* that mimics and unsettles this one. Readers of *Moby Dick* among you will recall that the tattooed Polynesian harpoonist, fully expecting to die after contracting a fever, has the Pequod's skilled carpenter knock him up a coffin; when he unexpectedly recovers, he adorns the redundant coffin with the lines and traces covering his body, copying them from the living organic surface to the dead one. These tattoos, you might further recall, represent the layout of the earth and heavens, and the transit between these, according to Queequeg's people's belief, and thus form 'a mystical treatise on the art of attaining truth'. Yet, as they cover his whole body, Queequeg cannot see them, and so needs to copy them – that is, himself – onto another surface, projecting space in the manner of a cartographer.

For the INS, it is no coincidence that the surface he projects onto is that of death, or at least its synecdoche, the coffin: marker of a death imperfectly experienced, deferred. That Captain Ahab, watching the 'rude' Queequeg, shakes his fist at heaven is no less telling: Ahab, too, is projecting himself narcissistically towards the whale, hoping to etch himself out across its skin, to behold himself on that white screen as whole, complete, an avenging hero, even if – or perhaps because – that trajectory can only resolve itself at the point of death. Ahab thus embodies an eminently Western fantasy of subjectivity as heroic authenticity. For all its 'rude' primitiveness, Queequeg's little art project, in its futility, both mirrors and parodies Ahab's own, and that of Western man in general. This, ultimately, is what the Great American Novel has to tell us: space, in the end, will not lie flat and form a passive surface for our narcissism, our self-projections, the realisations of our grand and aggrandising narratives. A book that devotes so many of its pages to the sheer materiality of what lurks on the horizon and beneath the surface – their fat, sperm, bones, bile, livers and so on – can only have one winner. The whale's materiality, its excessive weight, shatters the Pequod, rendering all self-projections void – or, to put it another way, the screen becomes blubber.

Today, we want to advance a set of proposals, of numbered theses, that will state categorically – catechistically even – some core elements of INS doctrine. These statements, like all INS propaganda, should be repeated, modified, distorted and disseminated as the listener sees fit.

1. We begin with the experience of failed transcendence, a failure that is at the core of the General Secretary's novels and the Chief Philosopher's tomes. Being is not full transcendence, the plenitude of the One or cosmic abundance, but rather an ellipsis, an absence, an incomprehensibly vast lack scattered with debris and detritus. Philosophy as the thinking of Being has to begin from the experience of disappointment that is at once religious (God is dead, the One is gone), epistemic (we know very little, almost nothing; all knowledge claims have to begin from the experience of limitation) and political (blood is being spilt in the streets as though it were champagne).

2. For us, art is the consequence and experience of failed transcendence. We could even say, borrowing defunct religious terminology, that it produces icons of that failure. An icon is not an original, but a copy, the copy of another icon. Art is not about originality, but about the repetition of the copy. We'll be coming back to this point repeatedly.

3. In order to grasp its place within INS doctrine, the experience of failed transcendence must be elucidated with reference to the classical philosophical opposition of form and matter. For Plato and Aristotle, nothing was more real than form. Knowledge of a thing, for Plato, is knowledge of the *form* of that thing, which is what makes that thing the thing it is, what Plato called *eidos*. For Aristotle, it is the essence or form of a thing that makes it the thing it is, what he called *ousia*. For Plato, higher than the material world and more real than the material world stands the world of forms, the world of ideas. For Aristotle, essence stands higher than existence.

4. Christianity imbibes, divinises and somatises this thought. If, for Plato, the highest knowledge was knowledge of the form of the Good, then for Christianity, the highest knowledge is of God. God is the most real thing there is, and if knowledge of God is impossible because of our fallen state, then our soul should strive to love God and love God alone and above all else.

5. If form is perfect, if it is perfection itself, then how does one explain the obvious imperfection of the world, for the world is not perfect *n'est-ce pas*? This is where matter – our undoing – enters into the picture. For the Greeks, the principle of imperfection was matter, *hyle*. Matter was the source of the corruption of form, of the corruption of the visible world. In Christianity, the imperfection of matter is made much sexier as the imperfection of the material world after the Fall and most of all the imperfection of the flesh, which drove St. Paul into such ecstasies of self-denigration or mortification (we like that), as when he speaks of 'the body of this death', of the law of sin that rages in the body's members.

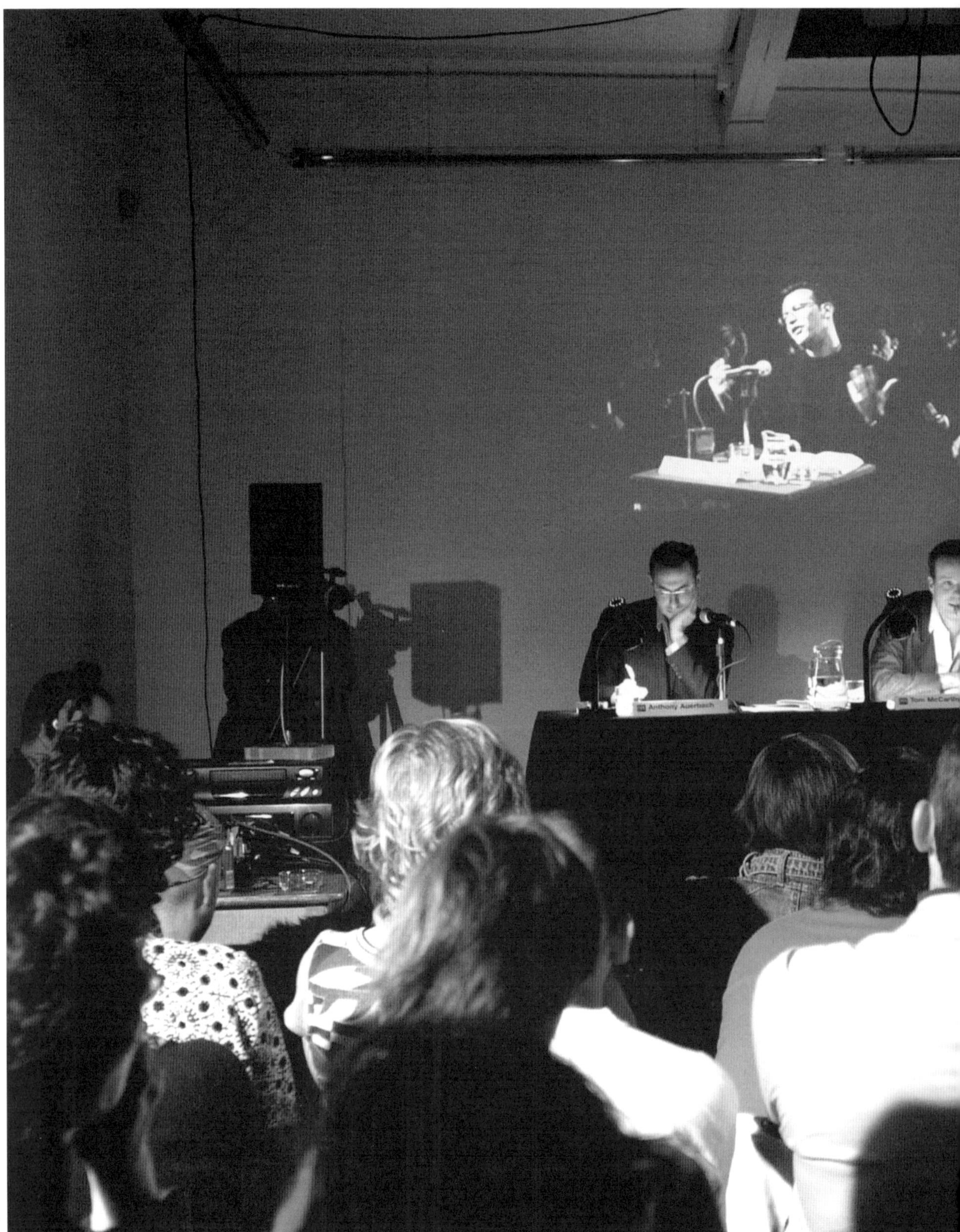
Anthony Auerbach

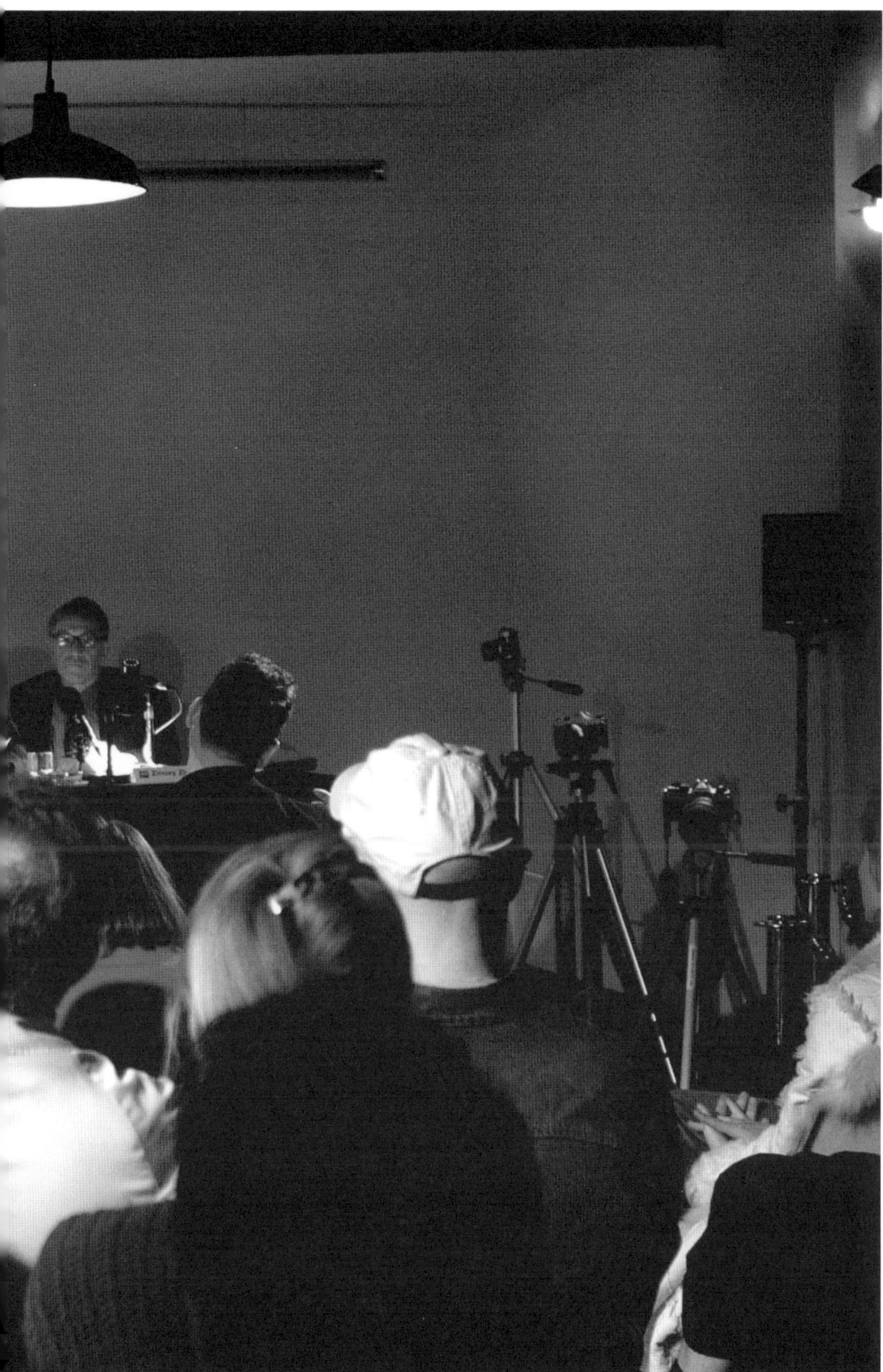

INS First Committee Delegation at the International Necronautical Society's Second First Committee Hearings: *Transmission, Death, Technology* at Cubitt, London, Saturday 16 November 2002

6. For us – necronauts, modern lovers of debris, radio and jetstreams – things are *precisely* the other way round: what is most real for us is not form, or God, but matter, the brute materiality of the external world. We celebrate the imperfection of matter and somatise that imperfection on a daily basis.

7. How do we let matter matter? How is the mattering of matter to be muttered and uttered? How is it to be formed? Following one of our heroes, Maurice Blanchot, we can isolate two tendencies, two temptations, two sloping *pistes* of possibility:
(7.1) One temptation is to try and ingest all of reality into a system of thought, to eat it all up, to penetrate and possess it. This is what Hegel and the Marquis de Sade have in common: the desire to assimilate all reality to the subject through the power of the Concept. This is the idealistic rage of the belly turned mind where matter is soaked up into concepts that function like blotting paper. This is what Deleuze had in mind when he said that philosophy was one long ass-fuck. On this view, language is a sort of murder and Adam was the first serial killer when he wandered around the Garden of Eden giving names to material things.
(7.2) The other option is to let things thing, to let matter matter, to let the orange orange and the flower flower. On this second slope, we take the side of things and try and evoke their nocturnal, mineral quality. This is, for us, the essence of poetry as it is expressed in Francis Ponge, the late Wallace Stevens, Rilke's *Duino Elegies* and some of the personae of Pessoa, of trying (and failing) to speak about the thing itself and not just ideas about the thing, of saying 'jug, bridge, cigarette, oyster, fruitbat, windowsill, sponge'.
(7.3) Sponge
(7.4) Sponge

8. In a sense, and this is the point that Blanchot makes so powerfully, all art and literature is divided between these two temptations: either to extinguish matter and elevate it into form or to let matter matter by making form as formless as possible. The INS delivers itself solidly to the second temptation: to let matter matter, to let form touch absence, ellipsis and debris. Like Flaubert at the end of *The Temptation of St. Antony*, who says he wants to ' ... flow like water, vibrate like sound, gleam like light, to curl myself up into every shape, to penetrate each atom, to get down to the depth of matter – *to be matter'*. But instead of seeing the radiant face of Christ like the tortured saint, Flaubert disintegrates into the void like Madame Bovary on her back in the woods, rifled by a man's organ, her eyes burnt by the fire of a star.

9. Thus our other heroes: not the Dorian Gray who projects such a perfect figure out into the world, but the rotting flesh-assemblage hanging in his attic; not the Frankenstein who would, through his creation, see himself in the likeness of God, who stands like Caspar David Friedrich on high mountaintops to contemplate the sublime – but his morbid double who confronts him there with the reality of industry, the stench of meat-packing factories; not the imperial dreams in the head of the polar explorer Ernest Shackleton but rather his blackened, frostbitten toes which, after the white space into which he'd ventured and on which he hoped to write his name

solidified and crushed his boat, he and his crew were forced to chop from their own feet, cook on their stove and eat. Necronauts are poets of the antipodes of poetry, artists of art's polar opposite, its Antartica.

10. In short, against idealism in philosophy and idealist or transcendent conceptions of art, of art as pure and perfect form, we set a doctrine of poetic or necronautical materialism akin to Bataille's notion of *l'informe* or 'the formless': a universe that 'resembles nothing' and 'gets itself squashed everywhere, like a spider or earthworm'. This is the universe that must be navigated. And, as *Moby Dick*'s narrator Ishmael knows all too well as he floats on the decorated coffin that has become his life raft, navigation is a difficult art.

11. Question: how do we navigate? How do we deal with matter? Answer: *inauthentically*. This brings us to a further central element in INS doctrine that we want to propagate today. In relation to the form/matter distinction, the dominant modern response to this dilemma is to believe that one can form oneself as a unified, autarkic, autonomous subject. This is the modern dream of authenticity: that, after the failure of metaphysical transcendence, the *self* can rise up, complete, godlike even, as a heroic subject and many such heroes can band together into a unified people. We choose to abandon the idea of the people and the individual subject. On the contrary, the necronaut is a dividual.

12. For us, inauthenticity is the core to the self, to what it means to be human, which means that the self has no core, but is an experience of division, of splitting. As such, all cults of authenticity, whether traditionally religious, political, new age or neo-Buddhistic that attempt to recuperate some notion of authenticity, should be abandoned.

13. We want to advance the concept of originary inauthenticity, which we freely adapt from Heidegger. The thought is that human existence is formed in relation to a brute material facticity that cannot be mastered. Any attempt at authenticity slips back into an inauthenticity from which it cannot escape, but which it would like to evade. It is in this movement of evasion, of the self's turning away from itself, that our fatal embeddedness in materiality is revealed. Inauthentic existence is experienced as a burden, a weight, something to which I am riveted without being able to know why or know further, like Racine's Phaedra rooted to the fact of her erotic longing for her stepson from which she longs to escape. Or like Ibsen's Hedda Gabler, languishing within an unsatisfied desire, an unbearable physical weariness whose only escape is her father's pistol. Inauthentic existence has the character of an irreducible *thatness*, what Heidegger calls '*das Daß seines Da*'. I feel myself bound to the 'that of my there', to the sheer fact of my facticity, in a way that demands a response.

14. However, from this point onwards we part company with Heidegger. For us, the nature of this response cannot be the authentic decision of existence that comes into the simplicity of its fate (*Schicksal*) by 'shattering itself against death' as Heidegger melodramatically puts it. The response will not be the heroic mastery of our

inauthentic state in the authentic present of what he calls the *Augenblick* or 'moment of vision', which produces an experience of ecstasy and rapture. On the contrary, for us, the response to the materiality of our inauthentic state is a more passive and less heroic decision. This calls for comic acknowledgement rather than tragic affirmation.

15. Let us explain. Ever since Kant, the tragic-heroic paradigm has dominated the modern philosophical, aesthetic and psychoanalytic traditions. The tragic is the aesthetic genre that reconciles the freedom of the subject with the causal necessity of the material world. Oedipus, for example, is defined by a free acceptance of his determination by necessity: that he did murder his father and marry his mother is necessity, and the dramatic process is the free acceptance of that. As such, the tragic hero can live the identity of freedom and law and die authentically.

16. For us, though, the key aesthetic genre is not the tragic, which always conveys meaning and authenticity on life through the control of death, but comedy, which is the mechanical splitting of the self, the dividuation or disintegration of the self into insubstantiality. This is why Hegel's *Aesthetics* ends with comedy rather than tragedy. For him, comedy is the end of art and the passage to philosophy; for us, it is the truth of art that reveals what philosophical conceptuality always misses, the mattering of matter, the vast *Klang* of the pyramids, the black stone of Mecca.

17. This sense of the comic is best articulated by the likes of Bergson and Baudelaire. For Bergson, comedy lies in the duplication that undermines uniqueness. Two similar faces, a repeated action – these things are funny. For Baudelaire, it lies in a twofold fall: the fall from the divine into the human *and* the pratfall. I watch another man trip on the pavement and I laugh in sudden glory. Baudelaire goes on to claim that what distinguishes the poet or philosopher from others is that he can laugh at himself. That is, he can simultaneously be the one who trips and the one who watches the trip: he can split himself in two – what Baudelaire calls *dédoublement*. However, as de Man points out in his essay on Baudelaire, once you're split and reproduced you're not unique anymore: you're fake. The ironic self-awareness of the poet or philosopher can only be that of his own inauthenticity, repeated at increasingly conscious levels, and 'to know inauthenticity is not the same as to be authentic'.

18. What's more, the falling man is, to quote de Man, 'a thing in the grip of gravity', the end point of all gravity being the grave. Thus comedy confronts us with 'the temporal reality of death'. Tragedy does this too, of course – but whereas the tragic hero strides into death in order to confer transcendent meaning on their life, the comic one dies badly, incompletely. Wiley Coyote gets blown up by dynamite and falls off cliffs, Sylvester the Cat gets electrocuted and squashed by trucks, but both come back and die again, and again and again.

19. Broken-hearted romantics dream of an authentic death, on the model of Empedocles extinguishing himself in the flames of Mount Etna, Socrates discoursing calmly with his followers as the hemlock does its inexorable work, or Christ in the bloody joy and Pelican-like self-consummation of his Passion. On the contrary, the necronaut does

not die well, at the right time or in the right way. That is, the necronaut dies almost without noticing, feeling a twig in his back instead of a bullet, stung on the neck by a flying insect and succumbing to the resulting fever, like Max Stirner, or tripping over a bronze utensil in the night, like Xenocrates. Sometimes the necronaut does not die at all.

20. Do not misunderstand us. We are not advocating cowardice or compromise. The captured *Résistance* member who refuses to betray his comrades and dies shouting 'Vive la liberté' is the one whom we would welcome to our organisation, not his collaborating counterpart. But what is his experience of that moment? We submit that it is neither divine transcendence nor an ecstatic spasm of self-fulfilment, but rather an angle of the sunlight on the wall of the execution yard, a clump of earth, a beetle trying to mount a stick and falling off repeatedly.

21. In his stunning short paper on humour, Freud writes of a prisoner condemned to be hanged. On the morning of his execution he is escorted from his cell and led out to the courtyard. Seeing the gallows ahead, he looks up at the sky and says, 'Na, die Woche fängt gut an' – 'Well, the week's beginning nicely.' *That's* our necronaut.

22. I am, but I do not have myself. Humour is the highest expression of the principle of dividuation, of an ever-divided self-relation, of our essential lack of self-coincidence. In other words, I find myself ridiculous, which is to say that I do not find my *self*, whatever that might mean, but rather see myself from outside and laugh. This is what Beckett calls the *'risus purus'*, 'the laugh laughing at the laugh, the beholding, the saluting of the highest joke, in a word that laugh that laughs – silence please – at that which is unhappy'.

23. How does one die properly? Mustn't Wiley Coyote long for a simple death to come and free him from his suffering, from its endless repetition? Beckett's Vladimir and Estragon, torn between waiting for Godot's arrival, which would save them, and hanging themselves, which would at least give them a hard-on, re-enact the scene of cruelty they witnessed between Pozzo and Lucky on the previous day. 'Was I sleeping,' Vladimir asks, 'while the others suffered?'

24. For Maurice Blanchot, who was himself lined up in front of a firing squad but reprieved at the last moment, there is a distinction between death and dying, or *'la mort'* and *'le mourir'*. If death is something that can be affirmed ecstatically in an act of tragic heroism, then dying is something we cannot control, a process of finite neutral drifting, a movement of absenting. The paradox of suicide is that at the moment of kicking away the chair and hanging oneself, what the suicide feels is the rope tying them ever more tightly to the existence they wanted to leave. Thus, for the Blanchot of *The Writing of the Disaster*, dying is the opposite of death: it is 'the incessant imminence whereby life lasts, desiring.' He continues: 'If death is the real, and if the real is impossible, then we are approaching the thought of the impossibility of death.'

25. Comedy over tragedy: that is, repetition, incompleteness, rupture and mess over neatness, uniqueness and transcendence. Indeed, on closer scrutiny we see the comic already inscribed within the tragic. Next to the body of *Cordelia*, the Fool, hanged with a rope, *une corde*. Consider the botched deaths of Hamsun's Nagel in Mysteries, who downs his poison only to discover he's been sold lemonade or Conrad's *Nostromo*, who misses his own heroic immolation and wanders around town like a beggar; or Faulkner's Quentin in *The Sound and the Fury*, continually distracted from the moment of his death while riding trams, his father's admonition that 'tragedy is second hand' ringing in his ears, what we call 'the tinnitus of existence'; or that of Addie Bundren in *As I Lay Dying*, who takes so long about it that her actual death-scene doesn't even make the novel's final cut, starts to reek and then gets substituted, replaced.

26. As Blanchot points out, the disaster doesn't have a writing: it has no accurate transcription – rather, it de-scribes, un-draws. And yet make no mistake, we are living under the sign of the disaster. Whether you take the disaster to be the Pequod's wreck, the death of God, the fall of communism, the 2000 electoral coup in Florida and subsequent invasion of Iraq, or the exorbitant price of fish is your affair; but you'd be hard pressed not to see that there is wreckage one must navigate through – or, like Ishmael, on.

27. Thinking begins with disaster – or, more precisely, with the forgotten origin of a trauma that clefts the self in twain and in whose ripples all subsequent thinking must find its contours. That is, thinking awakes in the wake of something unthinkable.

28. Trauma confers on those who experience it a feeling of inauthenticity: subsequent life does not seem 'real'. This feeling clouds the trauma-victim's entire world-view. To quote Warhol: 'Before I was shot, I suspected that instead of living I'm just watching TV. Since being shot, I'm certain of it.'

29. Trauma bequeaths a propensity to repeat. The trauma-moment, expelled from proper memory, plays itself out in a chain of repetitions that I instigate, modulating them even as I repeat them. We submit that almost all art, from Aeschylus' *Oresteia* to Sterne's *Tristram Shandy*, to the novels and plays of Beckett or the images of Warhol, can be interrogated along the lines of trauma.

30. Art is governed by what Mark E. Smith of the mighty Fall calls the three R's: repetition, repetition and repetition. As a consequence, we think artists should continue to do what they have always done: *steal*. Art is a repetitive mechanism that functions through theft, forgery, copying and embedding.

31. As McLuhan puts it, the true content of each medium is the previous medium. Or as we would say, Apache attack seven times the speed of sound. When you are in the cloud you can see nothing.

32. Skiing on art's first slope of possibility, art attempts to extinguish matter and achieve authenticity as a hypnotic, monotonous, endless recurrence of repetition. This produces the trance-like stasis and intense psychic tingling that we sometimes think of as aesthetic pleasure. At times it almost feels real. Then again, so can masturbation.

33. But art's dirty secret is inauthenticity all the way down, a series of repetitions and re-enactments that attempt to cover over the traumatic event of materiality. As Joyce realised in *Finnegans Wake*, literature is rich trash to be recycled and adapted in a commodius vicus of recirculation. Yet, there is always a remainder that remains: a shard, a leftover, a trace, a residual. Everything must leave some kind of mark. The attempt to coincide with reality is always undone by the material mark of an event, an accident of which we remember very little ... almost nothing.

34. Listen: the world is a sign of restless visibility, greater than six miles.

35. Listen: Ovid 251 Fight the Chimera. Winds aloft extended decode. Seminole. Going once going twice.

36. Listen: S.A.F.A. taxes may apply. Other taxes may apply.

37. Listen: between cities, countries and continents, we are going to crash.

38. We are sometimes asked: How do I join? How does one become a necronaut? Wrong question. As paragraph three, lines five and six of the INS's First Manifesto make clear, 'We are all necronauts, always, already.' Our mission here tonight is to disseminate that fact: not as conceptual knowledge but rather in the way that Molly Bloom fills her husband's mouth with seedcake, then repeats that moment, with a silent Yes.

39. As modern lovers of debris, radio and jetstreams, go spread the seed, tune into and repeat it until its signal echoes up and down the balconies, taken up by barking dogs, muttering bums, music traffic down windy streets, across parks and soccer fields. Illusion is a revolutionary weapon. Thank you for listening.

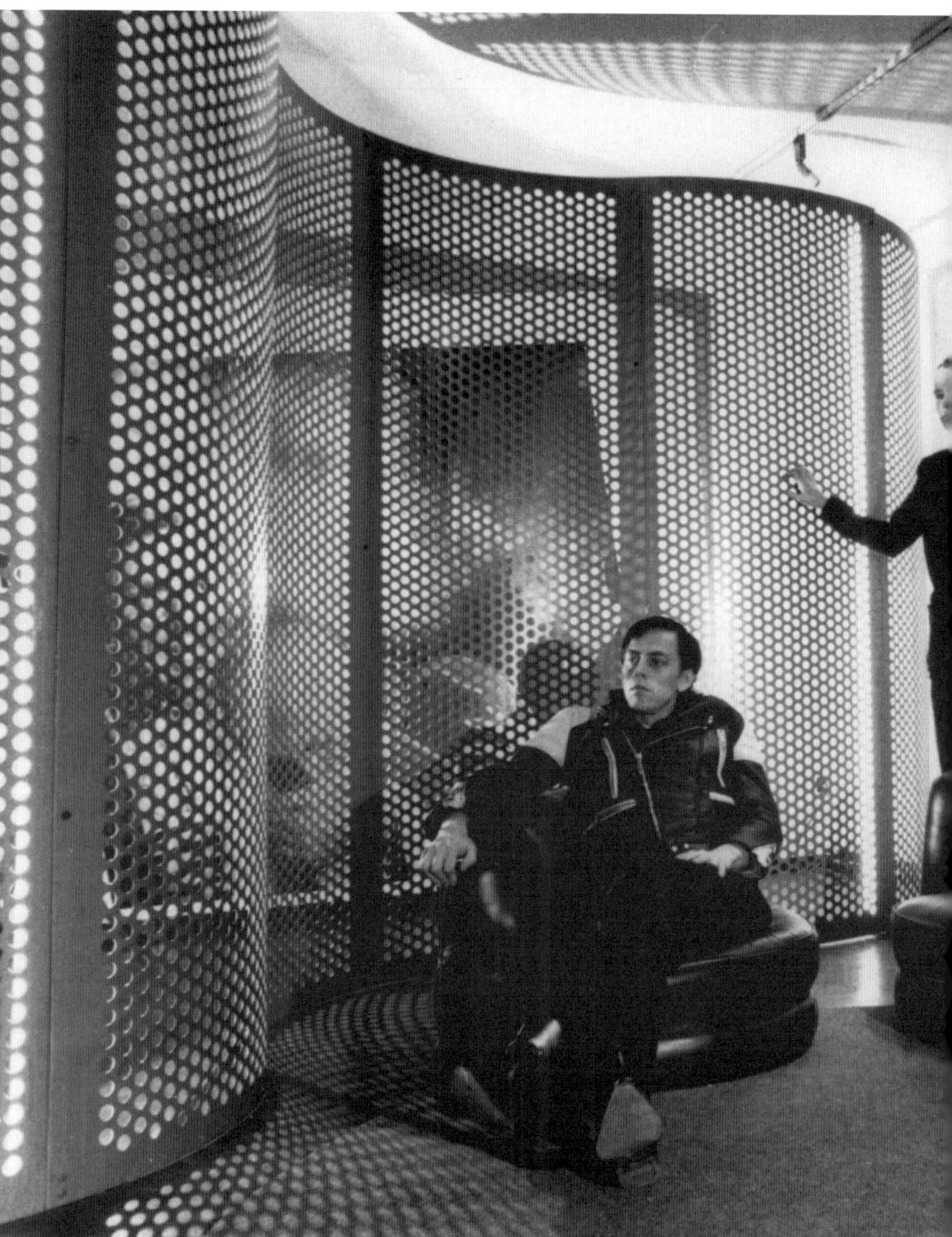

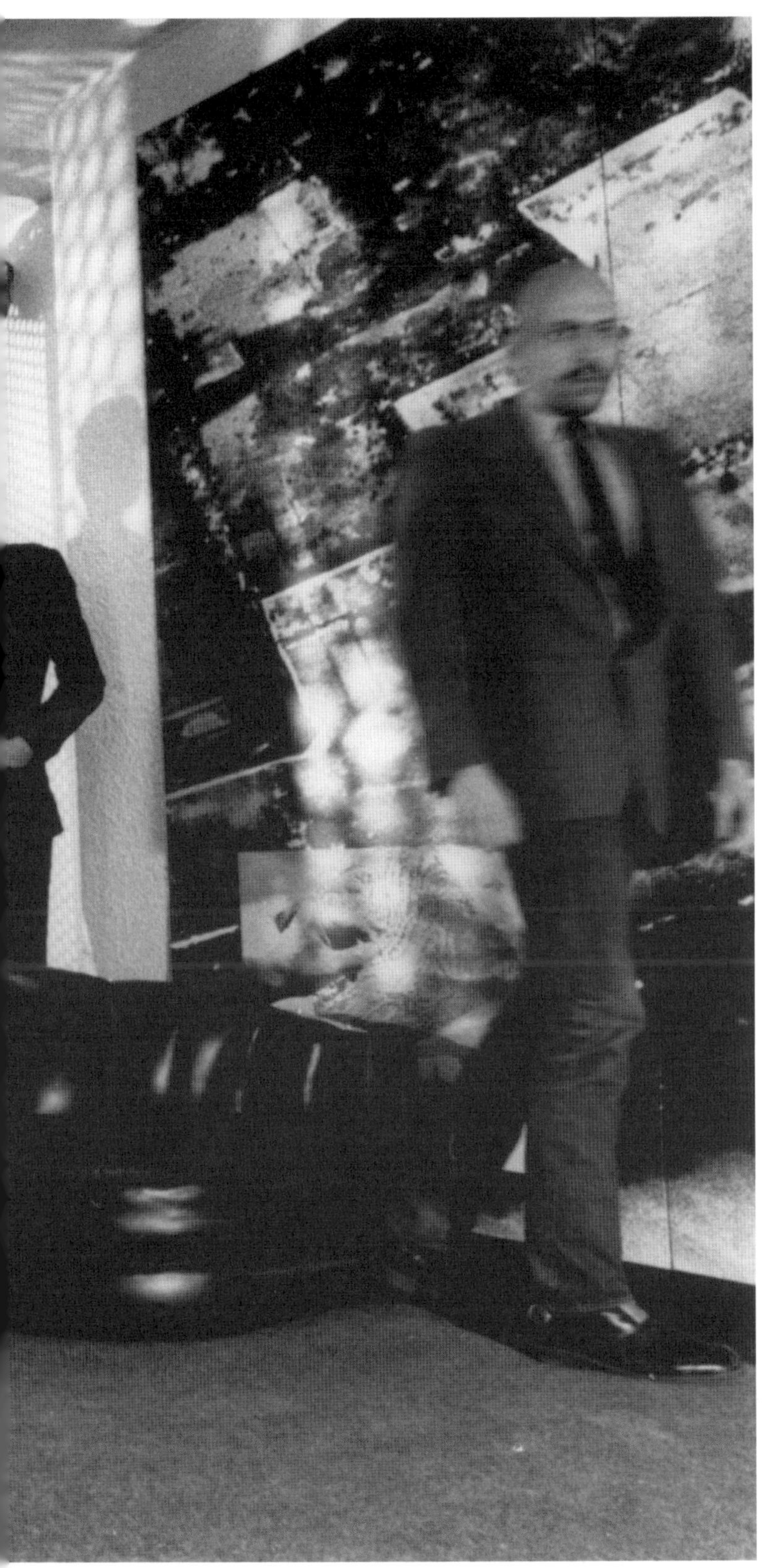

A.A. BRONSON, **FELIX PARTZ**, and **JORGE ZONTAL** (seen here in *Reconstructing Futures* 1977) collaborated as **GENERAL IDEA** across a variety of media for twenty-five years until the deaths of **ZONTAL** and **PARTZ** in 1994. The artists' practice – which used video, performance and forms of publishing to examine the relationship between the artist and mass media – is epitomised in this photograph: an ironic take on the group's own position as purveyors of artistic glamour. Their video work has been shown widely since the 1970s and continues to be shown today.

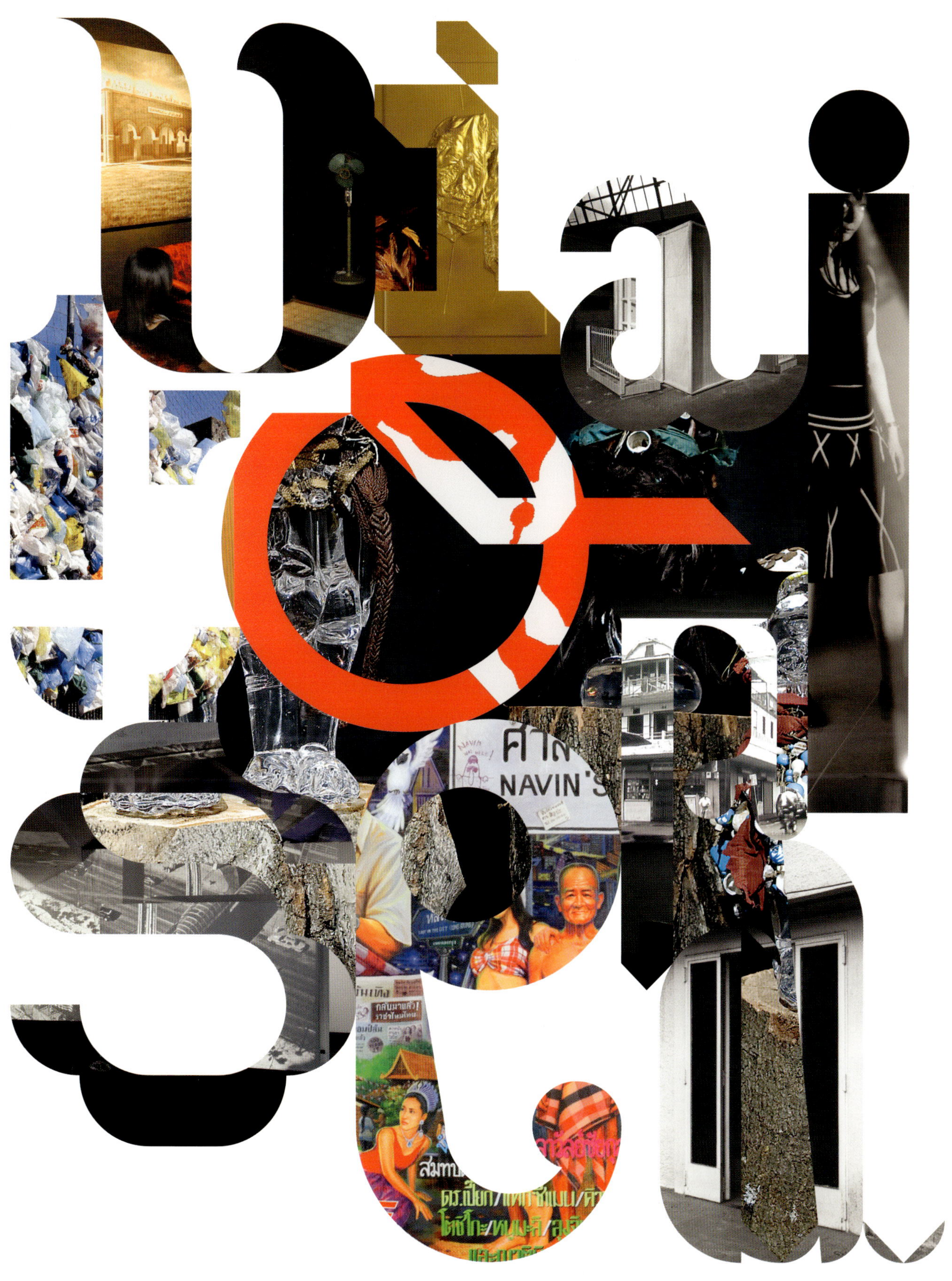
NAVIN'S

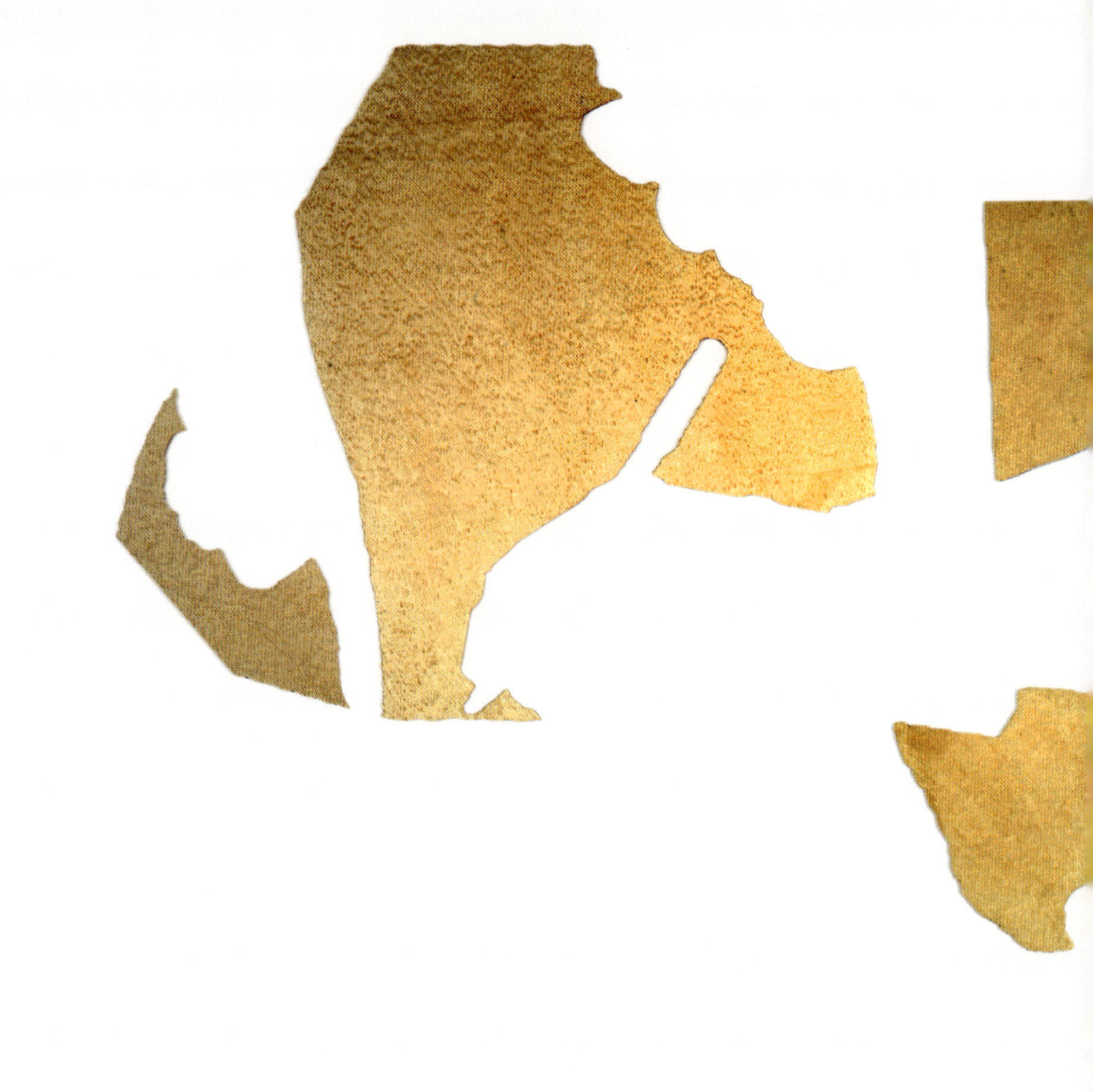

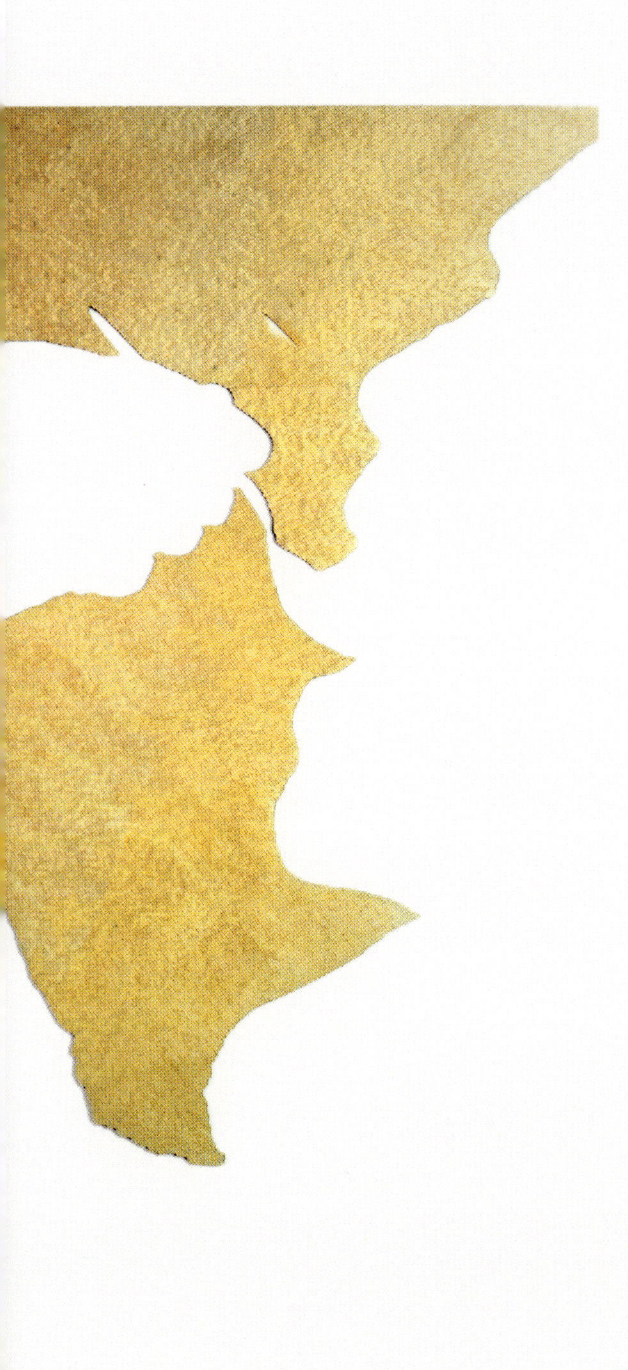

Seth
PRICE

If architecture is the model in Western metaphysics, we are in some sense the inhabitors of older buildings, and ours is the business of living in a ruined house. It's useful to take a hard look at the word *ruin*, a word that splits. On the one hand, it could refer to the sorts of ancient structures cherished in the early nineteenth century: squalid, overgrown, graffiti-covered, surveyed at sunset for best effect. Yet it might also indicate those same ruins today: sandblasted free of graffiti, restored and conserved, made lucrative, seen only in the full daylight of 'open hours' [...]

Come what may, everything is reused. Artists rummage through the toolkits of past artists for approaches they may make use of. The task is to take these instruments and fashion new tools. You want a fine art approach, you borrow the tool from commodity culture. Look for the use, not the meaning! And if it's done wrong, no problem, there is produced a nostalgia for the done-right way. For these reasons, the modern idea of a renovated ruin may be more relevant for art than the nineteenth century model of picturesque decay.

Extract from Décor Holes, *in* Colonial *magazine, 2005*

seth price — ***Untitled*, 2007**, 4 parts, prima birdseye maple and butternut walnut and plexi, 220 × 375, courtesy Friedrich Petzel Gallery, New York

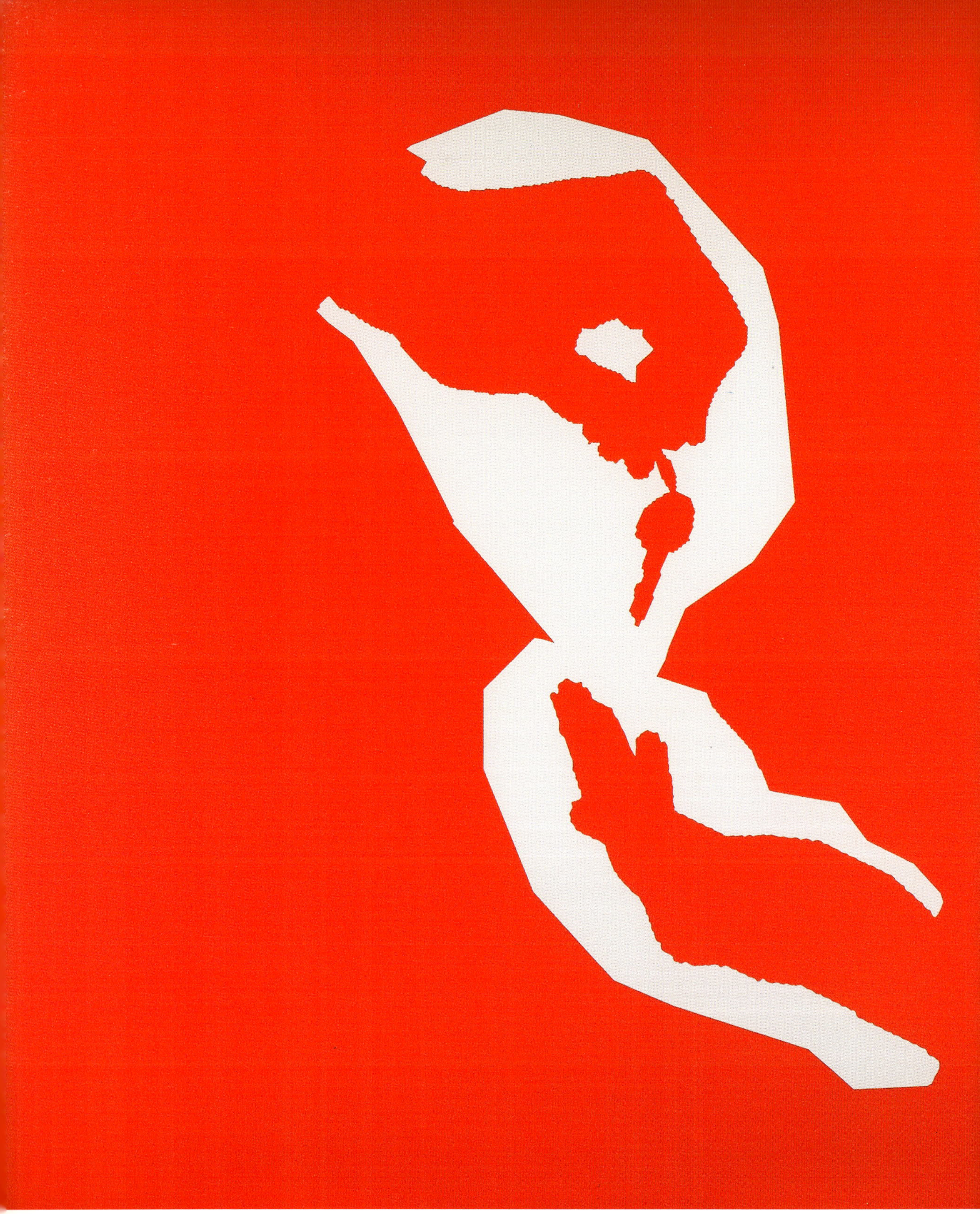

SETH PRICE — [LEFT] *Gold Key,* 2008, ink on dibond, 120.7 × 120.7, [RIGHT] *Vintage Bomber,* 2008, vacuum formed high impact polystyrene and synthetic enamel, 243.8 × 121.9, courtesy Friedrich Petzel Gallery, New York

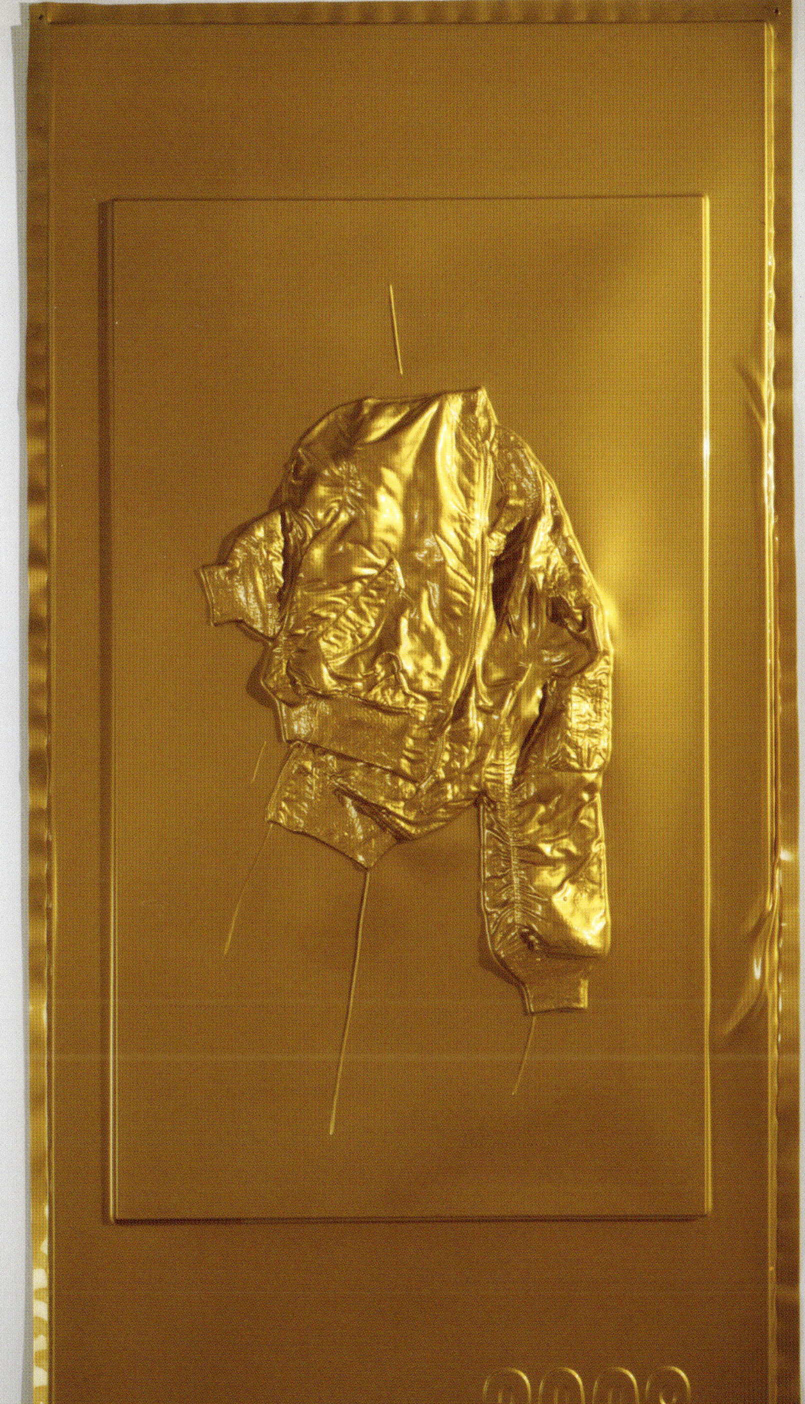
2008

Navin RAWANCHAIKUL

Dear navin,

I'm beginning to realise that what distinguishes you from the majority of today's artists is this very abundance, this productivity, this generosity of iconography: perhaps we've gotten too used to a certain dry-spell of thought, to a certain retention, to the rarity of signs; in contrast, profusion frightens. But nothing stops us from liking both Samuel Beckett and the Ramayana, Michael Asher and Mike Kelley. Indian visual culture, the memory of which seems not to have been erased by your successive migrations, operates through excess: vivid and intense colors, iconographic saturations, proliferation of surroundings and figures. Instead of highlighting this tradition as such, like those bad artists who have

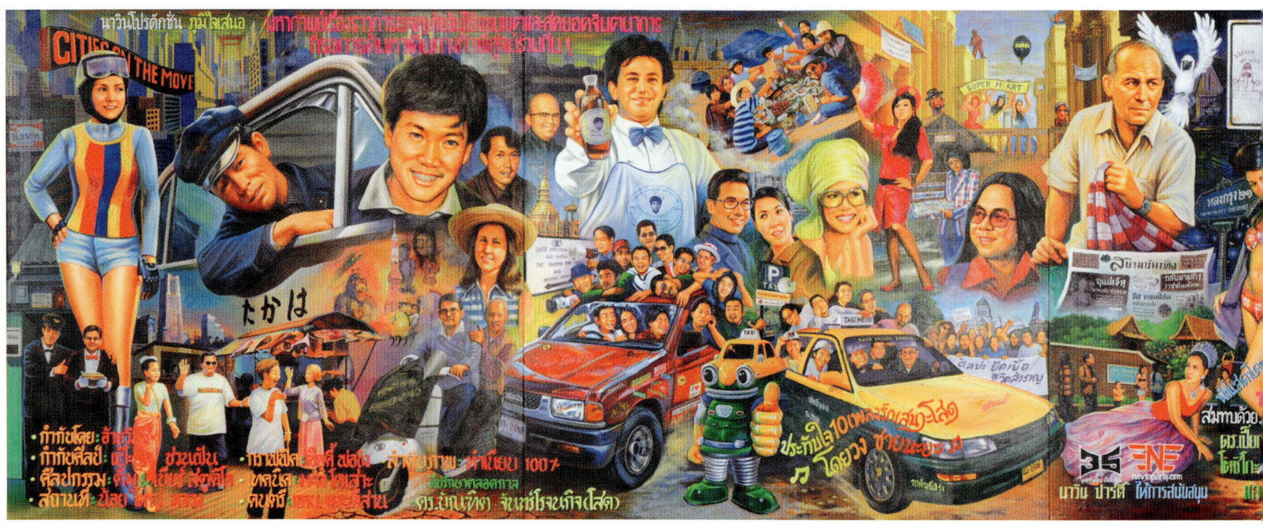

navin rawanchaikul — *Navin's Sala*, 2008, acrylic on canvas, 170 × 900, courtesy Navin Production and Galleri Niklas Belenius, Stockholm

no other ambition than to conform to what the market demands of them, i.e. to become representatives of national folklore, you've succeeded in connecting these patterns and figurative protocols with a complex set of issues. You use Bollywood to talk about immigration, you compose a little Mahabharata of contemporary art ... I remember having felt this way at Bangkok's About Café, in July 2004, when I attended a show that you staged: an astonishing crossbreed between contemporary debate and stage design that could have existed five hundred years earlier.

Nicolas Bourriaud

From 'Letter to the editor', in Navin's Sala, *Navin Production 2008.*

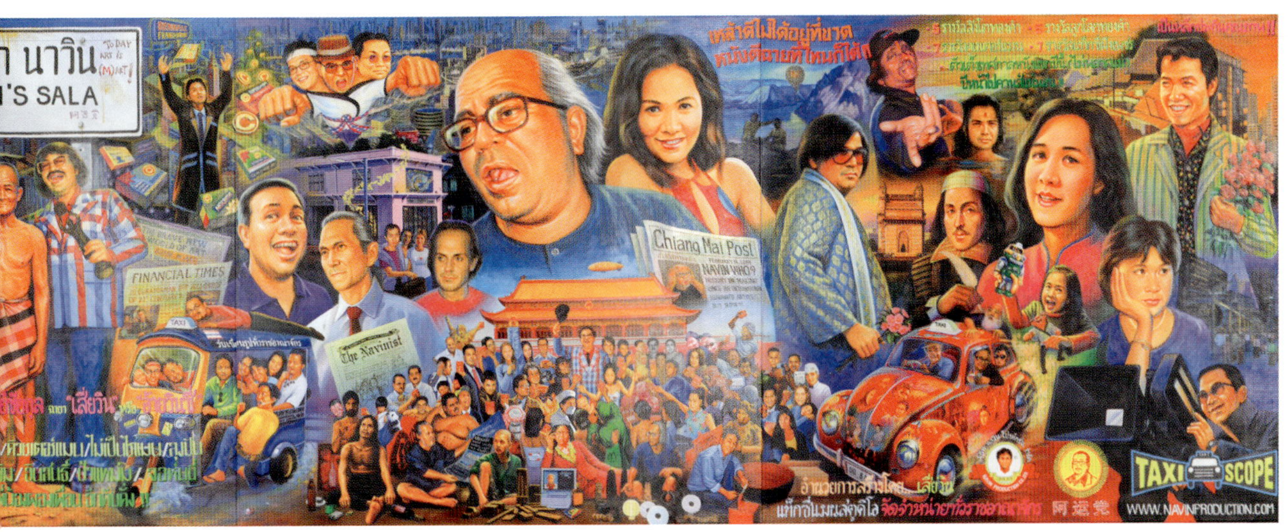

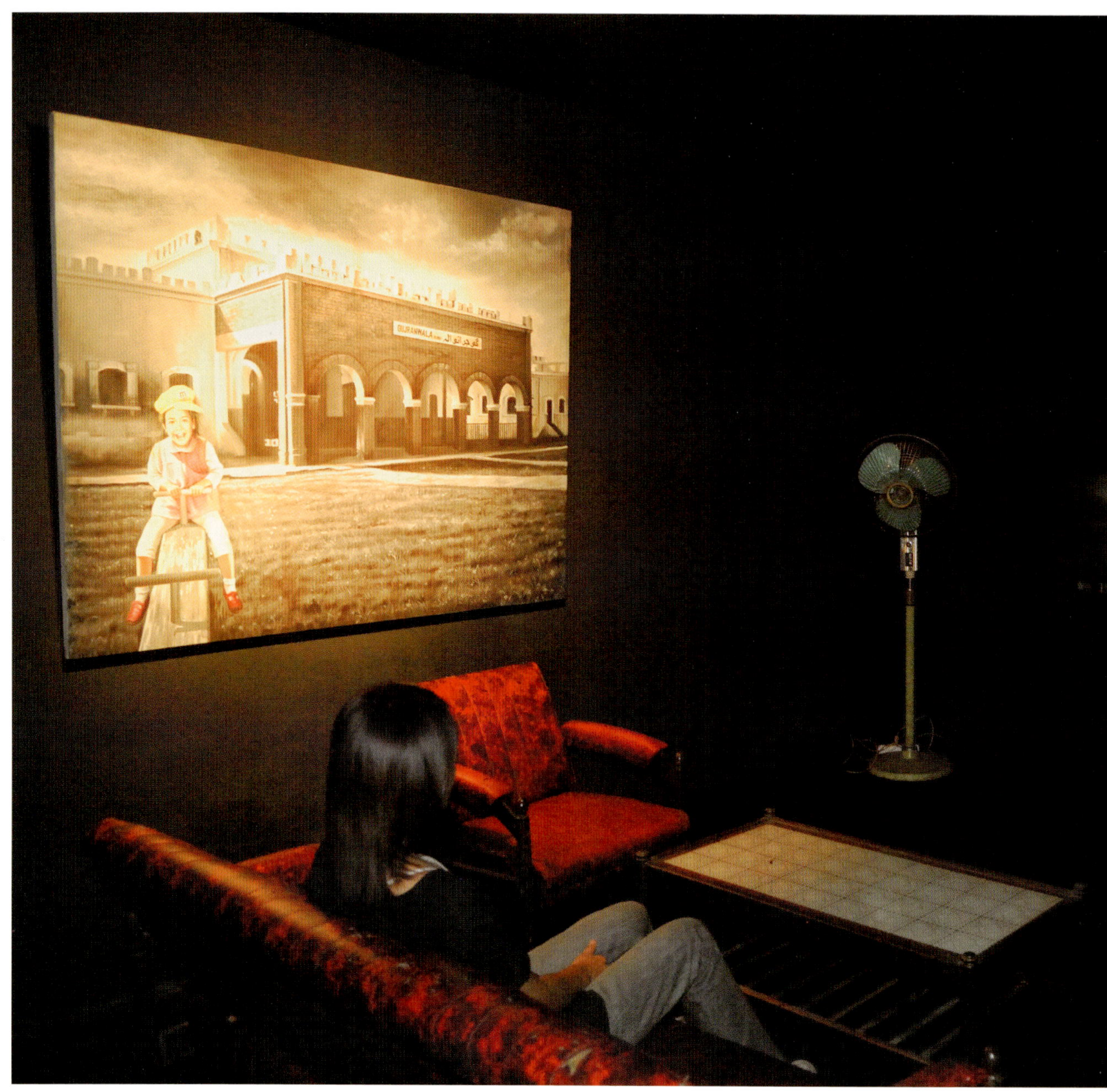

NAVIN RAWANCHAIKUL — ***Hong Rub Khaek,*** **2008**, a living room with two paintings (*Khaek* and *Mario Sisters*) and single-channel video, dimensions variable, courtesy of Navin Production and Gallery Soulflower, Bangkok

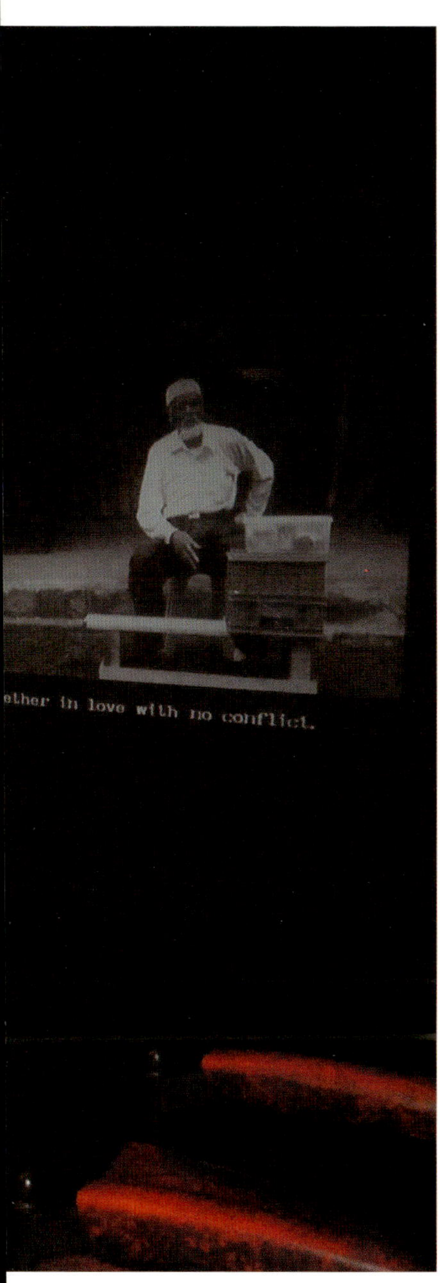
ether in love with no conflict.

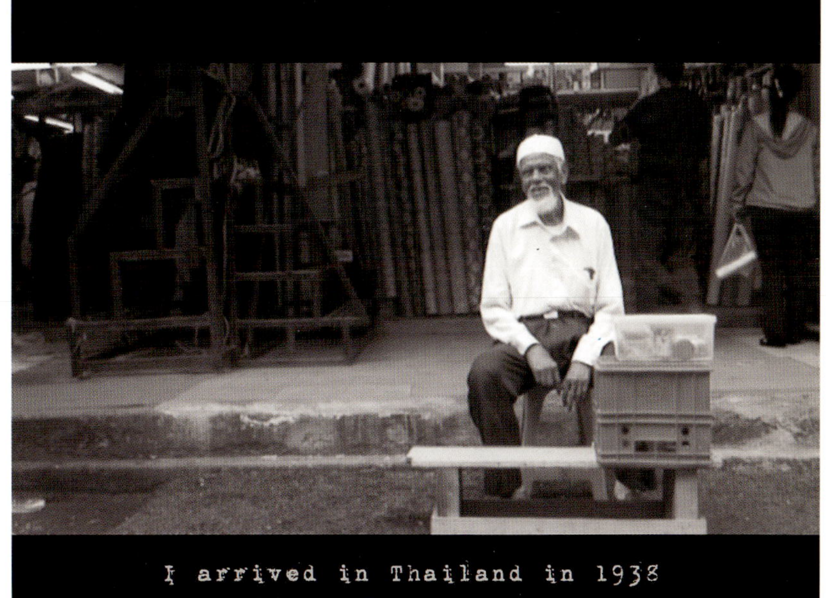
I arrived in Thailand in 1938

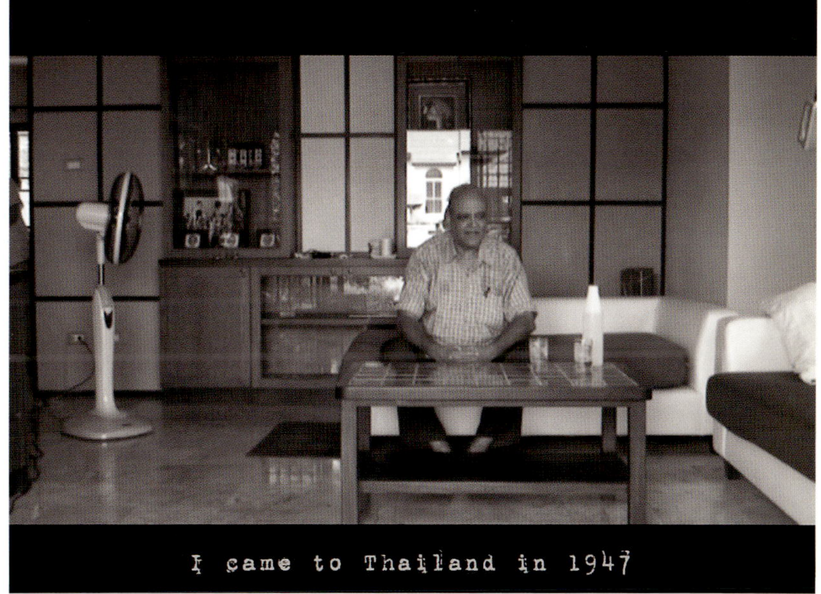
I came to Thailand in 1947

Lindsay SEERS

TRAVELLING BEYOND REASON

As she stands in the doorway with her suitcase, for a brief moment I'm unsure of whether the artist I've come to know so intimately is just arriving or just leaving this time. When she says goodbye, I recall her current travel route, but it occurs to me that 'that which travels' in her is not subject to the linear purpose and schedule that she nevertheless carries in her hand-luggage. She has requested from me that in her temporary absence I explain to those who ask why she is constantly travelling. How can I address her travels without addressing that which really travels in her when she travels?

On the surface it seems that the logistics of her plane journeys and appointments are like a modernist grid, where one set of crossing lines necessarily justifies the next, in line with a retrospective narrative. According to this logic, one thing has led to the other in a linear narrative that has taken Lindsay Seers from England to Holland, to Paraguay, Mauritius and, more recently, Italy and Sweden. Her tracing of the history, ontology and epistemology of photography has followed the principles of a first person empiricism in overlaying the historical with the autobiographical (for example through her 'becoming a camera'). But if we look a bit closer, the *logos* of the causal chain, ('Going to Holland led me to go to Mauritius', etc.) is not the real instigator of the travels of Lindsay Seers. 'That which travels' is outside the artist; not as an overarching principle of investigative reason, but as *nomos*, understood as immanent necessity. The 'nomadic' element of her work then is what drives her to travel, not the retrospective logic of the narratives themselves, which has linked photography to ventriloquism, cinematic projection, alchemy and theatre, all through so many personal stories. If the modernist travelled towards a utopian future and the postmodernist borrowed from the travel kits of various pasts, the artist Lindsay Seers's travels are dictated by a virtual, already existent future. How can this be?

Being in a foreign country can have a peculiar effect on anybody's assessment of the particular and the generic. Generic objects like houses, cups, chairs, or living beings, like farm animals, still exist abroad, but are slightly or radically different from the particular versions of them that we are familiar with from home. Only temporarily do we perceive this as strange before we resort to the thought that a particular object is but a foreign example of the generic Platonic Idea of 'cup' or 'house', etc. But through the lenses of Lindsay Seers, this momentary strangeness supports a much more radical doubt in the indexical status of the object. The thing as particular Thing and as an evidence in a staging of events is put in doubt because the indexical mark as a premise for cognition is put in doubt, as is the notion of stable generic ideas.

This refusal to believe in the common sense idea of the index is particularly evident in Lindsay's work as a projector. According to the conventional theory of perception, light moves in through the retina of the eye, triggering electrical changes in the optical nerves, which then stimulate the brain to produce an internal image, while nothing moves out. It follows that if this process is always the same, it must be so through the authority of the thing emitting light, what we could call the 'indexical source'. Paradoxically, at the same time as there is this unquestioned trust in the existence of the 'thing itself' (realism), it is also presumed that the image of the thing only exists in our brains (idealism). Alongside this model, the status of the camera is to be an apparatus mimicking the mechanics of perception. But when Lindsay Seers becomes a projector, a different model of perception replaces this insular one-way system. Vision becomes a two way process, an inward movement of light but also an outward movement of projected images. The world is no longer confined to our heads, but is where we perceive it to be, all around us as the mind literally reaches out beyond the brain through projection. There is a further radical aspect to this vision. In the model of perception presented by the artist, there is no storehouse of indexical marks in the mind or fixed indexical emitters in the world either. Every image appearing in the world is then genuinely a new configuration of totality; different neural pathways, different projections of memory coming together for each particular configuration of an object and therefore also for each configuration of past events.

Through becoming a *projector*, and presenting a new model of perception, the status of photography in the artist's world is also open to alteration. Photography no longer stands for a mechanistic process, but for a depth of time, where an unquantifiable whole produces both index and cognition simultaneously. The notion of a storehouse of indexical marks is replaced by an idea of fiction. If we imagine that all the fictions we can invent already exist ready for download as part of a virtual future, a non-manifest aspect of the real here and now, then they are no less real than 'factual' documentaries. According to this vision, the immediate past is constantly reconfigured from a virtual future. It is in this sense that Lindsay Seers's travels are dictated by an already existent future, in a process where there are no fixed indexical marks for cognition or photography.

But Lindsay Seers's work is not a spotless vision of pure 'duration'. The human drive for cohesive narratives is still subject to a desire to 'stabilise the present' or 'break with the past'. So although in the work there is a 'nomadic' drive towards a univocal vision of temporal flow without fixed indexical references, there is also the struggle to comprehend individuation and separation. Therefore there is not just the *nomos* of what drives her to travel, but also the *logos* of retrospection and narrative structure, whether linear or web-like. But the many identities that present themselves in the video narratives,

LINDSAY SEERS — *Extramission 4 (Black Maria)*, 2007, film still, courtesy the artist

through Seers's own person or through other associations, are always framed against the backdrop of *theatrum mundi*. In contrast to the micro-political freezing of identities in the oppositional language of 'critical theory', here identities are always performed. It is interpersonal staging that determines their stability. If we consider the longing for immediacy of perception and the projection of creative futures onto the photographic moment, the link between alchemy and photography, found in recent work by the artist, should not be understood as an analogy between the index and a transcendent Platonic reality. Because the world of the artist lacks indexical security and is merely the immediate projection of virtual futures, it is clear that the preoccupation with alchemy represents a quest for a vision where the sign and its referent are one and the same manifestation. The alchemical symbol in this context does not represent a Platonic world, but embodies the immediate talismanic power of the world as it is created at every moment. In the hunt for this vision, an excess of stories of people and places are produced and given coherence. In the narratives, the character of the artist struggles to disentangle personal emotional incentives from the experience of new visions of temporality and immediacy, because travelling beyond reason is to travel in the depth of time, where narrative logic and patterns are constantly removed from the idea of the indexical evidence in order to reveal the immanent and immediate manifestation of a fictional future created in every present moment.

To this close friend of the artist, the woman in the doorway embodies an army of possible versions of Lindsay Seers, constantly coming and going. The cameras in her suitcase make up a travelling alchemist's kit. They are tools of unique reconfigurations as well as talismans of perception. As for any adept dabbling with the virtual future, each time the kit is put to work, ghosts and messages appear. These spectral personas ensure that the world goes on and that the narrative of the world's creation as a unique new character always has plenty of interesting transitory sidekicks in people, objects, places and moments. But in the web of the artist, even the most accidental encounter eventually becomes another signpost in the route map towards the true source of photography.

Ole Hagen

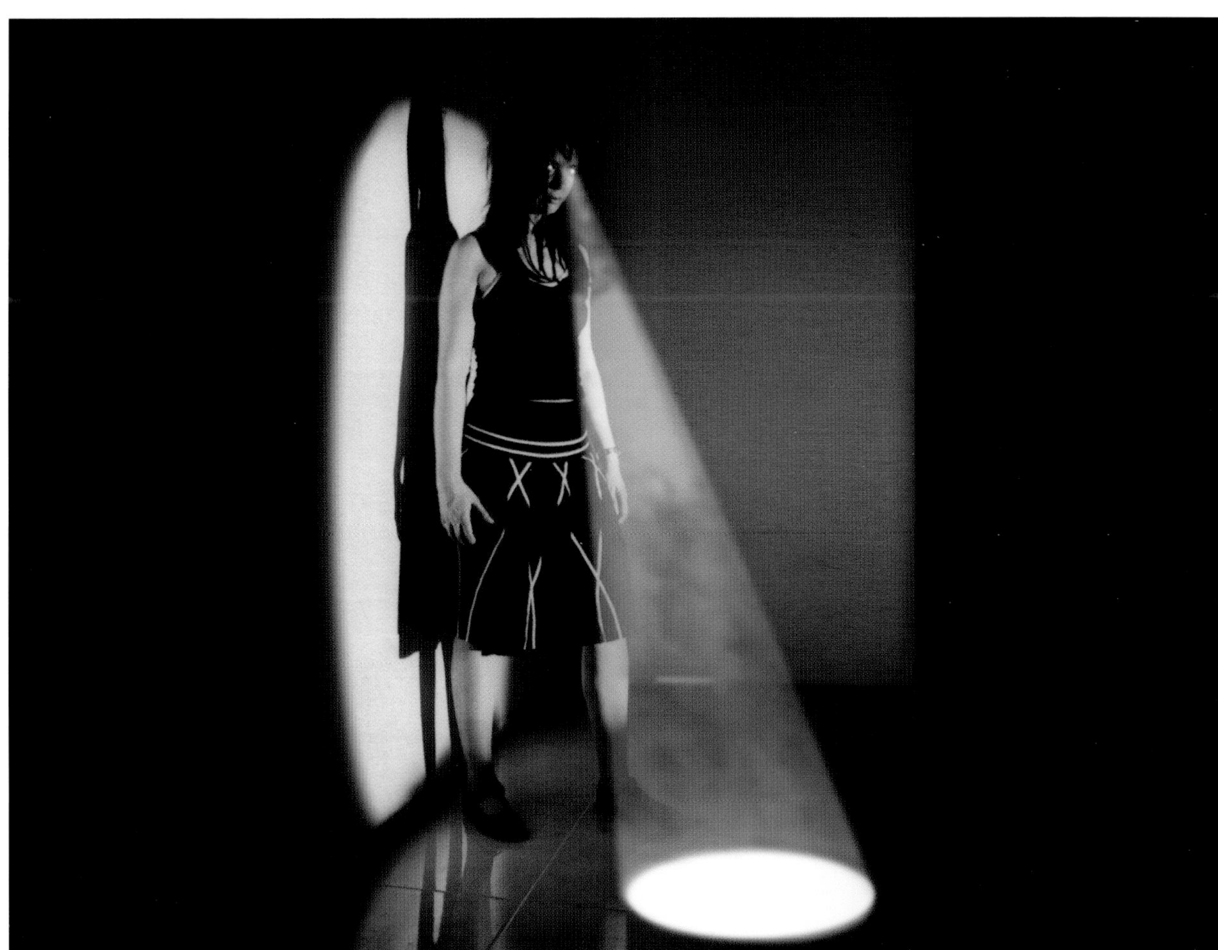

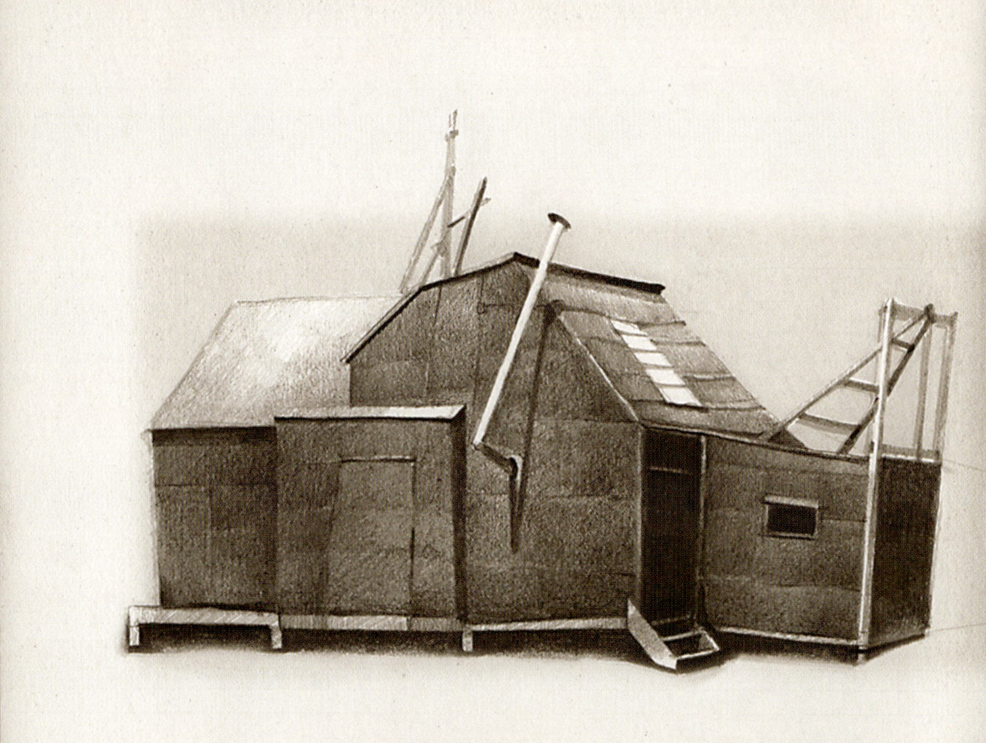

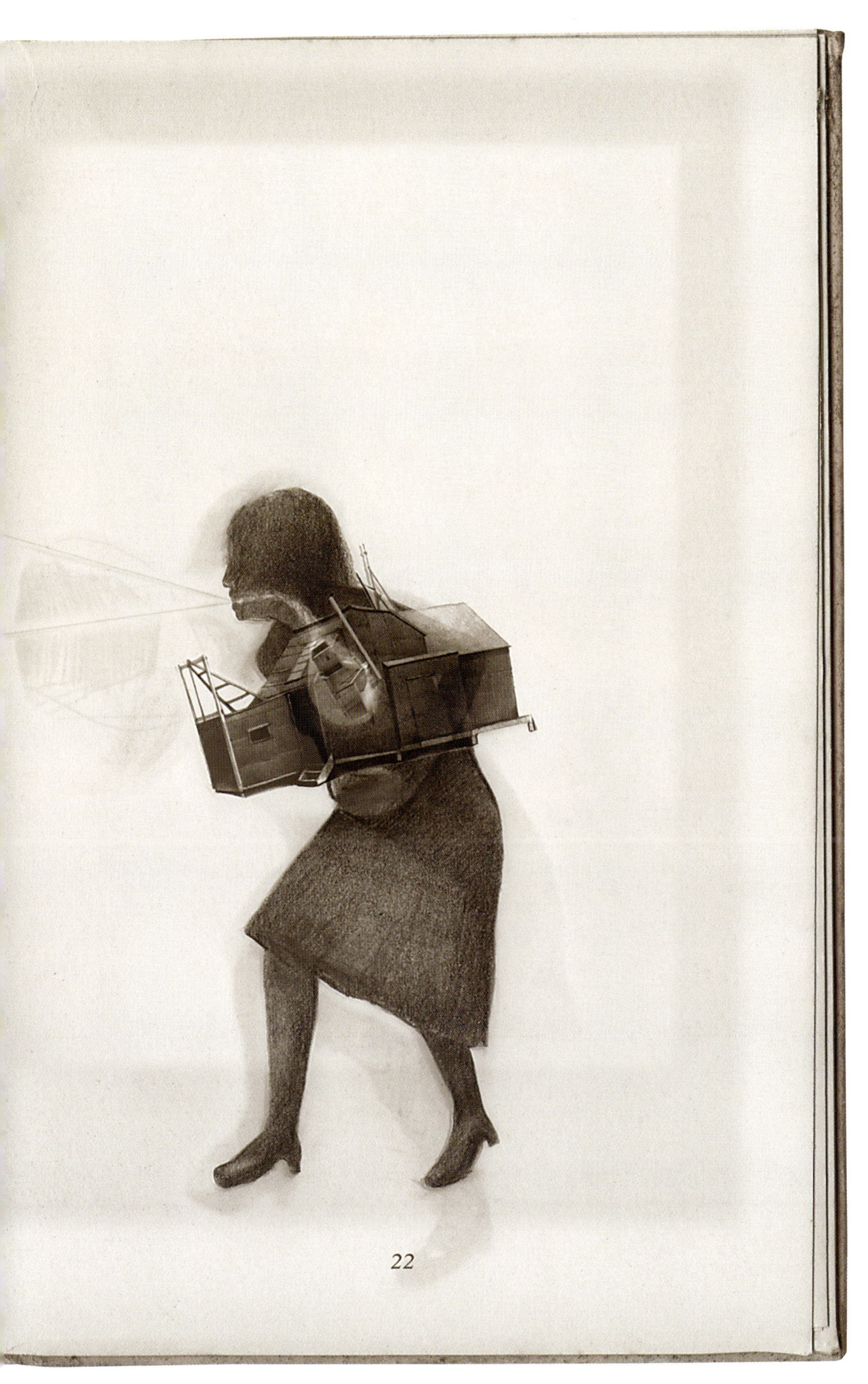

LINDSAY SEERS
— ***Swallowing Black Maria,***
2006,
photograph,
courtesy the artist

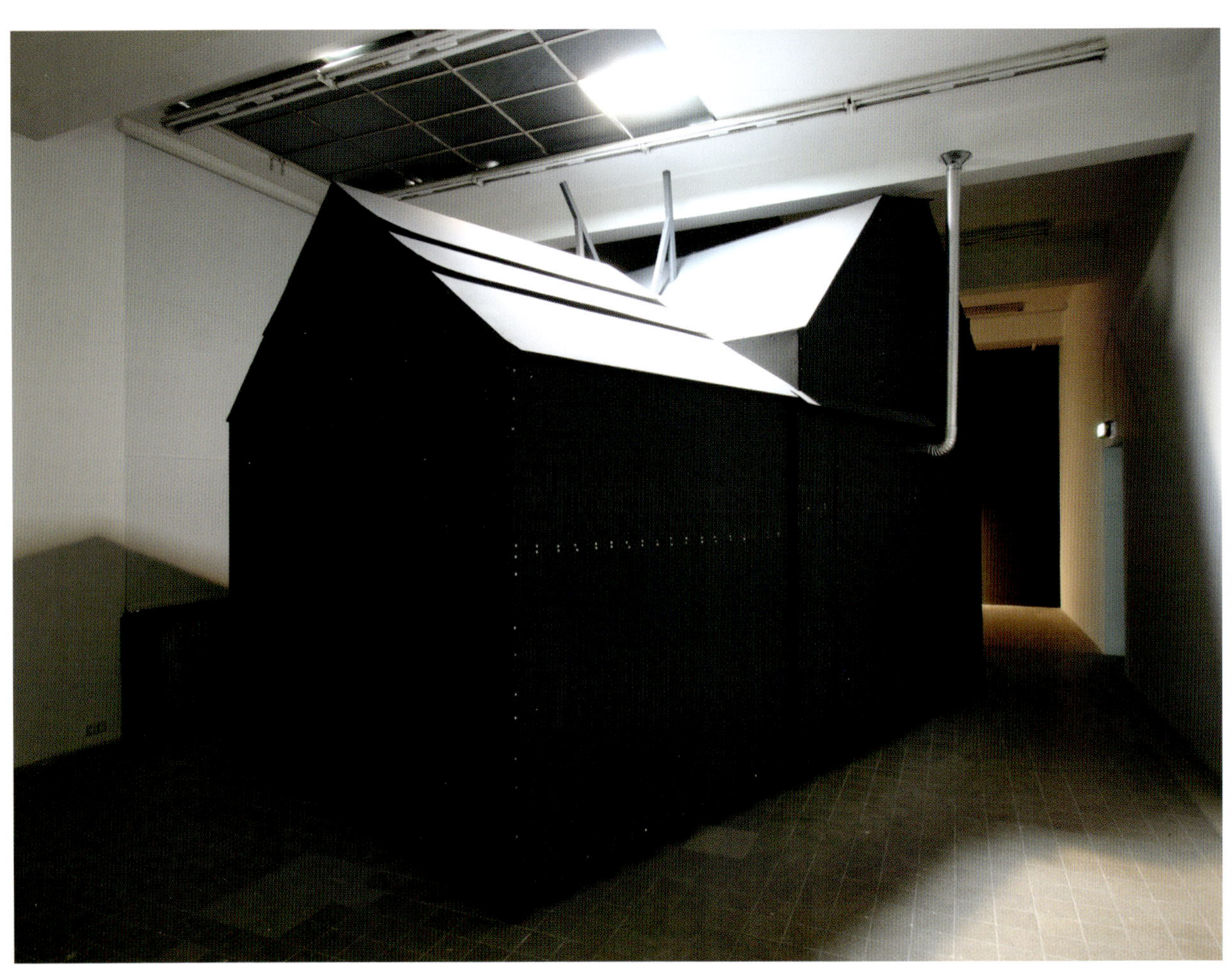

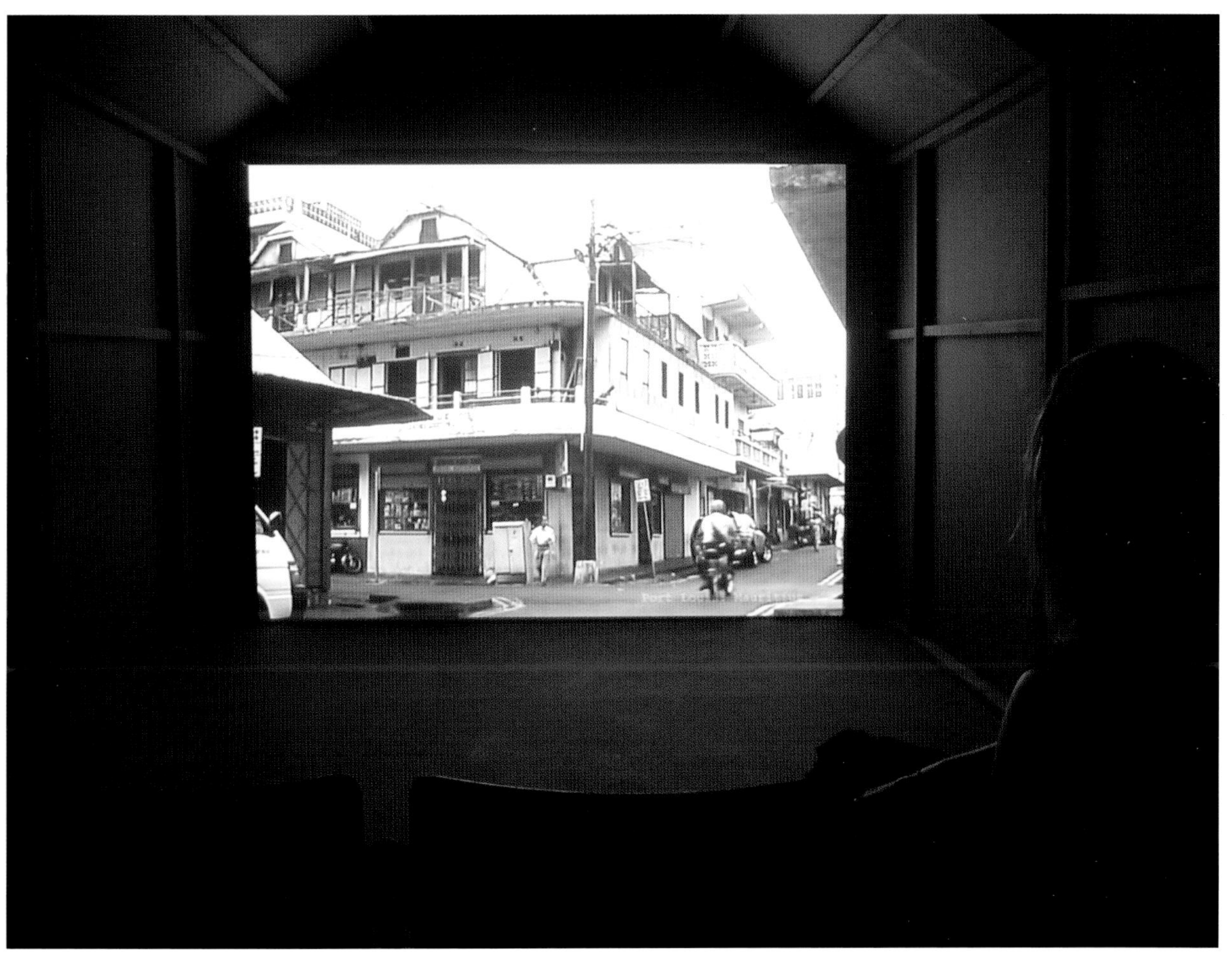

LINDSAY SEERS — *Extramission 4 (Black Maria)*, 2007, interior/exterior installation shots, courtesy Smart Project Space

Simon
STARLING

SIMON STARLING — ***Ballroom Doors, Manik Bagh Palace, Indore (open)*, 2007,**
Platinum/Palladium print 50.8 × 40.5
This photograph and the three subsequent are all extracts from ***Three Birds, Seven Stories, Interpolations and Bifurcations* 2008**, courtesy the artist and Galleria Franco Noero, Turin

Nearly all of the fixtures and fitting for Manik Bagh Palace were fabricated in Berlin.* The painted steel doors and windows were manufactured by Konrad Lindhurst, Berlin-Oberschöneweide and were fitted with grey/black tinted glass from Gustav Schulze & Jost, Berlin.

**The original design for Manik Bagh Palace (Garden of Precious Stones) was by the English architects McKensie & Co. The German architect Eckart Muthesius, commissioned by the Maharaja in 1929, absorbed part of this unfinished structure into his own design adding rust-red awnings (now defunct) in part to obscure the Jacobean style veranda that remained from the original building.*

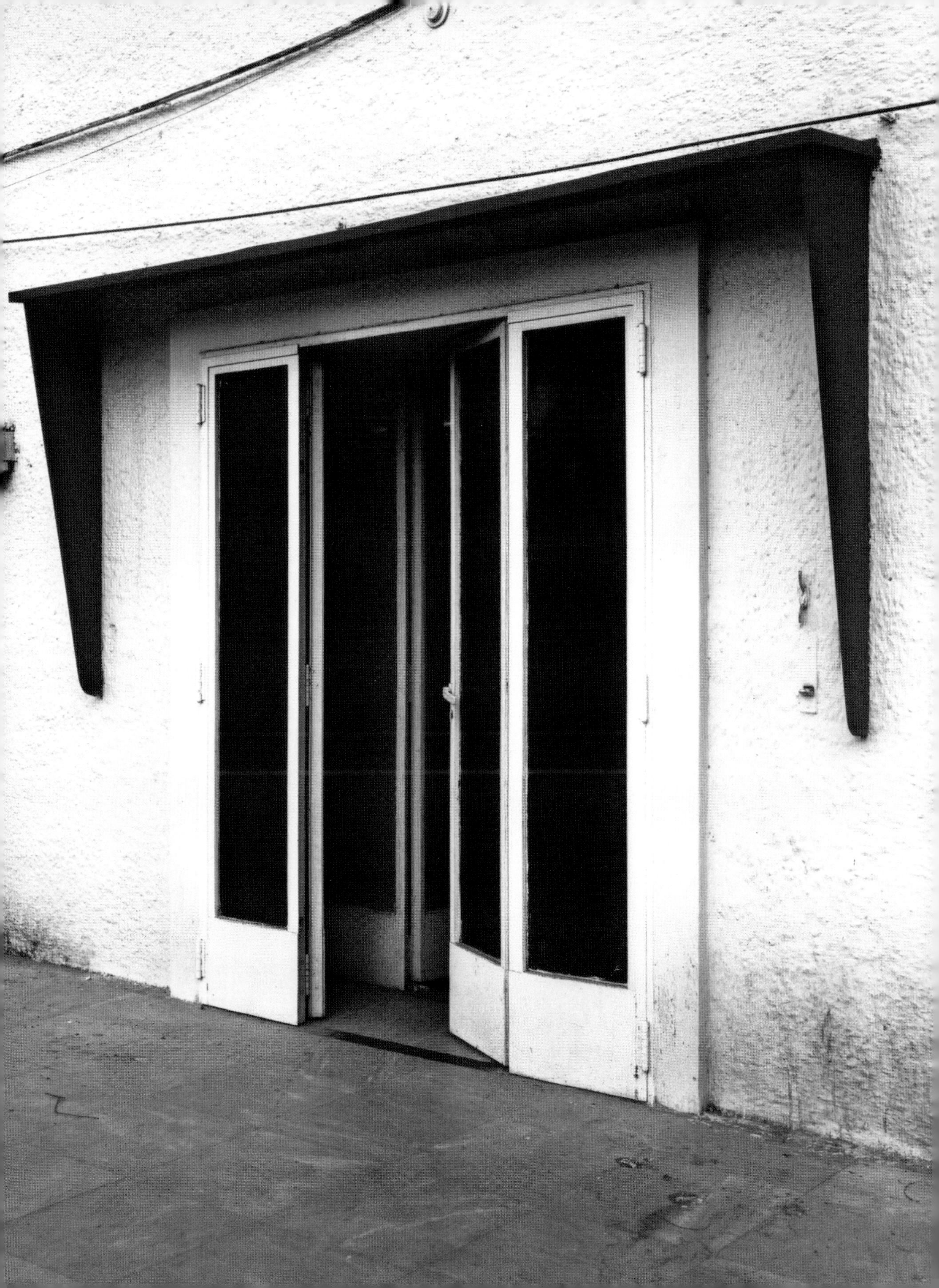

SIMON STARLING

1:1 scale model of the 5th Floor of 9 Via Giulia di Barolo, Turin (La Fetta di Polenta) built at Uferstrasse 8, Berlin,
2008, Platinum/Palladium print
40.5 × 50.8

The seven-story house at 9 Via Giulia di Barolo, locally known as the ***Fetta di Polenta,*** sits on just 40 sqm of land. The 16 metre-long house is at its widest point a mere 435 centimetres across and at its narrowest just 57 centimetres across. Its wedge-like form can be traced back to the partial demolition of a building that once blocked the end of Via Giulia di Barolo (formerly Via dei Macelli) that was carried out according to plans laid down by the architect Alessandro Antonelli in 1854.* The sliver of building that remained was converted into a simple three-story house with a flat roof. In 1859 this modest house was acquired by Francesca Scaccabarozzi, Antonelli's wife and he then asked for planning permission to add a further two stories. Once this permission had be granted the architect, as was his habit,* altered the design once more to include a further attic floor surrounded by a continuous small balcony. Each floor of the 23-metre-high house is accessed by a single trapezoid-shaped staircase. As well as the seven stories above ground, there are two basement floors including a kitchen and below that an elaborately decorated sauna.

**Alessandro Antonelli is most famous for his design for Turin's tallest building, the Mole Antonelliana. The original plans for this tower, originally designed as a synagogue, and now housing Turin's Film Museum were for a 67-metre-high tower but by the time it was complete it measured a total of 167 metres.*

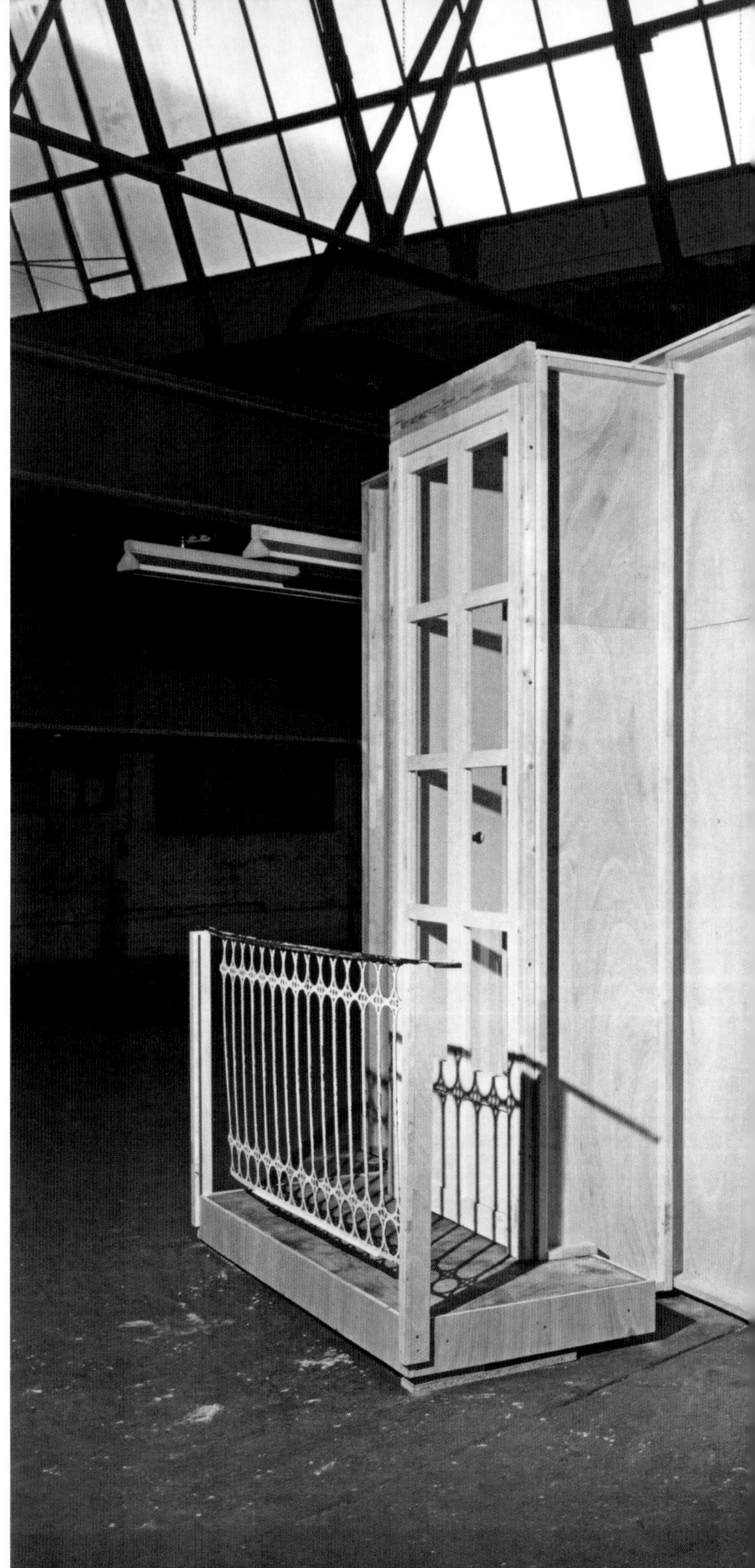

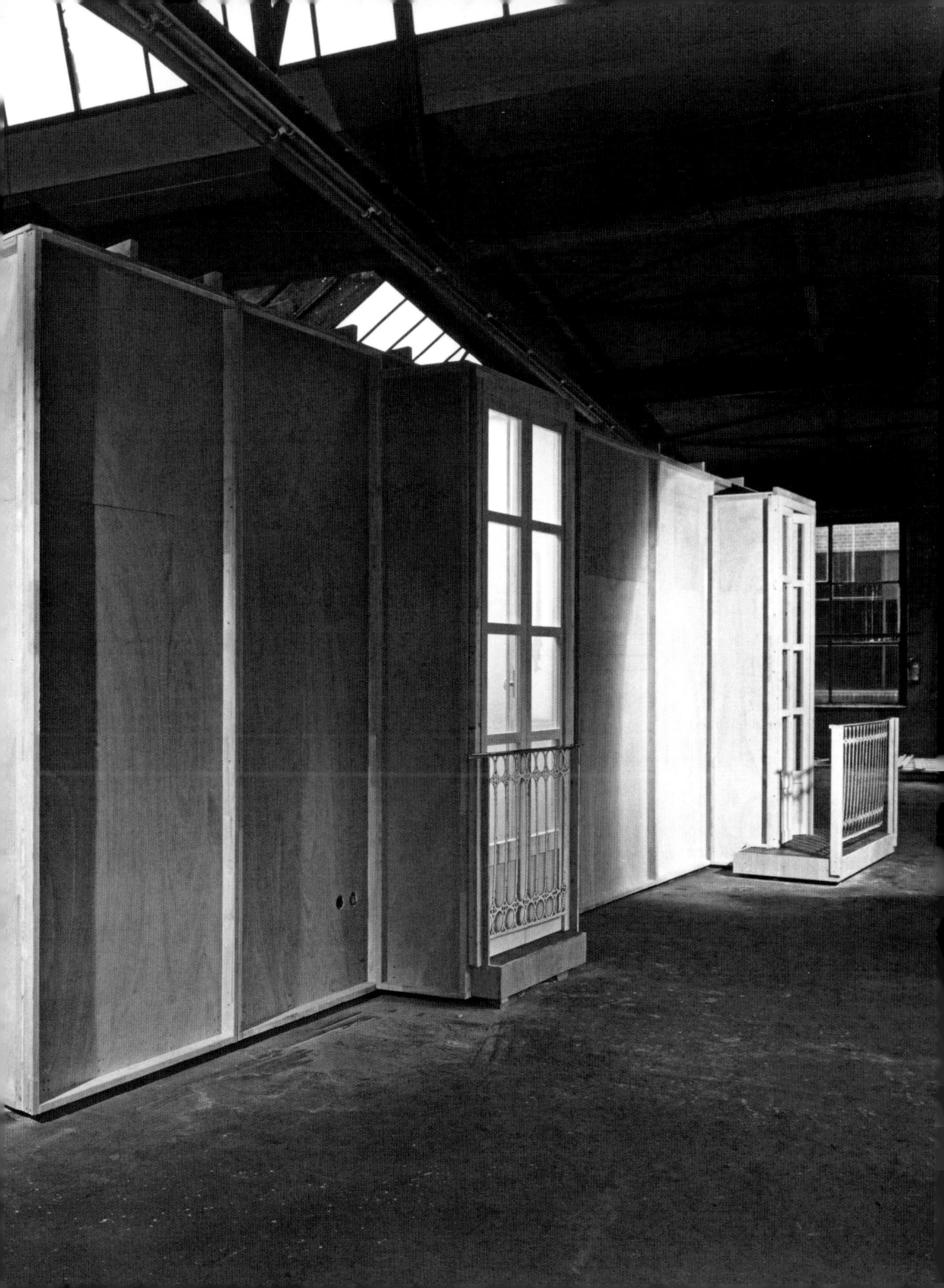

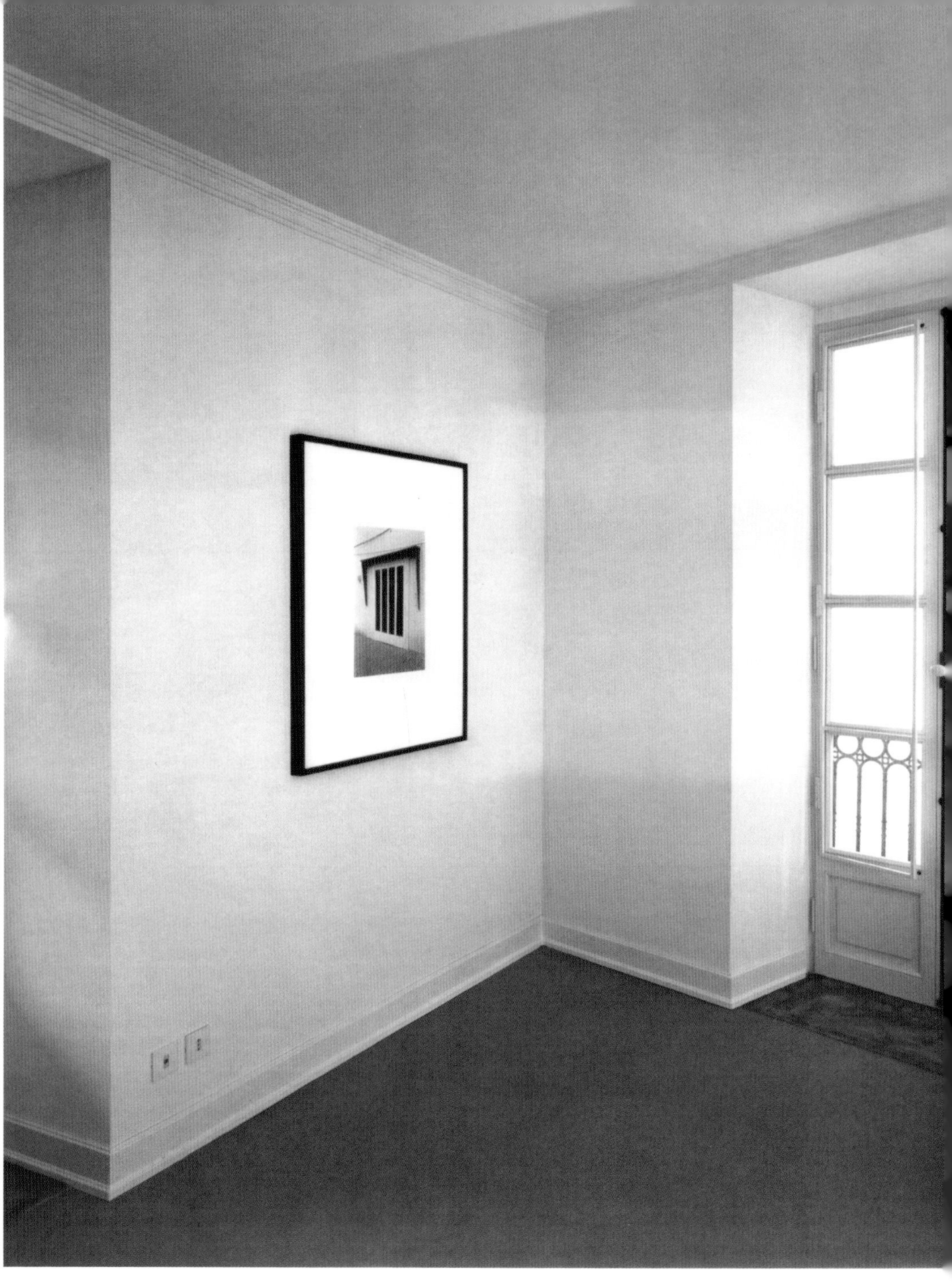

SIMON STARLING — [LEFT] ***Ballroom Doors, Manik Bagh Palace, Indore (closed),* 2008**, Platinum/Palladium print 50.8 × 40.5. Re-photographed in a 1:1 scale model of the fifth floor of Via Giulia di Barolo 9, Turin (*La Fetta di Polenta*) built at Uferstrasse 8, Berlin, by Annette Ueberlein, Jan Bleicher, Jan Dunkel and Antje Blumenstein. [RIGHT] ***Ballroom Doors, Manik Bagh Palace, Indore (closed),* 2008**, Platinum/Palladium print 50.8 × 40.5. Re-photographed in a 1:1 scale model of the fifth floor of Via Giulia di Barolo 9, Turin (*La Fetta di Polenta*) built at Uferstrasse 8, Berlin, by Annette Ueberlein, Jan Bleicher, Jan Dunkel and Antje Blumenstein. (Installation view, seventh floor, Via Giulia di Barolo 9, Turin [*La Fetta di Polenta*])

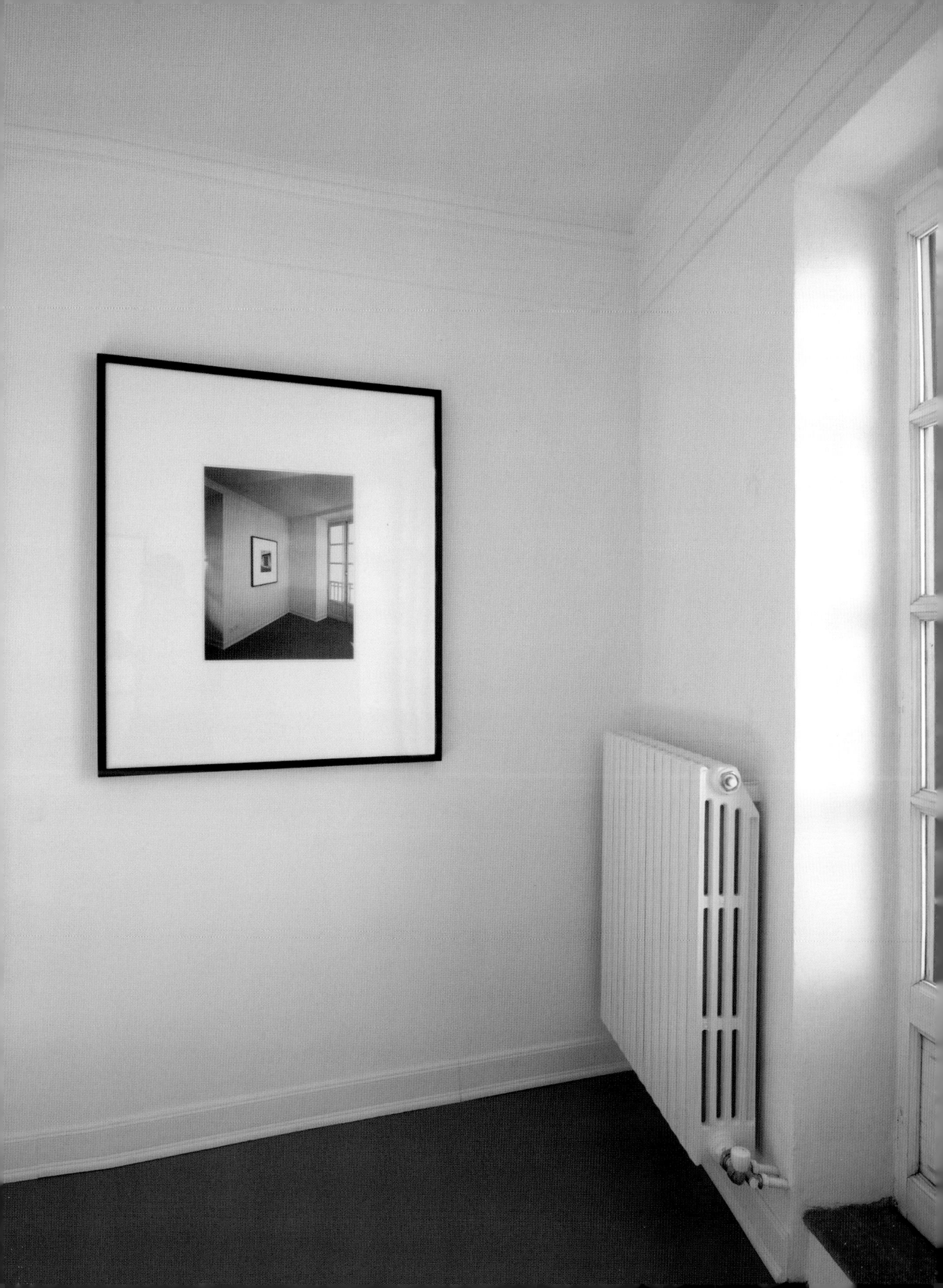

Pascale Marthine TAYOU

'MODERNITY' or 'contemporaneity' is the reflection of the present world in the mirror of the future, the past being the architectural model of our common histories – either known or still to be discovered.

It is therefore a matter of drawing up new frameworks of negotiation between different cultures, of mapping routes and coming up with new formulas so as to achieve the kind of globalisation in which development rhymes with humanity. For other 'modernities' are indeed possible at a time when the 'altermodern' might well become the bridge between the 'postmodern' and the 'modern'.

The other day, when I was in discussion about the great importance of the future in the construction of the past, we stressed the point that the birth of various 'alterglobalist' movements had come about thanks to encounters between heterogeneous groups around the world. There is well and truly a new modern culture. Every day and at every moment new construction sites are being created here and there; when all is said and done everything depends on us as individuals, on me as an identity in the midst of other thoughts. The magic that nature offers us opens up our field of operation ever wider. Every day new motorways are being built that lead to new places – there are many different ways of getting to Rome or Mecca, *omnes viae Roman ducunt* or *omnes viae Meqam ducunt*.

The world changes, it has always changed.

In the end, there are just so many gods!

Does modernity have to be truly global and why should it necessarily be so?

And if, instead of being simply a 'postmodern', I had the potential to be 'postglobal' or a 'postglobalist', would I seek to be as critical towards my African 'roots' as towards the colonial West?

Is this approach a critique of my African 'roots' or of the colonial West? And what in fact does one mean by critique?

My African origins are of course a fact of birth; there is no GPS where I come from, but my gaze fans out from my continent along the routes of the world: breaking out of the prison of my origins means making use of the spiritual in order to subvert the dogmas hidden in traditional thought. It is a matter of rifling through my ways and customs for elements that combine the useful with the agreeable, extending my roots under a foreign soil, making the network as wide as possible, exploding the boundaries, embracing the world.

But this as an approach that in no way constitutes a slogan or a profession of faith.

It is my delirium from the perspective of the African multitude when faced with the other world, the throng of the global village on the opposite bank.

By delirium I mean the adoption of intellectual, political ... artistic, plastic or hyper-plastic standpoints.

I am not a torch that lights up the cave; I am not a standard-bearer in Venice who awaits his Golden Lion.

Since everything is muddled and fuzzy, our common history is a combination of twists made up of innumerable knots.

My means of expression (which, to give it its 'ism', I call 'TAUDISME' – 'taudis' being the French word for a hovel or slum) has always been marked by a rejection of the inhuman, liberty not being synonymous with libertinism.

A popular Cameroonian proverb says that 'Money calls for Money' and one could also say that 'criticism calls for criticism', 'objects call for objects', 'makers call for makers'... and it is indeed the maker (until proved otherwise) who chooses his path, and it's equally straightforward and prudent to critique oneself before publicly critiquing others.

In the past, the exhibition of objects has largely tended to recall Western-style set design. If I am the representative of a culture, that implies that I accept the notion of national, regional or continental identity, in other words that I represent the sum of all the other identities built around a common discourse, and that such a discourse is aimed at a certain 'shared ideal', or an ideal supposedly shared by all or by the majority of the chosen batch.

Such an approach is indeed difficult to accommodate in the field of creation or procreation since it doesn't take into account the identities that are shunted to one side, consigned to the dungeons of the edifices of the 'majority'.

I therefore reject the notion of representing a group. I refuse to participate in it. You are automatically part of a group, and those that carry you and believe in you are your representatives, whether they're from here or from elsewhere. I am against the romantic viewpoint of exhibitions constructed on the model of humanitarian aid; such a practice distorts the true exotic meaning of the word 'exoticism', which in my opinion is the kingdom of curiosity, the encounter of the unknown, the question marks that one finds in cartoon bubbles.

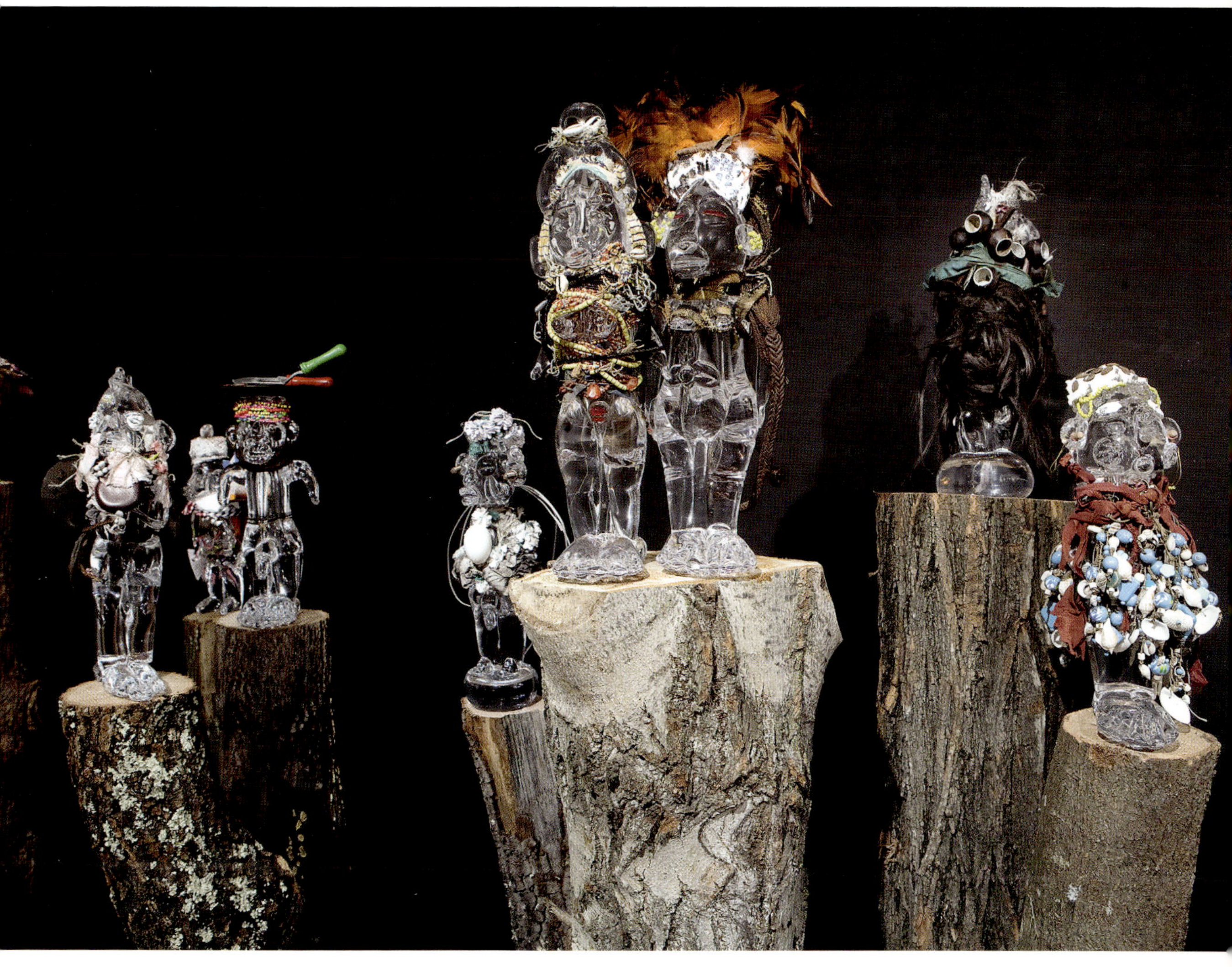

PASCALE MARTHINE TAYOU — ***Poupées Pascales*, 2008**, crystal, mixed media, view of the exhibition ***Jungle Fever***, Galleria Continua, San Gimignano, courtesy Galleria Continua, San Gimignano/Beijing/Le Moulin

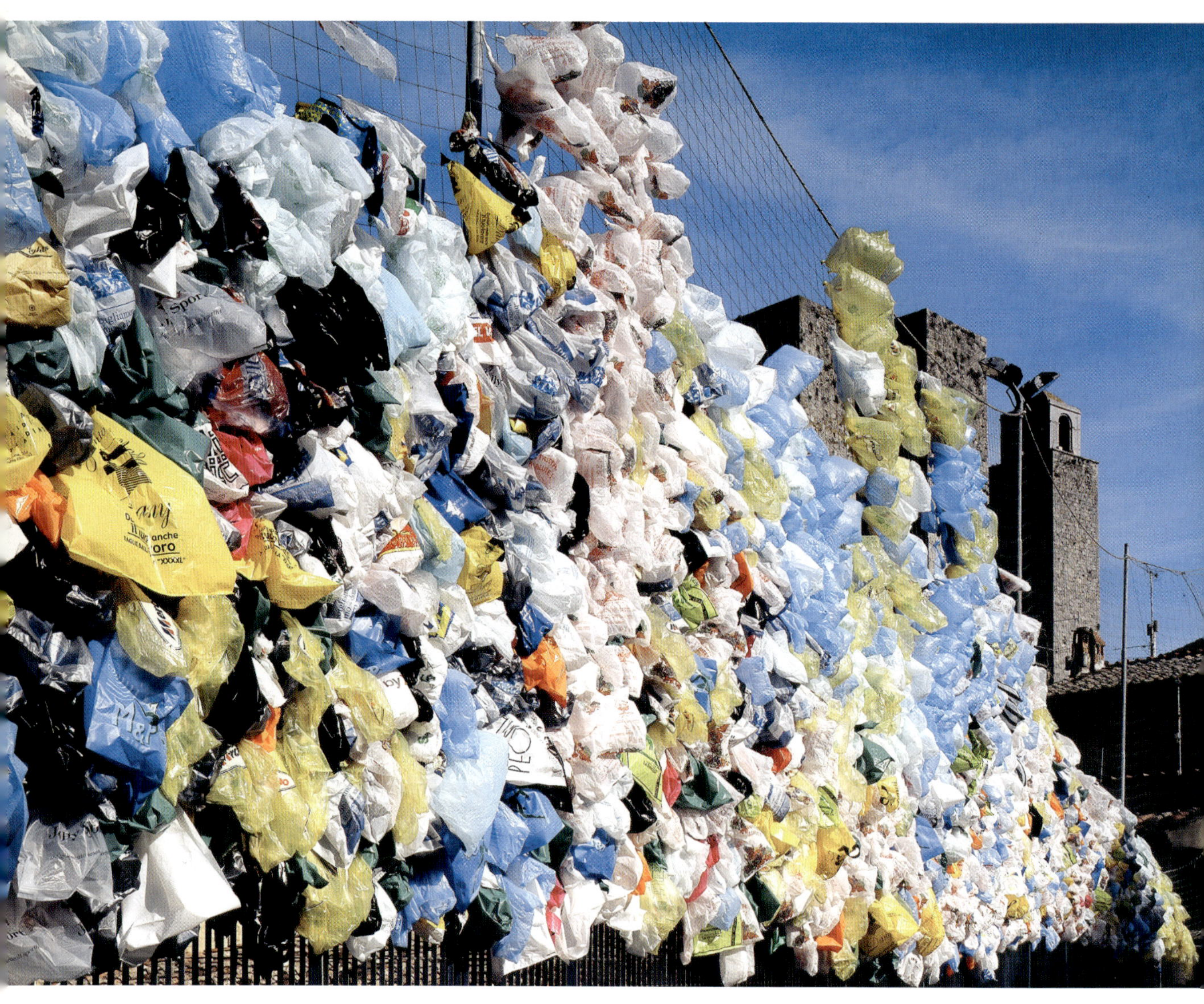

PASCALE MARTHINE TAYOU — [LEFT] ***Plastic Bags,* 2001**, plastic bags, variable dimensions, installation for ***Voices Over*** – installation view at Arte all'Arte 6, San Gimignano
[RIGHT] Foreground ***Matiti A,* 2008**,
foam polystyrene, pencils, felt pens, chalks, adhesive tape, 125 × 120 × 80,
background from left: ***Chalk G, Chalk H*** and ***Chalk E,* 2008**, wood, chalks, 165 × 212 × 7,
view of the exhibition ***Jungle Fever***, Galleria Continua, San Gimignano,
courtesy Galleria Continua, San Gimignano/Beijing/Le Moulin

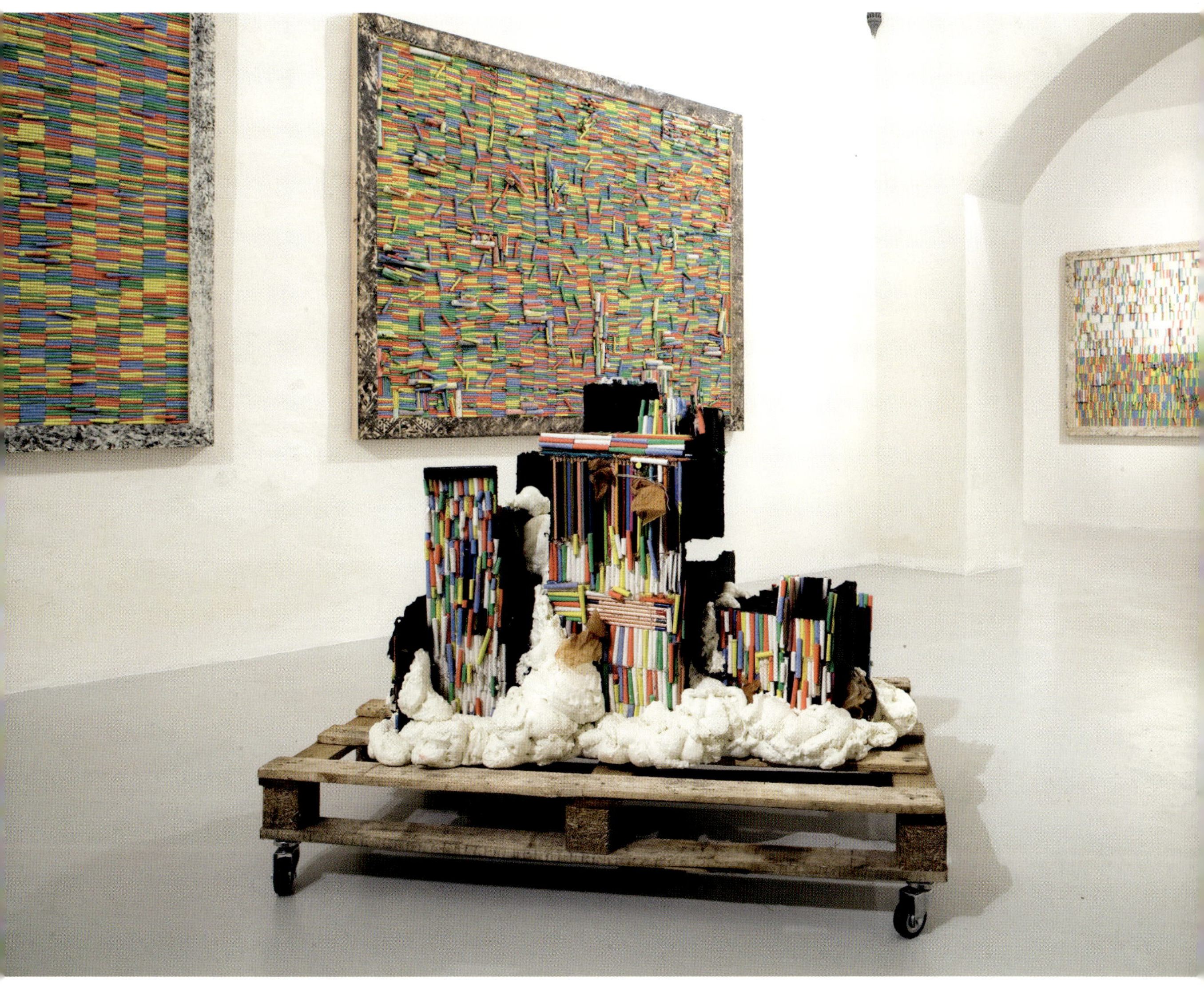

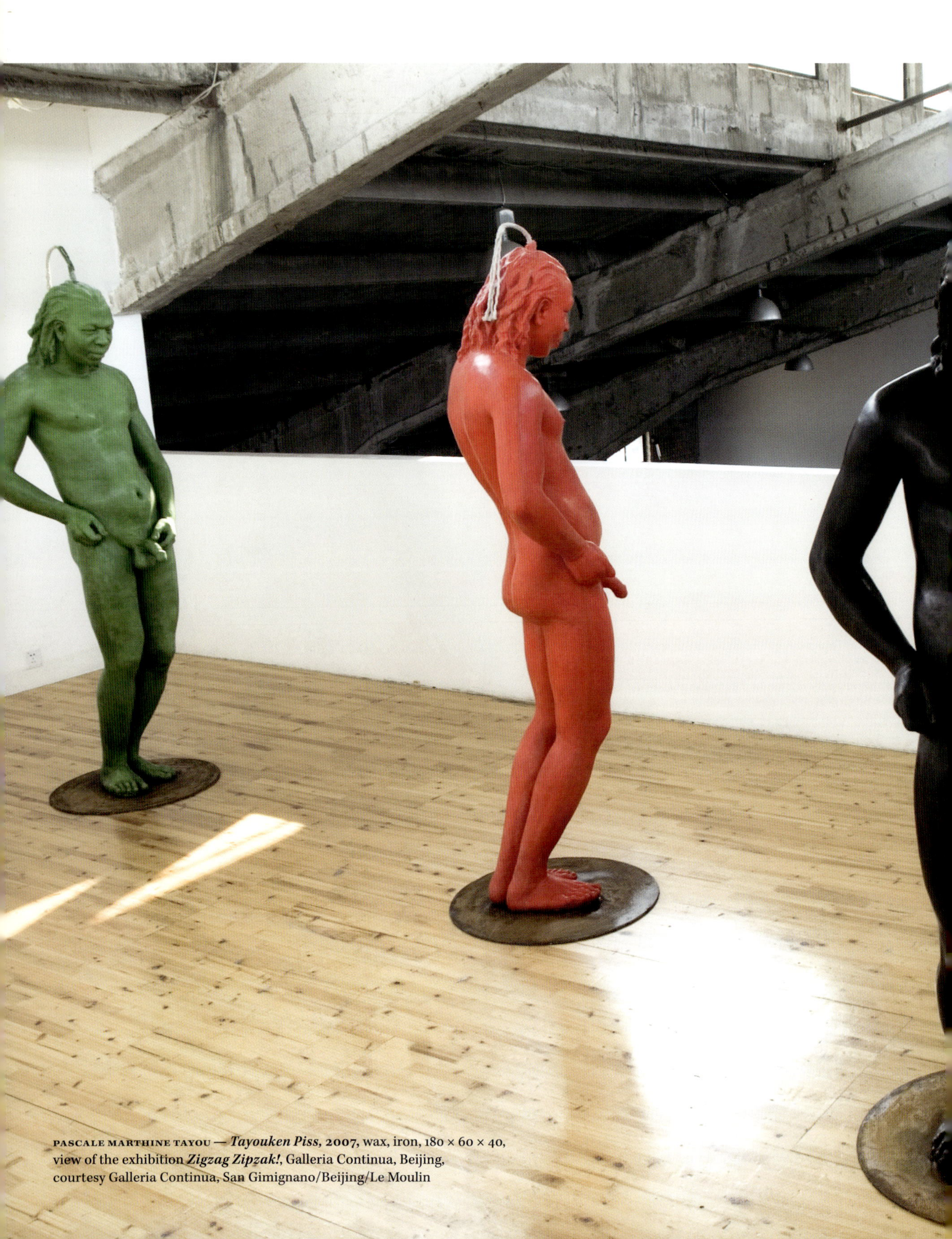

PASCALE MARTHINE TAYOU — *Tayouken Piss*, 2007, wax, iron, 180 × 60 × 40, view of the exhibition *Zigzag Zipzak!*, Galleria Continua, Beijing, courtesy Galleria Continua, San Gimignano/Beijing/Le Moulin

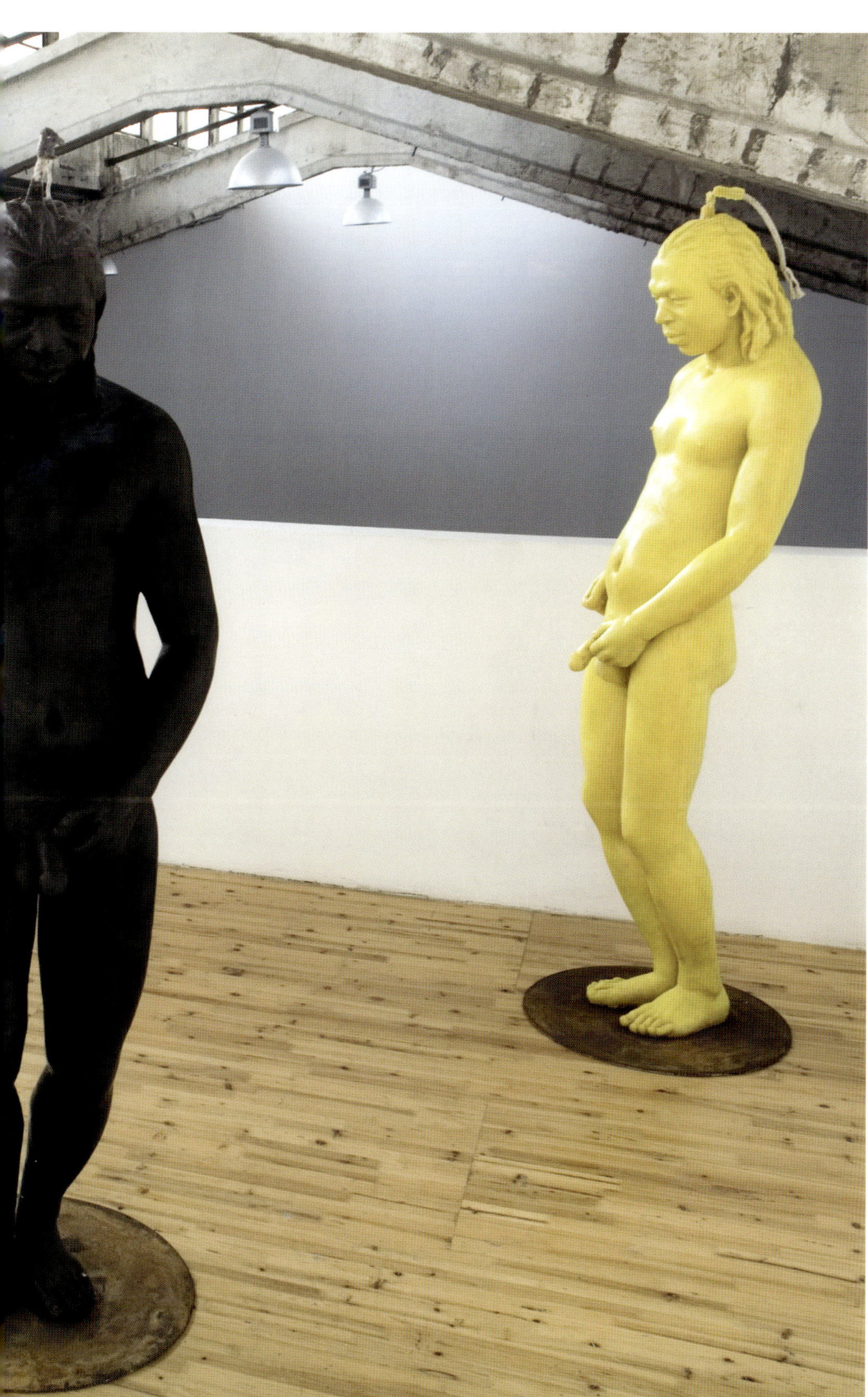

Tris VONNA-MICHELL

01:17AM. It's late, got an early start. Off to Limehouse to unload my studio space. With regards to personal history and narration – I feel that as an adult I'm experiencing the reflection of personal history through so many accelerated forms, therefore the decision to let my works or monologues be conveyed similarly was a natural consequence. But it's not something I'd embrace. I like the idea of narratives aging over time, becoming more vintage and fragile. Either way, in response to your question – yes, travel is a form in itself. I've just run over time: **01:21AM.** It's the confrontation of a moment and place that really propels me. That's where the challenge is, not necessarily the egg-timer. The verbalisation or sculpting of time or urgency is only a decoy to avert any dominant mental dispositions and/or realign my thoughts into a full and useful set of ideas. I always ignore time. **01:23AM.** Guess not, finished just on time. I wish I could end some things, but it just doesn't happen – despite most of my works starting with the intention of an ending ... or at least questioning the notion of an ending, I often never get anywhere near one. And when an ending somehow finds its way within my work or life I immediately try to comprehend it ... hence prolongation. Another question, followed by an attempt to answer it with a self-imposed time limitation: abbreviation or detour? A leather notepad kept open by a Pilot black ink pen. Irrelevancies and time-counters; locators for an ongoing and invisible or adjacent script, similar to that of non-existent questions or markers or indeed attractions. Places that are below or racing by, too aloof for examination and too ajar from reality for appreciation. Directives take prescience: from maps comprising of routes and itineraries to route describers. I know how to describe a route better than a destination, but then again, perhaps the journey is over-emphasised, and if so, best to be able to locate the act of description over the memory of arrival. Since most arrivals look the same and end.

Dual sight-seeing and travelogueing – *doing* and *seeing* become one, as announcements punctuate the scenery with convictions. Filling in the gaps with guide-books at later dates whilst endorsing the discontinuity between me, the spectator-traveller, and the space of the landscape that I'm passing through; airport digits evoking places that are abbreviated and consumed readily, just in time for departure – places that exist only through the words that evoke them. Words create the image and procure the myth: abbreviation. Egg-timer ... as a decoy, most of the time. Occasionally it's useful to amplify the present moment of delivery – to really intensify the whole experience (for the audience) thus allowing me to remove myself from it. Slide projectors or certain objects/props ... Well, projections – really depends on which work. As for objects – depends on certain past and present relationships with them. Not sure how long I have to answer this question, but I'm sure it's no more than three minutes ... At the beginning there was less repetition, perhaps no repetition – spoken word narratives lasted longer and the inherent content had more rough-edges ... which needed to be filtered through many live or reflective processes. Gradually core words or associations lost or found their form, paving way to new meaning within the overall structure of the work. The detective work is perhaps merely self-articulating; it's a way for me to find the perfect word or wording within a fast and ever-changing narration. Intimation: during a performance, faces of the audience become much more pictorial – I've bad eyesight, can't see much beyond two metres, but I don't wear glasses. Lost too many pairs. I work off their presence, and within the framework decided (collectively sometimes, although deceptively so) they induce the sculpting process, which is quite physical. Afterwards my awareness returns to the present state – I look at a mass of people, grateful that they are still present. As for reactions, well – **01:31AM** – I barely ever see their faces, similar to an author and his readers – but of course the presence of readership is massive, in my case it's the same, running over time – **01:32AM** – but I often hope that despite a performance lasting just five minutes (yet being developed over five years) that the audience will have a similar memory or perception of experiencing a certain disproportion in time.

With thanks to Sarah Kim

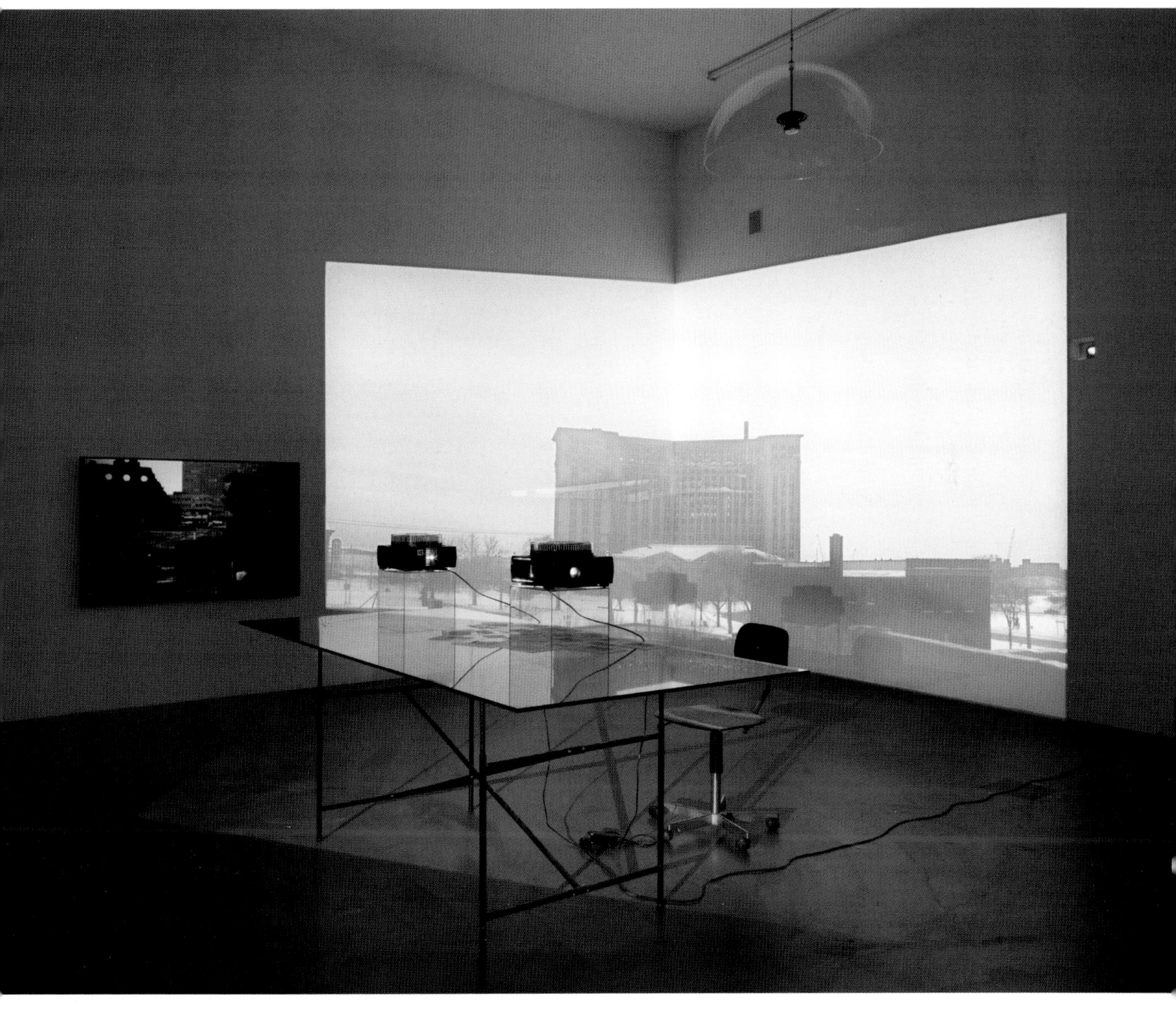

TRIS VONNA-MICHELL — ***Seizure*, 2007–8**, (from the work *hahn/huhn*, 2003 – ongoing) 35mm slide projections, 6 × 7 slide projection, audio-collage, printed papers, dimensions variable, exhibition at Kunsthalle Zürich, 2008

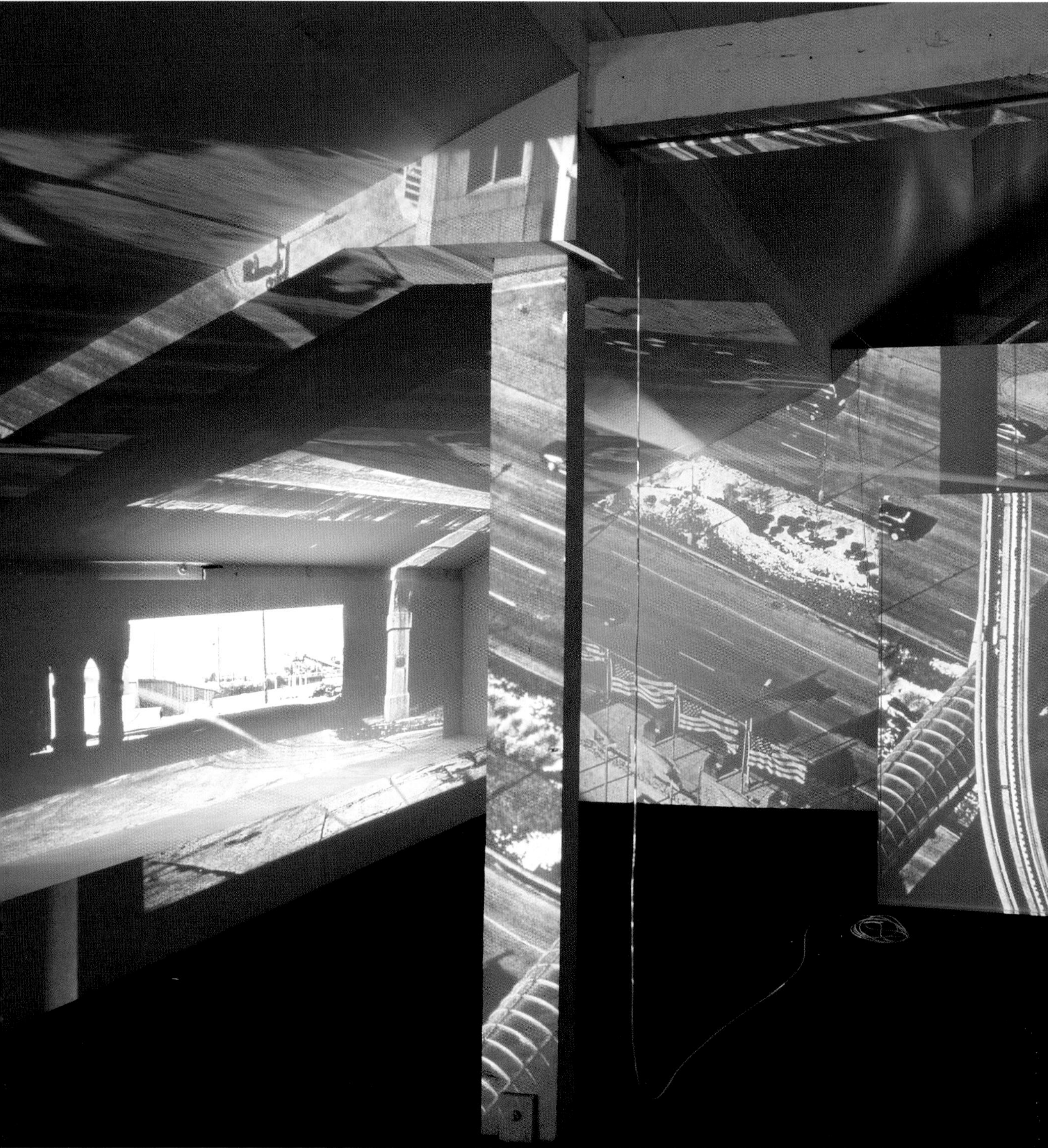

TRIS VONNA-MICHELL — *Studio A,* 2008, installation, mixed media and objects, dimensions variable, exhibition at the fifth Berlin Biennial for contemporary art, KW Institute for Contemporary Art, Berlin, 2008

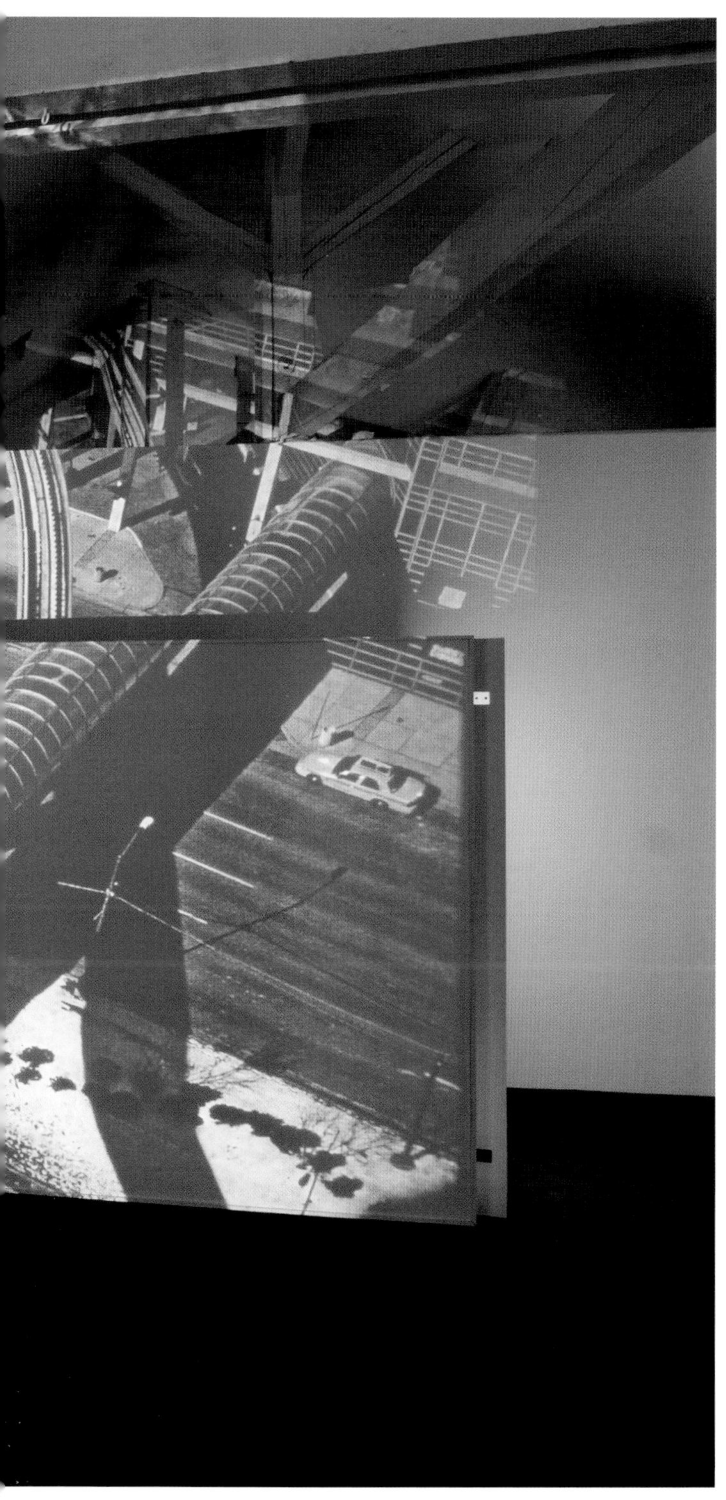

Appendices

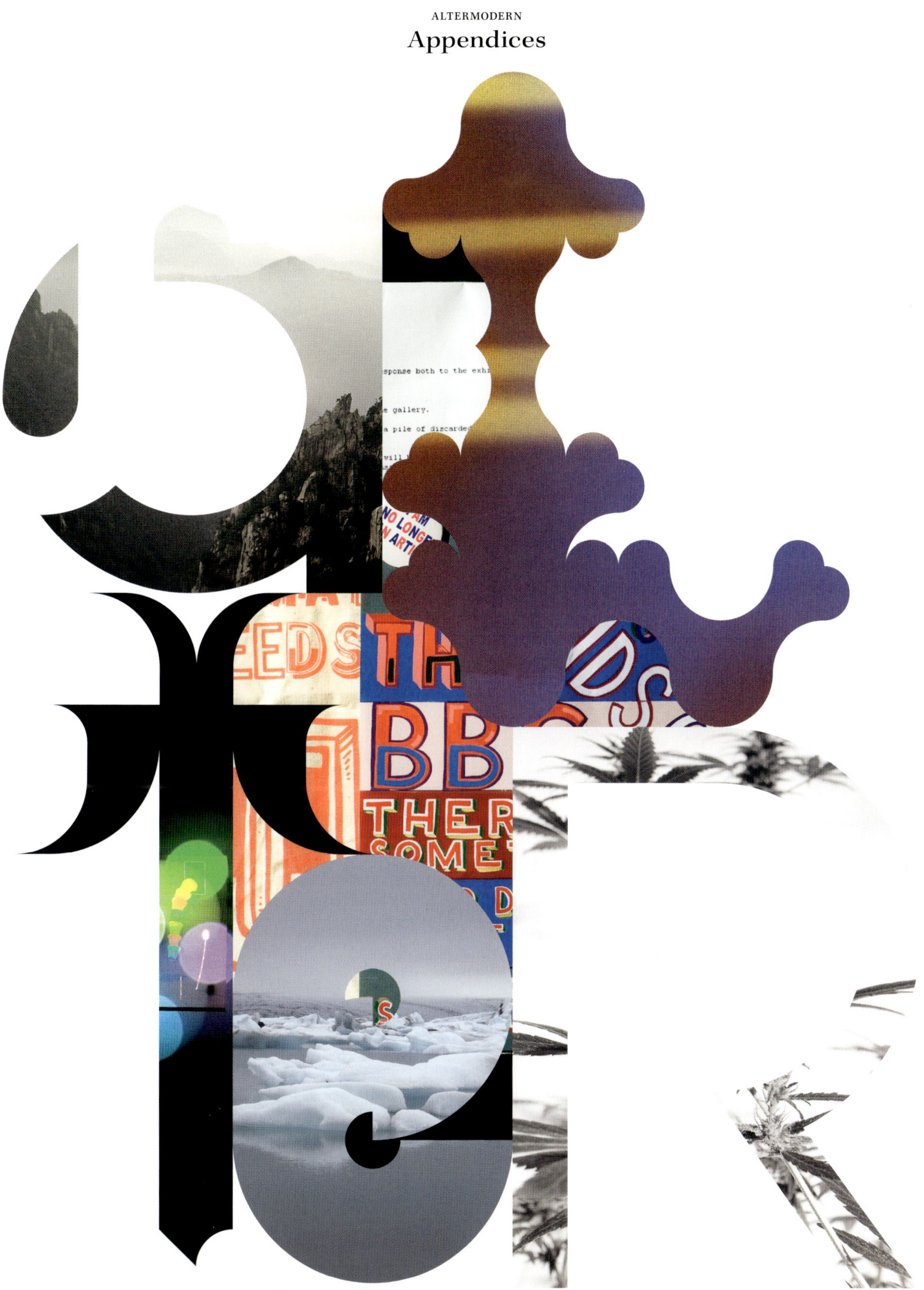

FRANZ ACKERMANN
b. 1963, Neumarkt St. Veit, Germany

'Gateway' – Getaway
2008–9
Room installation, mixed media, wall painting, oil on canvas and watercolour
Dimensions variable
Courtesy the artist

DARREN ALMOND
b. 1971, Wigan

FullMoon@Huangshan
2008
C-print on paper
276 × 127
Courtesy the artist, Galerie Max Hetzler, Berlin and Jay Jopling/White Cube, London

Dragon's Eye, 2008
C-print on paper
183 × 183
Courtesy the artist, Galerie Max Hetzler, Berlin and Jay Jopling/White Cube, London

Fullmoon@the Sea of Clouds, 2008
C-print on paper
183 × 183
Courtesy the artist, Galerie Max Hetzler, Berlin and Jay Jopling/White Cube, London

CHARLES AVERY
b. 1973, Oban

Aleph Nul Head, 2008
Plaster
425 × 220 × 500
Courtesy the artist

Installation of drawings
Pencil, ink and gouache on card and paper; wood, glass, and brass plates
Dimensions variable
Courtesy the artist

WALEAD BESHTY
b. 1976, London

Transparency (Positive) [Fuji Provia Color Film: October 19 – October 21, 2007 ORD/LAX LAX/ORD]
Epson Ultrachrome K3 archival ink jet print on Museo Silver Rag paper
151 × 111.8
Courtesy Wallspace, New York and China Art Objects Galleries, Los Angeles

Transparency (Negative) [Kodak NC Color Film: May 8 – May 18, 2008 ORD/LHR LHR/IAD IAD/JFK LGA/DCA DCA/ORD]
Epson Ultrachrome K3 archival ink jet print on Museo Silver Rag paper
151 × 111.8
Courtesy Wallspace, New York and China Art Objects Galleries, Los Angeles

Transparency (Negative) [Kodak NC Color Film: December 5 – December 9, 2007 ORD/MIA MIA/ORD]
Epson Ultrachrome K3 archival ink jet print on Museo Silver Rag paper
151 × 111.8
Courtesy Wallspace, New York and China Art Objects Galleries, Los Angeles

Transparency (Negative) [Kodak NC Color Film: October 15 – October 19, 2008 LAX/LHR LHR/LAX]
Epson Ultrachrome K3 archival ink jet print on Museo Silver Rag paper
151 × 111.8
Courtesy Wallspace, New York and China Art Objects Galleries, Los Angeles

Transparency (Positive) [Fuji Provia Color Film: April 7 – April 13, 2008 ORD/LAX LAX/ORD]
Epson Ultrachrome K3 archival ink jet print on Museo Silver Rag paper
151 × 111.8
Courtesy Wallspace, New York and China Art Objects Galleries, Los Angeles

FedEx Medium Kraft Box R4578, International Priority, Los Angeles-Tijuana trk# 8652 8205 8011, October 29–31, 2008
Glass with safety glass laminate, silicon and cardboard
50.8 × 50.8 × 50.8
Courtesy Wallspace, New York and China Art Objects Galleries, Los Angeles

FedEx Medium Kraft Box R4578, International Priority, Los Angeles-Tijuana trk# 8652 8205 8022, October 29–31, 2008
Glass with safety glass laminate, silicon and cardboard
50.8 × 50.8 × 50.8
Courtesy Wallspace, New York and China Art Objects Galleries, Los Angeles

FedEx Medium Kraft Box R4578, International Priority, Los Angeles-Tijuana trk# 8652 8205 8000, October 29–31, 2008
Glass with safety glass laminate, silicon and cardboard
50.8 × 50.8 × 50.8
Courtesy Wallspace, New York and China Art Objects Galleries, Los Angeles

FedEx Medium Kraft Box R4578, International Priority, Los Angeles-Tijuana trk# 8652 8205 7997, October 29–31, 2008
Glass with safety glass laminate, silicon and cardboard
50.8 × 50.8 × 50.8
Courtesy Wallspace, New York and China Art Objects Galleries, Los Angeles

SPARTACUS CHETWYND
b. 1973, London

Hermitos Children, 2008
DVD; TV wall
Courtesy the artist and Herald St, London

MARCUS COATES
b. 1968, London

The Plover's Wing, 2008
HDV
22 min
Courtesy the artist and Workplace Gallery

PETER COFFIN
b. 1972, Berkeley, California

Untitled (Tate Britain), 2009
Animation and works from Tate Collection
Courtesy the artist and Andrew Kreps Gallery, New York; Galerie Perrotin, Paris and Herald St, London

MATTHEW DARBYSHIRE
b. 1977, Cambridge

Palac, 2009
Mixed media
Dimensions variable
Courtesy the artist and Herald St, London

SHEZAD DAWOOD
b. 1974, London

Feature, 2008
DVD
55 min
Courtesy the artist and Paradise Row
Feature received Funding from Arts Council England East, and Wysing Arts Centre and was realised with completion funding from Arts Council England London and the support of Film London Artist's Moving Image Network and further support from the Arts and Humanities Research Council.

TACITA DEAN
b. 1965, Canterbury

The Russian Ending, 2001
Photogravure on paper
20 images; each 45 × 68.5
Tate. Presented by the artist 2002

RUTH EWAN
b. 1980, Aberdeen

Squeezebox Jukebox, 2009
Giant accordian constructed by Giancarlo Francenella in Castelfidardo, Italy 2000
Once a day for the duration of the exhibition two volunteers will play a selection of songs from Ewan's ongoing archive of protest and political songs: *A Jukebox of People Trying to Change the World*, 2003 –
Courtesy the artist and Ancient & Modern, London

LORIS GRÉAUD
b. 1979, Eaubonne, France

Tremors Where Forever (Frequency of an Image, White Edit), 2008
Modified micro vibrators, software, plexiglass console and white paint
Dimensions variable
Courtesy GréaudStudio and Yvon Lambert Paris/New York

SUBODH GUPTA
b. 1964, Khagaul, Bihar, India

Line of Control, 2008
Stainless steel and steel structure, stainless steel utensils
1000 × 1000 × 1000
Courtesy the artist, Arario Gallery, Beijing and Hauser & Wirth Zurich/London

RACHEL HARRISON
b. 1966, New York

Second Voyage, 2008
Suite of 58 digital inkjet prints
40.6 × 29.2
Courtesy Greene Naftali, New York

A Whole New Game, 2008
Wood, chicken wire, styrofoam, Parex, acrylic, photograph, ping pong balls
157.5 × 129.5 × 68.6
Courtesy Greene Naftali, New York

Bike Week at Daytona, 2008
Wood, plastic, Parex, cement, acrylic, cinder block, ribbon, DVD player and bike week video
251.5 × 35.6 × 147.3
Courtesy Meyer Kainer Gallery and Greene Naftali, New York

JOACHIM KOESTER
b. 1962, Copenhagen

The Hashish Club, 2008
16 mm film animation, lamps and photograph
6 min
Courtesy the artist and Galerie Jan Mot, Brussels

NATHANIEL MELLORS
b. 1974, Doncaster

Giantbum, 2008
Video installation with animatronic sculpture
Dimensions variable
Courtesy the artist and Matt's Gallery, London

GUSTAV METZGER
b. 1926, Nuremberg

Liquid Crystal Environment, 2006
Mixed media
Dimensions variable
Tate. Purchased 2006

MIKE NELSON
b. 1967, Loughborough

The projection room (Triple Bluff Canyon), 2004
Constructed room with video projection
300 × 500 × 400
Originally commissioned as part of the installation Triple Bluff Canyon at Modern Art Oxford
Courtesy the artist, Galleria Franco Noero, Turin; Matt's Gallery, London and 303 Gallery, New York

DAVID NOONAN
b. 1969, Ballarat, Victoria, Australia

Untitled, 2008
Silkscreen on jute and linen collage
30.4 × 21.4
Courtesy the David Simkins Collection

Untitled, 2008
Silk screen on jute, wood and steel in 5 parts
Dimensions variable
Courtesy the artist and HOTEL, London

KATIE PATERSON
b. 1981, Glasgow

All the Dead Stars, 2008
Etched metal
200 × 300
Courtesy the artist and Albion, London

OLIVIA PLENDER
b. 1977, London

Machine Shall be the Slave of Man, but We Will Not Slave for the Machine, 2008
Mixed media
Dimensions variable
Courtesy the artist

SETH PRICE
b. 1973, East Jerusalem

Untitled, 2008
Cherry Burl and diamond acrylic, laser-cut from jpeg
Dimensions variable
Private Collection, courtesy Capitain Petzel, Berlin

Untitled, 2008
Burled Carpathian elm and diamond acrylic, laser-cut from jpeg
Dimensions variable
Private Collection, courtesy Capitain Petzel, Berlin

Untitled, 2008
Vavona Redwood and diamond acrylic, laser-cut from jpeg
Dimensions variable
Private Collection, courtesy Capitain Petzel, Berlin

NAVIN RAWANCHAIKUL
b. 1971, Chiang Mai, Thailand

From Puk-kun to Mari, 2008
Pencil on paper
30 × 84
Courtesy the artist

Hong Rub Khaek, 2008
Single video channel
16 min
Courtesy the artist
Places of Rebirth 2009
Acrylic on canvas
220 × 720
Courtesy the artist

LINDSAY SEERS
b. 1966, Mauritius

Extramission 6 (Black Maria), 2009
Mixed media and DVD projection
1000 × 400 × 500
Courtesy the artist

BOB & ROBERTA SMITH
b. 1963, London

Off Voice Fly Tip, 2009
Mixed media
Dimensions variable
Courtesy the artist and Hales Gallery, London

SIMON STARLING
b. 1967, Epsom

Three White Desks, 2008–9
Mixed media
225 × 75 × 55
Courtesy the artist

PASCALE MARTHINE TAYOU
b. 1967, Yaoundé, Cameroon

Plastic bags, 2001–9
Plastic bags
Dimensions variable
Courtesy Galleria Continua, San Gimignano/Beijing/Le Moulin

TRIS VONNA-MICHELL
b. 1982, Rochford

Monumental Detours / Insignificant Fixtures, 2008–9
From the work, hahn / huhn, 2003 – ongoing
Dimensions variable
Courtesy the artist and Cabinet, London

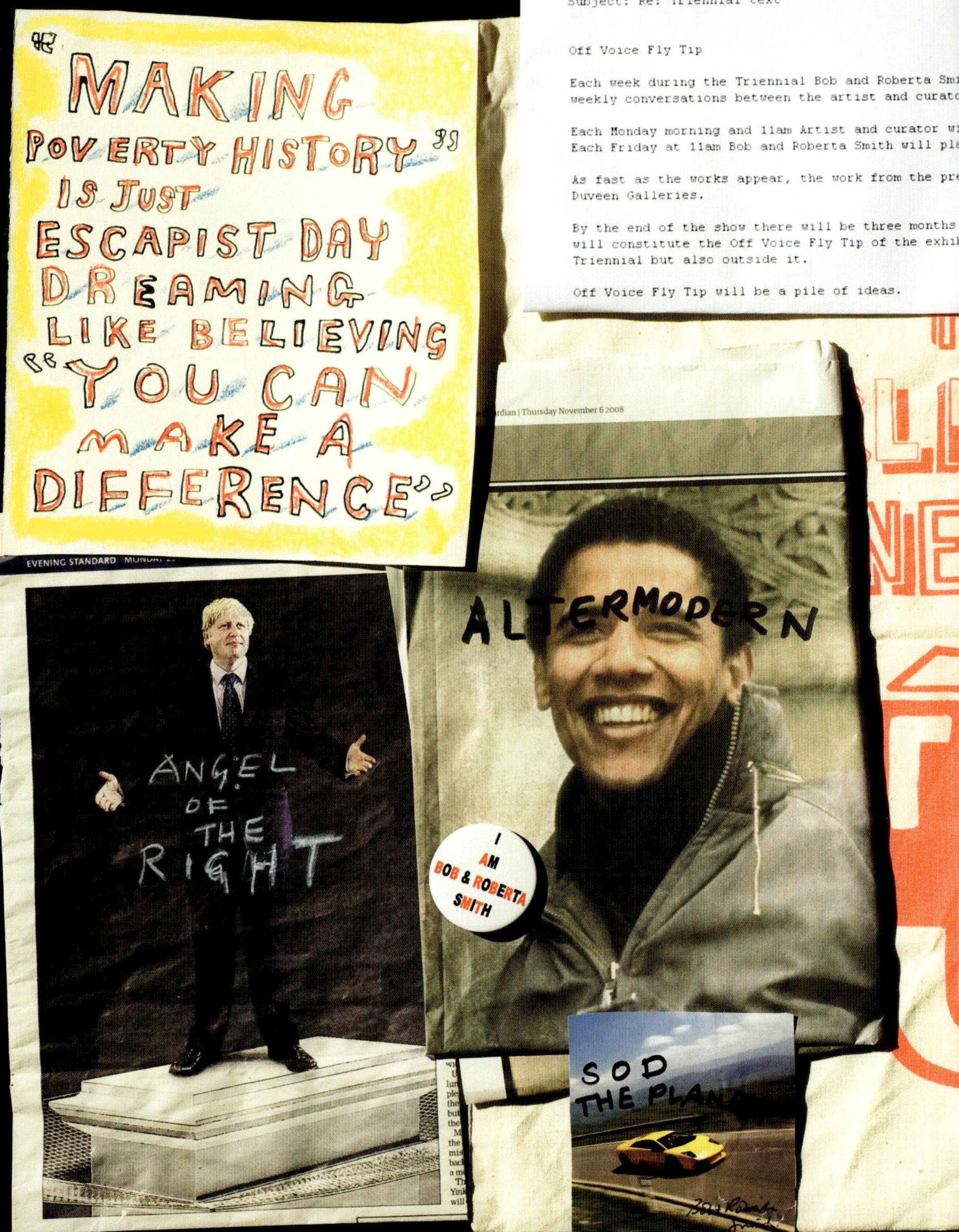
-----Original Message-----
From: Bob Smith
Sent: 10 November 2008 20:54
Subject: Re: Triennial text

Off Voice Fly Tip

Each week during the Triennial Bob and Roberta Smi
weekly conversations between the artist and curato

Each Monday morning and 11am Artist and curator wi
Each Friday at 11am Bob and Roberta Smith will pla

As fast as the works appear, the work from the pre
Duveen Galleries.

By the end of the show there will be three months
will constitute the Off Voice Fly Tip of the exhib
Triennial but also outside it.

Off Voice Fly Tip will be a pile of ideas.

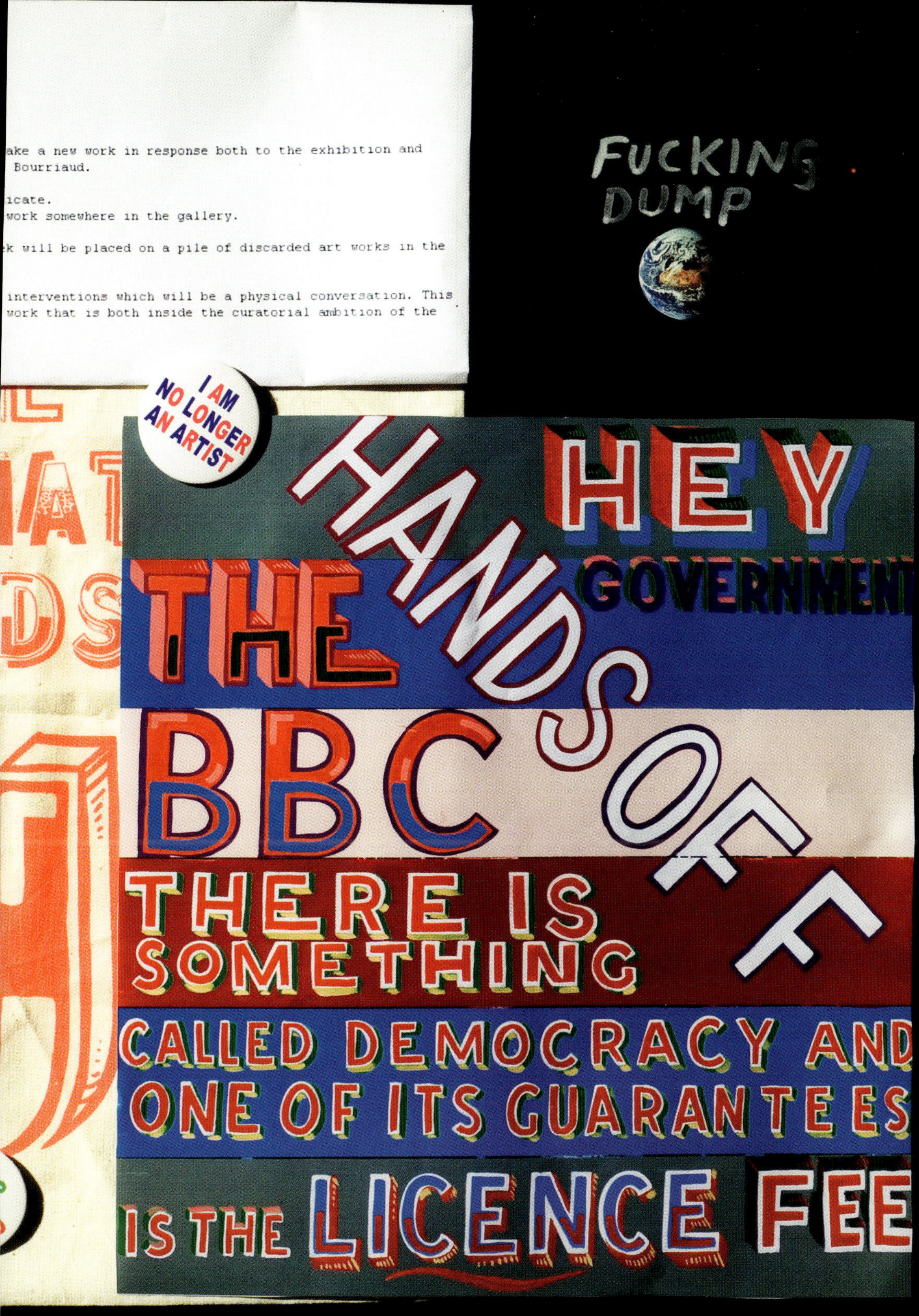

ake a new work in response both to the exhibition and
Bourriaud.

icate.
work somewhere in the gallery.

k will be placed on a pile of discarded art works in the

interventions which will be a physical conversation. This
work that is both inside the curatorial ambition of the

FUCKING
DUMP

I AM
NO LONGER
AN ARTIST

HEY
GOVERNMENT
HANDS OFF
THE
BBC
THERE IS
SOMETHING
CALLED DEMOCRACY AND
ONE OF ITS GUARANTEES
IS THE LICENCE FEE

PHOTOGRAPHIC CREDITS

213
Stefan Altenburger

146; 147, *bottom*
Thorsten Arendt/artdoc.de

104, *top*; 105, *bottom*
Thierry Bal

207, 209
Ela Bialkowska

97, *bottom*
Lisa Byrne

18, *top*
Courtesy James Cohan Gallery, New York

64–5
Nick David

156–7, 158–9
Alex Delfanne

174–5
Eugenie Dolberg/INS

105, *top*; 104, *bottom*
Ruth Ewan

150–1
FBM Studio, Zürich

30
Courtesy Gladstone Gallery, New York

29, *top*
Courtesy Thomas Hirschhorn and Gladstone Gallery, New York

17, *top*
Hulton Archive/Getty Images

198, 199
Gerjan Konings

18, *bottom*
Courtesy Yvon Lambert

208
Attilio Maranzano

29, *top*
Werner Maschmann

147, *top*; 148–9
Roman Mensing/artdoc.de

38
Courtesy Navin Production

166
Norbert Miguletz

86, *left*
Courtesy Flávia Müller Medeiros

134, 135
Zoran Naskovski

102–3
Nisi Audiovisivi di Castelfidardo (AN)

108–9
Olivier Pasqual

62
Jo Ramirez

14
Reprinted by permission of The Random House Group Ltd

96; 97, *top*
Lewin St Cyr

107
Sophie Soula

99–101
Tate Photography © Tate

28; 31; 35; 78; 81; 85; 86, *right*; 125; 126; 129; 130; 133
Richard Eaton

210–11
Oak Taylor-Smith

29, *bottom*
Courtesy Guy Tillim and Michael Stevenson, Cape Town

167
Enrique Touriño

214–15
Uwe Walter, © Berlin Biennial for Contemporary Art

56
Mark Woods © 2008

ARTISTS' COPYRIGHT

Unless specified, all images of work © the artists, except:

18, *bottom*
© ARS, NY and DACS, London 2008

23, 99–101
© Tacita Dean, courtesy Frith Street Gallery, London and Marian Goodman Gallery, New York/Paris

182–3
© Estate of General Idea

18, *top*
© Estate of Robert Smithson/DACS, London/VAGA, New York 2008